Religions of South Africa

Religions of South Africa explores the religious diversity of the region, organizing it into a single coherent story and providing the first comparative study and introduction to the topic. The author emphasizes the fact that the complex distinctive character of South African religious life has taken shape within a particular economic, social and political history, and pays special attention to the religious creativity of people who have suffered under conquest, colonialism and apartheid.

David Chidester begins with an overview of African traditional religion and looks at Christian missions and African innovations during the nineteenth century. Though religious life in South Africa has been dominated by a series of Protestant establishments, Roman Catholics, Jews, Hindus, Muslims and other religious movements have managed to build significant religious communities in South Africa. Against this background of religious pluralism, Dr Chidester explores the ambivalent role of religious symbols, myths, rituals and traditions in South African politics, showing how religion has been used to support political domination, but has also inspired struggles for human liberation from oppression.

Religions of South Africa combines up-to-date theory in comparative religion with the latest developments in the history and anthropology of South Africa. With its full documentation and references, and bibliographies at the end of each chapter, the book will be of great value to students and teachers of religious studies, history, anthropology, sociology, political studies, black studies and African studies.

The Library of Religious Beliefs and Practices

Edited by John Hinnells
University of Manchester
and Ninian Smart,
University of California Santa Barbara

This series provides pioneering and scholarly introductions to different religions in a readable form. It is concerned with the beliefs and practices of religions in their social, cultural and historical setting. Authors come from a variety of backgrounds and approach the study of religious beliefs and practices from their different points of view. Some focus mainly on questions of history, teachings, customs and ritual practices. Others consider, within the context of a specific region or geographical region, the inter-relationships between religions; the interaction of religion and the arts; religion and social organization; the involvement of religion in political affairs; and, for ancient cultures, the interpretation of archaeological evidence. In this way the series brings out the multi-disciplinary nature of the study of religion. It is intended for students of religion, ideas, social sciences and history, and for the interested layperson.

Already published

The Ancient Egyptians
Their Religious Beliefs and
Practices
A. Rosalie David

Jews
Their Religious Beliefs and
Practices
Alan Unterman

The Sikhs
Their Religious Beliefs and
Practices
W. Owen Cole and Piara Singh Sambhi

Zoroastrians
Their Religious Beliefs and
Practices
Mary Boyce

Theravāda Buddhism
A Social History from Ancient
Benares to Modern Colombo
Richard Gombrich

The British
Their Religious Beliefs and
Practices
Terence Thomas

Mahāyāna Buddhism
Paul Williams

Muslims
Their Religious Beliefs and
Practices
Andrew Rippin

Religions of South Africa

David Chidester

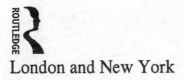

London and New York

First published 1992
by Routledge
11 New Fetter Lane, London EC4P 4EE

Simultaneously published in the USA and Canada
by Routledge
a division of Routledge, Chapman and Hall, Inc.
29 West 35th Street, New York, NY 10001

Typeset by Michael Mepham, Frome, Somerset
Printed and bound in Great Britain by
Mackays of Chatham plc, Chatham, Kent

British Library Cataloguing in Publication Data
Chidester, David
  Religions of South Africa.
  1. South Africa. Religions
  I. Title II. Series
  291.0968

Library of Congress Cataloging in Publication Data
Chidester, David.
  Religions of South Africa/ David Chidester.
  p. cm. – (The Library of religious beliefs and practices)
  Includes bibliographical references and index.
  1. South Africa – Religion. I. Title. II. Series.
  BL2470.S6C45 1992
  291'.0968—dc20   91–3329
                                                          CIP

ISBN 0–415–04779–X
     0–415–04780–3(pbk)

To Careena

Contents

Acknowledgements

I thank colleagues and students at the University of Cape Town for contributing to my South African education. Among those at the University of Cape Town, and elsewhere, to whom I am indebted, I acknowledge John Cumpsty, John de Gruchy, Shaan Ellinghouse, Jan Hofmeyr, Pat Lawrence, Tom Leeuw, Edward Tabor Linenthal, Welile Mazamisa, James McNamara, Gordon Mitchell, Ebrahim Moosa, Itumeleng Mosala, Tillay Naidoo, Nan Oosthuizen, Martin Prozesky, Christopher Saunders, Gabriel Setiloane, Milton Shain, Bernard Steinberg, Abdulkader Tayob, Charles Villa-Vicencio, Charles Wanamaker, and Peter Waugh. Thanks also to Ninian Smart and John Hinnells for their editorial trust. Especially, I thank Darrel Wratten for his editorial and research assistance, and I thank Susan Sayers, mapmaker. Once again, I pay tribute to the Board of Directors for continuing to exist.

Preface

This book is an introduction to the history of religions in South Africa. It summarizes and interprets the history of the many religions that have occupied the one geographical region that came to be called South Africa. While it is a work of comparative religion, I also see this book as a place where anthropologists, historians, theologians – and anyone who cares about human beings, for that matter – can meet and think about the nature of religion in this particular place. Religion has allowed people to experiment in different ways of being human. Not only humanizing, however, religion has also been implicated in forces of dehumanization in South Africa. Religion has been entangled with economic, social, and political relations of power that have privileged some, but have excluded many from a fully human empowerment. The religions of South Africa, therefore, must be considered within a general history of South Africa. Religion must be allowed to appear within a history of the relations of domination, resistance, and recovery that have made being human in this particular place meaningful. By placing comparative religion within the general history of South Africa, I hope this book has collected important resources for thinking once again about what it means to be human, not only in South Africa, but also in the world.

An introduction to the religions of South Africa might take the form of a simple inventory of religious traditions. For example, 1980 census figures suggested that out of a total population of roughly 30 million people in South Africa 76.6 per cent were affiliated with some form of Christianity. As an inherently plural category, Christianity was divided among many different denominations. African independent or indigenous churches, organized in as many as 4,000 denominations, accounted for over 20 per cent of the total population and over 30 per cent of the black population in South Africa. Dutch Reformed churches, sometimes called Afrikaans-speaking churches, accounted for 15.9 per cent, the largest being the Nederduitsch Gereformeerde Kerk with about 13.9 per cent of the total population. English-speaking Protestant churches accounted for 23 per cent of the total population. The largest English-speaking churches were Methodist (8.5 per cent) and Anglican (6.5 per cent), but other Protestant churches included Lutherans (3.4 per cent), Presbyterians (2.0 per cent), United Congregationalists (1.6 per cent), and Baptists (1.0 per cent). Finally, the Roman Catholic Church had a following of 9.5 per cent of the total population of South Africa. Along with smaller denominations, such as Seventh Day Adventists, Jehovah's Witnesses, and various Pentecostal groups, an inventory of these churches would necessarily suggest the rich variety of Christianity in South Africa.

In addition to Christianity, however, other 'world religions' in South Africa accounted for 4.5 per cent of the total population. In the 1980s, South Africa was home for religious traditions – Hindus (519,380), Muslims (328,440), Jews (125,000), Confucians (16,040), and Buddhists (10,780) – that in many cases had formed strong, local religious communities in a country ruled by a government that professed to be Christian. In conflict and accommodation, those religious traditions at the very least presented a vital religious pluralism in South Africa. Finally, there were people who adhered to beliefs and practices of a traditional or ancestral African religion. Unfortunately, those who practiced some form of African religion were excluded from the 1980 census. They were only included among the nearly 6 million people whose religious affiliation was identified as 'other or none.' Nevertheless, African religion continued to provide vital religious resources, often in new, unexpected ways, for many people in South Africa.

An inventory of the religions of South Africa might proceed to survey the beliefs, practices, and institutions of these various religious traditions. While such a survey might be useful, it would not capture the most important features of the religions of South Africa. The complex, distinctive character of South African religious life has taken shape within a particular economic, social, and political history. Instead of an inventory, therefore, I propose a history of religions that is set within the general history of South Africa. While attentive to religious difference, I have tried to locate the history of religions in South Africa in the context of a single, coherent narrative of the region's history. Certainly, the general history of South Africa has been told in many different ways. In this book, I propose a retelling of South African history that will expose and explore its most significant religious dimensions. Before beginning, let me briefly outline that story as I have chosen to tell it in this book.

I start with what the census has omitted, the practice of traditional or ancestral African religion. Since precolonial history remains largely a matter of conjecture, the history of African religion must be imaginatively reconstructed. I have suggested that African religion can be imagined in terms of three spheres: the homestead, the chiefdom, and the disciplines of sacred specialists. The homestead was the basic unit of economic production and social reproduction, while the chiefdom was a larger political order that encompassed homesteads. Between homesteads and chiefdoms, sacred specialists – healers, diviners, and ritual experts – offered professionalized religious services to both. During the nineteenth century, however, all three of these spheres of African religion were fundamentally altered under the pressures of colonial encroachment, military conquest, and the advance of capitalism. The history of African religion, therefore, is a story of both persistence and change. Chapter One introduces the history of African religion.

Nineteenth-century colonialism, conquest, and commerce were intertwined with an aggressive Christian mission to southern Africa. Christian involvement in the region can be traced back to the visits of the Portuguese explorer Bartholomew Dias in 1488. A more permanent Christian presence began with the establishment of a refreshment station by the Dutch East India Company at the Cape in 1652 and the Company rule over the Cape Colony until 1795. Christian missions, however, were undertaken on a large scale only after the British took control of the Cape Colony in 1804. While Christian missionaries proclaimed a gospel of sin and salvation, they also advanced certain colonial and commercial interests. As a result, they have often been viewed as agents in the nineteenth-century conquest of southern Africa. But the history of the missions was also a history of creative African appropriations of Christian religious resources. Certainly, African responses were varied. Initially, prior to the destruction of independent political, social, and economic life, most people simply ignored the missions. At the same time, however, African religious innovators during the nineteenth century drew upon the new, symbolic, cultural resources of the missions to forge both religious resistance and accommodation to a changing world. Chapter Two surveys Christian missions and innovative African responses during the nineteenth century.

At the beginning of the twentieth century, as Christian churches turned from frontier missions to church-building, South Africa underwent the most rapid period of Christian conversion in its history. Christian conversion in South Africa coincided with the nearly complete conquest of African societies, the expansion of colonial administration, the emergence of a modern state, and the advance of industrial capitalism. In particular, Africans were increasingly incorporated into new economic relations of power that followed the mineral revolution in South Africa. The discovery of diamonds in 1867 and gold in 1886 marked the beginning of an expanding, industrial capitalism that came to dominate South African society. In this historical context, particularly under the government of the Union of South Africa formed in 1910, Protestant churches tended to provide religious legitimation for the extensive capital accumulation in gold mining and other industry. As a result, Protestant churches, controlled by white, middle-class, male leadership, became entangled in the racial, class, and gender relations of industrial capitalism in South Africa. With particular attention to those relations, therefore, Chapter Three examines Protestant churches in the first half of the twentieth century.

During this same period, however, new churches emerged in South Africa under black leadership. Often called African indigenous or independent churches, these new religious movements began forming at roughly the same time that large numbers of black South Africans were turning to Christianity. Although several different types might be identified, independent churches are perhaps best understood in the historical context of their formation. In the new urban centers of the 1890s, independent churches emerged to assert black equality with whites in matters of religious leadership. Often called 'Ethiopian' churches, these new churches tended to be founded by educated black Christians who were increasingly excluded from economic, social, and political opportunity. During the 1920s and 1930s, however, new religious movements emerged that focused on the loss of land, economic deprivation, and endemic poverty reinforced by South African legislation. While a few millenarian movements promised a sudden, apocalyptic recovery of the land, other movements, such as the Israelites, Nazarites, and the Zion Christian Church, provided alternative land bases for their followers. By the 1960s, however, the Zion Christian Church, as well as many other 'Zionist,' 'Apostolic,' or 'Pentecostal' churches, had begun a period of rapid expansion that continued into the 1990s. Concentrating primarily on religious healing, these churches provided small enclaves of spiritual purity in a defiling and dehumanizing world. With special attention to the history of their formation, therefore, Chapter Four provides an overview of independent churches in South Africa.

South African history has been dominated by a series of Protestant establishments. The Cape Colony under the Dutch East India Company (1652–1795) prohibited any other religion at the Cape besides the Dutch Reformed Church until it permitted Lutherans to worship in public in 1778. This denial of religious pluralism was lifted during the brief reign of the Batavian Republic (1803–6), and religious pluralism was permitted in principle under the British rule that began in 1806. Nevertheless, the Cape Colony continued to provide financial support to ministers and churches until 1875. Likewise, the Colony of Natal was closely aligned with the Anglican and Methodist Churches. In the Transvaal and Orange Free State, Dutch Reformed churches received support from the governments of the Boer Republics. Close alignments between church and state continued in the Union of South Africa, particularly between the Dutch Reformed Church and the National Party government that came to power in 1948. In spite of this history of Protestant establishments, however, Roman Catholics, Muslims, Hindus, and Jews built religious communities in South Africa. Conflict and accommodation with dominant Protestant establishments was an important facet of their histories. Focusing on the unique positions of Catholics, Muslims, Hindus, and Jews in South Africa, Chapter Five explores important dimensions of religious pluralism.

Religion has been drawn upon to justify various economic, social, and political projects throughout South African history. But the National Party government that came to power in 1948 was particularly adamant that its policies were consistent with Christianity. The National Party legitimated its political power, capital accumulation, and programs for social engineering in the specifically ethnic, racial, and religious terms of a Christian Afrikaner nationalism. Although attributed with a divine origin, Afrikaner nationalism was a historical product of ethnic mobilization that assumed different forms at different points in South African history. Adopting the racialist slogan of apartheid, the National Party government embarked upon a program of legislating racial and ethnic separations in South Africa. In many respects, that program continued earlier policies of racial discrimination. Under National Party rule, however, racial discrimination, domination, and exclusion were invested with an aggressive religious legitimation by both the state and the Dutch Reformed Church. Chapter Six examines the dynamics, as well as some of the unexpected consequences, of that history of religious legitimation in twentieth-century South Africa.

Religion was invoked in attempts to legitimate political, social, and economic domination; but it was also drawn into struggles for liberation from domination. In particular, the ambivalent role of Christianity became a prominent feature of South African religious history in the twentieth century. Black Christians initiated new ways of reappropriating, subverting, or inverting the very Christian symbols that were used to legitimate their oppression. In the work of liberation, religious resources were drawn into the formation of a new African nationalism. Like Afrikaner nationalism, African nationalism had a religious character, particularly as it was formulated by the Youth League of the African National Congress in the 1940s. Unlike Afrikaner nationalism, however, African nationalists frequently proclaimed a liberation from the divisive categories of race and ethnicity that had proven to be so oppressive and ultimately dehumanizing in South Africa. Although supported by developments in African theology, black theology, and liberation theology, that African nationalism promised a liberation in a new, non-racial, democratic, and just South Africa that seemed in itself like a promise of religious and political redemption. Chapter Seven charts the history of religion, politics, and struggles for liberation within African nationalist movements during the twentieth century.

This book was written during a moment in South African history that seemed to call for cautious optimism. Early 1990 saw political organizations unbanned, prisoners freed, and even a 'New South Africa' promising to be born. While this book provides grounds for both optimism and caution, both hope and despair, I see it primarily as a work of historical recovery and revisioning. As the Afrikaner nationalist Paul Kruger and the African nationalist Anton Lembede both insisted, 'One who wants to create the future must not forget the past.' In creating a future, however, we will need new ways to remember the past. I hope this book provides an opportunity for remembering and rethinking the many experiments, denials, and recoveries of humanity that have been at the heart of the history of religions in South Africa.

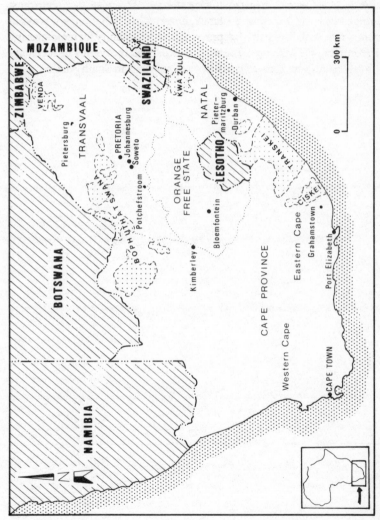

South Africa

1 African religion

Religious beliefs and practices of the indigenous inhabitants of southern Africa have usually been called traditional African religion. These terms, however, require some clarification. First, the term 'traditional' has often implied something timeless and unchanging, as if it were a closed set of beliefs, practices, and social customs handed down from the past. Such an implication is misleading. Although achieving a certain degree of continuity with the past, a religious tradition necessarily changes in different historical situations and circumstances. Therefore, the term 'tradition' might better be understood, not as something handed down, but as something taken up, as an open set of cultural resources and strategies that can be mobilized in working out the meaning and power of a human world. Like any religion, traditional African religion has generated persistent, yet also always changing ways of being human in the world. The term 'tradition,' therefore, should not be used to obscure the dynamic, changing, and even inventive processes of religion in Africa (Hobsbawm and Ranger, 1983; Spiegel and Boonzaier, 1988).

Second, the term 'African,' referring to a geographical location, raises questions about the relation between the general and the particular in the study of African religion. Is there a general 'African' religion that can be discerned amidst the observable differences in the beliefs, practices, and social institutions of particular historical groupings in Africa? Differences among historical groupings have been distorted and reified by the notion of 'tribalism,' which has treated African political groupings as if they were permanent 'tribal,' 'ethnic,' or 'racial' groups. Conventionally, the classification of these groupings has been based on political alignments that emerged in the midst of nineteenth-century colonial history, but were frozen in the 'retribalization' of African societies under colonial rule during the nineteenth century and under apartheid domination in the twentieth century (Southall, 1970; Mafeje, 1971; Saul, 1979; Hall, 1984; Vail, 1989).

Unfortunately, academic classifications of people in southern Africa have reinforced the notion of 'tribalism.' Academic classifications have been based on three basic distinctions that have been much more fluid than they might suggest. Scholars have made the following distinctions: (1) a basic distinction between Khoisan and Bantu-speakers; (2) a division of people speaking Bantu languages into Nguni, Sotho–Tswana, Tsonga, and Venda groupings; and (3) the further differentiation of Nguni-speakers (Cape Nguni, Zulu, and Swazi) and Sotho–Tswana-speakers (Southern Sotho, Northern Sotho, and Western Sotho or Tswana). Arguably, these distinctions have been invented or imagined. Even the one-time government ethnographer N. J. van Warmelo insisted that these classifications were 'fictions' (1974: 60). As historians Shula Marks and Anthony Atmore have noted, they have been 'flags of convenience' for historians and anthropologists (1970: 125). But these classifications of people have also been hard, potent fictions for those who have maneuvered within the apartheid ideology of separate ethnic groups or have suffered from the consequences of apartheid domination. In any case, all of the people designated by these classifications basically underwent a similar, although not uniform, historical experience as their precapitalist social worlds were to one degree or another incorporated into a capitalist economic and political system in South Africa.

The basic distinction between Khoisan and Bantu has been made primarily on linguistic grounds. But scholars in the past tried to correlate differences in language with differences in basic physical characteristics or cultural traits. Khoisan has referred to a cultural complex comprised of Khoikhoi (formerly called Hottentots) and San (formerly called Bushmen) who occupied the Cape region. Khoikhoi lived by herding and the San by hunting and gathering, but all Khoisan were displaced, incorporated, or exterminated by the encroachment of European settlement in southern Africa beginning in the seventeenth century (Elphick, 1985; Marks, 1972). Khoisan religion will only be outlined briefly here.

Khoisan religion seems to have posited a supreme god – Tsui//Goab – who presided over the collective life of the community. This good god was worshiped through regular rituals for making rain or celebrating a harvest. In opposition to the good god of life was an evil god, //Gaunab. This evil god was an independent, superhuman agent that brought illness, misfortune, and death. Khoisan myth, therefore, assumed the form of a cosmic dualism in which good and evil gods operated in the universe. While Tsui//Goab protected Khoisan communities, the ancestor–hero, Heitsi-Eibib influenced the good fortune of individuals. Khoisan myth and legend recorded many tales of the adventures of this cultural hero, particularly relating the stories of the numerous times that Heitsi-Eibib died and came back to life. The graves of Heitsi-Eibib, scattered throughout the region, were represented by piles of stones, or cairns, by pathways or river crossings, at which individuals could stop and add stones for good luck whenever they passed. In the superhuman persons of gods and the ancestor–hero, therefore, Khoisan religion developed mythic resources for understanding the conflicts of individual and social life (Hahn, 1881; Bleek and Lloyd, 1911; Schapera, 1930; Carstens, 1975; Barnard, 1988).

Probably the most important Khoisan ritual practice was the medicine dance. This ritual dance was celebrated for healing, fertility, and the spiritual power that could be achieved through altered states of consciousness in trance (Marshall, 1962; 1969). This form of shamanism through which spiritual knowledge and power could be gained in trance states seems to have been particularly important in the religion of San hunters and gatherers. Archaic rock art found throughout southern Africa has been interpreted as evidence of San shamanism, representing symbols of ecstatic dancing, trance visions, and images of power associated with sacred animal forms (Lewis-Williams, 1980; 1981).

The term 'Bantu' was originally a linguistic classification proposed in the nineteenth century by the philologist W. H. I. Bleek. But it developed into a conventional term applied to all black southern Africans. Evidence of Iron Age settlements based on herding and agriculture has contradicted the European 'myth of the vacant land' which suggested that 'Bantu' groups had been recent immigrants to the region (Marks, 1980; Maylam, 1986: 2–19). Precolonial history, however, has remained largely a matter of conjecture. Any attempt to reconstruct precolonial African religion, therefore, must also remain conjectural. Nevertheless, certain elements of African religious worlds can be assumed to have had a fairly long history, even though their form and content certainly changed under the pressures of colonialism during the nineteenth century.

In very general terms, the traditional or ancestral religion of Bantu-speaking people in southern Africa can be inventoried. Despite widespread, general beliefs in a high god, African religious beliefs and practices concentrated on the role of ancestors – the 'living dead' – as superhuman persons active in bestowing blessings, as well as occasionally bringing misfortune to their descendants. Every homestead head was a priest in performing the domestic rituals – rituals of thanksgiving, rituals for healing – that invoked the deceased, yet spiritually present and active relatives of the homestead. Besides rites of thanksgiving and healing, another set of rituals – rites of passage, marking the major life-cycle transitions of birth, initiation, marriage, and death – were also important in the religious life of the homestead, as well as in the larger network of social relations. On a larger social scale, rites of power were performed to reinforce the political order and power of a chiefdom, through rituals of rainmaking, fertility, or strengthening the power of chiefs and armies. Sacred specialists, particularly diviners, also played important roles in African religion, offering their professional services to individuals, homestead heads, and chiefs. Finally, a symbolism of evil in terms of witchcraft and sorcery was a highly developed and persistent feature of religion. Although many particular, regional differences in beliefs and practices have been observed, the elements of this basic inventory provide a general outline of traditional African religion (Eiselen and Schapera, 1934; Hammond-Tooke, 1974b).

This simple inventory of basic elements of African religion, however, is inadequate because it does not begin to suggest how these elements were related to each other. Did these elements fit together in a coherent system? One way of organizing religious elements into a system has been to regard African religion as a set of symbolic maps. For example, Cape Nguni religion orchestrated its various elements in terms of a symbolic, cognitive, or mental map that opposed the domestic sphere of the homestead with the wild, uncontrollable, and potentially dangerous region of the natural world beyond. Within the centered space of the homestead, the ancestors and ancestor spirits maintained order, bestowed blessings, and protected the family from evil. Beyond the boundaries of that centered world, however, the wild forest region held evil spirits, demons, and witch familiars that threatened to unsettle the domestic order anchored in the homestead.

Between domestic order and wild chaos, however, a middle region was associated with the rivers in which spirits also lingered, especially the 'River People,' who were ambivalent, sometimes beneficial, sometimes harmful, in their interactions with human beings. In this symbolic map, therefore, religious actors could be located. Ritual elders built up the homestead by invoking the ancestors. Witches and sorcerers performed evil acts by contacting familiar spirits of the forest. In between the homestead and the forest, diviners contacted ancestors, fought witches, but also conversed with the spiritual forces associated with the river (Hammond-Tooke, 1975).

With some variation, a similar symbolic map, opposing the domestic, ancestral sphere of the homestead to the wild, dangerous, and uncontrollable periphery outside, could be drawn for Sotho–Tswana tradition (Comaroff, 1980; 1981; 1985: 54–60). In simple outline, these maps suggest the meaningful ways in which elements of traditional African religion might have been coordinated into a relatively coherent, systematic worldview. While these maps are helpful, however, they need to be supplemented by a further analysis of the power relations involved in the ongoing creation of religious worlds. By paying attention to power relations, it might be possible to outline three basic domains of power that operated in traditional African religion – the homestead, the chiefdom, and the disciplines of sacred specialists.

The homestead was a symbol of the world, a central arena in which the symbolic relations of persons and place were negotiated. The home was the nexus of symbolic and social relations among the living and between the living and deceased relatives of the household who continued to live as ancestors or ancestor spirits. It was a place for being human. Although a human person was characterized by a moral or spiritual character, symbolized as a person's shadow (*isithunzi, sereti*), a person was also regarded as a human person as a result of interpersonal relations, relations among the living, as well as relations between the living and the dead (Du Toit, 1960). As a center of power relations, however, the homestead was supported by religious beliefs and practices that reinforced unequal, hierarchical relations between males and females, adults and children, and the older and younger members of the homestead. The oldest, adult, male member of the homestead performed the role of ritual elder, but he also had an interest in the labor power and reproductive power of his subordinates in the homestead. Invoking the jural authority of the ancestors, ritual elders implicated ancestor religion in those relations of power that controlled the homestead, the basic unit of production in economic and social life.

The chiefdom represented a larger sphere of political authority that encompassed homesteads. But often that authority extended only to a chief's claim to being the wealthiest homestead head among a coalition of homesteads. Nevertheless, religious beliefs and practices associated with a chiefdom were also implicated in power relations, especially when chiefs sometimes held a centralized power to distribute land and cattle to subjects. On this larger social scale, the chief stood at the apex of power relations that were simultaneously religious and political, responsible not only for political authority, legal administration, or military defence, but also for the ritual strengthening of the land. In the nineteenth century, the rise of powerful states, such as the Zulu, Swazi, or Pedi kingdoms, was invested with the emergence of royal ideologies that distinguished between 'aristocratic' and common chiefdoms in a new kind of political order, but also subjugated or excluded chiefdoms on the periphery (Guy, 1979; Bonner, 1983; Delius, 1983). The power relations of political authority, therefore, involved religion in a different range of symbolic, social projects than the ancestor religion anchored in a single homestead.

Between homestead and chiefdom, however, sacred specialists offered their services to both. While the ritual work of the homestead head was involved in familial relations and the religion of the chief was involved in communal, political relations, the sacred specialist pursued professional relations with clients that could be drawn from either sphere. In this respect, diviners in particular held a marginal position in which they claimed access to spiritual power that could heal, protect, and strengthen either the homestead or the chiefdom; but that power belonged to neither domain because it was achieved through the specialized, privileged initiation and discipline of the sacred specialist.

In an important sense, therefore, attention to power relations allows traditional African religion to appear as different spheres of interest that might even be regarded as three different religions. Those three African religions represented the different religious interests of homestead heads, chiefs, and those specialists who exercised sacred knowledge and techniques in ways that were made available to both homestead and chiefdom but belonged to neither. Although all three spheres were conversant with similar symbols, myths, and rituals, these different domains of African religion, or different religions, each advanced different symbolic and material interests in the power relations of social life.

MYTH

At the highest degree of abstraction, the existence of a high god overarched all the diverse religious interests in traditional African religion. The high god in African religion was an ultimate divinity beyond time, space, or human control. In general, however, no prayer, worship, or sacrifice was directed toward the high god (Nürnberger, 1975). Terms for the high god varied – *umDali* or *uQamatha* (Xhosa), *Umvelinqangi* or *Unkulunkulu* (Zulu), *Modimo* (Sotho–Tswana), or *Raluvhimba* (Venda) – but in most cases these god names referred to a remote, transcendent power beyond human understanding (Hodgson, 1982; Wanger, 1923–6; Setiloane, 1976; Schutte, 1978). Usually, there was no direct connection between the high god and ancestral spirits. However, Sotho–Tswana ancestors (*badimo*) might have been understood as mediators between human beings and the high god, *Modimo* (Mönnig, 1967: 57; Willoughby, 1928: 206–7) ; while the Zulu *Unkulunkulu* ('the great, great one') or *Umvelinqangi* ('the first to emerge') was perhaps identified as the first ancestor (Callaway, 1868–70: 47). Since ancestors had priority of place in ritual, the high god was not an object of ritual attention but a mythic reference point for explaining the origin of the human world (Smith, 1961).

Creation myths accounted for human origins in three basic ways. First, human beings emerged in the beginning from a hole in the ground. This emergence myth has been recorded among the Mpondo (Alberti, 1968: 13), among the southern Sotho (Casalis, 1861: 240), and among Tswana informants who could point to a particular hole in a rock at Lowe, near Mochudi, from which the original ancestors emerged, leaving their footprints in the rock at the beginning of the world. Venda and Tsonga traditions also recorded this creation myth of emergence from a hole in the ground (Stayt, 1931: 236; Junod, 1927: II: 349). Second, human beings originated from a bed of reeds, breaking off from that original source of life. This myth of origins from a bed of reeds also had a wide distribution throughout southern Africa, with accounts collected in Zulu, Swazi, Xhosa, Tsonga, and southern Sotho traditions (Callaway, 1868–70: 2; Kuper, 1947: 191; Brownlee, 1916: 116; Junod, 1927: II: 348; Ashton, 1952: 10). Third, human beings were fashioned in the beginning through the work of the high god. In this myth, attributed particularly to northern Sotho tradition, the high god Kgobe created the world, while his son, Kgobeane, created humans like a potter molding a vessel from clay (Mönnig 1967: 46).

Another widespread origin myth accounted for the origin of death in a primordial breakdown in communication between the spiritual world and the human world. In this myth, the high god sent a message of immortality to human beings, a message carried by the chameleon. The chameleon, however, was slow, stopping along the way, so that the message of life was delayed. Displeased, the high god sent a second message, a message of death, carried by the swifter lizard, who quickly and directly reached the human world with the message that human beings would have to die. In this myth, death entered the world through a breakdown in communication between humans and the spiritual realm represented by the high god. As a result, human beings had to die, but communication could be restored with the spiritual dimension of the world through the medium of ancestors and ancestor spirits who continued to live after death (Callaway, 1868–70: 3–4; Abrahamsson, 1951; Zahan, 1979: 36–52).

In addition to providing explanations for human origins, however, myth was also a medium for working out a particular understanding of the social and political conditions of the present world. Myth was a type of cultural work, a discourse for making sense out of the present in terms of a primordial past. For example, a Zulu creation myth related in the 1850s described how the high god Unkulunkulu brought human beings into the world. In the beginning, Unkulunkulu created males and females, but he also produced black and white human beings and assigned them to different spheres. According to this myth, Unkulunkulu said: 'The white men may live in the midst of the water, in the sea. He gave them clothing'; but 'the black people shall live within this land.' Anticipating conflicts to come, Unkulunkulu said, 'the white men shall carry guns'; but 'the [black] men shall carry spears.' Obviously, this myth was a creative improvisation on observable oppositions in the nineteenth-century Zulu world. Certain oppositions in that world – white/black, sea/land, guns/spears – were clarified, but they were also transcended by placing all those oppositions under the supreme authority of Unkulunkulu. In this creation story, therefore, myth was a medium for a particular kind of cultural work that not only explained the conflicts of the present world, but also validated black entitlement to the land in terms of the ultimate authority of the high god (Bleek, 1952: 3–4).

A similar nineteenth-century Zulu creation myth, however, explained black subordination to white domination. According to this account, black people emerged from the bed of reeds in the beginning and went out to fend for themselves in the world. White people also emerged, but they remained longer in the bed of reeds, learning wisdom, recording laws, and acquiring the technology of writing, wagons, ploughs, and guns. When they finally emerged with this knowledge and power, therefore, they were easily able to dominate the black people. However, this myth implied, if black people would submit and learn, they also could gain access to the knowledge and power that white people had gained in the original creation (Callaway, 1868–70: 76–80). Obviously, neither of these myths could be described as ancient or primordial. They might have improvised on older mythic themes, but these myths were specifically located in the cultural disruptions and conflicts of colonial southern Africa. In different ways, therefore, myth was a type of cultural work engaged in trying to make sense out of the new power relations and social conditions of the colonial world.

During the nineteenth century, the fundamental social condition addressed in myth was the expanded scale of economic and political interactions. Arguably, the increased scale of social interaction caused by population movements, expanding trade, new labor relations, and military conflict increased the mythic importance of supernatural beings that were of a correspondingly larger scale. Superhuman powers had to be everywhere, rather than anchored in a specific homestead, chiefdom, or region of the country. In southern Africa, Christian and Muslim missionaries introduced precisely such a mythic solution to the increased scale and complexity of social relations by proclaiming transcendent supreme beings who presided over the entire world. But African high gods also seem to have expanded to assume similar positions in response to a changing social, economic, and political environment. Not only under the influence of Christian missions, therefore, but also in response to a changing world, African understandings of a high god seem to have expanded in scope and significance during the nineteenth century (Horton, 1971; 1975; Hexham, 1981; Etherington, 1987: 88–9).

African religious worldviews were populated by other spirits besides high gods and ancestors. Cape Nguni traditions included river spirits, the 'people of the river,' who were sometimes harmful, but could be appeased by offerings. The river people also played an important role in the initiation of diviners (Hunter, 1936: 263; De Jager and Gitywa, 1963: 110). Zulu tradition included a nature goddess – Nomkhubulwana, 'Princess of Heaven' – who was honored by young, unmarried women through seasonal rituals

(Gluckman, 1963: 112–18; Berglund, 1976: 64–74). Sotho–Tswana tradition included certain 'demigods' – Lôwê, Tintibane, Matsieng, and Thobêga – to whom offerings were occasionally made (Willoughby, 1932: 36–40; Brown 1926: 101). These spirits were associated with the wild, the forest, or the river, positioned beyond the relatively stable domestic domain. The most important representatives of the spirit world, however, clearly were the ancestors, or ancestor spirits, who provided the focus for the domestic rituals of the homestead.

ANCESTOR RITUAL

In simplest terms, ancestors were regarded as relatives who had died, yet continued to show an interest in their surviving descendants. Ancestors could be relatives in either the male or female line of descent, but male ancestors tended to play the dominant role in Nguni and Sotho–Tswana ancestor religion, while both paternal and maternal ancestors featured in Tsonga and Venda ritual. Ancestors were most frequently referred to in religious discourse and ritual in the pl ral. When an individual ancestor spirit was singled out for special attention, it was usually because that paternal or maternal relative had been discer.:ed as the cause of some illness, misfortune, or affliction, chastising his or her surviving descendants for some neglect or breach of the moral order. That communicating ancestor spirit, therefore, had to be addressed through ritual in order to reestablish harmony between the living and the dead.

An example of such an ancestral ritual can be briefly outlined (Kuckertz, 1983: 124–31). At a Xhosa-speaking homestead in the eastern Cape, relatives gathered for an ancestral ritual in response to the illness suffered by a young woman in the household. A diviner, a sacred specialist expert in communicating with the ancestors, had been consulted by the homestead head to determine the cause of the young woman's illness. Since the cause was determined to have been an ancestral spirit, a lineage ritual was arranged to restore harmonious communication between the homestead and the ancestors. The ritual was designed to honor, appease, and communicate with the ancestors, as well as to restore the afflicted young woman to health.

The ritual drama began at the cattle enclosure. A cow had been selected for sacrifice. The animal was thrown to the ground, consecrated, and then speared by the second eldest man in the lineage group. The bellowing of the sacrificial animal was crucial to the ritual, because that cry opened up communication with the ancestors. The animal's cry carried the words of the ritual elder, as he stood next to the afflicted woman at the entrance to the cattle enclosure and invoked the ancestors, calling on them to intercede on behalf of the young woman of his household. Although in this case the cry of the sacrificial animal invoked the ancestors, in other cases the same ritual effect could be accomplished through an offering of beer, shared by the participants and poured out in the cattle enclosure for the ancestors. In either case, the offering of sacrificial animal or beer was a means of establishing communication with the ancestors and the ancestor spirit responsible for causing the particular misfortune that was being addressed in the ancestral ritual.

After the invocation of the ancestors, the focus of ritual action moved to the main house of the homestead. The house was not merely a home for the living, but also a sacred place inhabited by the dead, a domestic space in which the ancestors resided or visited. The round, thatched house was kept dark and cool for the ancestors' comfort. Certain places in the house – the back, the hearth, and the thatch over the single door – were especially identified as places charged with the presence of the ancestors. As the ancestral ritual moved into the main house, the ritual elder, the young woman, and all the women of the lineage gathered inside. A piece of fat from the slaughtered animal was placed by the ritual elder on the fire to be wholly consumed for the ancestors. Then a small piece of meat was placed on the fire as an individual offering to the communicating ancestor spirit. While the meat burned, silence was observed in the house.

As the sacrificial animal was being skinned, prepared, and cooked by the men at the cattle enclosure, a special muscle from below the armpit of the animal's right foreleg was extracted and brought to the main house. This meat, referred to as the *intsonyama*, was used in a ritual of healing. The ritual elder cut a long thin strip and roasted it on the fire, the smoke filling and consecrating the house and the people inside. In the midst of this smoke, and in the presence of the ancestor spirit, the ritual elder offered the roasted *intsonyama* to the young woman. Receiving the meat on the back of her hands, she sucked it and then threw it away toward the back of the house, signifying that she was discarding her sickness or misfortune. She then received a second piece. Holding the meat on the back of her right hand, motionless, the young woman was vigorously criticized and ridiculed for the disrespect she had shown to the living and the dead. Finally, the ritual elder instructed the young woman to eat. As she ate the *intsonyama*, the people in the house began to cheer, congratulating the young woman for having 'eaten the ancestor.' In a spirit of celebration, the ritual elder, the young woman, and the people in the house went outside to return to the cattle enclosure. There the remaining portions of the *intsonyama* and the meat of the sacrificial animal were shared in a festive communal meal. At that meal, no other food or beer was served. The meat of the sacrificial animal was eaten, the ritual concluding with the burning of its bones.

However, as noted, the entire ritual could have been performed with beer as the offering used to establish ritual communication with the ancestors. In that case, the ritual followed roughly the some pattern, except that invocations and prayers at the cattle enclosure by the ritual elder were preceded by passing around specially brewed beer and followed by pouring out beer toward the center of the cattle enclosure as an offering for the ancestors. The ritual in the main house also involved criticism of the afflicted person for disobeying the ancestors, but criticism might be followed by a kind of ritual catharsis in which the afflicted person sang, confessed, and danced to the rhythmic clapping of the participants. Whether the medium was beer or an animal, the point of ancestral ritual was not merely to open communication with the ancestors, but also to restore individuals to a state of harmony with the spiritual dimension and social norms they represented. Illness or misfortune were interpreted as signs of being out of harmony with the ancestors of the homestead. Ancestral ritual, therefore, reflected several layers of African religious worldviews that revolved around the domestic space of the homestead.

First, ancestor religion provided an explanatory system that accounted for affliction. Illness or misfortune could be attributed to the inscrutable acts of the high god, or to the evil, harmful acts of witches or sorcerers, or to some impersonal pollution, darkness, or hotness a person might contract by unintentionally violating some ritual rule of conduct. Among these explanations for affliction, the ancestors were attributed with the power to chastise their descendants for acts of disobedience. In this respect, one explanation for illness or misfortune was the displeasure of an ancestor spirit at the disrespect shown by a descendant (Kiernan, 1982).

Second, therefore, ancestor religion provided a symbolic system that supported the authority of elders in the homestead. It reinforced their jural authority and rights over junior members of the extended family. In its emphasis on obedience to elders, ancestor religion gave superhuman sanction to the jural authority of elders, particularly the authority of senior men over the labor power of younger men and the labor power and reproductive power of younger women (Fortes, 1965).

Finally, ancestor religion identified a spiritual dimension of the world that effectively dissolved death. In ancestral ritual, death was not a barrier between the living and the 'living dead' who continued to interact and communicate with their descendants. Although the precise location of the ancestors might not have been clearly specified, perhaps living under the earth, in the sky, or beyond the horizon, their presence in and around the homestead was activated through ritual attention (Kuckertz, 1981).

Other questions, however, have been raised about the role of ancestors in traditional African religion. Considerable controversy has been generated over whether or not ancestors were worshiped. The answer to this question has turned to a large extent on what might be understood by 'worship,' but some commentators have argued that ancestors were not worshiped but were treated with the same kind of attention that was owed to living elders. In that case, they were treated with respect and deference, but not with the kind of worship that might be directed toward a supreme or divine being (Kopytoff, 1971; Brain, 1973).

Nevertheless, ritual attention directed to ancestors did represent a sustained, concentrated interaction with the presence and power of superhuman persons. Although some rituals were performed out of respect for the ways of the ancestors, other rituals – rites of thanksgiving, rites of healing – were clearly designed to invoke the presence of the ancestors in a communal meal that had all the characteristics of an act of worship (Hammond-Tooke, 1978). To be more accurate, however, the ancestors performed a number of different roles in the religion of the homestead. At different times and on different ritual occasions, ancestors represented lineage elders, jural authority, superhuman persons, and the spiritual realm beyond death in the religious beliefs and practices that built up the world of the homestead (Kuckertz, 1984: 11–16).

In the ancestral rituals of the homestead, sacrifice was the primary ritual act. What was the significance of sacrifice? In the history of religions, sacrifice has been interpreted in a number of different ways, depending upon which aspect of the ritual has been emphasized. Sacrifice can involve the killing, offering, expenditure, or consumption of something with highly charged symbolic value, whether that value lies in the 'having,' the 'being,' or the 'consuming' of that object. If the value lies in 'having,' then the sacrifice might be regarded as the exchange of some valued possession, giving that offering to the ancestors in expectation of some return. If the value lies in 'being,' then the sacrifice might be an act of substitution, replacing an animal or an object in sacrificial offering for the life of a human being. If the emphasis is on 'consuming,' however, then the point of the sacrifice is a communal meal shared among the living and between the living and the dead. In southern African ancestral ritual, this last emphasis, on consuming a shared, communal meal, seems to have been the primary focus of sacrifice. In this respect, an offering of sanctified beer could work just as well as the ritual killing of an animal to establish communication and communion with the ancestors, certified by the sharing of a meal between the living and the dead (Heusch, 1985).

Historically, ancestor religion has operated as a force of conservatism, maintaining lifestyles and social relations associated with the past. In the colonial context, however, ancestor religion emerged as a medium of political resistance. In the 1850s, for example, W. H. I. Bleek observed that his Zulu attendant would often seem to be talking to himself. When Bleek asked what he was saying, however, his servant always answered, 'I am not speaking to you, I am praising the *Amadlozi* [ancestors]' (Bleek, 1965: 38). This brief exchange merely suggested the potential of the ancestors for providing a frame of reference that could discount the white, colonial presence in South Africa. In that respect, it might be argued, ancestor religion assumed a new, more urgent character in the nineteenth century. Identified with the homestead, the land, and a specific locality, the ancestors might have become even more crucial as a spiritual anchor that tied people to places that were being threatened and destabilized by European colonial encroachment.

As a medium of resistance to European influence and expansion, ancestor religion continued to be mobilized throughout the twentieth century in southern Africa. In the eastern Cape, for example, the so-called Red, traditional communities mobilized ancestral beliefs and practices as a way of carving out an independent enclave in a larger economic, social, and political world. Therefore, the ancestors represented not only an ancient world but also a more recent way of life that was being undermined. Within that context, adherence to ancestor religion was a particular strategy of resistance to displacement and domination in South Africa (Mayer, 1980b; McAllister, 1986).

Ancestor religion, however, also adapted to social and economic change. For example, as many young men and women chose or were forced to enter the migrant labor market, the scope of ancestor religion expanded to address the dangers of leaving home, living in a strange environment while away at work, and then returning to the homestead with money and other alien symbols of wealth. In response to migrant labor, the entire cycle of leaving and returning to the homestead became an initiatory rite of passage, a ritual that was in many cases formalized as an integral part of ancestor religion. As ritual practice changed to adapt to new conditions of migrant labor, the spiritual power and authority of the ancestors was invoked to protect the worker while away from home. But that spiritual authority was also invoked to reincorporate any wealth gained through migrant labor back into the homestead. In one respect, these rituals of migrant labor allowed homestead elders to assert a certain measure of control over the labor-power and wages of migrant workers. However, ancestral rituals of migrant labor also represented a vital, innovative adaptation of religious beliefs and practices to new challenges, suggesting that ancestor religion was something both persistent and changing in African religious life (McAllister, 1980; 1985).

SYMBOLISMS OF EVIL

In the forms of illness or misfortune, evil could enter human experience as a result of ancestral chastisement for violating ritual or ethical obligations. In addition, however, affliction could be accounted for as a result of the actions of evil agents – witches or sorcerers – who employed superhuman power against the symbolic order represented by the domestic homestead. While the ancestors might send misfortune, however, these wild, dangerous, evil agents were thought to be capable of using superhuman means to bring death. Furthermore, a person afflicted by misfortune from a communicating ancestor spirit had to assume personal responsibility, since misfortune was an evil consequence of some disobedience to the moral or ritual order reinforced by the ancestors. In the case of misfortune suffered as a result of the acts of witches or sorcerers, however, the victim was regarded as innocent. In one respect, therefore, witchcraft beliefs and practices identified the cause of misfortune suffered by innocent victims as the superhuman powers exercised by agents of evil.

In another sense, however, witchcraft beliefs and practices defined violence in African religious thought. If violence can be defined as direct harm to persons or property, then witches and sorcerers were sources of violence in the world, performing acts that harmed innocent victims. On the other hand, if violence can be defined as anything that violates humanity, then witches and sorcerers were also regarded as violent because they violated the domestic order of the homestead, using superhuman power to achieve antihuman ends.

Researchers have made a basic distinction between witches and sorcerers in traditional African religion (Mair, 1969: 23; Beidelman, 1971: 131–2). The witch has been defined as someone with the supernatural power to exert harm on people or their property; but that power depended on the witch's inherently evil character that produced violent effects in the human world. Therefore, the witch harmed others by means of an inherently evil disposition. The violence of the witch resulted from an evil psychic or superhuman power, often supported by grotesque or wild animal spirits, the witch's familiars. The witch's disposition toward violence was often thought to be inherited, sometimes unconsciously, as an evil, antisocial power to cause harm. By contrast, the sorcerer was not born into that role, but learned the techniques of causing harm by means of powerful medicines and acts. The sorcerer, therefore, could be an ordinary person, but a person who employed the superhuman power of strong medicines to cause harm to persons or property.

This distinction between witches and sorcerers, however, was not always so clearly defined in traditional African symbolisms of evil. One term tended to be used for both, such as *abathakathi* in Xhosa and Zulu, *baloi* in Sotho and Tswana. A widespread distinction in Sotho–Tswana tradition, however, marked the difference between 'day witches,' who, as sorcerers, used medicines, and 'night witches' of inherently evil character who used psychic power, animal familiars, grotesque beasts, and zombies dug up from graves to cause harm. For the most part, day witches tended to be men, employing the superhuman power of strong medicines in competition with other men, while night witches tended to be women (Hammond-Tooke, 1974c; 1981).

The entire complex of witchcraft and sorcery beliefs might be explained in several ways. First, this symbolism of evil can be analyzed as a way of accounting for interpersonal conflicts in the social world. In this respect, witchcraft and sorcery were expressions of competition, jealousy, and anger, in other words, reflections of social tension. Tension arose between jealous co-wives in polygynous households, between half-brothers competing for inheritance within a lineage, between commoners jealous of each others' success, or between men competing for advantage in the political order of a chiefdom. In all these cases, people could resort to strong medicines or techniques of sorcery as instruments of power. But they might also have been vulnerable to accusations of practicing witchcraft or sorcery by those who regarded themselves as victims of their jealousy or competition. In such cases, the symbolism of evil reflected in witchcraft and sorcery provided a framework in which social conflict between individuals came into focus (Kuper, 1947: 175).

Second, this symbolism of evil can be interpreted as a set of moral sanctions that reinforced social norms. Like ancestral sanctions, witchcraft beliefs and practices provided a vocabulary for identifying antisocial behavior. Since anyone perceived as antisocial – a lazy wife, a stingy man, an unpopular neighbor – was vulnerable to being accused of practicing witchcraft or sorcery, that symbolism of evil performed an important social function by encouraging people to observe basic social norms (Hunter, 1936 (1961 edn): 108).

Third, the symbolism of evil implicit in witchcraft and sorcery can be interpreted as a means by which individuals could marshal public support against a common public enemy. If a person was accused of evil, antihuman practices, the accuser had to make the case in public. Accusation, therefore, required gathering support from friends, relatives, and sacred specialists in witch detection to identify and expose the evil agent. In a successful prosecution, social support for an innocent victim of evil could build a unified front against the accused witch or sorcerer, demanding confession and reparation for any violence that had been committed. Situations in which public support was uncertain, however, resulted in a lower incidence of witchcraft and sorcery accusations. The work of evil agents might have been suspected, but the public accusation and prosecution of witches or sorcerers was rare because any accuser had to be unsure of being able to gather the necessary public support to put the accused through what has been called a 'ceremony of degradation' (Sansom, 1972).

When accusations of witchcraft or sorcery were made and sustained in public, a person identified as an evil agent was usually given the opportunity to confess or to reveal the evil medicines that had been used to cause harm. If the accused confessed, payment of damages and a sacrifice for purification could be sufficient to mark the reintegration of that person back into normal social relations. In other cases, however, the public discovery and prosecution of an evil agent required his or her exclusion from society. Under the political authority of a chief, exclusion could be accomplished by confiscating the property and banishing the person of the accused from the chiefdom. Only rarely, it seems, did the exclusion of an evil agent require execution.

Although evidence of the torture and execution of convicted witches and sorcerers has been recorded, execution seems to have been a ritual of exclusion of last resort. For example, as one observer in the eastern Cape noted in 1837, there might be only one execution for witchcraft during the course of any year in the entire region, with some years passing without a single execution (Peires, 1981: 206). As long as relatively independent African political systems were intact, the confiscation of possessions and banishment were adequate means of excluding someone identified as an antihuman, evil agent from society. With the destruction of those independent polities, the ritual killing of alleged witches became the only means of excluding evil agents from society, giving rise to an increase in witch-eradication activity requiring the execution of witches in African societies under colonial domination.

The symbolism of ancestors and witches provided a way of locating misfortune in terms of interpersonal relations, either in terms of the personal relations between the living and the dead that went into building up a homestead, or in terms of personal rivalries and conflicts that threatened its destruction. In this respect, ancestors and witches provided a symbolism of personal causation for evil. By contrast, African religion also generated impersonal symbolisms of evil. While the high god sometimes was credited with bringing misfortune, illness, or even death in ways that were beyond personal responsibility or human understanding, a more immediate, highly charged system of impersonal causation for misfortune was located in beliefs and practices relating to purity and pollution.

Symbols of pollution – dirt, blackness, or heat – represented boundaries on ordinary, everyday behavior. An important part of religious practice was the avoidance of situations or conditions of pollution, many of which were associated with birth, death, and the monthly cycle of women. But the automatic condition of defilement, blackness, or heat could be addressed through ritual means: Xhosa practice required ritual bathing to counteract impurity that was automatically contracted through certain kinds of prohibited contact, such as the contact between a man and a menstruating woman

(Hunter, 1936: 46). Zulu practice required techniques of purging and vomiting to expel 'blackness' (Ngubane, 1977: 77). Perhaps the most elaborate in this regard, Sotho practice used water, beer, ash, or the green chyme from the stomach of a sacrificial animal in order to 'cool' the condition of 'heat' that could be contracted at the death of a close relative, by certain types of sexual contact, during pregnancy, upon returning from a journey, or in other situations perceived as particularly dangerous (Schapera, 1979; Verryn, 1981; Hammond-Tooke, 1981: 112–22). In this symbolism of purity and danger, beliefs and practices relating to impurity, blackness, or heat provided another way of explaining and dealing with misfortune.

Even when they brought misfortune, the personal interventions of ancestors were part of building up the network of domestic relations centered in the homestead. The actions of witches and sorcerers, by contrast, were wild, uncontrollable, and dangerous forces threatening that centered world. Furthermore, although ancestors could bring illness, they did not bring death to their descendants. Only witches and sorcerers killed in the violent course of their evil work. Any untimely death tended to be explained as the result of the work of an evil agent, an attack on the centered stability of the homestead from the wild, evil forces that were mobilized beyond its periphery. A certain degree of protection from evil was gained by observing ancestral ritual, building up the spiritual power of the homestead, but it also had to be gained by recourse to sacred specialists who acted as counter-agents against witches and sorcerers. In African traditional religion, sacred specialists demonstrated a particular expertise in the types of knowledge and power that could counteract evil.

SACRED SPECIALISTS

Healing was an important dimension of African traditional religion. Doctors specialized in various healing techniques and practices. A general distinction has often been made between herbalists and diviners, practicing different healing arts, the herbalist adept in the use of medicines, while the diviner, often in addition to using medicines, was expert in various techniques for gaining spiritual knowledge and power over illness, misfortune, or evil. The herbalist's pharmacopia was primarily derived from plants and animals, but those medicines were prescribed according to rules that might be called a 'poetics of healing' that symbolized healing power through the similarity, contact, or association of the medicine with whatever effect was desired. Although herbalists often invoked the ancestors in their healing work, they basically operated as medical doctors who specialized in certain medicines and techniques for healing (Watt and Van Warmelo, 1930; Hoernlé, 1934; Hammond-Tooke, 1989).

Diviners, however, were sacred specialists with greater religious knowledge, power, and prestige. The diviner – *igqira* (Xhosa), *isangoma* (Zulu), or *ngaka* (Sotho–Tswana) – was the most important sacred specialist in African traditional religion. The diviner was expert in discerning the cause of any misfortune, whether that cause was the work of witches or the wrath of ancestors. The role of diviner was acquired by means of a special calling, often suggested by the onset of an illness thought to have been sent by the ancestors. Nguni diviners tended to be women, Sotho–Tswana diviners men, but either men or women could enter into the role of sacred specialist. The novice was initiated into the specialized knowledge and power of the profession by an experienced practitioner. The process of initiation involved an extended period of isolation, training, instruction in medicines, and, particularly in the case of the Nguni *igqira* or *isangoma*, the performance of certain dances and other techniques for inducing trance states that allowed the diviner to communicate directly with ancestral spirits (Callaway, 1871; Lee, 1969; Sibisi, 1975; Ngubane, 1981).

Nguni diviners further specialized in different fields, becoming expert in discerning the will of the ancestors, exposing witches and sorcerers, or finding lost property. In addition, diviners employed different techniques in their work: some became trance mediums for the voices of familiar or ancestral spirits, some used sticks or bones as tools for divination, while many diviners conducted question–and–answer sessions with a group of people to divine the truth behind some affliction that they suffered. Although diviners could employ these techniques in private consultations, they could also be employed in dramatic, public rituals performed and orchestrated by sacred specialists in divination.

An example of ritual divination conducted by a Xhosa-speaking diviner was recorded in the 1850s in the eastern Cape. This *umhlalo* ritual was designed for 'smelling out' witches, discerning and exposing some anti-social, evil agent in the community. After receiving permission from a chief, the diviner invited his clients to his homestead. The people formed two semi-circles. On one side sat the clients seeking assistance, on the other the diviner with supporters. While the clients beat spears on the ground, clapped their hands, or hummed, the diviner made statements about their misfortune. If the diviner's statements were accurate, the clients said, 'We agree,' while their drumming grew louder. By gauging their response, the diviner could discern how the clients perceived the cause of their affliction. On one level, therefore, the diviner conducted a type of inquest through this ritual drama (Hunter, 1936: 336).

However, the diviner also claimed specialized knowledge and power that could only be achieved by an inner sight or through contact with the spirit world. Having achieved clarity about the cause of the clients' distress, the diviner retreated into a hut. As the drumming continued, the diviner suddenly emerged to perform an ecstatic dance, going into a type of trance that signified a superhuman access to the knowledge and power of divination. At the climax of that ritual dance, the diviner spoke the name of the witch whose evil disposition had been responsible for bringing misfortune to the clients. Since that person was present at the ritual, the clients separated to leave the accused sitting alone, while the diviner described his evil acts. Exposed as an evil, disruptive agent in society, the accused then had the opportunity to confess, arrange for the performance of a sacrifice, and make a payment for guilt to the chief under whose jurisdiction the ritual had been performed. Whether the accused was reincorporated into society, or excluded through confiscation of property, banishment, or execution, the diviner had succeeded in employing specialized, sacred knowledge and power to resolve a crisis in human social relations (Warner, 1858: 88–92).

The most common Sotho–Tswana technique involved casting bones, sticks, or dice for divination. In many cases, the basis for this system of divination was a set of four specially carved dice, often combined with bones, shells, or stones. The four dice in this set usually represented an adult male, an adult female, a young male, and a young female. These ritual objects were thrown to produce different combinations that could be interpreted by the sacred specialist. Reading the pattern in their arrangement, the diviner was able to consult with clients about the cause of some misfortune, the location of lost property, or prospects for the future (Dornan, 1923; Eiselen, 1932; Laydevant, 1933; Junod, 1927, II: 603–8; Hammond-Tooke, 1981: 103–4).

Although divination through trance states, mediumistic contact with spirits, or ecstatic dancing was practiced by Sotho–Tswana diviners, these techniques seem to have been adopted from the basic Nguni pattern of divination. Certain South Sotho diviners were found to have appropriated characteristic techniques for inducing trance states practiced by Cape Nguni trance diviners. Some North Sotho, or Pedi, diviners specialized in achieving direct spiritual contact with the ancestors (Ashton, 1952: 283; Mönnig, 1967: 87). These examples suggest a degree of religious interchange between sacred specialists based in different regions.

Sacred specialists in African religion were involved in competitions over religious claims to sacred power, especially the power identified with the ancestors, that were conducted among homestead heads, chiefs, and diviners. Claims on ancestral authority made by the ritual elders of a family, clan, or lineage were anchored in the domestic order of the homestead. Claims made by chiefs were focused in the dynamics of reinforcing a political order. But sacred specialists assumed a relatively marginal position from which they could make their services available in either sphere, the homestead or the polity. In cooperation, the ritual elder of a homestead or the chief of a polity

could draw on the specialized knowledge and practices of diviners in reinforcing their authority over those different domains. Sometimes, however,
sacred specialists were involved in conflicts over power. For example,
whenever a Nguni diviner determined that a young woman's illness was an
initiatory sickness sent by the ancestors, the diviner risked undermining the
patriarchal authority of the homestead head by taking his daughter away to
become a novice in the specialized arts of divination.

In the political arena, diviners might also come into conflict with alternative claims on sacred authority, in this case the authority of chiefs. For
example, the early nineteenth-century Tswana chief Kgama I once set a test
for all the diviners under his jurisdiction. Announcing that he was sick,
Kgama invited all the doctors to divine the cause of his illness. After casting
their dice and bones, most specialists divined that the chief had been bewitched. Only two discerned that there was actually nothing wrong with him.
As a result of this test, Kgama declared that most of the diviners were ignorant
frauds. He decreed that they would be forbidden to continue in their practice,
ordering the burning of their divining bones and medicine bags. Only diviners
who lived in the wards of the two specialists who had divined correctly would
be allowed to continue practicing their arts. In this act, therefore, Kgama did
not merely indicate a certain skepticism about the practices of religious
specialists; he asserted his chiefly religious and political authority over the
sacred knowledge and power that those specialists represented (Schapera,
1970: 131–2). Between the domains of homestead heads and chiefs, therefore, sacred specialists operated to advance their own claims on sacred
knowledge and power.

In the twentieth century, sacred specialists continued to practice their arts.
Of the three spheres of power in African religion – the homestead, the
chiefdom, and the disciplines of specialists – the professionalized knowledge
and practice of sacred specialists was most suited to survive the social
disruptions that absorbed homesteads and chiefdoms in a larger, European-
dominated political economy. As professional specialists, herbalists and
diviners could still find clients, even in alien urban environments. Nevertheless, changes in the practices of sacred specialists also occurred. Under a
series of colonial and state laws, the detection of witches was proscribed as
an illegal act. Therefore, one of the primary roles of diviners, the detection
and exposure of evil agents in society, in other words, the identification of
criminals, came into conflict with the criminal code of the dominant legal
system in South Africa.

Certainly, specialists continued to perform this role, ignoring the risk of
being prosecuted under South African law. In many cases, however, the
criminological work of sacred specialists was replaced by an exclusive
emphasis on the medical and psychological services they provided for people

with limited access to other forms of health care. After years of condemning traditional healing practices, some western medical professionals gradually acknowledged the therapeutic potential of traditional healing. The grounds for this accommodation, however, were clearly medical and psychological, with no necessary connection to the social, spiritual, or ritual dimensions of the practice. Increasingly, this medicalization and psychologization of sacred specialists was also adopted by many African diviners and herbalists in reshaping their understanding of their specialized knowledge, power, and place as professionals in the health care market in South Africa (Bührmann, 1978; 1984).

RITES OF PASSAGE

Major life-cycle transitions – birth, adolescence, marriage, and death – were mediated through rites of passage. Although centered in the homestead and kinship relations, these rituals, particularly initiation and marriage, had wider social significance in linking the homestead with other homestead lineages or with the larger political sphere of the chiefdom. In this respect, rites of passage mediated both personal life-cycle transitions as well as social relations inside and outside the homestead.

Rituals marking birth and death attended the highly charged, dangerous transitions of the unborn and the recently deceased, requiring a ritual response to the mystery of the 'other world' from which human beings come and to which they return at death. Often, women played an important ritual role in the rites of passage surrounding birth and death, as, in Zulu tradition, a woman could be regarded as mother of birth (*umdlezane*) and mother of death (*umfelokazi*). This parallel between birth and death was acted out in ritual (Ngubane, 1976).

At birth, a child was obviously dependent on its mother, but it belonged to the father and his patrilineage. This conflict of interest was manifested in ritual restraints and restrictions placed on a mother during approximately the first 10 days after giving birth. She was required to remain in seclusion, in the company only of married women, because her association with new life was regarded as placing her in a dangerous condition of ritual pollution that endangered men, cattle, and crops. After this period of confinement, a sacrifice marked the entry of the child into the world. At the same time, however, the ancestral ritual of sacrifice signified the incorporation of the child into the patriarchal lineage represented by the ancestors of the homestead. In this sense, the first sacrifice performed for a child symbolized a transfer of rights over the child from the mother to the father, whose authority was represented by the patrilineal ancestors.

When a death occurred in the homestead, women also played an important ritual role in marking the transition of the deceased to the spiritual world of the ancestors. Like birth, death represented a condition of extreme pollution. In Zulu tradition, only married women could handle and prepare the corpse, delivering it to the men of the homestead through the doorway of the hut, like the delivery of a child from the womb. A married woman served as the principal mourner in funeral ritual, observing restrictions on her behavior that were analogous to the prohibitions surrounding birth. Ritual reversals of ordinary conduct also marked the dangerous transition of a recently deceased to the ancestral world. Women washed the corpse with their left hands, wore their dresses inside out, and walked backwards out of the hut, acting out ritual reversals that not only addressed the extraordinary condition of dangerous pollution associated with death but also signified the passage of the deceased into the reversed world of the ancestors beneath the earth where up was down, black was white, and the bitter gall of the sacrificial animal tasted sweet (Berglund, 1976: 364–81).

Entry into that world, however, was not achieved until a year after death, when a final ritual sacrifice for 'bringing home' the ancestor marked the incorporation of the deceased into the ancestral realm. In that event, the principal mourner, who had been observing ritual prohibitions on her conduct over the year, was reincorporated into the ordinary life of the homestead, as the deceased was incorporated into the company of its ancestors. Like birth, therefore, death required a ritual renegotiation of the familial, social, and spiritual relations out of which the world of a homestead was built (Gluckman, 1937).

The important passage from childhood to adulthood was marked by rituals of initiation, symbolizing a death and rebirth into an adult world. Although regional differences and historical changes in practice could be observed, initiation rituals followed a characteristic pattern that required the seclusion of the initiates, instruction in the sacred wisdom of myths, rituals, and ethical norms, and a ceremonial coming out that marked the reincorporation of the initiate in a new status as an adult. Historically, Sotho–Tswana chiefs assumed control over initiation rituals, while local headmen, parents, and sacred specialists organized Nguni initiations (Wilson and Thompson, 1969, I: 160). In either case, however, rituals of initiation reinforced a pattern of obedience to authority, particularly the authority of fathers, headmen, and chiefs, while instructing boys and girls in the norms that governed their roles as men and women in society.

Tswana initiation required two separate, but coordinated ritual sequences, the *bogwera* for boys and the *bojale* for girls, performed at roughly 4-year intervals or whenever a son or nephew of a chief was old enough to serve as regimental leader. Although initiation was the personal life-cycle transition of boys and girls into adulthood, it was also a political event that reinforced loyalty to a chief, who was regarded as the owner of the initiation. At the initiative of a chief, all the male regiments were assembled and sent out to hunt for their kin and bring them to the initiation. For boys, the first, or white, *bogwēra* proceeded through three stages. First, a phase of separation, lasting nearly a month, was spent in the bush outside of the village, under the supervision of senior men, occupied with singing, dancing, and making ceremonial kilts out of bark. Second, a transition phase required all the initiates to journey to the chief's court, where they were circumcised, remaining secluded in special lodges to learn dances, songs, and ethical norms emphasizing obedience to the chief, filial piety, and the domination of women. Finally, a phase of reincorporation into society, now, however, in a new status as an adult, was marked by rituals of reentry in which the initiates were revealed to the general population, received by the chief, and given their regimental name. Although ritual and ethical instruction was reinforced a year later in the second, or black, *bogwēra*, cycle, the first initiation admitted boys into adult society, entitling them to participate in the public, political activity that was the province of men (Willoughby, 1909; Comaroff, 1985: 84–114).

Female initiation was a shorter, less elaborate ritual cycle, synchronized to coincide with the final stages of the *bogwēra*. The *bojale* emphasized instruction in the private, domestic sphere of women, but also involved ritual phases of separation, transition, and reincorporation. While the initiates were secluded outside the village, their transition into adulthood was symbolically inscribed on their bodies by means of ritual operations – cutting the inner thigh, perforating the hymen – that marked their change in status. After a month of instruction in domestic wisdom, the initiates appeared in public at the chief's court to be reincorporated in a new adult status as women ready for marriage (Comaroff, 1985: 114–18).

Considerable variation in the practice of initiation rituals was observed during the nineteenth century. Sotho initiations revealed dramatic mysteries of masked dancers, sacred drums, and ritual objects, including the Beast (*Senkōkōyi*), that were associated with sacred power (Hammond-Tooke, 1981). Xhosa initiations focused on circumcision as the crucial rite, followed by a period of seclusion before a coming out ceremony (Ngxamngxa, 1971). Zulu practice discontinued circumcision, but continued to provide instruction and the formation of regiments that marked the passage into adulthood (Krige, 1936: 116–17). For all this diversity, however, initiation ritual defined the personal and political spheres in which the lives of adults were supposed to be conducted. Clearly, those roles were defined in the interests of adult, male elders – whether chief, lineage head, or homestead head – who were the owners of the initiation ritual that reinforced obedience to senior male authority in both the homestead and the chiefdom (Carstens, 1982).

The different roles assigned to males and females were also embedded in marriage ritual, particularly the ritualized payment of bridewealth *(lobola, lobolo, bohali)*. Conventionally paid in cattle to the father of the bride, bridewealth served a number of interlocking interests in sealing a marriage arrangement, not merely between two individuals, but between two extended family groups. In one respect, bridewealth was compensation paid to the father for the loss of his daughter's labor power in the agricultural production that was exclusively designated as women's work in the homestead economy. In addition, however, bridewealth represented security for the good conduct of husband and wife in marriage. If a husband mistreated his wife to such an extent that she returned to her father, the father might keep both the bride-wealth and the daughter; if the wife failed in obedience, agricultural work, or producing children, then the return of bridewealth might be demanded by the husband (J. L. Comaroff, 1980; A. Kuper, 1982; Haas, 1987; Burman, 1990: 59).

Arguably, however, the overarching interest at stake in this marriage transaction was male control over female labor power and reproductive power. As a cycle of exchange, the ritual of bridewealth allowed fathers to exchange the productive capacity and reproductive potential of their daughters for cattle. In turn, cattle provided a resource for acquiring rights over the labor and reproductive power of other women through marriage to sons of the homestead. This ritual cycle of exchange, therefore, contributed to building up the wealth of a homestead; but it also reinforced the social subordination of women through male control over their lives, labor, and reproductive power (Guy, 1990). In the world of the homestead, social relations – males/females, adults/children, seniors/juniors – were all reinforced by ritual, particularly by those rites of passage that marked the most intimate, personal transitions in the human life cycle and social relations.

RITES OF POWER

Encompassing the world of the homestead, the religious ideology of the chiefdom was also acted out through ritual. The most important ritual practices were performed to strengthen the fertility of the land and the political authority of rulers. Although varying under different historical conditions, these rites of power formed a religious repertoire of practices that were available to chiefs in asserting supernatural, sacred claims to political power. In this chiefly religious ideology, fertility and polity were often linked through ritual, with a chief assuming responsibility for the rain, crops, and harvest, as well as for the stable, strong order of the polity. Rituals for rainmaking, harvest, and strengthening the chief and army, therefore, could merge in a single religious ideology that reinforced the political power of rulers in a chiefdom.

Although assisted by sacred specialists, chiefs often assumed the ultimate responsibility for rainmaking. In most cases, the chiefly ancestors were invoked through ritual to bring rain. Through ancestral intercession, rainfall not only served the fertility of the fields but also indicated that the political order was operating in harmony with the spiritual realm that the ancestors represented. Communal rituals of rainmaking could require the participation of an entire chiefdom, as in the case of the Pedi annual ceremony in which young women from all over the region came to the capital with small pots of water from their local areas. They poured the water into large pots that were treated with rain medicines under the direction of chief and rainmaker. Then they refilled their small pots with the treated water and returned home to sprinkle it on their fields (Mönnig, 1967: 155–8). Such a ritual practice coordinated religious activity over a wide region under the jurisdiction of a chief. In other cases, however, even stronger claims were made for a political ruler's control over the rain. For example, in the nineteenth century Zulu kings claimed to exercise direct control over the heavens, while the Lovedu ruler – Mujaji, the 'Rain Queen' – was attributed with supernatural powers that regulated the heavens, controlled the seasons, and brought the rain clouds at her command (Krige, 1936: 320; Krige and Krige, 1943: 271). Whether attributed to a supreme being, ancestors, or the inherent sacred power of rulers, the fertility represented by rain was channeled through ritual into a symbolic reinforcement of the political order (Schapera, 1971).

Similarly, annual harvest festivals were often combined with rituals for strengthening chiefs and warriors. At the time of harvest, the chief assumed responsibility for a ceremonial 'biting' of the first fruits before new crops could be eaten by the people. An annual festival practiced in the eastern Cape, for example, was performed at the ripening of the first crops in February or March. Conducted by a reigning chief, the 3-day festival began with the gathering of the first fruits of the harvest, which were cooked on a sacred fire. This food was ritually tasted by the chief, then sampled by the adult males in attendance, in order of seniority. The next day, the army marched past the chief, with fighting songs and war cries, spitting medicines in the direction of enemies surrounding the chiefdom. Proceeding to a river, the warriors were washed and treated with protective, strengthening medicines. On the final day of the ceremony, warriors killed a black bull, signifying their triumphant military power. With a final doctoring of the army and chief by sacred specialists, the festival concluded, having completed a ritual drama of fertility and power, both revolving around the office and person of the chief (Hammond-Tooke, 1953).

This rite of power, however, was also an object of competition among contending claimants to political power and authority in a particular region. In that competition, the ritual seniority symbolized by first-fruits ceremonies might be claimed by several different chiefs, with conflict over the ritual sometimes even resulting in armed combat. Furthermore, ritual was entangled in two political developments – African state building and European colonial domination – that fundamentally altered the character of African rites of power in the nineteenth and twentieth centuries. Although these effects of power can be illustrated here by a Zulu example, their impact was experienced to one degree or another throughout southern Africa.

The rise of the Zulu kingdom in the early nineteenth century represented a concerted economic and military effort of state building, but it was also accompanied by significant religious and ideological projects. On the level of symbolic discourse and ritual practice, the role of Zulu king was elevated to a new preeminence in south-east Africa. Formerly referred to by the address-name 'dog's penis,' the small Zulu clan asserted itself during the nineteenth century as the center of a new royal ideology, appropriating the address-name, Nguni, that had been associated with ancient, legitimate political authority in the region (Wright, 1986: 108). By incorporating other clans and chiefdoms, the Zulu royal ideology replaced older rites of power that had distinguished chiefs from commoners. This new royal ideology placed Zulu and other 'aristocratic' chiefdoms at the center, incorporated 'commoner' chiefdoms as tributaries, and excluded chiefdoms on the periphery of the kingdom under the derogatory label, *amalala*, sometimes glossed as 'those who sleep (*ukulala*) with the fingers up their anuses' (Hamilton and Wright, 1990).

In ritual, these new political relations of state building – domination, incorporation, and exclusion – were reflected in the privileged, exclusive claims advanced by Zulu royalty to ownership of the first-fruits festival. As chief of chiefs, the Zulu king used the annual *umkosi* ceremony as an occasion to reinforce his privileged, hierarchical authority over all incorporated chiefs and commoners. For a few days prior to the ceremony, the king was treated with purifying, strengthening medicines. The king also acted out his domination by jumping over various objects that symbolized enemies of the kingdom. When people had gathered at the king's court for the festival, chanting, drumming, and striking shields and spears, the king emerged to dance with the army. The royal dance song contained the refrain – 'They hate him, they hate the king' – which placed the entire festival within the context of military conflict.

In the evening, a black bull that had been captured from an enemy group was sacrificed. Having been treated by a specialist, the meat was distributed to warriors, the gall to the king. At that point in the ceremony, the Zulu royal symbol, the *inkatha*, a ring wound together out of straw from the entrances of several huts, soil from footprints, grass on which the army had slept, and vomit from the royal family, was taken apart, treated with medicines, and rebound. Symbolizing Zulu unity, the *inkatha* also signified the privileged, dominant position of the royal household in this religious ideology of kingship. On the first day of the first-fruits festival, celebration was focused exclusively on the political and military power claimed by the king.

On the morning of the second day, the ritual addressed the fruits of the harvest. The king performed a ceremony with gourds that were taken from a basket to be thrown and shattered against the shields of the warriors. The king took the final gourd, threw it on the ground, and stamped on it to signify the crushing of an enemy. Taking the mush from the gourd, the king threw it toward the sun, invoking the favor of the heavens over enemies on earth. After the king was cleansed with medicines and a ritual bath, the festival ended with a feast, celebrated with dancing by the army and the king. At the conclusion of the feast, the king's councilor proclaimed new laws, an occasion that could allow for public discussion and dispute, but nevertheless a conclusion to the ceremony that reinforced the king's legal jurisdiction over the kingdom (Gluckman, 1938).

The martial opening and the legislative closing of the *umkosi* ceremony suggested that a first-fruits ritual had been incorporated into a new rite of power, as it was placed between military and legal ceremonies that reinforced the sacred, royal power of the king. Rather than celebrating the first fruits under the authority of a homestead, or a lineage, or even a chiefdom, this Zulu ceremony was a rite of power implicated in the power relations of state building. Fertility, therefore, while always having had political implications, was clearly submerged under the centralized military and legal authority of the king in this ritual enactment of Zulu royal ideology.

Ironically, that centralized authority was itself decentered by the destruction of the Zulu kingdom after 1879 (Guy, 1979). Under colonial domination, royal ritual assumed an ambivalent character, both resisting and accommodating new power relations. During the 1920s and 1930s, Zulu royalists tried to revive the religious status of the king. Under South African law, however, the Governor-General (later, the State President) had been declared 'Supreme Chief of All Natives,' holding the authority to appoint or dismiss all chiefs under his domain. South African law, therefore, represented new relations of power under which royal or chiefly ritual was submerged. At the same time that Zulu royalists were trying to gain recognition for their king, royal ritual was more successfully revived in the 1930s in the British Territory of Swaziland. In Swaziland as well, however, royal rituals of state building were performed in both resistance and accommodation to the power and presence of a colonial government (Kuper, 1947: 197–225; Gluckman, 1963; Beidelman, 1966; Apter, 1983; Lincoln, 1987). Obviously, under the military and legal force of colonialism, the politics of religious rites of power had changed radically by the twentieth century.

Likewise, economic changes brought about by the advance of capitalism altered the power relations of the chiefdom and the homestead. In particular, increasing involvement in migrant labor disrupted and transformed domestic and social relations. Various motives inspired Africans to enter the migrant labor market. Some became migrant laborers as a new way of serving older allegiances to chiefs or homestead heads, who in many cases continued to control any surplus wealth produced by younger workers. For many young men, a term of migrant labor became an extension of the initiatory rite of passage into adulthood. Many, however, were forced into the labor market by poverty that was caused or made worse by land reservation and taxation policies of the government. In some instances, however, people entered new labor markets or commercial enterprises as they internalized the religious values advanced by Christian missions. Linked with colonialism and capitalism, Christian missions were significant catalysts of change in southern Africa. During the nineteenth century, southern Africa became one of the most missionized regions of the world. Christian missions achieved little success, however, until the independent domains of the chiefdom and the homestead, along with the religious resources that supported them, became absorbed in a new colonial and capitalist order.

REFERENCES

Abrahamsson, Hans (1951). *The Origin of Death: Studies in African Mythology.* Uppsala: Almqvist.

Alberti, Ludwig (1968). *Ludwig Alberti's Account of the Tribal Life and Customs of the Xhosa in 1807.* Trans. William Fehr, Cape Town: A. A. Balkema (orig. edn 1810).

Apter, Andrew (1983). 'In Dispraise of the King: Rituals against Rebellion in South-east Africa.' *Man* 18: 521–34.

Argyle, W. John and Eleanor Preston-White (eds) (1978). *Social System and Tradition in Southern Africa.* Cape Town: Oxford University Press.

Ashton, Edmund Hugh (1952). *The Basuto.* London: Oxford University Press.

Barnard, Alan (1988). 'Structure and Fluidity in Khoisan Religious Ideas.' *Journal of Religion in Africa* 18: 216–36.

Beidelman, T. O. (1966). 'Swazi Royal Ritual.' *Africa* 36: 373–405.

Beidelman, T. O. (1971). *The Kagaru.* New York: Holt, Rinehart, & Winston.

Berglund, Axel Iver (1976). *Zulu Thought-Patterns and Symbolism.* London: C. Hurst.

Bleek, W. H. I. (1952). In: J. A. Engelbrecht (ed.) *Zulu Legends.* Pretoria: Van Schaik.

Bleek, W. H. I. (1965). *The Natal Diaries of Dr. W. H. I. Bleek, 1855–56.* Cape Town: A. A. Balkema.

Bleek, W. H. I. and L. C. Lloyd (1911). *Specimens of Bushman Folklore.* London: George Allen & Co.

Bonner, Philip (1983). *Kings, Commoners and Concessionaires: The Evolution and Dissolution of the Nineteenth-Century Swazi State.* Cambridge: Cambridge University Press.

Brain, James L. (1973). 'Ancestors as Elders in Africa: Further Thoughts.' *Africa* 43: 122–33.

Brown, J. Tom (1926). *Among the Bantu Nomads: A Record of Forty Years Spent among the Bechuana.* London: Seeley, Service.

Brownlee, Charles (1916). *Reminiscences of Kaffir Life and History.* 2nd edn. Lovedale: Lovedale Press (orig. edn. 1896).

Bührmann, Vera (1978). 'Tentative Views on Dream Therapy by Xhosa Diviners.' *Journal of Analytical Psychology* 23: 105–21.

Bührmann, Vera (1984). *Living in Two Worlds: Communications between a White Healer and Her Black Counterparts.* Cape Town: Human & Rousseau.

Burman, Sandra (1990). 'Fighting a Two-pronged Attack: The Changing Legal Status of Women in Cape-ruled Basutoland, 1772–1884.' In: Cherryl Walker (ed.) *Women and Gender in Southern Africa to 1945.* London: James Currey; Cape Town: David Philip. 48–75.

Callaway, Henry (1868–1870). *The Religious System of the Amazulu.* Springdale, Natal: A. J. Blair; New edn. London: Folklore Society, 1884; Cape Town: Juta.

Callaway, Henry (1871). 'On Divination and Analogous Phenomena among the Natives of Natal.' *Journal of the Royal Anthropological Institute* 1: 163–85.

Carstens, Peter (1975). 'Some Implications of Change in Khoikhoi Supernatural Beliefs.' In: M. G. Whisson and M. West (eds) *Religion and Social Change in Southern Africa.* Cape Town: David Philip. 78–95.

Carstens, Peter (1982). 'The Socio-economic Context of Initiation Ceremonies among Two African Peoples.' *Canadian Journal of African Studies* 16: 505–22.

Casalis, Eugène (1861). *The Basutos, or Twenty-Three Years in South Africa.* London: James Nisbet.

Comaroff, Jean (1980). 'Healing and the Cultural Order: The Case of the Barolong boo Ratshidi of Southern Africa.' *American Ethnologist* 7: 637–57.

Comaroff, Jean (1981). 'Healing and Cultural Transformation: The Case of the Tswana of Southern Africa.' *Social Science and Medicine* 15B: 367–78.

Comaroff, Jean (1985). *Body of Power, Spirit of Resistance: The Culture and History of a South African People.* Chicago: University of Chicago Press.

Comaroff, John L. (ed.) (1980). *The Meaning of Marriage Payments.* New York: Academic Press.

De Jager, E. J. and V. Z. Gitywa (1963). 'A Xhosa Umhlwayelelo Ceremony in the Ciskei.' *African Studies* 22(3): 109–16.

Delius, Peter (1983). *The Land Belongs to Us: The Pedi Polity, the Boers and the British in the Nineteenth-Century Transvaal.* Johannesburg: Ravan Press.

Dornan, S. S. (1923). 'Divination and Divining Bones.' *South African Journal of Science* 20: 504–11.

Du Toit, Brian M. (1960). 'Some Aspects of the Soul-Concept among Bantu-Speaking Nguni Tribes of South Africa.' *Anthropological Quarterly* 33: 134–42.

Elphick, Richard (1985). *Khoikhoi and the Founding of White South Africa.* Johannesburg: Ravan Press; 1st edn *Kraal and Castle: Khoikhoi and the Founding of White South Africa.* New Haven: Yale University Press, 1975.

Eiselen, W. M. (1932). 'The Art of Divination as Practiced by the BaMasemola.' *Bantu Studies* 6: 1–29, 251–63.

Eiselen, W. M. and Isaac Schapera (1934). 'Religious Beliefs and Practices.' In: Isaac

Schapera (ed.) *The Bantu-Speaking Tribes of South Africa.* London: George Routledge & Sons. 247–70.

Etherington, Norman (1987). 'Missionary Doctors and African Healers in Mid-Victorian South Africa.' *South African Historical Journal* 19: 77–91.

Fortes, Meyer (1965). 'Some Reflections on Ancestor Worship in Africa.' In: Meyer Fortes and Germaine Dieterlen (eds) *African Systems of Thought.* Oxford: Oxford University Press. 122–42.

Gluckman, Max (1937). 'Mortuary Customs and the Belief in the Survival After Death Among South-Eastern Bantu.' *Bantu Studies* 11: 117–36.

Gluckman, Max (1938). 'Social Aspects of First Fruit Ceremonies Among the South-Eastern Bantu.' *Africa* 11: 25–41.

Gluckman, Max (1963). 'Rituals of Rebellion in South-east Africa.' *Order and Rebellion in Tribal Africa.* London: Cohen & West. 110–36.

Guy, Jeff (1979). *The Destruction of the Zulu Kingdom: The Civil War in Zululand, 1879–1884.* London: Longman.

Guy, Jeff (1990). 'Gender Oppression in Southern Africa's Precapitalist Societies.' In: Cherryl Walker (ed.) *Women and Gender in Southern Africa to 1945.* London: James Currey; Cape Town: David Philip. 33–47.

Haas, M. de (1987). 'Is There Anything More to Say about *Lobolo*?' *African Studies* 46(1): 33–55.

Hahn, Theophilus (1881). *Tsuni-//Goam: The Supreme Being of the Khoi-Khoi.* London: Trubner & Co.

Hall, Martin (1984). 'The Burden of Tribalism: The Social Context of Southern African Iron Age Studies.' *American Antiquity* 49: 455–67.

Hamilton, Carolyn, and John Wright (1990). 'The Making of the *AmaLala*: Ethnicity, Ideology and Relations of Subordination in a Precolonial Context.' *South African Historical Journal* 22: 3–23.

Hammond-Tooke, W. D. (1953). 'The Function of Annual First Fruit Ceremonies in Baca Social Structure.' *African Studies* 12: 75–87.

Hammond-Tooke, W. D. (ed.) (1974a). *The Bantu-Speaking Peoples of Southern Africa.* London: Routledge & Kegan Paul.

Hammond-Tooke, W. D. (1974b). 'Worldview I: A System of Beliefs. Worldview II: A System of Action.' In: W.D. Hammond-Tooke (ed.) *The Bantu–Speaking Peoples of Southern Africa.* London: Routledge & Kegan Paul. 318–62.

Hammond-Tooke, W. D. (1974c). 'The Cape Nguni Witch Familiar as a Mediatory Construct.' *Man* 9: 128–36.

Hammond-Tooke, W. D. (1975). 'The Symbolic Structure of Cape Nguni Cosmology.' In: M. G. Whisson and M. West (eds) *Religion and Social Change in Southern Africa.* Cape Town: David Philip. 15–33.

Hammond-Tooke, W. D. (1978). 'Do the South-eastern Bantu Worship their Ancestors?' In: W. John Argyle and Eleanor Preston-Whyte (eds) *Social System and Tradition in Southern Africa.* Cape Town: Oxford University Press. 134–49.

Hammond-Tooke, W. D. (1981). *Boundaries and Belief: The Structure of a Sotho Worldview.* Johannesburg: Witwatersrand University Press.

Hammond-Tooke, W. D. (1989). *Rituals and Medicines: Indigenous Healing in South Africa.* Johannesburg: AD. Donker.

Heusch, Luc de (1985). *Sacrifice in Africa: A Structuralist Approach.* Trans. Linda O'Brien and Alice Morton. Manchester: Manchester University Press.

Hexham, Irving (1981). 'Lord of the Sky, King of the Earth: Zulu Traditional Religion and Belief in the Sky God,' *Sciences Religieuses/Studies in Religion* 10: 273–78.

Hobsbawm, Eric, and Terence Ranger (eds) (1983). *The Invention of Tradition.* Cambridge: Cambridge University Press.

Hodgson, Janet (1982). *The God of the Xhosa.* Cape Town: Oxford University Press.

Hoernlé, W. Winifred (1934). 'Magic and Medicine.' In: Isaac Schapera (ed.) *The Bantu-Speaking Tribes of South Africa.* London: George Routledge & Sons. 221–45.

Horton, Robin (1971). 'African Conversion.' *Africa* 41: 85–108.

Horton, Robin (1975). 'On the Rationality of Conversion.' *Africa* 45: 219–35, 373–99.

Hunter, Monica (1936). *Reaction to Conquest: Effects of Contact with Europeans on the Pondo of South Africa.* London: Oxford University Press. 2nd edn 1961. 3rd abridged edn Cape Town: David Philip, 1979.

Junod, H. A. (1927). *The Life of a South African Tribe.* 2 vols, 2nd edn. London: Macmillan (orig. edn 1912).

Kiernan, J. P. (1982). 'The 'Problem of Evil' in the Context of Ancestral Intervention in the Affairs of the Living in Africa.' *Man* 17: 287–301.

Kopytoff, Igor (1971). 'Ancestors as Elders in Africa.' *Africa* 41: 129–42.

Krige, E. J. (1936). *The Social System of the Zulus.* London: Longmans, Green.

Krige, E. J. and J. D. Krige (1943). *The Realm of the Rain Queen.* Oxford: Oxford University Press.

Kuckertz, H. (ed.) (1981). *Ancestor Religion in Southern Africa.* Cacadu: Lumko Missiological Institute.

Kuckertz, H. (1983). 'Symbol and Authority in Mpondo Ancestor Religion, Part One.' *African Studies* 42: 113–33.

Kuckertz, H. (1984). 'Symbol and Authority in Mpondo Ancestor Religion, Part Two.' *African Studies* 43: 1–17.

Kuper, Adam (1982). *Wives for Cattle: Bridewealth and Marriage in Southern Africa.* London: Routledge & Kegan Paul.

Kuper, Hilda (1947). *An African Aristocracy: Rank among the Swazi.* London: Oxford University Press.

Laydevant, F. (1933). 'The Praises of the Divining Bones Among the BaSotho.' *Bantu Studies* 7: 341–73.

Lee, S. G. (1969). 'Spirit Possession among the Zulu.' In: John Beattie and John Middleton (eds) *Spirit Mediumship and Society in Africa.* London: Routledge & Kegan Paul. 128–56.

Lewis-Williams, J. D. (1980). 'Remarks on Southern San Religion and Art.' *Religion in Southern Africa* 1(2): 19–32.

Lewis-Williams, J. D. (1981). *Believing and Seeing: Symbolic Meanings in Southern San Rock Paintings.* London: Academic Press.

Lincoln, Bruce (1987). 'Ritual, Rebellion, Resistance: Once More the Swazi Ncwala.' *Man* 22: 132–56.

McAllister, P. A. (1980). 'Work, Homestead, and the Shades: The Ritual Interpretation of Labour Migration among the Gcaleka.' In: Philip Mayer (ed.) *Black Villagers in an Industrial Society.* Cape Town: Oxford University Press. 205–53.

McAllister, P. A. (1985). 'Beasts to Beer Pots: Migrant Labour and Ritual Change in Willowvale District, Transkei.' *African Studies* 44: 121–35.

McAllister, P. A. (1986). 'Conservatism as Ideology of Resistance among Xhosa-speakers: The Implication for Oral Tradition and Literacy.' In: Richard Whitaker and Edgaard Sienaert (eds) *Oral Tradition and Literacy: Changing*

Visions of the World. Durban: Natal University Oral Documentation and Research Centre. 290–302.

Mafeje, Archie (1971). 'The Ideology of "Tribalism."' *Journal of Modern African Studies* 9: 253–61.

Mair, Lucy (1969). *Witchcraft*. New York: McGraw-Hill.

Marks, Shula (1969). 'Traditions of the Natal Nguni: A Fresh Look at the Work of A. T. Bryant.' In: Leonard Thompson (ed.) *African Societies in Southern Africa: Historical Studies*. London: Heinemann: 126–44.

Marks, Shula (1972). 'Khoisan Resistance to the Dutch in the Seventeenth and Eighteenth Centuries.' *Journal of African History* 13: 55–80.

Marks, Shula (1980). 'South Africa: The Myth of the Empty Land.' *History Today* 30(1): 7–12.

Marks, Shula, and Anthony E. Atmore (1970). 'The Problem of the Nguni: An Examination of the Ethnic and Linguistic Situation in South Africa Before the Mfecane.' In: David Dalby (ed.) *Language and History in Africa*. New York: Africana Publishing Corporation. 120–33.

Marshall, Lorna (1962). '!Kung Bushman Religious Beliefs.' *Africa* 32: 221–52.

Marshall, Lorna (1969). 'The Medicine Dance of the !Kung Bushmen.' *Africa* 39: 347–81.

Mayer, Philip (ed.) (1980a). *Black Villagers in an Industrial Society*. Cape Town: Oxford University Press.

Mayer, Philip (1980b). 'The Origin and Decline of Two Rural Resistance Ideologies.' In: Philip Mayer (ed.) *Black Villagers in an Industrial Society*. Cape Town: Oxford University Press: 1–80.

Maylam, Paul (1986). *A History of the African People of South Africa: From the Early Iron Age to the 1970s*. London: Croom Helm; Cape Town: David Philip.

Mönnig, H. O. (1967). *The Pedi*. Pretoria: Van Schaik.

Ngubane, Harriet (1976). 'Some Notions of "Purity" and "Impurity" among the Zulu.' *Africa* 46: 274–84.

Ngubane, Harriet (1977). *Body and Mind in Zulu Medicine*. London: Academic Press.

Ngubane, Harriet (1981). 'Aspects of Clinical Practice and Traditional Organization of Indigenous Healers in South Africa'. *Social Science and Medicine* 15B: 361–5.

Ngxamngxa, A N N. (1971). 'The Function of Circumcision among the Xhosa-speaking Tribes in Historical Perspective.' In: E. J. de Jager (ed.) *Man: Anthropological Essays Presented to O. F. Raum*. Cape Town: C. Struik. 183–204.

Nürnberger, Klaus (1975). 'The Sotho Notion of the Supreme Being and the Impact of the Christian Proclamation.' *Journal of Religion in Africa* 7: 174–200.

Peires, J. B. (1981). *The House of Phalo: A History of the Xhosa People in the Days of their Independence*. Johannesburg: Ravan Press.

Sansom, Basil (1972). 'When Witches are not Named.' In: Max Gluckman (ed.) *The Allocation of Responsibility*. Manchester: Manchester University Press. 193–226.

Saul, J. S. (1979). 'The Dialectic of Class and Tribe.' *Race and Class* 20: 347–71.

Schapera, Isaac (1930). *The Khoisan Peoples of South Africa: Bushmen and Hottentots*. London: George Routledge & Sons.

Schapera, Isaac (ed.) (1934). *The Bantu-Speaking Tribes of South Africa*. London: George Routledge & Sons.

Schapera, Isaac (1970). *Tribal Innovators: Tswana Chiefs and Social Change, 1795–1940*. London: Athlone Press.

Schapera, Isaac (1971). *The Rainmaking Rites of Tswana Tribes*. Leiden: Afrika Studiecentrum.

Schapera, Isaac (1979). 'Kgatla Notions of Ritual Impurity.' *African Studies* 38: 3–15.

Schutte, A. G. (1978). 'Mwali in Venda: Some Observations on the Significance of the High God in Venda History.' *Journal of Religion in Africa* 9: 109–22.

Setiloane, Gabriel (1976). *The Image of God among the Sotho–Tswana*. Rotterdam: A. A. Balkema.

Sibisi, H. (1975). 'The Place of Spirit Possession in Zulu Cosmology.' In: M. G. Whisson and M. West (eds) *Religion and Social Change in Southern Africa*. Cape Town: David Philip. 48–57.

Smith, E. W. (ed.) (1961). 'The Idea of God among South African Tribes.' *African Ideas of God*. 2nd edn. London: Edinburgh House Press (1st edn. 1950).

Southall, Aidan W. (1970). 'The Illusion of Tribe.' In Peter C. W. Gutkind (ed.) *The Passing of Tribal Man in Africa*. Leiden: E. J. Brill. 28–51.

Spiegel, Andrew, and Emile Boonzaier (1988). 'Promoting Tradition: Images of the South African Past.' In: Emile Boonzaier and John Sharp (eds) *South African Keywords: The Uses and Abuses of Political Concepts*. Cape Town: David Philip. 40–57.

Stayt, H. A. (1931). *The Bavenda*. London: Oxford University Press.

Thompson, Leonard M. (ed.) (1969). *African Societies in Southern Africa: Historical Studies*. London: Heinemann.

Vail, Leroy (ed.) (1989). *The Creation of Tribalism in Southern Africa*. Berkeley: University of California Press; London: James Currey.

Van Warmelo, N. J. (ed.) (1932). *Contributions towards Venda History, Religion and Tribal Ritual*. Pretoria: Government Printer.

Van Warmelo, N. J. (1974). 'The Classification of Cultural Groups.' In: W. D. Hammond-Tooke (ed.) *The Bantu-Speaking Peoples of Southern Africa*. London: Routledge & Kegan Paul. 56–84.

Verryn, Trevor (1981). '"Coolness" and "Heat" among the Sotho Peoples.' *Religion in Southern Africa* 2: 11–38.

Walker, Cherryl (ed.) (1990). *Women and Gender in Southern Africa to 1945*. London: James Currey; Cape Town: David Philip.

Wanger, W. (1923–26). 'The Zulu Notion of God According to the Traditional Zulu God-names.' *Anthropos* 18–19 (1923–4): 656–87; 20 (1925): 558–78; 21 (1926): 351–85.

Warner, J. C. (1858). 'Mr Warner's Notes.' In: John Maclean (ed.) *A Compendium of Kafir Laws and Customs*. Mount Coke: Wesleyan Mission Press. 57–109.

Watt, J. M. and N. J. van Warmelo (1930). 'The Medicines and Practices of a Sotho Doctor.' *Bantu Studies* 4: 47–63.

Whisson, M. G. and M. West (eds) (1975). *Religion and Social Change in Southern Africa*. Cape Town: David Philip.

Willoughby, W. C. (1909). 'Notes on the Initiation Ceremonies of the Becwana.' *Journal of the Royal Anthropological Institute* 39: 228–45.

Willoughby, W. C. (1928). *The Soul of the Bantu*. Garden City, NY: Doubleday. London: SCM Press.

Willoughby, W. C. (1932). *Nature-Worship and Taboo*. Hartford: Hartford Seminary Press.

Wilson, Monica and Leonard Thompson (1969). *The Oxford History of South Africa*: 2 vols. Oxford: Oxford University Press.

Wright, John (1986). 'Politics, Ideology, and the Invention of the "Nguni."' In: Tom Lodge (ed.) *Ideology in Settler Societies*, Southern African Studies, vol. 4. Johannesburg: Ravan Press. 96–118.

Zahan, Dominique (1979). *The Religion, Spirituality and Thought of Traditional Africa*. Chicago: University of Chicago Press.

2 Christian missions

A Christian presence in southern Africa can be dated back to the explorations of the Portuguese navigator, Bartholomew Dias, who in 1488 erected a limestone pillar, or *padrão*, in the eastern Cape. The Catholic ritual of the Mass might have been performed by priests accompanying the expedition. But the planting of the pillar itself, with its Christian cross and Portuguese coat of arms, signified a ritual act that was simultaneously religious and political (Brown, 1960: 1). As in the expedition of Bartholomew Dias, religion, politics, and commercial interests continued to be interwoven in the history of Christianity in southern Africa.

A more permanent Christian presence, however, was initiated with the establishment of a refreshment station at the Cape by the Dutch East India Company in 1652. Although this station was a commercial, political, and military venture, its establishment was also attributed with religious significance. Dutch interest in the Cape had been stimulated by reports from survivors of the shipwreck of the *Haerlem* in 1648, among whom was a man who would later become governor of the Cape Colony, Jan van Riebeeck. Emphasizing the commercial benefits of a Dutch establishment at the Cape, these survivors also suggested 'that some of the natives can be Christianised with the result, if God almighty chose to bless this beneficial action – many souls could be brought to the Reformed religion and God' (Moodie, 1960, I: 1–4). Four years later, this religious motive was enshrined in Article XIII of the Company Charter, linking commercial and religious interests by declaring that the Dutch East India Company in the Cape would create a settlement in which 'the name of Christ may be extended, and the interests of the Company promoted' (Du Plessis, 1911: 21).

Although expressly committed to extending Christianity, the Company's missionary efforts were limited for the most part to setting up slave schools. Resistance to Christian instruction, however, was reflected in a 1658 report that to 'stimulate the slaves to attention while at school, and to induce them to learn the Christian prayers, they were promised each a glass of brandy and two inches of tobacco, when they finish their task' (Du Plessis, 1911: 30). Slaveowners also resisted providing their slaves with Christian instruction due to uncertainty about the status of baptized slaves. The Calvinist Synod of Dort (1618–19) in the Netherlands had ruled that any slave who was baptized should be freed. Before 1770, no law in the Cape implemented this provision of the Reformed faith in the Netherlands. An ordinance in 1770, however, prohibited buying or selling slaves who had converted to Christianity. In response, slaveowners effectively excluded their slaves from Christian conversion or baptism in order to retain property rights over them. As a result, the Dutch Reformed Church minister responsible for slave missions in the 1790s, Michiel Christiaan Vos, wrote that he was not so much concerned with their condition of slavery, but that he was worried about 'the neglect of their immortal souls.' The 1770 statute was repealed in 1812 in hopes that efforts to convert slaves might be resumed (Elphick and Shell, 1989: 190–1).

Few Khoisan showed any interest in Christian conversion. The most notable convert was Krotoa, known as Eva, who was baptized and married in Christian rites, but succumbed to alcoholism, prostitution, and despair after the death of her husband, and died imprisoned on Robben Island in 1674 (Malherbe, 1990). The first sustained missionary work with the Khoisan in the Cape began with the arrival of the German Moravian missionary, George Schmidt, in 1737. Suffering under the disapproval of the Company, the Dutch Reformed Church, and the Classis of Amsterdam, however, Schmidt returned to Germany after 7 years, having achieved no enduring success in gaining converts to his Christian faith (Krüger, 1966).

A new era of Christian missions opened with the arrival of missionaries representing the London Missionary Society (LMS) in 1799. The LMS was followed by the entry of American, French, German, and Scandinavian missionaries into the field. Nineteenth-century Christian missions were obviously an international enterprise, but it was the British blend of political, commercial, and religious interests that established the framework for Christian missions and conversions. In that process, neither colonialism nor Christianity were uniform; nor did their extension represent a single, coherent project (J. L. Comaroff, 1989). Linked with commerce and conquest, however, Christianity assumed distinctive shapes and forms in southern Africa during the nineteenth century.

THE FRONTIER MISSION

Nineteenth-century missionaries embarked on their work preaching an evangelical Christian message, but also bearing certain class, cultural, commercial, and political interests that shaped the character of their mission.

For the most part, missionaries emerged from lower middle–class or laboring–class backgrounds, with experience as businessmen, tradesmen, craftsmen, artisans, or laborers. The first LMS missionary, J. T. Van der Kemp, a former soldier, medical doctor, and scholar, was an exception. John Philip, a former weaver, and Robert Moffat, a former hot-house gardener, were more typical of the class background of the missionaries. With little formal education or theological training, missionaries nevertheless placed a high value on literacy and education, exercising the power of the written word while in the field and in letters, journals, and publications for the benefit of patrons back in Europe.

For the missionaries, the most powerful written word was contained in the Bible, which the missionaries read under the influence of the evangelical revivals as if it contained a single, unified message of sin and salvation. Signs of saving grace were found in faith, devotion, and personal conversion. Influenced by the Industrial Revolution as well as the evangelical revival, however, the missionaries promoted a particular blend of 'Christian civilization' that identified signs of salvation in certain types of moral discipline and productive labor. At the cutting edge of an expanding colonial frontier, the mission station focused religious concerns that were interwoven with education and literacy (Ashley, 1974; 1980; 1982), trade and commerce (Beck, 1989), and the extraction and exploitation of African labor (Cobbing, 1988). In all these respects, Christian missionaries, regardless of their denominations or places of origin, became immediately caught up in local conflicts over meaning and power. In particular, nearly all eventually called upon British military force to support a mission of 'Christianity and civilization.' At the same time, the mission station itself became a ritual space for a particular kind of European, Christian worldview in Africa. European clothing, square houses, irrigation, fenced gardens, hammers, saws, and ploughs, all became ritual artifacts of that Christian worldview (Comaroff and Comaroff, 1989). In that way, a nineteenth-century, European gospel of Christian salvation was entangled with a particular cultural orientation embedded in certain forms and rhythms of everyday life.

Christian missions, therefore, were inherently multidimensional. On one level, missions involved European Christians in a cross-cultural argument, a theological debate between practitioners of different religions. Initially, missionaries entered that debate by denying the fact that Africans had any religion at all. J. T. Van der Kemp wrote back to London in 1800 about the Xhosa-speaking people he stayed with in the eastern Cape: 'I never could perceive that they had any religion, nor any idea of the existence of a God' (Van der Kemp, 1804b: 432). This discovery of 'no religion' among Africans became a recurring theme in missionary reports. Twenty years after Van der Kemp, the Methodist missionary to the Xhosa, William Shaw, argued that they 'cannot be said to possess any religion,' while Methodist missionary W. J. Shrewbury insisted that they were 'without any religion, true or false' (Shaw, 1860: 444; Williams, 1967: 79). Working with the southern Sotho, the French missionary Eugène Casalis complained about their 'endemical atheism,' while Thomas Arbousset reported that they were all atheists, 'with scarcely any idea of a Supreme Being' (Casalis, 1861: 238; Arbousset, 1968: 69). In the north, the Methodist T. L Hodgson reported that the Tswana 'appear to have no religious worship,' with 'no idea of a spirit' (Cope, 1977: 155, 367).

This initial, sweeping denial of African religion represented the South African mission field as if it were a clear space for Christian conversion. However, that denial could not long be sustained. By the 1850s, Christian missionaries had been forced by their engagement with African resistance to conversion into acknowledging that Africans did in fact have a religion, even if that recognition was made grudgingly, only allowing, in the words of the government agent in the eastern Cape, J. C. Warner, that Africans had 'a regular system of superstition which answers all the purposes of any other false religion' (Warner, 1858: 76). In admitting that Africans had a religion, the missionaries had to recognize that they were not introducing Christian beliefs and practices into a religious vacuum but into a contest of religions.

Certainly, that contest of religious worldviews was carried out on the level of theological debate. For example, Robert Moffat recorded an argument between himself and a Tswana sacred specialist in rainmaking. Impatient with Moffat's arrogant claims, the rainmaker offered a theological compromise. 'He said that my God dwelt in the South,' Moffat recalled, and 'that their God dwelt in the North.' Closing the debate, Moffat rejected this negotiated compromise by insisting on the universal scope of his religion. In Moffat's account, the rainmaker 'looked rather stupid when I informed him that my God ruled over all the earth' (Northcott, 1961: 77). In this exchange, a Christian exclusivism came into conflict with a more plural, adaptive, and accommodating African religious worldview. On the purely theological level, Africans were willing to select and adapt elements of the Christian message, even viewing the missionaries themselves as sacred specialists with knowledge and power that might be useful. Intolerant of such African adaptations, however, missionaries insisted on an exclusive, total domination of the religious field.

On the level of theological argument, therefore, Africans occasionally found aspects of the Christian message that were of value. For example, after hearing the Ten Commandments, Sotho Chief Moshoeshoe apparently told Eugène Casalis that the same ethical principles were 'written in all our hearts.' Although unfamiliar with the particular Christian doctrine of God, or the specific ritual observances of the Sabbath, Moshoeshoe concluded that 'in all the rest of your law we find nothing new' (Robinson and Smith, 1979: 51; Elphick, 1981: 275). More significant than this rare moment of religious recognition, however, were the many points of bafflement and incomprehension at the strange, mixed Christian message. Often that message was perceived to be in conflict with the normal order of things. Casalis reported that his students rejected his assertion that Jesus Christ would be joined in heaven with his apostles on twelve thrones because a king should not condescend to have his servants share his throne (Kuper, 1987: 150). On other occasions, however, missionary reports recorded the searching questions that Africans raised about internal contradictions in the Christian message. If God loved the world, why did he not send rain? If God was all powerful, why did he not destroy Satan? If Abraham was both good and rich, why was it hard for a rich man to enter heaven? (Etherington, 1978: 56). In the case of missionary and Bishop J. W. Colenso, in Natal from the 1850s, such questioning apparently led to his reconsideration of the literal inerrancy of the Bible (Guy, 1983). In most instances, however, missionaries interpreted such theological challenges as symptomatic of a stubborn, contentious resistance to the saving message of the gospel.

In any event, the contest of religions in which the missionary enterprise was entangled was not conducted primarily on the level of theological debate. No matter what religious concepts missionaries held when they entered the field, they were immediately involved in local, African contests of meaning and power. They may have come with a gospel of sin and salvation, but the missionaries immediately became engaged in contests over the local rituals of the chiefdom, the homestead, and the sacred specialists of African religion. On the level of ritual, therefore, missionaries consistently attacked African practices related to witchcraft detection in an effort to undermine the religious authority of sacred specialists. They attacked ancestor ritual, initiation, polygyny, bridewealth, and the ritualized relations of production and gender roles that went into building up a homestead. In those arenas of conflict, the Christian message came to be defined, not in general concepts of sin and salvation but in the more specific, localized terms of the African beliefs and practices that it opposed (Williams, 1967: 76–94).

The best illustration of the contest of religions was the intervention of missionaries in the political arena of the chiefdom by engaging in competitions with chiefs and rainmakers over the spiritual, religious, and political power associated with rain. Using rain as an environmental index for religious truth, both sides accused the other of being responsible for drought; and both sides claimed spiritual power that was demonstrated by access to rain (Grove, 1989). In the earliest account of a rainmaking contest, the missionary J. T. Van der Kemp reported that he had been requested by Chief Ngqika to employ his spiritual power to bring rain. Since the chief's rainmakers had failed, Ngqika had turned to the missionary as an alternative sacred specialist. Turning to foreign rainmakers was not uncommon in Xhosa religious practice, since they commonly employed Khoi rainmakers from the western Cape, and later Mfengu refugees from the southeast, as rainmaking specialists. However, Van der Kemp argued against African evidence and experience by insisting that human beings were incapable of making rain, because only his God had the power to grant or withhold that blessing. Nevertheless, he agreed to pray for rain, 'in subordination to the glory of God,' by speaking to Jesus Christ. In return, Chief Ngqika presented Van der Kemp with a cow in payment for his professional services as a rainmaker. The next day, according to Van der Kemp's account, his prayer was answered when 'it pleased the Lord to give us a plentiful rain.' By such events, Van der Kemp argued, 'this ignorant and obstinate nation... will be induced to embrace the Christian religion!' (Van der Kemp, 1804a: 426–28).

In this way, a Christian mission inserted itself into the local religious arena as an alternative 'environmental religion,' making contested claims on the rain as a symbol of religious truth, meaning, and power. Throughout southern Africa, Christian missionaries entered into similar environmental, religious contests over the rain. In 1826, the missionary Thomas Hodgson attacked the Tswana chief Sehonelo and his specialists for their 'vain pretensions' in claiming to make rain during a long period of drought. In this case, the missionary insisted that the absence of rain had to be interpreted as a sign of God's displeasure. 'Surely the Lord's hand is immediately in this,' Hodgson declared. 'May it convince the natives of the folly and wickedness of their pretensions' (Cope, 1977: 356–62). In 1829, the missionary William Shaw used the failure of a Xhosa chief, Phato, and his specialists to make rain to hold a prayer service for rain, declaring that 'times and seasons are in the hand of God, and that He can give or withhold rain as seemeth good to him.' When rains fell 2 weeks later, Shaw interpreted them as a sign of divine blessing, but also as confirmation of a Christian ownership of the rain (Shaw, 1972: 181–3). In 1861, a Methodist missionary in Natal, Joseph Jackson, Jr., reported the effect of the rains that fell following his Sunday service, claiming that people said, 'Our mouths are now stopped; we can answer you nothing; we see that God is, and that he hears prayers' (Etherington, 1978: 52). In this conflict over symbols, therefore, missionaries appropriated the African religious symbol of rain as a sign of their own exclusive, privileged religious authority and power (Reyburn, 1933).

However, because the rain was also an African symbol of chiefly, political power, missionary claims on divine ownership of the rain threatened to undermine the political authority of chiefs. In the case of Chief Ngqika, for example, Van der Kemp's rainmaking produced an allegory for the political destruction of an African world: After 7 days of rain, Van der Kemp reported,

Ngqika petitioned the missionary to stop the thunderstorms because his homestead had been washed away by the rains. In Van der Kemp's account, therefore, the rain represented not only a higher spiritual authority but also a force that could destroy an African political order (Van der Kemp, 1804a: 428).

Most missionaries entered the mission field with the ideal of achieving conversions through persuasion. After some time in the field, however, nearly all turned to advocate various instruments of economic, social, political, or military coercion to create the necessary conditions for Christian conversion. In this regard, the remarks of colonial administrator, J. C. Warner, in the 1850s were echoed by many missionaries who argued that the way 'God will make use of' in converting Africans would be 'the sword' of military force. Like many missionaries, Warner insisted that:

> the sword must first – not *exterminate* them, but – break them up as tribes, and destroy their political existence; after which, when thus set free from the shackles by which they are bound, civilization and Christianity will no doubt make rapid progress among them.

> (Warner, 1858: 108–9)

After the 1820s, missionaries became less willing to engage on relatively equal terms in contests over sacred symbols with chiefs, rainmakers, and other sacred specialists. Aligning themselves with colonial or imperial interests, missionaries increasingly invoked the military force and administrative presence of the British Empire into the work of Christian conversion. As missionary for the Glasgow Missionary Society John Comming observed during the War of the Axe in the 1840s on the eastern Cape frontier, chiefly 'power *must* be broken; and then there is a brighter prospect of the benign influence of the gospel being more generally diffused over those who may be spared from the judgements which are now abroad in the land' (Williams, 1959: 175). Likewise, American, German, and Scandinavian missionaries, who had hoped to create independent Christian communities, began to insist that the political power of chiefs had to be destroyed and replaced by British rule. 'While I would not advocate the policy of planting the gospel at the point of the bayonet,' an American missionary observed, 'I fully believe that the supremacy of English rule is necessary to the speedy and wholesome development of Christian missions in this half of "the dark continent"' (Cope, 1979: 16–17). But even the first black Anglican priest, Peter Masiza, in the eastern Cape during the late 1870s, called for coercion. Masiza insisted that 'it is absolutely necessary to subdue these savages to order and obedience by law and by physical force' (Goedhals, 1989: 20).

Although missionaries became increasingly devoted to the destruction of chiefly political power, African chiefs nevertheless pursued their own interests in relation to the missions. While independent African polities remained in power, with their economic and social relations intact, Christian missions made only minimal gains in converts. Nevertheless, chiefs frequently invited missionaries into their domains in pursuit of perceived material benefits that promised to advance their own military, political, and economic interests.

Perceived as agents of white, colonial society, missionaries seemed to provide the military advantage of firearms and ammunition. In the 1820s, that advantage was exploited by groups known as Griquas, Berengaars, and Bastards in the northern Cape. These ethnically mixed, diverse communities were ruled by warlords and armed horsemen, who maintained a Christian affiliation and close trading and military relations with missionaries. Their raiding expeditions were instrumental in the advance of Christian missions, not because they were Christians, but because their attacks in the 1820s and 1830s motivated certain African groups – the Sotho of Moshoeshoe, the refugees known as the Mfengu, and the Tswana in the north – to turn to missionaries for protection. Having observed the success of these Christians in raiding expeditions, Tswana chiefs to the north of the Cape Colony vied with each other, according to missionary Thomas Hodgson, over 'which of the tribes should possess the missionaries of peace' (Cope, 1977: 104–5).

Bringing guns and ammunition, these 'missionaries of peace' were sometimes sought by chiefs for the superior firepower that might advance their position in relation to other chiefs or provide protection in case of attack. As Hodgson reported, the Tswana chief with whom he worked was convinced that the advent of the missionary had deterred the chief's enemies from attacking him out of 'a dread of being resisted by firearms' (Cope, 1977: 295). Likewise, on the eastern Cape frontier, chiefs sometimes welcomed missionaries to enhance their prestige or deter attacks from rival chiefs (Williams, 1959: 77–8); while in the southeast in 1867 a chief requested that the Natal Colony 'send them a missionary to reside with them to be a protection and keep them right' (Etherington, 1978: 141).

In colonial political relations, chiefs often relied on missionaries for diplomatic services. On the eastern Cape frontier, Chief Ngqika finally accepted a permanent missionary presence for diplomatic rather than religious reasons. As an LMS missionary observed, Ngqika wanted 'to have one who can write for him to the Governor and read his answers, but he has manifested much hostility to the precepts of the word of God' (Williams, 1959: 71). In Zululand and Natal, missionaries were valued if they could prove that they had influence with the Natal Governor, Theophilus Shepstone. A Swazi chief in 1872 even turned down an Anglican request to establish a mission station in his territory on the grounds that Shepstone was 'Missionary enough for them' (Etherington, 1978: 50). This diplomatic role, however, placed missionaries in a somewhat ambiguous position between chiefs and colonial government. As a result, they were more often than not distrusted by both.

Finally, African chiefs often valued missionaries for the material and technological benefits they brought. Although some of these innovations, such as irrigation, well-digging, and ploughing, proved to be profoundly disruptive of African social relations, they nevertheless represented new skills and techniques that many chiefs showed considerable interest in acquiring. On the northern frontier, Robert Moffat declared that it was the 'Bible and plough, with all that they represent, that will regenerate Africa' (Smith, 1925: 147). Arguably more important than the Bible for the advance of Christian missions, the plough represented a technology that dramatically changed, if it did not regenerate, African social relations of production. In the division of labor of the homestead, women had been responsible for agriculture, tending the gardens and fields, while boys herded the cattle and men engaged in public, political, and ritual work. The plough, however, inserted a fundamental contradiction into this gender division of labor because it had to be drawn by oxen, literally yoking what had been separated as the male domain of cattle and the female domain of agriculture. In addition to drawing men into farming, the plough also increased the yield of crops to produce surplus that could be sold on the market. Although trade in agricultural surplus initially led to the emergence of successful peasant producers, it also created class divisions as wealthy individuals gained control over larger tracts of land for agriculture. As a result, African peasants were increasingly forced into wage labor in white-controlled farming and industry. The missionary gospel of the plough, therefore, although adopted by many chiefdoms and homesteads, had unexpected consequences in the breakdown of social and economic relations.

In spite of these supposed military, diplomatic, and material benefits, the predominant African reaction to Christian missions in the nineteenth century was resistance. In the battle over sacred symbols, African religious specialists engaged in counterattacks, such as the prolonged campaign led by the Xhosa rainmaker Mngqatsi in the late 1830s and early 1840s in the eastern Cape. This African sacred specialist conducted rituals near mission stations, often intentionally performed on Sundays, to disrupt the rituals of the missionaries and draw people back from the hold of the mission (Williams, 1967: 85; Peires, 1981: 71).

The homestead also provided a base of resistance to the missions. Homestead heads in Natal and Zululand might have allowed their children to attend mission schools, but they often removed them before they could be baptized. The vast majority of people, however, indicated their resistance to the Christian missions by simply ignoring them. As long as independent African polities were intact, the only people interested in the missions were social outcasts, misfits, and refugees. Statistics suggest this general lack of interest in the missions: In the eastern Cape, the first four mission stations housed 434 converts out of a surrounding population of about 32,000 (Williams, 1967: 93). Even in the southeastern region, the most missionized area in the world during the nineteenth century, fewer than 10 per cent of Africans in Natal were Christian by 1880, with only a few hundred converts in Zululand and Pondoland (Etherington, 1978: 24). Clearly, people retained loyalty to the homestead, the chiefdom, and their religion.

Many chiefs realized that Christian conversion robbed them of their subjects, since converts seemed to owe their loyalty to the alien political power of the British Empire or the colonial government that the mission represented. This problem of dual loyalty in Zululand was addressed in the 1870s by a royal decree that made conversion to Christianity illegal. As the Zulu King Cetshwayo's principal advisor observed, 'We will not allow the Zulus to become so-called Christians. It is not the King says so, but every man in Zululand.' This royal observer noted that people who went to mission stations tended to be accused or convicted criminals, or men who had eloped with a girl without obtaining parental consent, or men who wanted to avoid providing military or other service to the Zulu king, or men and women accused of witchcraft. The Christian mission had to be resisted, therefore, because its mission stations were inhabited by such antisocial people. Ultimately, however, the mission had to be resisted because it represented the vanguard of a foreign political power. 'The missionaries desire to set up another power in the land,' this Zulu royal advisor concluded, 'and as Zululand has only one King that cannot be allowed' (Cope, 1979: 12–13).

In the history of the missions, large-scale, mass conversion to Christianity was in fact linked to the destruction of independent African economic, social, and political life. This progress of destruction went through several stages. While African polities were still intact, missionaries were welcomed by chiefs, not for their gospel, but for the material benefits they might provide. The missionary teachings and practices, however, undermined the political authority of chiefs and subverted the social order of African societies. Gradually, missionaries advocated the replacement of chiefs by British rule in order to make way for 'Christian civilization.' Conquest or cooptation of African polities introduced the political authority of white magistrates, the penetration of a capitalist economy, but also the increasing authority of missionaries, who were agents of military conquest and economic change, as well as agents of a religious worldview that gained converts only when older religious beliefs and practices failed to make sense out of a changing political, social, and economic world. Even under those new conditions, Africans appropriated Christian beliefs and practices to serve their own interests. But it was nevertheless the case that widespread conversion did in fact depend on the breakdown of African social, economic, and political relations under conquest. The history of African conversions, appropriations, and innovations during the nineteenth century can be considered in each of the three major regions of Christian missionary activity.

THE EASTERN CAPE FRONTIER

Originally from Holland, the former army officer, medical doctor, and scholar J. T. Van der Kemp arrived in the Cape in 1799 as the first representative in southern Africa of the newly formed London Missionary Society. After 18 months with the Xhosa chief Ngqika, and 2 years in Graaff Reinet, Van der Kemp established the mission station of Bethelsdorp in 1803, near what later became the town of Port Elizabeth. Caught between settler farmers who regarded him as a troublemaker, and Xhosa chiefs who regarded him as a British agent, Van der Kemp collected a community at Bethelsdorp that was largely comprised of Khoi and former slaves. Although the station provided shelter for some refugees, education for the children of a few chiefs, and opportunities for trade, Xhosa-speaking people for the most part showed little interest in Van der Kemp's mission. Rather than converting the surrounding population, therefore, Van der Kemp and his associate James Read created a small, self-contained community over which Van der Kemp ruled as a chief or perhaps as a pope, as the missionary K. A. Pacalt observed, 'the pope is removed from Rome to Bethelsdorp' (Enklaar, 1988: 165). In 1806 Van der Kemp married a young woman, Sara Janse, a Muslim and former slave. Van der Kemp incurred the enmity of white settlers and farmers by making public accusations of their mistreatment of laborers, resulting in the 'Black Circuit' courts, inconclusive in their findings, that were instituted the year after his death in 1812.

Van der Kemp's Khoi following was comprised of people who by 1800 had become particularly vulnerable. Their land and cattle had been appropriated by European settlers; their survival increasingly depended upon being incorporated into the Cape labor market. On the one hand, their new Christian faith, with its millennial expectation of the end of the world, and promise of salvation, was attractive to people undergoing the experience of their world coming to an end. On the other hand, however, the Christian community at Bethelsdorp, or the settlement on the Kat River established by LMS missionary Joseph Williams in 1816, provided displaced and dispossessed Khoisan people some measure of protection from a new world of market relations and labor exploitation that was being born (Holt, 1954; Kirk, 1973). Van der Kemp's community at Bethelsdorp, in particular, was condemned by European colonial settlers as an obstacle to progress because it provided a refuge for people who might otherwise have been exploited as laborers in white-controlled herding and farming. Partly for this reason, Bethelsdorp was consistently criticized by settlers as a haven of idleness, fostering laziness and lacking in any signs of 'human industry' (Moodie, 1960: V: 21; Philip, 1828, I: 73–74, 92, 94, 99; Lichtenstein, 1930, I: 237–9). This lack of industry was partly due to the poor soil and water supply at the settlement. But it also seemed to have resulted from Van der Kemp's attempt to establish the mission station as a type of buffer between its displaced inhabitants and the demands of the colonial labor market. Nevertheless, after Van der Kemp's death, the mission station did become a type of reserve for labor for surrounding white-controlled economic interests. In that respect, the mission station anticipated the later South African reserve system in providing a reservoir of cheap, exploitable labor (Freund, 1973: 382–3; 1989: 343).

As the LMS expanded, the missionary John Philip was appointed from London to serve as superintendent. Arriving in 1819, Philip devoted his efforts to administration, supervision, and what might be regarded as public relations and propaganda for the missionary society. Based in the center of colonial power in the Cape, Philip became a spokesman for the advance of British imperial and commercial interests. As an advocate of empire, Philip called for the British annexation of Griqua territory by the Cape Colony during the 1830s. When that project failed, however, Philip drew up a charter for a Christian Griqua republic, an armed, feudal, Christian nation, with allegiance to the Colony, that would dominate the surrounding peoples and support Christian missions and British interests throughout the region. Philip regarded such a religious and political alliance as the key to the success of missions in South Africa (Ross, 1986: 174; Legassick, 1989: 397–402).

This blend of religious mission and political rule also held economic implications for people under its domain. Philip was an ardent proponent of proposed legislation in the Cape that would remove legal restrictions on Khoi, former slaves, and other 'free persons of color.' Although Philip advocated this measure on the basis of a liberal ideal of equality, he also argued that lifting restrictions would result in satisfying colonial demands for cheap labor. In its defense Philip argued:

> make the coloured population in your colony free... permit the natives to choose their own masters – secure to them, inviolate from the grasp of colonial violence, the right which God and nature have given them to their offspring – allow them to bring their labour to a free market, and the farmers will no longer have occasion to complain of a want of servants.
> (Philip, 1828: 329; Gailey, 1962; Newton-King, 1980: 198)

Philip's advocacy of state intervention in the Cape labor market was consistent with his recurring theme that Christianity, labor, and commerce were necessarily linked in the work of the missions. Insisting that one of the main purposes of Christian missions was to teach 'industrious habits,' Philip formulated a missionary motif that was almost endlessly repeated throughout the nineteenth century, 'the gospel of work.' Christian converts, however, were not merely laborers; they were also consumers. By instilling what Philip called 'artificial wants' – new desires for European clothing, tools, and other manufactured goods – Christian missions promised to contribute to the advance of British commercial interests. By advancing labor, commerce, and dependence on the Colony, Philip proclaimed the close cooperation of Christian missions with the expansion of British imperialism (Philip, 1828: ix–x; Trapido, 1980: 249).

Of greater immediate impact than missions, commerce, and settlements, however, British presence on the eastern Cape frontier was primarily military. A series of brutal, devastating wars was fought along that frontier during the hundred years from 1779 to 1880. Precolonial Xhosa warfare had not been particularly bloody; war had been largely a matter of cattle raiding, with ritual restraints on harming chiefs, crops, women, and children. The British army, however, introduced the indigenous people of the eastern Cape to a new kind of warfare – total war – that was targeted at the complete destruction of human and material resources. Rather than conquering and absorbing the Xhosa as subjects, colonial troops waged a total war to eliminate or expel them from the region in order to claim their land for white settlement. In this incomprehensible situation of death, destruction, and displacement, Xhosa prophets emerged to assume important leadership roles as religious visionaries struggling to make sense out of a changing world. Rather than representing pagan reactions to conquest, Xhosa prophets – particularly the militant Nxele and the pacifist Ntsikana – appropriated beliefs and practices from the Christian mission. In their new Christian visions, these prophets demonstrated that the missions could have unexpected consequences as a result of African initiatives and innovations in mobilizing Christian resources of symbolic meaning and power (Peires, 1979).

Nxele, also known as Makana, grew up on a Boer farm in the Cape Colony, where he was exposed to European, Christian cultural resources. When he began experiencing the initiatory symptoms of a diviner, Nxele withdrew to live in forests and fields, occasionally preaching against witchcraft. Following an experience that he described as an intervention by Christ, Nxele established his ministry at the homestead of chief Ndlambe, uncle and rival of Ngqika. There Nxele preached a Christian message about God – whom he called Mdalidiphu, creator of the deep – and his son, Tayi. In the name of Mdalidiphu, Nxele proclaimed a promise of the resurrection of the dead. Making common cause with the missionaries, Nxele preached against witchcraft, polygyny, adultery, and warfare. However, as Nxele complained to the missionary James Read, no one was interested in his ministry. For their part, the missionaries in and around the colonial outpost of Grahamstown also rejected Nxele for what one referred to as his 'metaphysical subtleties or mystical ravings' (Pringle, 1835: 279).

By 1816 Nxele's ministry began to change, as he started calling himself the younger brother of Christ. Embarking on a new phase of his ministry, Nxele invited people to witness an event at Gompo Rock where he promised that the dead would rise and witches would be buried. When this prophecy failed, Nxele blamed it on the disobedience of the people in attendance. Establishing his own homestead, Nxele's reputation as a man of spiritual power grew. Nxele began to paint his body with red ocher, to lead ritual dancing, and to demand payment in cattle for his services, all characteristics of traditional Xhosa diviners. But he continued to preach a particular kind of Christian message. However, the content of Nxele's gospel was modified to make symbolic sense out of the world-destroying conflict between whites and blacks that was raging around the Xhosa. Nxele depicted the world as a battleground between the God of the whites, Thixo (the Khoi, and later Xhosa, name for God used by the missionaries) and the God of the blacks, Mdalidiphu. According to Nxele, the whites had killed the son of their God. As punishment, they had been thrown into the sea. Now, they had arrived in search of land, but in the near future they would be forced back into the sea through the greater power of Mdalidiphu, who was not in some remote heaven, but underground with the ancestors. In the meantime, God was to be worshiped not through prayer, as the missionaries taught, but through celebration, dance, procreation, and spiritual preparation for war. In that last form of worship, Nxele served as war doctor for the forces of Ndlambe and his allies as they prepared to counterattack the British army.

In May 1819, confident in his spiritual power, Nxele led a contingent of as many as 10,000 warriors against Grahamstown only to suffer a dramatic defeat. Hoping to end British reprisals, Nxele surrendered 3 months later and was imprisoned on Robben Island. A year later, in an effort to escape, Nxele and his companions were drowned off the Cape coast. Refusing to believe he was dead, however, many of Nxele's adherents continued to expect his return. In his appropriation of Christian symbols, Nxele had formulated an apocalyptic message that promised an imminent victory out of the conflict between the opposing forces represented by two gods. After his death, Nxele himself became a symbol of militant black resistance to white domination in South Africa (Hodgson, 1985a, 1985b, 1986a).

By contrast, the Xhosa prophet Ntsikana proclaimed a pacifist Christian message of accommodation to the changing historical conditions of the eastern Cape. Head of a homestead in the chiefdom of Ndlambe, Ntsikana reportedly experienced a vision of a mysterious light shining on his favorite ox at the gate of his cattle enclosure. Afterwards, finding that he was incapable of participating in ritual dancing, Ntsikana washed himself in a stream for purification and went to Ndlambe to offer his spiritual services to the chief. Since Nxele was already established as spiritual advisor to Ndlambe, however, Ntsikana's offer was declined. As a result, Ntsikana went to Ngqika, Ndlambe's rival, and was accepted, initially distinguishing himself for his vocal opposition to the teachings of Nxele. Through contacts between 1816 and 1818 with Joseph Williams, who at the time was serving as missionary to Ngqika, Ntsikana seems to have gained familiarity with Christian symbols. In Christian terms, therefore, Ntsikana argued that Nxele was not merely wrong, but that he had perverted Christian doctrine. Opposing the rival prophet, Ntsikana argued that 'Nxele is wrong in saying that God is on earth: God is in the heavens. He is right in saying that there are two Gods, but they are not Tayi and Mdalidiphu, but Thixo and his son' (Peires, 1979: 59). Like Nxele, Ntsikana also had an apocalyptic message, but it was a promise of a reign of peace that would be brought by the Messiah – the Broad-Breasted One – who would establish a kingdom of God.

In the meantime, Ntsikana advised the Xhosa to accept the Bible, beware of money, and discard their weapons. His closest followers were called the Poll-headed, like oxen without horns, because of their pacifism. Subjects of Ngqika might have found this acceptance of the colonial military situation easier to support because the British military government had somewhat arbitrarily set up their chief as paramount in the region. Nevertheless, when he was unsuccessful in restraining Ngqika's warriors from battle, Ntsikana warned that they would be destroyed. Proclaiming submission to the will of God, and accommodation to the presence of whites, Ntsikana represented a position that was particularly congenial to the Christian missions. Before his death, Ntsikana instructed his closest followers to join a nearby mission station and many were absorbed in that alternative social world. But he also told them to remain united, like a ball of scrapings from tanned hide, maintaining their cultural unity even as they submitted to the regimen of the missions. Although Ntsikana stood as a symbol of accommodation to the religious and political world represented by the Christian missions, the example, message, and evocative hymn that he left represented a distinctively African appropriation of Christian faith (Hodgson, 1980; 1985a).

Nxele's resistance and Ntsikana's submission persisted as models for relating with the Christianity of the missions in the eastern Cape. Ntsikana's followers became absorbed into the life of the mission station, wearing European clothing, building square houses, attending church and school, and working hard. Ntsikana's disciple, Soga, was an exception, as he remained outside of the mission station and built up a prosperous homestead by exploiting new techniques of ploughing, irrigation, and the new economy based on money and payment of wages to his followers. As an important transitional figure, Soga adhered to his Christian faith, with its economic, as well as religious implications, while he took several wives, occasionally consulted diviners, and allowed his followers to participate in ancestral rituals. Nevertheless, Soga conducted regular prayer services at his homestead, insisting, however, that only the prayers and hymns of Ntsikana be performed. Ntsikana's son, Dukwana, became an evangelist and leader in the life of the Chumie mission station, pursuing a Christian ministry that spanned nearly 50 years. Likewise a transitional figure, Dukwana remained loyal to the missions but opposed the colonial government's confiscation of Xhosa lands (Hodgson, 1986b).

During the 1840s and 1850s missionary work expanded. In addition to the work of the London Missionary Society and the Glasgow Missionary Society, the Wesleyan Methodist Missionary Society had established a string of seven mission stations by 1845 (Shaw, 1860: 337–64, 468–518). A seminary for the training of teachers had been founded in 1841 by the Free Church of Scotland mission at Lovedale which would become a center for Christian education (Young, 1902; Shepherd, 1940). A Methodist school was established at Healdtown (Hewson, 1959). However, the Christian gospel and education were primarily received by the displaced refugees from Natal who came to be known by the collective name of Mfengu, a name given to any refugee who identified with the aims of the missions or the colonial government (Moyer, 1976). Mfengu groups were placed by the colonial government in land confiscated from Xhosa chiefdoms, serving as a buffer between displaced Africans and white settlements. With Mfengu allies and on the authority of a series of military governors, British troops subjected Xhosa chiefdoms to a reign of terror during extensive colonial wars of extermination (Maclennan, 1986). One religious implication of this situation was the common perception among Xhosa-speaking people that two religions, or two gods, were being proclaimed by the Christian missions. Many apparently asked: 'How many are these gospels that you preach?... We ask because [Lt. Col. Henry] Somerset came and said 'stop doing evil,' and yet he kills people every day' (Williams, 1967: 60). One Christian convert asked his missionary, 'Why do not the missionaries first go to their own countrymen and convert them first' (Peires, 1981: 77). In this context, most Xhosa-speaking people were committed to religious and military resistance.

Resistance was mobilized in the frontier war of 1850–53 by the war doctor and witch detector Mlanjeni, who in preparation for war ordered people to sacrifice all yellow and dun-colored cattle to counteract the evil spells under which the country was suffering. As an African religious innovator, Mlanjeni prayed to the sun as symbol of the high god who would give power over the white colonial invaders, while he provided powerful medicines that promised to make warrior's invincible and turn bullets into water (Brownlee, 1916:

169; Chalmers, 1877: 51–4; Govan, 1875: 119). Fighting alongside Mlanjeni's Xhosa warriors, Khoi Christians from the Kat River Settlement prayed, read the Bible, and sang hymns before battle. Their leader, Willem Uithaalder, called upon his followers to trust in the Lord and seize the opportunity for rebellion in the name of God, motherland, and freedom (Peires, 1987: 59). In a variety of ways, therefore, religious symbols were mobilized as instruments of power in resistance to white military domination in the eastern Cape, with traditional, Christian, and innovative religious symbols invoked in common cause against a common enemy.

In the desperate situation that followed defeat in Mlanjeni's war, people in the eastern Cape even looked to foreign aid from Russians who were fighting the British in the Crimean War. Apparently, many Xhosa believed that 'Russians are black people like ourselves, and they are coming to assist us to drive the English into the sea' (Chalmers, 1877: 102). In this context of despair, mixed with hope of redemption, a councilor of the Xhosa chief Sarhili, by the name of Mhlakaza, reported that his teenaged niece, Nongqawuse, had seen a vision of strange people – some Russians, some Xhosa ancestors – who appeared with many cattle and promised to return to drive away the white invaders and restore land, cattle, and prosperity to the people. Before the ancestors could return, however, the living had to put away witchcraft, those evil practices that divided the unity and disrupted the harmony of the social order. As evidence that they had renounced witchcraft and trusted in the promise of redemption, Mhlakaza drew on the authority of his young niece's vision to instruct people that they had to sacrifice all their cattle in anticipation of the resurrection of their ancestors and the overthrow of white domination (Brownlee, 1916: 128–9).

From April 1856 to May 1857, the vast majority of Xhosa homesteads responded to the prophecy by sacrificing their cattle and destroying their crops. An estimated 400,000 cattle were sacrificed in expectation of the imminent return of the ancestors. When the prophecy failed, Mhlakaza and Nongqawuse were able to blame its failure on the disbelief and witchcraft of those non-believers who had refused to sacrifice. By that point, however, 40,000 people had died of starvation, while at least another 40,000 had been forced to leave their homes in search of food or work in the colonial labor market. After years of resistance, Xhosa independence was finally destroyed by what might appear as a ritual of national, sacrificial suicide. To the believers, however, the cattle killing appeared as a reasonable response to the desperate conditions of the colonial frontier. They were predisposed to place their hope in a prophecy of redemption by the prolonged colonial warfare that had already turned the frontier into a region of death, as colonial troops systematically killed people, raided cattle, and destroyed crops in a campaign of extermination. In addition, a devastating lung-sickness epidemic in 1854 had caused the death of countless cattle throughout the region, in many areas leaving few cattle still alive to be sacrificed. Since the world of the Xhosa had already become a region of death, therefore, it must have seemed reasonable to many believers that the dead would rise and return to reclaim it.

The redemptive return of the ancestors and cattle, however, was thought to be prevented by the impurity of the land. The region had been defiled by defeat in battle and by the death of cattle from an illness attributed to the evil work of witches. In counteracting the pollution caused by enemies and witches, it made sense to believers to sacrifice cattle in order to restore the necessary condition of purity. In this respect, Mhlakaza and Nongqawuse mobilized traditional religious resources – belief in ancestors, renunciation of witchcraft, and ritual sacrifice for purification – in the cattle-killing movement. At the same time, however, their emphasis on an apocalyptic resurrection of the dead indicated that those religious resources were orchestrated around a new, Christian understanding of redemption.

The cattle killing provided another, dramatic illustration of the unexpected consequences of the Christian mission. Rather than representing a pagan reaction, the movement actually appropriated Christian symbols of meaning and power. Mhlakaza had been a Christian convert, who from 1849 to 1852 had served Archdeacon Nathaniel J. Merriman of Grahamstown. During that time, Mhlakaza not only became conversant with Christian beliefs, but he also aspired to becoming a minister and missionary for the Anglican church. Rejected by Nathaniel J. Merriman, however, Mhlakaza turned to a different Christian gospel that promised the imminent advent of the messiah, Sifuba-Sibanzi, the Broad-Breasted One of whom the prophet Ntsikana had spoken. Many believers in the cattle-killing movement were convinced that the appearance of this messiah and the return of the dead were consistent with biblical accounts of resurrection. Arguing that the return of the ancestors and cattle was no more unlikely than many stories in the Bible, believers adopted the prophetic promise as an even greater spiritual knowledge and power than the Bible because it was a new revelation that specifically addressed the historical situation of the Xhosa on the eastern Cape frontier. Nevertheless, that new, apocalyptic revelation had tragic consequences in the death and destruction that ensued. As a result of the cattle killing, survivors were even more vulnerable to colonial domination, absorption into the labor market, and conversion to the Christianity represented by the mission stations (Peires, 1989; Ralston, 1976; Zarwan, 1976; Keller, 1978; Thorpe, 1984).

In 1857, Tiyo Soga, son of the elder Soga who had followed Ntsikana, returned after 5 years of ministerial training in Scotland to establish the Mgwali mission station among the people of Ngqika in a region devastated by the recent cattle killing. As the first black South African to be ordained as a minister, under the auspices of the United Presbyterian Church of Scotland and the Glasgow African Missionary Society, Tiyo Soga was well positioned to gather a following of displaced Xhosa and Mfengu converts. With his Scottish wife Janet and Ntsikana's son Dukwana, Tiyo Soga built up the Mgwali mission station as a thriving religious center, often referring to it as Mount Zion. By 1866 the Mgwali mission station was surrounded by 30 preaching and praying homesteads. Tiyo left Mgwali in 1868 to found another station, where he died 4 years later, at the age of 42.

Like other missionaries, Tiyo Soga attacked traditional religious practices and interpreted the catastrophe of the cattle killing as an opportunity for gaining Christian converts. Nevertheless, he represented the vanguard of a new, educated, black elite in an emerging African nationalism. Tiyo Soga advised his children to 'take your place in the world as colored, not as White men, as [Africans] not as Englishmen.... For your own sakes never appear ashamed that your father was [an African], and that you inherited some African blood' (Soga, 1983: 6). Although certainly caught in the racial and class contradictions of his position, Tiyo Soga also suggested the possibility of a new African consciousness that by the end of the nineteenth century would provide an important frame of reference for the self-understanding and identity of many black Christians in South Africa.

By the 1880s, the Christian mission had become a site for defining basic class divisions in the black population of the eastern Cape. The population was deeply divided between 'school people,' who were affiliated with the missions, and the 'red people,' also known as 'blanket people,' who self-consciously tried to adhere to what they regarded as older, traditional ways of life. Resisting the religion of the missions, the so-called 'red' Xhosa referred to converts as *amagqoboka* – 'people having a hole' – indicating that the 'school' people had opened a hole in the nation through which white enemy forces had entered. For their part, the 'school' people were committed to the discipline and self-improvement represented by education, wage labor, and participation in the colonial cash economy. But the 'red' people were also subject to the changing economic relations, as even their red ocher and blankets had to be obtained from white traders (Mayer, 1980).

Nevertheless, the 'school' people were positioned to take advantage of new opportunities in peasant farming, skilled trades, transport, and other occupations in the eastern Cape. Within the 'school' community, however, a class division emerged with the rise of an educated elite, who aspired to westernized values, lifestyles, and citizenship. Leaders of the educated elite, such as John Tengo Jabavu, Pambani Mzimba, and Elijah Makiwane, argued that they should hold all the civilized rights and privileges of colonial citizens. For example, in response to denials of their equality on racial grounds, Elijah Makiwane asserted that 'notwithstanding the 2,000 years of christianity and civilization there are individuals even in the higher callings to whom some [blacks] may be compared without fear' (Davis, 1979: 29). Like many of the educated elite, Makiwane had been a product of the Lovedale missionary school. Lovedale's director, James Stewart, disagreed with Makiwane by insisting that Africans were 'a race as yet intellectually dormant and far behind in the race of nations' (Ashley, 1982: 57).

Stewart was an ardent proponent of the Christian gospel of productive labor. 'The gospel of work does not save souls, but it saves peoples,' Stewart declared. 'Lazy races die or decay. Races that work prosper on earth. The British race, in all its greatest branches, is noted for its restless activity. Its life motto is Work! Work! Work!' (Wells, 1908: 216). On these terms, James Stewart advocated schooling blacks for labor that would serve British commercial and industrial interests, thereby incorporating blacks as subservient workers in the advance of capitalism and Christianity. On terms of equality, however, the 'school' elite requested admittance into the colonial society. The Native Educational Association, founded in 1879, provided one forum for advancing the interests of the educated elite. As their aspirations were increasingly frustrated, however, some members of the educated elite explored the formation of independent Christian churches as an alternative avenue for advancing their religious and political interests.

THE SOUTH-EASTERN FRONTIER

In the early 1820s, British adventurers, travelers, and traders entered southeastern Africa during a time of intense political disruption. This time of turmoil has conventionally been referred to by historians as the *mfecane* – the 'crushing' – that resulted from aggressive Zulu military projects of state building. However, more recent historical analysis has suggested that the widespread social dislocation and migrations associated with the *mfecane* resulted not from wars of conquest initiated by the Zulu King, Shaka, but from the extraordinary pressures placed on African societies by the slave-raiding expeditions that fed captives into the Portuguese slave market to the north in Delgoa Bay. In any case, British entrepreneurs took advantage of an unstable political situation by publishing propaganda that portrayed Shaka as a bloodthirsty tyrant, faking treaties that ceded to whites vast tracts of coastal and inland territory, and, in the case of H. F. Fynn, even establishing by 1827 an African fiefdom with over 2,000 subjects and extensive holdings in cattle and land (Cobbing, 1988; Stuart and Malcolm, 1950; Gardiner, 1836).

In this context, the account of a religious discussion between King Shaka and the traveler Nathaniel Isaacs should probably be read with some skepticism. Shaka listened attentively as Isaacs described God as the supreme being and expressed astonishment when Isaacs recounted the Christian story of creation. Shaka was so moved by this information, according to Isaacs, that he said 'he had discovered we were a superior race and that he would give the missionaries abundance of cattle to teach him to read and write' (Isaacs, 1836, I: 119–20). Before that could happen, however, Shaka was murdered in 1828 by a conspiracy that supported the interests of one of the claimants to the Zulu throne, Dingane. Nine years later, in 1837, Francis Owen was the first British missionary to visit Dingane's court. The missionary preached to the king about sin, salvation, and the word of God, but Dingane was apparently baffled by the fact that this white person had come so far and gone to such trouble simply to relate such an unlikely story. Like Shaka, Dingane also asked to be taught how to read, but immediately followed that request with a request for gunpowder (Cory, 1926: 40).

Most Zulu speakers initially found the message of the Christian missionary incomprehensible. In response to his theological language about 'the chief above,' Owen encountered skeptical reactions: 'Is there one? Can he see us if he is in the air? He must be a good climber.' In general, Owen found a fundamental misunderstanding of his message, as people 'did not know I was speaking of God, they thought I was talking of King George.' Even Dingane was understandably confused when Owen talked about God as supreme chief. Dingane asked, 'Was God among the English Kings?' (Cory, 1926: 39; 103). In these theological discussions, Zulus seemed to be trying to understand a basic tenet of the new religion in terms of the more familiar religious concept of Unkulunkulu, the first ancestor. For their part, the missionaries appropriated the term Unkulunkulu to refer exclusively to their own notion of God. While Zulus initially found this theological argument useless, they did show considerable interest in acquiring technology, writing, firearms, and horses from the missionaries. This practical interest was evident in Dingane's response to Owen's sermon on the resurrection. The Zulu king told the missionary not to worry about the dead but to provide medical care, because healing the sick was easier than raising the dead (Cory, 1926: 74).

During the same year, a different style of Christian message was preached to Dingane by Piet Retief, a leader of white emigrants from the Cape who came to be known as Voortrekkers. Referring to the Ndebele chief recently defeated in battle, Retief warned the Zulu king that the 'great Book of God teaches us that kings who conduct themselves as Umsilikazi [Mzilikazi] does are severely punished, and it is not granted to them to live or reign long; and if you desire to learn at greater length how God deals with bad kings, you may enquire concerning it from the missionaries who are in your country' (Bird, 1888, I: 362–4). Although Retief had condemned missionaries on other occasions as 'interested and dishonest,' he nevertheless invoked their authority to threaten the Zulu king with the vengeance of a more powerful divine king. A month later, in December 1837, the Zulu king asserted his own royal, religious ideology at a first fruits ceremony, at which, according to the diary of the missionary Owen, attendants praised Dingane by declaring, 'Who can fight with thee? No king can fight with thee! They that carry fire cannot fight with thee' (Cory, 1926: 89). In an attempt to forestall Voortrekker settlement in the region, but also perhaps as a ritual act in this conflict of religious claims on spiritual, royal power, Dingane killed Retief and his company in February 1838.

However, that act did not end the contest. At the end of the year, on 16 December 1838, a Voortrekker commando, with wagons encircled in laager formation, armed with muskets and cannons, defeated a Zulu army of 10,000, killing 3,000 without suffering a casualty in an engagement that came to be known as the Battle of Blood River. This battle was later invested with considerable religious significance by Afrikaner nationalists as a demonstration of the superior power of the Voortrekkers' God, particularly in the legendary accounts of their prayers, covenant, and promise to build a church if God gave them victory (Thompson, 1985: 144–88). But the defeat of Zulu warriors at Blood River at least demonstrated the superior power of the weapons that these white invaders could deploy against African forces in the region.

Although their exploits later came to be clothed in a religious aura in the ideology of Afrikaner nationalism, the Voortrekkers had ventured into Zulu territory accompanied by no ordained minister of religion, largely because the clergy of the Dutch Reformed Church had disapproved of their departure from the Cape Colony. In 1841, the Voortrekkers hired the American missionary, Daniel Lindley, to serve as their predikant, or minister. Lindley had originally entered the region in the hope of establishing a Zulu mission, but he claimed to have found the Voortrekkers an even greater challenge. 'Unless they come under religious instruction,' Lindley wrote back to America about the Voortrekkers, 'they will overturn everything in this country.' But Lindley also saw them as providing an opportunity for advancing his Zulu mission, noting that 'the cheapest, speediest, easiest way to convert the heathens here is to convert the white ones first' (Smith, 1949).

During the nineteenth century, nine different missionary societies operated in the south-eastern region, establishing over 75 mission stations in Natal, Zululand, and Pondoland. A detailed analysis of the varied reasons for residing at a mission station has found that out of 177 individuals for whom motives were recorded, only about 12 per cent claimed purely religious reasons for joining a mission. Of the rest, 33 per cent were refugees, 26 per cent came for employment, 15 per cent joined family members, and 14 per cent had accompanied a missionary when he moved to a new location. Although these statistics only suggest the mixed motives that brought people to the Christian mission, they do indicate that the vast majority of converts entered the mission for pressing social or economic reasons (Etherington, 1977: 35).

As in the eastern Cape, mission stations were places of refuge for people either escaping or excluded from African homesteads and chiefdoms. Those who were refugees might have been young women avoiding an arranged marriage, young men refusing royal service, or men and women accused of witchcraft. As a result, Africans tended to view the mission stations as 'sinks of iniquity,' evil places that harbored criminals, witches, social misfits, and rebellious men and women. Even the missionary Henry Callaway had to admit that 'it is not the elite of [African] society, which first gathers around a missionary; it is not even an average specimen of the natives' (Etherington, 1978: 87).

Those who came to the mission for land, employment, or economic opportunity tended to be viewed by Africans as antisocial individualists. As the Zulu King Cetshwayo observed, 'they do nothing but work – serving neither their own chiefs nor the Government. They live only for themselves' (Etherington, 1978: 81). From its inception, therefore, the mission station was a separate enclave, religiously, socially, and economically isolated from the larger African social world. For the most part, mission-station residents came to be regarded as aliens. From the perspective of the homestead and chiefdom, as one African witness testified in evidence at a government commission in the 1880s, people of the mission stations 'have become as white men' (Etherington, 1978: 68).

Missionaries exploited African social and economic motivations in their efforts to gain converts and increase the populations of their missions. Besides providing a haven for refuge and land for farming, however, the missionaries also advanced their own social and economic interests. In this regard, the career of Henry Callaway is instructive. Medical doctor, ethnographer, and comparative religionist, Henry Callaway was a missionary with a particular sensitivity to traditional African religious life (Etherington, 1987). Based on his detailed investigations into African religion, Callaway argued that Africans were, 'in every respect, possessed of the same intellectual, moral, and religious potential as ourselves' (Callaway, 1874: 24). To realize that potential, however, Callaway insisted that Africans had to adopt new values and disciplines of 'time, labour and skill.' Callaway preached this gospel of work with such enthusiasm that residents at his mission station referred to the plough as his wife. In Callaway's Christian mission, therefore, the Protestant work ethic was essential to the process of conversion (Etherington, 1978: 119).

While Callaway insisted that his African converts needed to work, he also wanted Africans converted into laborers who would satisfy colonial labor needs. 'How are 8,000 widely scattered whites,' Callaway asked, 'to compel 200,000 [blacks] to labour, against their will?' (Benham, 1896: 88). Various colonial enactments – land reservation, pass systems, hut taxes, and forced labor – provided legalized instruments of coercion that compelled many Africans into the labor market in Natal. Ultimately, however, military intervention provided a more direct form of coercion. Although he had resented the encroachments of white settlers in the 1850s, Callaway eventually converted to the colonial gospel of commerce and civilization, arguing that it was not right 'to keep out the struggling, hard-working white man for such an unprogressive people as this' (Benham, 1896: 152–3). Finally, by 1873, Callaway was advocating direct military intervention by British troops, who represented, he declared, 'the God-sent power' that would effect change in the region (Benham, 1896: 309–10; Etherington, 1978: 44). In the career of Henry Callaway, therefore, missionary work was obviously entangled in the social, economic, and political interests of an emerging colonial order.

The link between Christianity and commerce in Natal produced some unexpected consequences for both missionaries and converts. The Wesleyan missionary James Allison had gathered a following of people from diverse backgrounds over two decades before settling in 1851 at Edendale, near the colonial capital of Pietermaritzburg. Allison's community at Edendale was divided by religion, comprising 150 converts, 270 believers, and 160 non-believers, but it was unified in a common economic venture as residents pooled their resources to purchase a large tract of land for the mission station. Ten years later, however, when the land had been paid off, the residents were outraged to discover that the title to the land was in Allison's name. Refusing to worship with a minister who was so dishonest in business, the people of Edendale succeeded in driving Allison from the village and making their own arrangements for a ministerial replacement (Meintjes, 1990: 126–9). Fifteen years later, James Allison was still remembered as a model of missionary deceit for:

> cheating his people about their land which they had bought with their own money, he was no longer in good odour with them when he died, they called him a deceiver, and he had ceased to worship with their village.
>
> (Etherington, 1978: 142)

Unexpected consequences of the connection between Christianity and commerce also appeared in the work of the American missionary Aldin Grout. In 1861, Grout triumphantly reported from his mission station at Mvoti that religious conversion had resulted in the kinds of commercial involvement that he and other missionaries associated with Christian civilization. With 'an increase of religious interest among a heathen people,' Grout observed, 'we naturally expect a corresponding increase in the direction of civilisation.'

Grout found evidence of civilization in the ploughs, wagons, upright houses, and European clothing adopted by his converts (Etherington, 1978: 116). These objects appeared to the missionary as the outer signs of a Christian conversion. Although non-Christians also took advantage of new economic opportunities, converts in particular adapted to the colonial economy by internalizing the Protestant ethic of hard work, discipline, and frugality. In many cases, as at Mvoti, converts had considerable success in their new ventures, achieving a certain measure of wealth and economic independence (Vilakazi, 1962: 118–21).

Economic independence, however, conflicted with the basically feudal arrangement of the mission station. Replacing the older institutions of chiefdom and homestead in the lives of his converts, the missionary tried to operate as both chief and father. At Mvoti, the feudal, paternalistic authority of missionary Aldin Grout came to be resented. In 1869, residents rebelled against that authority, declaring, 'Heretofore we have been children and have followed our missionary, now we are men and may think and act for ourselves' (Etherington, 1978: 142). Apparently, mission station residents also wanted to think and act for themselves in matters of religion. As Aldin Grout observed, 2 years before leaving the mission field in despair, 'enterprise in business makes enterprise in religion' (Etherington, 1978: 145). Reversing his earlier argument that conversion led to commerce, Aldin Grout concluded 10 years later that African converts who had achieved a certain degree of economic independence also wanted to assume greater control over their religious lives. Religious initiative was demonstrated by African converts in the nineteenth century. The careers of converts, however, suggested the different trajectories that African innovators could take in response to the missions: rejecting, accepting, or creatively adapting the new symbolic resources of the Christian religion.

As one of the first converts of the Anglican Bishop J. W. Colenso, William Ngidi charted a course that ultimately led to a complete rejection of the Christian religion. While still a Christian, William Ngidi assisted Colenso in translating the Bible into Zulu. It was his searching questions about biblical narratives that apparently led to Colenso's rejection of the literal accuracy of the entire Christian scriptures. Similarly, William Ngidi's defense of ancestral customs, particularly polygyny and lobola, must have contributed to Colenso's relatively tolerant attitude toward those African institutions. After his conversion, William Ngidi, like his fellow convert Mgema Fuze, took second wives. Certainly, economic considerations influenced these Christians to become polygynists, as Fuze later noted, 'a man with one wife only is a poor fellow.' But both converts could also cite the biblical precedent of the ancient patriarchs of Israel (Etherington, 1978: 137–8). William Ngidi initially tried to accommodate both Christian and African religion. He undertook a short-lived missionary campaign of his own, traveling to mission stations and defending African customs on Christian grounds. When this effort failed, however, William Ngidi rejected Christianity, retreated to a remote region of Natal, and lived as an ardent proponent of non-Christian religion and customs (Etherington, 1978: 43, 135, 158).

By contrast, Mpengula Mbande, one of the first two black Anglican priests ordained by Henry Callaway, enthusiastically accepted the new religious and political order represented by the Christian missions. Mbande had been born in a chiefly family, but when his family came under suspicion he fled to the mission station of J. L. Döhne. There he married a young woman who had run away to the station to avoid an arranged marriage. When Döhne departed the region in 1857, Mpengula Mbande and his wife went to Callaway at Springdale (Etherington, 1978: 108–9). Mbande served not only as deacon but also as Callaway's principal informant in his investigations of traditional African religion. Although a diligent ethnographer, Mbande also inserted Christian editorials into his accounts of traditional religion, observing, for example, that Zulus did not 'possess the truth' when they placed trust in ancestors rather than Christ (Callaway, 1868–70: 27–8). In adopting Christianity, however, Mbande also assumed the superiority of European civilization. Even accepting the divine authority of white colonial domination, Mbande preached that all Africans, Christian and non-Christian, as one missionary reported in 1872, had to 'submit themselves to our government, for the power we exercise is given to us by God. And, that if they did not abandon their old customs and imitate our industrial habits, they will soon as a people cease to exist' (Etherington, 1978: 164). In Mpengula Mbande, therefore, Christian missionaries found a convert who had fully embraced their social, economic, and political interests in the new colonial order.

In between total rejection or acceptance of the new order represented by the missions, many converts worked out creative accommodations. By the 1870s, African Christians took over greater responsibility for conducting evangelism relatively independent of white control. Black Methodist lay evangelists preached throughout the region, acquiring the name, *Nontlevu*, 'the people who go about talking too much' (Etherington, 1978: 151). Drawing on the experience of black lay evangelists, the people of Edendale founded their own mission society in 1875. Although affiliated with the Methodists, and maintaining Methodist doctrine and discipline, this society, known as Uzondelelo, operated independent of direct white supervision or control. A certain degree of doctrinal innovation, however, was also evident, as black evangelist Ira Nembula, in 1875, was reported to have been preaching a kind of African theology in which he told his audiences that 'he held the faith of their own people. They believed in righteousness and conscious existence after death. He believed the same truths as brought into clearer light

in Christ' (Etherington, 1978: 145–6). In addition to organizational innovations, therefore, black Christians were advancing new theological
formulations to accommodate both African and Christian religious resources.

THE NORTHERN FRONTIER

In the northern regions, Sotho–Tswana communities were also incorporated
in new colonial relations during the nineteenth century. With the breakdown
of the extensive polity dominated by the Rolong clan in the previous century,
several smaller chiefdoms emerged. The largest chiefdom was the Tlhaping
which controlled a multi-ethnic society from a large, centralized settlement
roughly the size of Cape Town, with a population estimated at 16,000. The
Tlhaping, however, competed for political power in the region with the
emergent states controlled by warlords of the diverse groups known as
Griqua, Berengaars, and Bastards. The Griqua employed guns, horses, and
Christianity in an effort to build states and extend control over Khoisan and
Sotho–Tswana communities in the region. As the traveler Henry Lichtenstein
noted, the Griqua were 'educated in Christianity: they learnt to sing psalms
and to read: and were, even to receiving the sacrament of baptism, as good
Christians as the offspring of Europeans' (Lichtenstein, 1930, II: 241).
Although they had developed stable trading relations with the Tlhaping, the
Griqua were also interested in breaking the Tlhaping monopoly on trade with
Sotho–Tswana communities to the north-east. The Griqua were determined
to strengthen ties with the Cape Colony, especially in trading for guns and
ammunition, and to extend their domination over the northern frontier. In
both those projects, they enlisted the aid of Christian missionaries.

The LMS missionary Robert Moffat entered the northern frontier along
the Orange River in 1819. Although missionary William Anderson had been
in the area, invited by the Bastards in 1801, and Van der Kemp's associate
James Read had established a Sotho–Tswana mission at Dithakong after
1816, Moffat came to play a pivotal role in the frontier conflict. For the
British public, Moffat represented a heroic figure of evangelism, the former
gardener planting seeds of the gospel in a savage wilderness. With a profound
disdain for traditional African religion, however, Moffat showed his con-
tempt for his potential converts by declaring that 'indifference and stupidity
form the wreath on every brow – ignorance, the grossest ignorance of Divine
things, forms the basis of every action; it is only things earthly, sensual, and
devilish, which stimulate to activity and mirth' (Moffat, 1842: 284–5).
Lacking confidence in African moral, intellectual, and spiritual potential,
therefore, Moffat resorted to techniques of coercion from the beginning of
his Christian mission.

Moffat's first dramatic victory in the mission field was the conversion of the Griqua warlord Jager Afrikaner, who Moffat brought back to Cape Town as evidence of his success, but also to arrange for horses, guns, and ammunition for the people of his new convert. By 1821, Moffat had begun a mission to the Tlhaping, eventually establishing a station at Kuruman that attracted a diverse, but small group of residents. During the 1820s, the government agent John Melvill and the missionary Robert Moffat maintained common cause with the Griqua, Berengaar, and Bastard warlords in their armed raids on surrounding communities for cattle, but also for captives that could be turned over to the colonial labor market in the Cape. Professing humanitarian motives in protecting Sotho–Tswana communities from nebulous, probably fictitious marauders called 'Mantatees,' Robert Moffat played an instrumental role as a middleman trading in the ivory, cattle, and prisoners obtained through the raiding expeditions of the Griqua. Understandably, Moffat disguised his role in these raids, due to the recent illegality of slave trading. But he nevertheless participated in sending captives to be sold, indentured, or simply handed over as forced labor in the Cape Colony (Cobbing, 1988).

The Tlhaping chief Mothibi formed an alliance with Robert Moffat to obtain horses, guns, and ammunition through the missionary. From his base at Kuruman, however, Moffat took over control of the Tlhaping chiefdom, becoming in effect a chief himself. Resisting this domination, or perhaps seeking alliance with a more powerful warlord, Mothibi took some of his Tlhaping followers in 1830 to Griquatown, while other Tlhaping under his brother Mahura moved to the north-east to be farther away from missionary influence. This exodus left Moffat with a small community of refugees at Kuruman (Legassick, 1969: 374).

As Griqua warlords sought to extend their domination during the 1830s, competition between Griquatown and Kuruman resulted in a kind of religious warfare between two Christian missions. From 1834 to 1840, LMS missionaries Peter Wright and Isaac Hughes at Griquatown defended the work of Griqua warlords in extending political control and religious conversion. Robert Moffat, on the other hand, accused Wright and Hughes of trying to build up their own power base by increasing the Christian population of Griquatown. Moffat complained that they admitted anyone who merely professed Christianity, rather than observing the stricter requirements for baptism enforced at Kuruman. By the end of the 1830s, Sotho–Tswana observers, understandably confused by this religious conflict between mission stations, frequently asked if there were in fact two Christian gods, one for Griquatown, the other for Kuruman (Legassick, 1989: 403).

For their part, however, Griqua leaders claimed that Christian spiritual power actually belonged to them. The warlord Andries Waterboer informed Peter Wright that since the Griqua now had the *bongaka*, the power of healing souls, they no longer needed white missionaries. Griqua evangelists undertook independent, far-ranging missionary work among Sotho–Tswana communities, drawing increasing numbers of Tlhaping to Griquatown. These evangelists insisted on Griqua political and religious independence. In 1838, a Griqua evangelist by the name of Nicholas Kruger even argued that his nation ought to be independent and powerful like the United States of America, because the Griqua 'began to receive the Gospel at the very same time the colonisation of America commenced.' Toward this end, Nicholas Kruger announced Griqua plans to drive all other missionaries out of the region and convert the Sotho–Tswana communities to the north-east who would have to hear and obey the Griqua Christian gospel (Legassick, 1989: 403). In the early 1840s, concerted resistance by those Sotho–Tswana communities forced the Griqua to abandon plans for extending their particular form of Christian domination over the northern frontier. Where the Griqua failed, however, British and Boer forces eventually succeeded during the nineteenth century in enforcing a Christian presence in the region.

To the north-east of the Tlhaping, Wesleyan Methodist missionaries were in contact during the 1820s with other branches of the extended Rolong clan. At Plaatberg, on the Vaal river, Rolong chiefdoms – Seleka, Tshidi, and Ratlou – joined together to form a large settlement in the early 1830s seeking refuge from the raiding expeditions of mounted riflemen. In 1833, the Wesleyans James Archbell and John Edwards claimed to have obtained permission from the southern Sotho Chief Moshoeshoe to establish a mission settlement on a large tract of land. Moshoeshoe himself had been motivated to gain missionary support, finally acquiring Eugène Casalis and Thomas Arbousset of the Paris Missionary Society, for protection against raids by armed Berengaar horsemen who had terrorized his villages. Under the same pressure, Rolong chiefdoms agreed to move to the new Wesleyan missionary settlement that came to be known as Thaba 'Nchu (Watson, 1977). There the chiefs attempted to establish a settlement along traditional religious and political lines; but the missionaries erected their headquarters at the center of the settlement. From that central point, the missionary Samuel Broadbent waged a campaign against traditional religious beliefs and practices, gradually creating divisions between a small group of converts who had adopted *sekgoa*, the worldview and ways of the whites, and those who defended the older order, which by contrast came to be known as *setswana*, or Tswana culture (Comaroff, 1985: 25). In this religious conflict, therefore, a traditional Tswana religion came to be objectified in opposition to the alien religion of the Christian mission. While most chiefs defended this Tswana religion, one junior member of the Tshidi royal household, Molema, became a Christian convert, eventually emerging as a powerful leader of a new Tswana Christian community based at Mafikeng.

During a period of expansion for the Thaba 'Nchu settlement at the end of the 1830s, the region was invaded by Voortrekker immigrants. Voortrekkers initially received support and cooperation from the chiefs and missionaries at Thaba 'Nchu, particularly in common cause against the Ndebele chiefdom of Mzilikazi that had been established to the north on the Molopo River. In 1837, joint military expeditions, in alliance with the Griqua, succeeded in driving the Ndebele out of the region. Subsequently, however, that area became a contested frontier, as both Tswana and Boers asserted claims on the land. As Rolong chiefs left Thaba 'Nchu and established themselves along the Molopo River, they remembered the usefulness of missionary representatives in relations with the Boers. In 1848, Chief Montshiwa sent his Christian half-brother Molema to acquire a Wesleyan missionary; 2 years later Joseph Ludorf arrived at Montshiwa's capital. By contrast, conflict between British and Boers in the region apparently inspired an anti-Christian reaction among Moshoeshoe's southern Sotho. After 1848, most people in the chiefdom rejected the missionaries and their religion, reviving polygyny, circumcision, and ritual dancing (Thompson, 1975: 145–51). Under pressure from similar border conflicts, however, the pagan Montshiwa turned to a Christian mission (Molema, 1966).

After the 1852 Sand River Convention at which the British granted independence to a Boer Republic, Joseph Ludorf played an increasingly significant role in trying to negotiate with the Boers on behalf of Tswana interests. With the discovery of diamonds in 1867, however, conflict over the land intensified. Boer, British, Griqua, and Sotho–Tswana factions all made claims to legitimate ownership. A government commission in 1871 awarded the land to the Griqua, largely because the Griqua had already agreed to cede the contested territory to the British. In response, Ludorf drew up plans for the creation of a united Tswana nation, for which he would serve as commissioner and diplomatic agent. A few weeks later, however, Ludorf died before his plans could be implemented. Nevertheless, the work of Ludorf suggested that a missionary could perform a vital political role in defending African independence in the midst of conflicts over land, cattle raiding, labor recruitment, and other competing interests on the northern frontier (Comaroff and Comaroff, 1986: 6–7).

In the 1870s, Tswana chiefdoms were caught between two expanding domains – the diamond fields of Griqualand West and the political domination of the Boer Republics. Rejecting the claims of both the Cape Colony and the Boer Republics, the missionary John Mackenzie advocated imperial annexation of all Tswana territories. As a missionary imperialist, Mackenzie insisted that Tswana interests could only be protected from both colonial and Boer encroachment if all the chiefdoms in the region were ruled directly from London. In 1878, a coalition of southern Tswana chiefs rebelled against this situation, directing armed attacks against the mission stations that symbolized their predicament. 'We accepted the Word of God in our youth,' Tlhaping rebels around Kuruman apparently said, 'but we did not know all that was coming behind it' (Mackenzie, 1887, I: 76). After this rebellion was suppressed by British troops, Mackenzie intensified his campaign to interest the British government in extending imperial rule over the Tswana chiefdoms. Largely through the propaganda efforts of the missionary, the Protectorate of British Bechuanaland was created in 1885 (Dachs, 1972).

In the Transvaal, the extensive northern Sotho polity known as the Pedi kingdom defended its independence against the demands for land, cattle, and labor made by the expanding Boer Republics. In this context, in 1861, the Pedi chief Sekwati admitted Lutheran missionaries from the Berlin Missionary Society into his domain. Led by Andrew Merensky, the German missionaries established stations in the Pedi kingdom under the jurisdiction of its new king Sekhukhune, who assumed power after the death of Sekwati in 1862. As elsewhere in southern Africa, these mission stations initially attracted marginal people, refugees, outcasts, and suspected witches. Gradually, however, a few former clients of Sekwati, such as Martinus Sewushane, joined the mission, perhaps because it provided an alternative power base. More serious from Sekhukhune's perspective, however, the mission gained one of his wives and his half-brother Johannes Dinkwanyane as converts, causing divisions of loyalty within the royal family. Although Sekhukhune initially welcomed the mission, the conversion of royal family members, clients, and political rivals caused him to reconsider.

As elsewhere on the northern frontier, the Christian mission introduced religious conflict into the Pedi social order of the homestead and chiefdom. In failing to perform important rituals of the homestead, such as the appropriate rites of passage at the death of a relative, converts were accused of placing the people and the land in a dangerous condition of spiritual pollution or heat. Of more direct political implication, converts refused to participate in rainmaking, harvest, or other rituals of the chiefdom, thereby weakening its collective spiritual power. Since the definition for such dangerous, antisocial behavior was witchcraft, opponents of the mission understandably suspected Christian converts of being witches. In response to this tension, Sekhukhune threatened the convert Martinus Sewushane with exposure as a witch. 'All the people say that the believers have bewitched them,' the chief warned the convert, 'and divination also points to you' (Delius, 1983: 115).

Not only a threat to his religious authority, the mission was also perceived by Sekhukhune as an alien force that undermined his political authority. 'I am no longer king in this country,' he apparently told Merensky. 'You have taken my people from me' (Wilson and Thompson, 1969, I: 440). Sekhukhune accused the missionaries of acting as spies for the Boers. In this respect, the Pedi king was not entirely mistaken, because Merensky had in fact been appointed as an agent of the Transvaal Republic. Furthermore, the Berlin Missionary Society, like most other missionary organizations in southern Africa, was committed to the political destruction of African chiefdoms. The official publication of the society observed in 1861 that it was 'certain that in a country where God's judgement has broken the people politically the seed of evangelism is most conveniently sowed, that is where missionaries enjoy the legal protection of the colonial government' (Delius, 1983: 118–19).

Under these religious and political pressures, Sekhukhune banished the mission from his territory in 1865. Led by Merensky and Johannes Dinkwanyane, the Pedi Christians purchased a farm in Boer territory and established the mission station of Botshabelo. Over the next 10 years, the station gathered a population of around 1600. The convert Martinus Sewushane assumed responsibility for its religious life, Johannes Dinkwanyane for its political life, but both religion and politics were subsumed under the supreme authority of the missionary Merensky at Botshabelo. Insisting that divine law, moral discipline, productive labor, and an elaborate system of fines, tithes, and payments for religious services would be the rule of the station, Merensky operated, in the words of one colonial official, as 'a great chief more than a mere teacher of the gospel' (Delius, 1983: 162). An even greater power over the station, however, was held by the Boer Republic that extracted taxes and unpaid labor from the residents.

In 1874, to escape these exactions of tithes, taxes, and forced labor, many residents left the mission station and established a separate Christian community (Delius, 1983: 175). Under the leadership of Johannes Dinkwanyane, this new community, called Mafolofolo, maintained Christian preaching, prayers, and baptisms, independent of any resident missionary. When the independence of the Mafolofolo community was rejected by the Boer Republic, Dinkwanyane placed his community under the jurisdiction of the Pedi polity of Sekhukhune. Because of its independence from the missions and its links with Sekhukhune, Mafolofolo became the primary target for the Boer military campaign launched in 1876 to destroy the Pedi kingdom. Apparently, the missionaries concurred in that objective, as Merensky's associate Albert Nachtigal observed that 'it would be best for the mission if a foot is placed on the necks of the blacks' (Delius, 1983: 176). Prior to the Boer attack on the community of Mafolofolo, Johannes Dinkwanyane sent a letter that expressed his African Christian resistance to Boer domination:

> I will address you Boers, you men who know God; do you think there is
> a God who will punish lying, theft and deceit? I ask you now for the truth,
> I pray for the truth because I also speak my whole truth. I say: the land

belongs to us, this is my truth, and even if you become angry I will nonetheless stand by it.

(Delius, 1983: 178)

A few months later, Johannes Dinkwanyane was killed by combined Boer and Swazi forces that invaded and destroyed his Christian community. The war concluded in 1878 with the capture and imprisonment of Sekhukhune. Amidst the ruins of the Pedi polity, the Berlin Missionary Society almost immediately established a new mission at Sekhukhune's capital. Unexpectedly, however, the new missionary, J. A. Winter, opposed the political policy of the Berlin Missionary Society, defended Pedi religious independence, and adopted a Pedi life style. As a result, Winter was expelled from the missionary society, but he remained in the region, and eventually, in 1889, supported the formation of the Pedi Lutheran Church, one of the first independent African Christian churches in South Africa (Mönnig, 1967: 32). The precedent for an independent African church, however, had already been set by the example of the Christian community that had been led by Johannes Dinkwanyane at Mofolofolo.

Christian missions, therefore, were catalysts for change in the nineteenth century. Clearly, religious change was interlinked with the economic, social, and military advance of European colonial interests. In different ways, and with differing intentions, Christian missionaries appeared as agents of conquest (Majeke, 1952). The implication of Christian missions in conquest gave rise to the common aphorism that 'when the white men came to Africa, the black men had the land and the white men had the Bible, [but] now the black man has the Bible and the white men the land' (Zulu, 1972: 5). This brief review of the history of Christian missions, however, has suggested that their cultural project did not produce uniform results on passive subjects. African initiatives in conflicts over sacred meaning and power during the nineteenth century produced new and unexpected religious responses to the uneven penetration of colonialism, capitalism, and Christianity in southern Africa. Under increasingly difficult conditions, religious initiatives continued to be advanced in the twentieth century.

REFERENCES

Arbousset, Thomas, with F. Daumas (1968). *Narrative of an Exploratory Tour to the North-east of the Colony of the Cape of Good Hope.* Trans. John Croumbie Brown. Cape Town: Struik (orig. edn 1846).

Ashley, M. J. (1974). 'African Education and Society in the Nineteenth-Century Eastern Cape.' In: Christopher Saunders and Robin Derricourt (eds) *Beyond the Cape Frontier: Studies in the History of the Transkei and the Ciskei.* London: Longman. 199–212.

Ashley, M. J. (1980). 'Universes in Collision: Xhosa, Missionaries and Education in Nineteenth-Century South Africa.' *Journal of Theology for Southern Africa* 32: 28–38.

Ashley, M. J. (1982). 'Features of Modernity: Missionaries and Education in South Africa, 1850–1900.' *Journal of Theology for Southern Africa* 38: 49–58.

Beck, Roger B. (1989). 'Bibles and Beads: Missionaries as Traders in Southern Africa in the Early Nineteenth Century.' *Journal of African History* 30: 211–25.

Benham, Marian S. (1896). *Henry Callaway M.D., D.D., First Bishop of Kaffraria: His Life History and Work. A Memoir*. London: Macmillan.

Bird, John (1888). *Annals of Natal*. 2 vols. Pietermaritzburg: Davis.

Boas, Jack (1973). 'The Activities of the London Missionary Society in South Africa, 1806–1836: An Assessment.' *African Studies Review* 16: 417–35.

Brock, Sheila (1974). 'James Stewart and Lovedale: A Reappraisal of Missionary Attitudes and African Response in the Eastern Cape, South Africa, 1870–1905.' PhD dissertation, University of Edinburgh.

Brown, W. E. (1960). *The Catholic Church in South Africa*. London: Burns & Oates.

Brownlee, Charles (1916). *Reminiscences of Kafir Life and History*. 2nd edn Lovedale: Lovedale Press (orig. edn 1896).

Callaway, Henry (1868–70). *The Religious System of the Amazulu*. Springdale: A. J. Blair.

Callaway, Henry (1874). *A Fragment on Comparative Religion*. Natal: Callaway.

Casalis, Eugène (1861). *The Basutos, or Twenty-Three Years in South Africa*. London: James Nisbet.

Chalmers, John A. (1877). *Tiyo Soga: A Page of South African Mission Work*. Edinburgh: Andrew Elliot.

Cobbing, Julian (1988). 'The Mfecane as Alibi: Thoughts on Dithakong and Mbolompo.' *Journal of African History* 29: 487–519.

Comaroff, Jean (1985). *Body of Power, Spirit of Resistance: The Culture and History of a South African People*. Chicago: University of Chicago Press.

Comaroff, Jean, and J. L. Comaroff (1986). 'Christianity and Colonialism in South Africa.' *American Ethnologist* 13: 1–22.

Comaroff, Jean, and J. L. Comaroff (1989). 'The Colonization of Consciousness in South Africa'. *Economy and Society* 18: 267–96.

Comaroff, John L. (1989). 'Images of Empire, Contests of Conscience: Models of Colonial Domination in South Africa.' *American Ethnologist* 16: 661–85.

Cope, R. L. (ed.) (1977). *The Journals of the Rev. T. L. Hodgson*. Johannesburg: Witwatersrand University Press.

Cope, R. L. (1979). 'Christian Missions and Independent African Chiefdoms in South Africa in the Nineteenth Century.' *Theoria* 52: 1–23.

Cory, George, ed. (1926). *The Diary of Rev. Francis Owen*. Cape Town: Van Riebeeck Society.

Cragg, D. G. L. (1974). 'The Role of the Wesleyan Missionaries in Relations between the Mpondo and the Colonial Authorities.' In: Christopher Saunders and Robin Derricourt (eds) *Beyond the Cape Frontier: Studies in the History of the Transkei and Ciskei*. London: Longman. 145–62.

Dachs, Anthony J. (1972). 'Missionary Imperialism: The Case of Bechuanaland.' *Journal of African History* 13: 647–58.

Davis, R. Hunt (1979). 'School versus Blanket and Settler: Elijah Makiwane and the Leadership of the Cape School Community.' *African Affairs* 78(310): 12–32.

Delius, Peter (1983). *The Land Belongs To Us: The Pedi Polity, the Boers and the British in the Nineteenth Century Transvaal.* Johannesburg: Ravan Press.

Du Plessis, J. (1911). *A History of Christian Missions in South Africa.* London: Longmans Green; rprt. Cape Town: Struik, 1965.

Elphick, Richard (1981). 'Africans and the Christian Campaign in Southern Africa.' In: Howard Lamar and Leonard Thompson (eds) *The Frontier in History: North America and Southern Africa Compared.* New Haven: Yale University Press. 270–307.

Elphick, Richard and Hermann Giliomee (eds) (1989). *The Shaping of South African Society, 1652–1820.* Cape Town: Maskew Miller Longman.

Elphick, Richard, and Robert Shell (1989). 'Intergroup Relations: Khoikhoi, Settlers, Slaves and Free Blacks, 1652–1795.' In: Richard Elphick and Hermann Giliomee (eds) *The Shaping of South African Society, 1652–1820.* Cape Town: Maskew Miller Longman. 184–239.

Enklaar, Ido H. (1988). *Life and Work of Dr. J. Th. Van der Kemp, 1747–1811: Missionary Pioneer and Protagonist of Racial Equality in South Africa.* Cape Town: A. A. Balkema.

Etherington, Norman (1971). 'The Rise of the Kholwa in Southeast Africa: African Christian Communities in Natal, Pondoland, and Zululand, 1835–1880.' PhD dissertation, Yale University.

Etherington, Norman (1977). 'Social Theory and the Study of Christian Missions in Africa: A South African Case Study.' *Africa* 47: 31–40.

Etherington, Norman (1978). *Preachers, Peasants, and Politics in Southeast Africa, 1835–1880: African Christian Communities in Natal, Pondoland, and Zululand.* London: Royal Historical Society.

Etherington, Norman (1987). 'Missionary Doctors and African Healers in Mid-Victorian South Africa.' *South African Historical Journal* 19: 72–92.

Freund, William (1973). 'The Career of Johannes Theodorus Van der Kemp and his Role in the History of South Africa.' *Tijdschrift voor Geschiedenis* 86: 376–90.

Freund, William (1989). 'The Cape Under the Transitional Governments, 1795–1814.' In: Richard Elphick and Hermann Giliomee (eds) *The Shaping of South African Society 1652–1820.* Cape Town: Maskew Miller Longman. 324–57.

Gailey, Harry A. (1962). 'John Philip's Role in Hottentot Emancipation.' *Journal of African History* 3: 419–33.

Gardiner, Allen (1836). *Narrative of a Journey to the Zoolu Country.* London: Crofts.

Goedhals, Mandy (1989). 'Ungumpriste: A Study of the Life of Peter Masiza, First Black Priest in the Church of the Province of Southern Africa.' *Journal of Theology for Southern Africa* 68: 17–28.

Govan, William (1875). *Memorials of Rev. James Laing.* Glasgow: David Bryce & Sons.

Grove, Richard (1989). 'Scottish Missionaries, Evangelical Discourses, and the Origins of Conservation Thinking in Southern Africa 1820–1900.' *Journal of Southern African Studies* 15: 163–87.

Guy, Jeff (1983). *The Heretic: A Study of the Life of John William Colenso 1814–1883.* Johannesburg: Ravan Press.

Hewson, Leslie A. (1959). 'Healdtown: A Study of a Methodist Experiment in African Education.' PhD thesis, Rhodes University.

Hodgson, Janet (1980). 'The "Great Hymn" of the Xhosa Prophet, Ntsikana: An African Expression of Christianity, 1815–1821.' *Religion in Southern Africa* 1(2): 33–58.

Hodgson, Janet (1984). 'Do We Hear You Nyengana? Dr. J. T. Vanderkemp and the First Mission to the Xhosa.' *Religion in Southern Africa* 5(1): 3–48.

Hodgson, Janet (1985a). 'Ntsikana: History and Symbol. Studies in a Process of Religious Change among Xhosa-speaking People.' PhD thesis, University of Cape Town.

Hodgson, Janet (1985b). 'A Study of the Xhosa Prophet Nxele (Part I).' *Religion in Southern Africa* 6(2): 11–36.

Hodgson, Janet (1986a). 'A Study of the Xhosa Prophet Nxele (Part II).' *Religion in Southern Africa* 7(1): 3–24.

Hodgson, Janet (1986b). 'Soga and Dukwana: The Christian Struggle for Liberation in Mid 19th Century South Africa.' *Journal of Religion in Africa* 60: 187–208.

Holt, Basil (1954). *Joseph Williams and the Pioneer Mission to the South-Eastern Bantu*. Lovedale: Lovedale Press.

Hutchinson, Bertram (1957). 'Some Social Consequences of Nineteenth-Century Missionary Activity among the South African Bantu.' *Africa* 27: 160–77.

Isaacs, Nathaniel (1836). *Travels and Adventures in Eastern Africa*. 2 vols. London: Edward Churton.

Keller, B. B. (1978). 'Millenarianism and Resistance: The Xhosa Cattle Killing.' *Journal of Asian and African Studies* 13: 95–111.

Keto, C. Tsheloane (1976). 'Race Relations, Land and the Changing Missionary Role in South Africa: A Case Study of the Zulu Mission, 1850–1910.' *The International Journal of African Historical Studies* 10: 600–27.

Kirk, Tony (1973). 'Progress and Decline in the Kat River Settlement, 1829–54.' *Journal of African History* 14: 411–28.

Krüger, Bernard (1966). *The Pear Tree Blossoms: A History of the Moravian Mission Stations in South Africa*. Genadendal: Provincial Board of the Moravian Church in South Africa.

Kuper, Adam (1987). *South Africa and the Anthropologist*. London: Routledge & Kegan Paul.

Lamar, Howard and Leonard Thompson (eds) (1981). *The Frontier in History: North America and Southern Africa Compared*. New Haven: Yale University Press.

Legassick, Martin (1969). 'The Griqua, the Sotho–Tswana and the Missionaries, 1780–1840: The Politics of a Frontier Zone.' PhD dissertation, University of California, Los Angeles.

Legassick, Martin (1989). 'The Northern Frontier to c.1840: The Rise and Decline of the Griqua People.' In: Richard Elphick and Hermann Giliomee (eds) *The Shaping of South African Society, 1652–1820*. Cape Town: Maskew Miller Longman. 358–420.

Lichtenstein, Henry (1930). *Travels in Southern Africa in the Years 1803, 1804, 1805, and 1806*. 2 vols. Trans. A. Plumptre. Cape Town: Van Riebeeck Society (orig. edn 1812–15).

Mackenzie, John (1887). *Austral Africa: Losing It or Ruling It*. 2 vols. London: Sampson Low.

Maclennan, Ben (1986). *A Proper Degree of Terror: John Graham and the Cape's Eastern Frontier*. Johannesburg: Ravan Press.

Majeke, Nosipho (1952). *The Role of the Missionaries in Conquest*. Johannesburg: Society of Young Africa.

Malherbe, V. C. (1990). *Krotoa, Called 'Eva': A Woman Between*. Cape Town: University of Cape Town, Centre for African Studies.

Marks, Shula, and Anthony Atmore (eds) (1980). *Economy and Society in Pre-industrial South Africa*. London: Longman.

Mayer, Philip (1980). 'The Origin and Decline of Two Rural Resistance Ideologies.' In: P. Mayer (ed.) *Black Villagers in an Industrial Society*. Cape Town: Oxford University Press. 1–80.

Meintjes, Sheila (1990). 'Family and Gender in the Christian Community at Edendale, Natal, in Colonial Times.' In: Cherryl Walker (ed.) *Women and Gender in Southern Africa to 1945*. London: James Currey; Cape Town: David Philip. 125–45.

Moffat, Robert (1842). *Missionary Labours and Scenes in Southern Africa*. London: John Snow.

Molema, S. M. (1966). *Montshiwa, Barolong Chief and Patriot, 1815–1896*. Cape Town: Struik.

Mönnig, H. O. (1967). *The Pedi*. Pretoria: Van Schaik.

Moodie, Donald (1960). *The Record: A Series of Official Papers Relative to the Condition and Treatment of the Native Tribes of South Africa*. 5 vols. Cape Town: A. A. Balkema (orig. edn 1838–41).

Moyer, R. A. (1976). 'A History of the Mfengu of the Eastern Cape, 1815–65.' PhD thesis, University of London.

Newton-King, Susan (1980). 'The Labour Market of the Cape Colony, 1807–28.' In: Shula Marks and Anthony Atmore (eds) *Economy and Society in Pre-Industrial South Africa*. London: Longman.

Northcott, Cecil (1961). *Robert Moffat, Pioneer in Africa*. London: Lutterworth Press.

Peires, J. B. (1979). 'Nxele, Ntsikana and the Origins of the Xhosa Religious Reaction.' *Journal of African History* 20: 51–62.

Peires, J. B. (1981). *The House of Phalo: A History of the Xhosa People in the Days of their Independence*. Johannesburg: Ravan Press.

Peires, J. B. (1987). 'The Central Beliefs of the Xhosa Cattle-Killing.' *Journal of African History* 28: 43–63.

Peires, J. B. (1989). *The Dead Will Arise: Nongqawuse and the Great Xhosa Cattle-Killing Movement of 1856–7*. Johannesburg: Ravan Press.

Philip, John (1828). *Researches in South Africa*. 2 vols. London: James Duncan; rprt. New York: Negro University Press, 1969.

Pringle, Thomas (1835). *Narrative of a Residence in South Africa*. London: Maxon; rprt. Cape Town: Struik, 1966.

Ralston, Richard D. (1976). 'Xhosa Cattle Sacrifice, 1856–57: The Messianic Factor in African Resistance.' In: David Chanaiwa (ed.) *Profiles in Self Determination*. Northridge, CA, California State University. 78–105.

Reyburn, H. A. (1933). 'The Missionary as Rainmaker.' *The Critic* 1: 146–53.

Robinson, David, and Douglas Smith (1979). *Sources of the African Past: Case Studies of Five Nineteenth-Century African Societies*. New York: Africana Publications.

Ross, Rodney (1986). *John Philip (1775–1851): Missions, Race and Politics in South Africa*. Aberdeen: Aberdeen University Press.

Schreuder, D. M. (1976). 'The Cultural Factor in Victorian Imperialism: A Case Study of the British "Civilising Mission."' *Journal of Imperial and Commonwealth History* 4: 281–317.

Shaw, William (1860). *The Story of My Mission in South Eastern Africa*. London: Hamilton Adams.

Shaw, William (1972). In: W. D. Hammond-Tooke (ed.) *The Journal of William Shaw*. Cape Town: A. A. Balkema.

Shepherd, Robert H. W. (1940). *Lovedale, South Africa: The Story of a Century, 1824–1955*. Lovedale: Lovedale Press.

Sillery, Anthony (1971). *John Mackenzie of Bechuanaland, 1835–1899: A Study in Humanitarian Imperialism*. Cape Town: A. A. Balkema.

Smith, Edwin W. (1925). *Robert Moffat, One of God's Gardeners*. London: SCM Press.

Smith, Edwin W. (1949). *The Life and Times of Daniel Lindley*. London: Epworth Press.

Soga, Tiyo (1983). In: Donovan Williams (ed.) *The Journal and Selected Writings of the Rev. Tiyo Soga*. Cape Town: A. A. Balkema.

Stuart, James, and D. M. Malcolm (1950). *The Diary of Henry Francis Fynn*. Pietermaritzburg: Shuter and Shooter.

Thompson, Leonard (1975). *Survival in Two Worlds: Moshweshwe of Lesotho, 1786–1870*. London: Clarendon Press.

Thompson, Leonard (1985). *The Political Mythology of Apartheid*. New Haven: Yale University Press.

Thorpe, S. A. (1984). 'Religious Response to Stress: The Xhosa Cattle Killing and the Indian Ghost Dance.' *Missionalia* 12(3): 129–37.

Trapido, Stanley (1968). 'African Divisional Politics in the Cape Colony, 1884 to 1910.' *Journal of African History* 9: 78–98.

Trapido, Stanley (1980). '"The Friends of the Natives": Merchants, Peasants, and the Political and Ideological Structures of Liberalism in the Cape, 1854–1910'. In: Shula Marks and Anthony Atmore (eds) *Economy and Society in Pre-Industrial South Africa*. London: Longman. 247–74

Van der Kemp, J. T. (1804a). 'Transactions of Dr. Van der Kemp in the Year 1800.' *Transactions of the [London] Missionary Society*. Vol 1. London: Bye & Law. 412–31.

Van der Kemp, J. T. (1804b). 'An Account of the Religion, Customs, Population, Government, Language, History, and Natural Productions of Caffraria.' *Transactions of the [London] Missionary Society*. Vol 1. London: Bye & Law. 432–41.

Vilakazi, Absolom (1962). *Zulu Transformations: A Study of the Dynamics of Social Change*. Pietermaritzburg: University of Natal Press.

Warner, J. C. (1858). 'Mr. Warner's Notes.' In: John Maclean (ed.) *A Compendium of Kafir Laws and Customs*. Mount Coke: Wesleyan Mission Press. 57–109.

Watson, R. L. (1977). 'Missionary Influence at Thaba Nchu, 1833–1854: A Reassessment.' *The International Journal of African Historical Studies* 10: 394–407.

Wells, James (1908). *Stewart of Lovedale: The Life of James Stewart*. London: Hodder and Stoughton.

Williams, Donovan (1959). 'The Missionaries on the Eastern Frontiers of the Cape Colony 1799–1853.' PhD dissertation, University of the Witwatersrand.

Williams, Donovan (1967). *When Races Meet: The Life and Times of William Ritchie Thomson, Glasgow Society Missionary, Government Agent, and Dutch Reformed Church Minister, 1794–1891*. Johannesburg: APB Publishers.

Williams, Donovan (1978). *Umfundisi: A Biography of Tiyo Soga 1829–1871*. Lovedale: Lovedale Press.

Wilson, Monica, and Leonard Thompson (eds) (1969). *The Oxford History of South Africa*. 2 vols. Oxford: Oxford University Press.

Young, R. (1902). *African Wastes Reclaimed: The Story of the Lovedale Mission.* London: J. M. Dent.

Zarwan, John (1976). 'The Xhosa Cattle Killings, 1856–57.' *Cahiers d'études africaines* 16: 519–39.

Zulu, Alphaeus (1972). *The Dilemma of the Black South African.* Cape Town: University of Cape Town.

3   Protestant churches

By the beginning of the twentieth century the Christian focus in South Africa had turned from frontier missions to church building, as Christian leaders concentrated on building local congregations and regional organizations (Gerdener, 1958: 7). However, with the closing of the frontiers, South Africa entered into the most dramatic period of Christianization in its history. Statistics merely hint at this transformation. In 1911 roughly 25 per cent of the black population incorporated in the new Union of South Africa regarded themselves as Christians. Twenty-five years later, however, Christians made up nearly 50 per cent of the black population. Although most of this increase could be attributed to the emergence of the independent African churches (considered in Chapter Four), and the growth of the Roman Catholic Church (considered in Chapter Five), the more established Protestant denominations also recorded increases in black membership during this period. Even missionary organizations, although they remained under white control, depended on black Christian involvement in preaching and pastoral work. As a survey of forty-eight mission organizations in 1928 revealed, close to 80 per cent of the ministers and almost all of the nearly 20,000 lay preachers in mission work were black South Africans (Taylor, 1928: 500; Elphick, 1987: 68).

Increases in Christian affiliation coincided with the dramatic structural changes in South African society that followed the discovery of diamonds in 1867 and gold in 1886. Exploiting those mineral resources, an emergent industrial capitalism demanded an exploitable supply of labor to serve white-controlled interests in mining, industry, and the new, expanding urban centers of South Africa. Christian churches were directly implicated in that process of social and economic change. However, Christianity played an ambivalent role in that process. First, for black Christians who had internalized the missionary 'gospel of work,' the Protestant values of discipline, labor, and personal advancement provided one set of motivations for entering into wage labor in white-controlled farming, industry, mining, domestic service, or public-service occupations. In addition to overwhelming economic pressures caused by taxation, land reservation, and rural poverty, many black Christians had a religious interest in joining the labor market. Second, Christian churches operated in the city as one amongst a number of systems of social control designed to adapt black workers to the demands of urban life. A new type of urban mission emerged that was directed toward producing disciplined, obedient, and docile workers who would serve white-controlled economic interests. Although church pronouncements sometimes protested the harsh and inhumane exploitation of black workers, churches were more often aligned with capital interests in creating and controlling a stable supply of labor. Finally, however, Christian churches provided a set of symbolic resources that could also be appropriated in resistance to exploitation, urban alienation, and white domination. Ironically, the same religion that legitimated their oppression could be reversed by black Christians to symbolize their predicament and signal a promise of their liberation.

Conventionally, Protestant churches in South Africa have been separated by language (Hofmeyr and Cross, 1986). Churches speaking Dutch, and later Afrikaans, have been distinguished from English-speaking churches (Hinchliff, 1976). Although the Roman Catholic Church in southern Africa eventually came to be aligned with the English-speaking Protestant churches, the Catholic Church will be treated in the context of religious pluralism because of its history of exclusion by dominant Protestant establishments in South Africa. The largest and most influential English-speaking churches have been the Anglican and Methodist churches (Hinchliff, 1963; Hewson, 1950). In addition, however, the category of English-speaking churches has included Congregationalists (Briggs and Wing, 1970), Presbyterians (Shepherd, 1940), Baptists (Hudson-Reed, 1977), and Lutherans (Florin, 1967). Among the Afrikaans-speaking churches in the twentieth century, the Nederduitse Gereformeerde Kerk (referred to in English as the Dutch Reformed Church) had the longest history and largest following (Moorrees, 1937; Kinghorn, 1986). In the middle of the nineteenth century, however, the Nederduitse Gereformeerde Kerk drew some competition from two new Dutch Reformed churches, the Nederduitsch Hervormde Kerk (founded 1853) and the Gereformeerde Kerk (founded 1859). These churches remained relatively small, based in the Transvaal or the Orange Free State, but they lent considerable support to the development of the ideology of white supremacy, Afrikaner nationalism, and apartheid in the twentieth century. The distinction between English-speaking and Afrikaans-speaking churches, however, became increasingly ironic in the twentieth century as the growing number of South African Christians were people who spoke African languages.

Protestant churches assumed their modern form during the first half of the twentieth century in the context of emerging industrial capitalism and large-scale incorporation of blacks as workers in a white-controlled economy. In fact, this context generated the central contradictions in South African Protestant churches, the contradictions of race, class, and gender. Put simply: while membership of Protestant churches in the Union of South Africa came to be comprised predominantly of blacks, workers, and women, control of those churches remained in the hands of white, middle-class men, aligned for the most part with the interests of capitalist expansion. Although Protestant denominations had different historical origins, and followed different historical trajectories, they all adapted during the period from 1910 to 1940 in the same context of racial, class, and gender relations in South Africa.

DUTCH REFORMED CHURCHES

Distant historical background for the Dutch Reformed churches in South Africa can be found in the rise of a militant Calvinism during the sixteenth-century religious wars in the Netherlands. Influenced by the German Reformation, many people in the Netherlands had adopted forms of the new Protestant faith, placing themselves in conflict, however, with the political and religious control of the region then exercised by the forces of the Catholic King of Spain. After 1556, King Phillip II of Spain enforced Catholic creeds and observances on the Netherlands, requiring Catholic conformity in the region with increasing strictness after 1564. Two years later, beginning in August 1566, a popular revolt against Spanish domination broke out in the central and northern provinces of the Netherlands. Although the revolt was against Spanish political control, its initial target was the Catholic Church, as Calvinist preachers, assuming leadership in the early stages of the revolt, led angry mobs in destroying statues, paintings, and other religious images in Catholic churches. Developing into armed conflict, this revolt against Spain continued until a truce was declared in 1609, with a final settlement, the Peace of Munster in 1648, at which Spain officially recognized the Dutch Republic (Geyl, 1958; 1961; Schöffer, 1961).

A militant, politicized Calvinism, therefore, played a significant role in the independence of the Netherlands. During this period of religious warfare, Dutch Calvinists had worked out orthodox positions on Christian doctrine and practice at the Synod of Dort (1618–19). Emphasizing the Calvinist doctrine of predestination, the Dutch Reformed Church at Dort was defined as a community of the elect. After the Peace of Munster, the Dutch Reformed Church succeeded by 1651 in gaining recognition as state church. Nevertheless, Calvinists of the Dutch Reformed Church continued to coexist, often in conflict, with other Protestants and Roman Catholics in the Netherlands.

As a commercial extension of the state, the Dutch East India Company that established its refreshment station at the Cape in 1652 was in a position also to establish the Dutch Reformed Church. During the administration of the Cape by the Dutch East India Company (1652–1795), the Dutch Reformed Church was organized as a branch of government. Ministers (*predikanten*) were ordained by the Classis of Amsterdam, hired by the Company, and appointed to churches in the Cape. They acted as ministers of religion, but also as officials of the Company government. As local congregations emerged, they were administered by relatively independent councils comprised of the predikant, two Company officials, and four local citizens. The Dutch Reformed Church was legally established by the government as the only permitted religious organization in the Cape until 1778 when Lutherans were allowed to worship in public (Wilson and Thompson, 1969, I: 229).

Even with government backing, however, the Dutch Reformed Church did not have a monopoly on the religious life of the Cape, nor did orthodox Calvinism necessarily determine the beliefs and practices of members of the Dutch Reformed Church. The Bible, along with the rituals of prayer, baptism, and eucharist (*nagmaal*), provided the basic contours of Christian beliefs and practices at the Cape. But evidence is lacking of a strict Calvinist orthodoxy (Elphick and Giliomee, 1989b: 527). The Huguenots who arrived in 1688 were strict Calvinists. It is unclear, however, to what extent Calvinism permeated the Dutch Reformed Church or religious life at the Cape. In fact, reports of visitors to the Cape occasionally suggested that there was a general lack of interest in either religion or the services of the Dutch Reformed Church. In 1714, for example, Reverend François Valentyn visited the Cape Town church and was surprised by the small congregation. Apparently, no government officials and very few citizens were church members, owing, Reverend Valentyn complained, to their 'stupidity and insolence.' In addition, Reverend Valentyn's distress at this lack of participation in the Dutch Reformed Church was made worse by his suspicion that there were many Lutherans among the servants of the Company (Valentyn, 1973, II: 259).

Nevertheless, the Dutch Reformed Church gradually expanded in the Cape, establishing a network of local churches beginning with the Groote Kerk in Cape Town in 1666, and adding five other churches by 1792. Relations with the state of the Netherlands were broken with the first British occupation of the Cape in 1795, but close ties with the Dutch Reformed Church in the Netherlands persisted. Cape ministers continued to be trained in the Netherlands, where they were not only exposed to Calvinism, but also to evangelical piety and the liberal ideas of the European Enlightenment. Without evidence of doctrinal uniformity in the Cape Dutch Reformed Church, it seems safe to assume that it was divided amongst factions that supported, to one degree or another, a Calvinist theology or a pietist theology, with occasional agreement between Calvinists and pietists on the danger of 'foreign ideologies' such as liberal humanism.

In 1824 the Dutch Reformed Church in the Cape formed its own synod and became institutionally independent of the church in the Netherlands. Theologically, however, it continued in conversation with the European church. The 1834 Calvinist revival in the Netherlands, led by Groen van Prinsterer, generated some interest among Cape clergy of the Dutch Reformed Church. Insisting on strict Calvinist standards of orthodoxy, going back to the Synod of Dort, Groen van Prinsterer adopted the motto – 'In isolation is our strength' – and founded a new Reformed Church for his small following. Under the influence of this Calvinist revival, some of the Dutch Reformed Church clergy in the Cape were influenced by Groen van Prinsterer's insistence that all aspects of social and political life had to be governed in accordance with the Bible. On that basis, modern trends toward secularization and democracy had to be resisted. In particular, education had to have a biblical, Christian, and national basis in order to counteract those modern trends. Prior to the 1870s, however, such Calvinist themes gained only a small following in the Netherlands as well as in South Africa (Schutte, 1987).

Although some clergy identified with this Calvinist revival, a majority were eventually swept up in the enthusiasm of the evangelical revivals led by Andrew Murray, Jr. From Scottish background, Murray became a leading figure of the nineteenth-century Dutch Reformed Church, serving as moderator of its synod on six occasions. As an evangelical pietist, Murray advocated a fervent, emotional revivalism for bringing people to Christian conversion and faith that was in tension with the orthodox Calvinist doctrine of predestination. Furthermore, Murray argued against mixing religion with politics, concentrating on cultivating a Christian piety that was removed from the political arena. In this separation of religion and politics, Murray's followers in the Dutch Reformed Church were also in tension with the minority of politicized Calvinists throughout the nineteenth century (Du Plessis, 1919).

In 1837 the synod of the Dutch Reformed Church in the Cape denounced the emigration of the farmers and cattle herders who came to be known as the Voortrekkers. The Voortrekkers left the Cape, partly in protest to the recent freeing of slaves, but definitely to escape the British rule that had enforced the abolition of slavery at the Cape. The church synod also refused permission for any of its ordained ministers to accompany the emigrants on their trek out of the Cape. Without benefit of clergy, however, those trekkers seemed to have taken with them a basic kind of biblical faith. In contrast to the disinterest in religion at the city of Cape Town described by Reverend

Valentyn in 1714, Boer farmers in the countryside a century later seemed to place importance on their Christian religion. As the German medical doctor Henry Lichtenstein observed on a tour during 1803–6, a Boer religious service involved prayer, psalm singing, foot washing, and readings from a book of sermons and the Bible, the only books that Lichtenstein found in the house (Lichtenstein, 1930, II: 447).

The American missionary Daniel Lindley, eventually hired as minister by the Voortrekkers, described them in 1837 as having 'no minister, no teacher for their children, almost no books and almost nothing to keep them from sinking into the depths of heathenism' (Smith, 1949: 162–3). However, at least some among the Voortrekkers claimed explicitly Christian motives for their departure from the Cape. In a letter written in 1843, Voortrekker leader Piet Retief's niece, Anna Steenkamp, tried to explain that the Christian religion had been prominent among their reasons for emigrating from the Cape. It was not so much the freeing of the slaves that they had found objectionable, Anna Steenkamp recalled:

> as their being placed on an equal footing with Christians, contrary to the laws of God and the natural distinction of race and religion, so that it was intolerable for any decent Christian to bow down beneath such a yoke; wherefore we rather withdrew in order thus to preserve our doctrines in purity.

> (Bird, 1888, I: 459)

In the Boer republics formed in the South African interior, this search for doctrinal purity had organizational consequences for the Dutch Reformed Church. In 1853, Voortrekker leader of the new South African Republic, Andries Pretorius, initiated a separation from the Cape Dutch Reformed Church that resulted in the formation of a new church, the Nederduitsch Hervormde Kerk. Although served by predikants from the Netherlands, this new church operated as a national church, or *volkskerk*, for the white South African Republic in the Transvaal. Not all followed this new church, however. Many remained with the Dutch Reformed Church based in the Cape, while a few in 1859 founded the Gereformeerde Kerk as a strict, orthodox Calvinist church. Also known as the 'Dopper' church, this conservative church remained small, but had a certain amount of influence through a few powerful members, such as President of the South African Republic in the Transvaal, Paul Kruger.

The two new Dutch Reformed churches in the 1850s were established as essentially white churches. The new constitution of the Nederduitsch Hervormde Kerk specifically excluded blacks from membership. But the synods of the Dutch Reformed Church in the Cape had officially ignored racial differences, providing, in principle, a single church for all members, regardless of race or color. At its 1857 synod, however, perhaps anticipating the competing claims on membership made by the new white Reformed churches, the Cape synod of the Dutch Reformed Church introduced a policy of separation based on race. Describing this policy as an accommodation to 'the weakness of some,' the Cape synod announced that 'the heathen' would henceforth 'enjoy its privileges in a separate building or institution' (De Gruchy, 1979: 8). Although not all congregations complied with this policy, some initially maintaining common worship regardless of race, this official position of the Dutch Reformed Church initiated a division of Christians into separate places of worship on the basis of race.

Despite the emigrations of the Great Trek, the Dutch Reformed Church in the Cape expanded from fourteen congregations in 1824 to forty-nine in 1854 (A. Du Toit, 1987: 37). In the 1860s, theological concern returned to a renewed conflict between liberal and strict Calvinists. The victory of the strict Calvinists in a controversial heresy trial at the theological seminary at Stellenbosch, recently founded in 1857, indicated that orthodox, conservative Calvinists were reasserting themselves in the life of the Dutch Reformed Church (Wilson and Thompson, 1969: I: 277). Conservative Calvinists responded to crucial developments in the Netherlands during the 1870s, as the theologian and politician Abraham Kuyper expounded a Neo-Calvinism that promised to provide a complete formula for personal, social, and political life. Developing the Calvinism of Groen van Prinsterer, Abraham Kuyper reaffirmed the sovereignty of God over all spheres of human life. This theology of 'sphere sovereignty' suggested that different spheres of life, such as family, church, and state, were independent of each other, governed by different divine laws, but were all under the supreme will of God. In the Netherlands, Kuyper's influence extended over a political party, labor unions, and education through the founding of the Free University of Amsterdam in 1880, where many South African Dutch Reformed Church ministers subsequently went for training.

Although Kuyper represented a minority position in the Netherlands, his Dutch Christian nationalism provided intellectual resources for those Dutch Reformed clergy who supported an Afrikaner Christian nationalist movement in South Africa. In 1875 the Genootskap van Regte Afrikaners (Fellowship of True Afrikaners) was formed in the Cape as a cultural organization dedicated to protecting the rights of Afrikaans-speakers in South Africa (Hofmeyr, 1987: 95–9). In one respect, this Afrikaans language movement was a response to a recent history of tension between English and Afrikaans cultural interests in language, education, and religion. In the 1860s, the use of English at the main Dutch Reformed church in Cape Town, the Groote Kerk, and an attempt by British liberals to pass legislation making English the only medium of instruction in education, had caused some resentment among Afrikaans-speakers in the Cape. In 1870 Anglican Bishop Robert Gray had even proposed union with the Dutch Reformed Church in the Cape. Resistance to domination by British language and culture intensified in the reactions of many Dutch Reformed clergy to the campaign led by British liberal Saul Solomon to end state grants to all the churches of the colony. Although the Dutch Reformed Church was no longer state church, this campaign to cut all political and economic ties with the Cape government was seen by many as a British attempt to undermine its position. First introduced in 1854, a 'voluntary bill' ending state financial support for churches finally passed into law in the Cape in 1875. From the perspective of many Dutch Reformed Church leaders, the disestablishment of the church marked a victory for British liberalism (Trapido, 1980: 274).

On one level, therefore, the involvement of some Dutch Reformed Church clergy in emerging Afrikaner organizations was a defensive reaction to British dominance in language, culture, and religion. On another level, however, conservative Dutch Reformed Church clergy perceived a real danger of losing political and religious authority as their youth turned to British language, culture, and education as avenues of advancement in a society increasingly dominated by British economic interests in an emerging industrial capitalism. In this sense, Afrikaner nationalist organizations mobilized against British dominance in the economy. Nevertheless, on both the cultural and economic levels, the Dutch Reformed Church had an ambivalent relationship with this new nationalism. Initiatives in creating an Afrikaner nationalism shifted away from the Cape and the Dutch Reformed Church. British annexation of the Transvaal in 1877 and the Transvaal War of Independence against the British in 1881 mobilized a militant Afrikaner nationalism, with its own sacred history and sense of divine destiny, in the Transvaal South African Republic (A. Du Toit, 1985). Founder of the Afrikaner Bond, Reverend S. J. du Toit, often credited as the father of Afrikaner nationalism, broke with the Dutch Reformed Church in the Cape to align himself with this new nationalism. Du Toit's Calvinist nationalist theology, drawing on the work of Abraham Kuyper, failed to achieve widespread support in the mainstream of the Dutch Reformed Church in the 1880s; it would, however, resurface in the 1930s as a dominant element in the church's nationalist theology and the doctrine of apartheid adopted by the Dutch Reformed Church.

As independent synods of the Dutch Reformed Church emerged in the Transvaal, Orange Free State, and Natal, the Cape synod remained dominant until the 1930s. Major institutional changes, however, formalized divisions within the church that had followed the creation of separate congregations in 1857 on the basis of race. In 1881, the Dutch Reformed Mission Church – the Sendingkerk – was formed for so-called 'Coloured' members, people regarded as coming from mixed racial backgrounds. Although dependent on the Dutch Reformed Church for financial support and clergy, the Sending-kerk was established as a separate church organization. In 1910, when black South Africans made up as much as 10 per cent of Dutch Reformed Church membership, the first synod of a separate church for blacks, the NGK in Afrika, met in the Orange Free State. This racial division of the Dutch Reformed Church continued throughout the twentieth century. Eventually, the church was divided by racial classifications into four separate churches: the white Nederduitse Gereformeerde Kerk, the Sendingkerk, the NGK in Afrika, and the Indian Reformed Church.

Although church leaders in 1881 explained the formation of the Sending-kerk as an organizational expedient, by the time the Indian church was formed in 1951 racial separation had become a matter of theological prin-ciple. Church leaders in the 1950s argued that 'according to our policy of apartheid we ought to minister separately to these groups' (Kinghorn, 1990: 63–9). The racial division of the church came to be defended as a policy based on the Bible. Biblical defense of apartheid in the church became common in the synods of the Dutch Reformed Church. As the 1974 Federal synod of the Dutch Reformed Church announced, 'The existence of separate Dutch Re-formed Church affiliations for the various population groups is recognized as being in accordance with the plurality of church affiliation described in the Bible' (B. Du Toit, 1984: 623). What in 1857 and 1881 had been provisional arrangements eventually became matters of religious doctrine in the theology of the Dutch Reformed Church.

This transition to a theology and church organization that incorporated racial separation as a crucial ingredient occurred during the 1930s, as clergy of the Dutch Reformed Church played an active role in formulating the doctrine and policy of apartheid. A general mission committee meeting of the Dutch Reformed Church, held in Bloemfontein in 1926, issued a state-ment of commitment to interracial cooperation that affirmed 'the divine dignity of natives as men and women created in the image of God.' Based on this theological affirmation that blacks and whites were equally created in the image of God, the mission committee concluded that blacks 'shall never be used as instruments to be exploited in order to enrich others.' In this policy statement, based on theological principle, church leaders opposed racial inequality and class exploitation (Kinghorn, 1990: 60).

During the next few years, however, a new generation of Dutch Reformed Church clergy, committed to racial separation, joined this mission commit-tee. By 1935 they had succeeded in getting the Federal Council of the Dutch Reformed Church to adopt a new racial policy. Insisting that this new policy was consistent with Afrikaner tradition, church leadership stated that the 'traditional fear among the Afrikaner of 'equalisation' of black and white stems from his abhorrence of the idea of racial admixture and anything that may lead to it.' To avoid racial mixing, blacks and whites had to be kept separate in both society and church. Therefore, rejecting social equality of blacks and whites in South Africa, the Dutch Reformed Church announced its intention 'to promote social differentiation and spiritual or cultural segregation.' Three years later, one of the leaders in this reformulation of church policy on race introduced the term, apartheid, to represent this commitment to racial separation (Kinghorn, 1990: 60–1).

Although apartheid became a political slogan for Afrikaner nationalists, this doctrine of racial separation at the same time became entangled in the theology of the Dutch Reformed Church. As we will see in Chapter Six, complex economic factors were crucial to the emergence of the racial ideology of apartheid. But theologians and church leaders in the Dutch Reformed Church were also heavily influenced by nationalist and racialist ideologies that were flourishing in Europe at the end of the nineteenth and the beginning of the twentieth centuries. In that respect, however, the Dutch Reformed Church had much in common with the English-speaking churches in South Africa.

ENGLISH-SPEAKING CHURCHES

British roots of South African English-speaking churches can be found in the sixteenth-century English Reformation in which the Church of England emerged as a state church, retaining most of the basic Catholic forms of ritual and organization, but gradually incorporating many of the theological insights of the Protestant reformers. The centralized, hierarchical structure of the Church of England, under the authority of monarch, archbishops, and bishops, reinforced uniformity in religious practice and a close cooperation between church and state in both the religious and political realms. During the seventeenth century, Puritan resistance to the episcopal system of the Church of England produced several experiments in alternative church organization. Among those experiments, the congregational model, in which church membership was comprised of individuals who claimed a personal experience of divine grace, with church leadership elected from among those members, represented a nonconformist challenge to the episcopacy of the Church of England. Under the reign of the Stuarts (1603–49), several congregational groups separated from the Church of England, even emigrating to Holland or North America to pursue their religious experiments free from the hierarchical authority of the established church. Those who remained succeeded in establishing the Puritan Commonwealth of the mid-seventeenth century that nearly ended the episcopal system (Whiteman, 1962: 48). With the settlement of 1661–2, however, the Church of England restored and even strengthened its episcopacy in response to nonconformist challenges to the sacramental order of the church. In the 1830s, the Oxford Movement, with its emphasis on the authority of the church hierarchy and the uniformity of church discipline, further revitalized the Anglican episcopacy in ways that would be influential to the development of the Anglican Church in southern Africa.

Beginning in the 1740s, the Methodist movement of John Wesley emphasized a personal, emotional Christian practice that concentrated on the salvation of souls. Dismissing matters of theological doctrine or church organization as irrelevant, Wesley and his followers stressed a personal religious experience of guilt for sin, acceptance of Christ, assurance of forgiveness, and individual sanctification. Although social concern was evident in self-help, mutual aid, and social service schemes, an emphasis on the salvation of individual souls remained paramount in the Methodist movement. In the context of the Industrial Revolution, however, this emphasis on the individual was linked to a revitalized Protestant work ethic, particularly demanding discipline, productive labor, and frugality from an emerging urban working class. As historian E. P. Thompson noted, the Methodist movement was instrumental in 'promoting loyalty in the middle ranks as well as subordination and industry in the lower orders of society' (Thompson, 1968: 386). Although the production of loyal middle classes and subservient working classes served their interests, rural agriculturalists, professionals, and aristocrats largely ignored the Methodist revivals (Warner 1930: 165).

Nevertheless, the evangelical enthusiasm of Methodism permeated British Protestant life, contributing to an increase in church attendance that reached over 50 per cent of the population by the middle of the nineteenth century (Carwardine, 1990: 228). Methodist concern for personal salvation led to an ambivalence about the relation between Protestant religion and British politics in the nineteenth century. On the one hand, the influential Methodist leader Jabez Bunting argued in the 1830s that Christians were to stay out of politics, remaining 'quiet in the land,' although Bunting did betray a conservative, Tory political commitment by insisting that 'Methodism hates democracy as much as it hates sin' (Hempton, 1987: 204–13). On the other hand, however, Methodist emphasis on service to others was translated into involvement in various nineteenth-century reform movements, advocating the abolition of slavery, the promotion of free trade, the discipline of temperance, and the disestablishment of the Church of England. A similar concern for saving souls and social welfare generated Methodist support for the extension of Christian missions in southern Africa and elsewhere.

From 1827 to 1847 Anglican congregations and ministers in southern Africa lacked local episcopal supervision, although they were under the control of the government in the Cape. In the expanding colonial world of the Church of England, southern African Anglicans were placed under the religious jurisdiction of the bishop of Calcutta. With the consecration of Robert Gray as Bishop of Cape Town in 1847, however, the Anglican church in southern Africa began a period of rapid institutional expansion. In 1853 bishops were assigned to Natal and Grahamstown; in 1863 a bishop was assigned to Bloemfontein; and in 1870 the church was incorporated as the Church of the Province of Southern Africa under the jurisdiction of the Archbishop of Cape Town. During the 1850s Robert Gray claimed that he had 'transplanted the system and organization of the Church of England to this land' (De Gruchy, 1979: 17). In the 1870 constitution of the Church of the Province of Southern Africa, however, a certain degree of independence from London was asserted on matters of doctrine, practice, and church discipline. Defending that independence in synod debates in 1883, one archdeacon argued that 'we desire this church to be indigenous, not exotic' (Lewis and Edwards, 1934: 185–6). Nevertheless, what it meant to be an 'indigenous' church was worked out in the context of expanding British political, social, and economic domination in southern Africa during the nineteenth century.

First, an 'indigenous' church did not necessarily mean a church serving the interests of the indigenous African inhabitants of the region. For the most part, the Anglican church hierarchy supported British conquest and dominion over the people of southern Africa. In this cooperation between church and state, Bishop Henry Cotterill, serving Grahamstown since 1857, argued that any clergyman who ignored 'the rightful authority of the Civil Government' was 'unfitted, whatever might be his other qualifications, for the office of a missionary.' Any refusal to cooperate with the state in extending the authority of British rule over the indigenous population was regarded by Bishop Cotterill as 'a dereliction of the duty a Christian owes to the government of his country' (Goedhals, 1989b: 107). With few exceptions, Methodist ministers and missionaries were in agreement with the Anglican hierarchy on the political imperative of loyalty and obedience to the colonial government.

Second, an 'indigenous' church did not mean a church that adapted Christian beliefs and practices to indigenous patterns of African religion. The Anglican hierarchy was in complete sympathy with the general missionary project of rooting out indigenous African religious beliefs and practices in order to replace them with a new Christian faith and lifestyle. In an attempt to replace African with British Christian culture, Bishop Robert Gray in 1858 founded an educational institution in Cape Town, Zonnebloem College, for the education of sons and daughters of African chiefs in the arts and sciences of British learning. By separating them from what he regarded as 'heathen and barbarous' influences, Gray hoped to transform future African leaders into cultivated products of Anglican religion and British culture. Twenty years later, however, after mixed results, this experiment in the transformation of culture for an African elite at Zonnebloem had largely been replaced by industrial training. But the motive of undermining indigenous African religion and culture remained (Hodgson, 1979; 1987).

Objection to the campaign against African religion had been voiced by Bishop of Natal J. W. Colenso when he rejected a church policy toward Africans that tried 'to uproot altogether their old religion, scoffing at the things which they hold most sacred' (Guy, 1983: 45). Colenso was exceptional in arguing for greater tolerance of African religious beliefs and practices. Affirming the common humanity of Africans and Europeans, Colenso suggested the possibility of a uniquely African Christianity. On this point, however, Bishop Gray disagreed, insisting that Africans could be 'reclaimed from the indolence of barbarism – if only they were Christianised and civilized' (Guy, 1983: 49).

In the 1860s, Bishop Gray entered into a more intense conflict with Bishop Colenso, not over African religion, but over the nature of the scriptural revelation at the basis of Anglican faith and church discipline. Colenso's innovative critical biblical scholarship, which called into question the literal, historical accuracy of the Pentateuch, generated controversy in Britain, as well as in southern Africa, where Gray ironically branded Colenso as a 'heathen' for his critical biblical scholarship. In the southern African context, however, the conflict was not merely over theology but also over Bishop Gray's authority to enforce church discipline in the region. In Cape Town, Gray asserted his authority by having Colenso convicted of heresy, excommunicated, and replaced as Bishop of Natal. Colenso's refusal to leave Natal, however, resulted in an Anglican split that divided Gray's Church of the Province of Southern Africa from Colenso's smaller Anglican community that came to be called the Church of England.

Third, an 'indigenous' church did not mean a church in which blacks assumed any role in leadership. No black delegates were in attendance at the first provincial synod of the Church of the Province of Southern Africa in 1870 (Nuttal, 1970). Black Anglican clergy, however, showed considerable interest in the imitation of British models. For example, Peter Masiza, the first black priest in the Church of the Province of Southern Africa, attacked traditional initiation ritual as 'the most wicked and horrible custom' and conducted his choirs so they would be 'just like the English service' (Goedhals, 1989a: 26–27). In this respect, Methodists, as in Victorian England, were essentially supplementary to the Anglican church (G. M. Young, 1964: 65). Although black involvement in both Anglican and Methodist churches expanded, particularly with the initiative of black Methodist evangelists and lay preachers, white religious models and institutional controls remained firmly in place, even when they were challenged at the end of the nineteenth century by the emergence of independent, indigenous Christian churches under black leadership.

During the 1870s, black economic, social, and political involvement in the Cape was supported by white liberal activists who had strong connections with the English-speaking churches. Liberal 'friends of the natives,' such as Saul Solomon, W. P. Schreiner, and J. X. Merriman, defended the limited franchise for blacks in the Cape. By encouraging Christian, educated blacks to participate in electoral politics, Cape liberals hoped to complete the civilizing work of the colonial missions. As John Noble claimed in 1877, 'The aim of the policy of the Colonial Government since 1855 has been to establish and maintain peace, to diffuse civilisation and Christianity, and to establish society on the basis of individual property and personal industry' (Noble, 1877: 334–5). In addition to what has been called the 'great tradition' of Cape liberalism, based on the values of liberal Christianity, human rights, and free enterprise, a 'small tradition' of liberalism in the Cape was based in the 1870s on alliances between black peasants and white merchants and traders in taking advantage of new economic opportunities. Arguably, however, the liberalism that was influential in English-speaking churches contributed to the cooptation of a class of black peasants, artisans, and entrepreneurs into market relations that remained under the control of white economic and political interests (Trapido, 1980: 258; Bundy, 1972; 1979).

Nevertheless, the more liberal franchise gave blacks some limited room to maneuver in the politics of the Cape. For many black Christians in the English-speaking churches, British colonial rule was a political reality to be embraced as an integral part of a divine pattern of salvation. For example, the black newspaper *Isigidimi SamaXhosa*, edited by Elijah Makiwane, and later by John Tengo Jabavu, depicted the last war on the eastern Cape frontier, from 1877 to 1881, as a battle between Christendom and heathendom, fought by British forces that these black Christians described as 'our troops, the troops of Victoria, Child of the Beautiful,' against heathen villains who persisted in 'hostility to the Word' (Hogan, 1980: 277). Similarly, the black Christian editors of the newspaper, *Imvo*, identified both Christian interests and black interests with British imperial rule. 'Direct imperial control,' *Imvo* stated in 1897, 'is the talisman engraved on the heart of every native in the land' (Willan, 1982: 242).

Black educated Christians in the diamond city of Kimberley celebrated British religion, nationalism, and culture in the 1890s. Educated black Christians, such as Sol Plaatje, Isaiah Bud-M'belle, and the Reverend Gwayi Tyamzashe, formed the South African Improvement Society in the hope that it would help their advancement in the colonial society. At a celebration in honor of Queen Victoria in 1891, Isaiah Bud-M'belle, high-court interpreter in Kimberley, observed that, when the Queen came to the throne, few blacks could write and none were ministers. 'Now thousands could write,' Bud-M'belle declared, 'and there were about five hundred Native ministers. There were also flourishing Native educational institutions' (Willan, 1982: 243). For these black Christians, British language, education, and culture promised an avenue of advancement beyond what seemed to them as the limits presented by either Boer or native society. At the same time that black Christians were embracing British religion and nationalism, however, economic advantages associated with British rule were being closed, as, ironically, the last black allowed by law to hold a diamond claim was the Lovedale graduate and Free Church of Scotland minister, Reverend Gwayi Tyamzashe (Turrell, 1982: 69). By the time Reverend Tyamzashe died in 1896, educated black Christians in South Africa were increasingly caught in the contradiction of being incorporated in a white-dominated political order, yet fundamentally excluded from equal citizenship or economic opportunity.

By the end of the nineteenth century, English-speaking churches were also caught in a contradiction, the contradiction between their humanitarian ideals and the dehumanizing racial, class, and gender relations that took shape in an emerging industrial capitalism. After the South African War (1899–1902), English-speaking churches were directly involved in supporting the creation and control of a black workforce that would serve capitalist interests in the new Union of South Africa. The cooperation among religion, government, and industrial capitalism was reinforced by the findings of the South African Native Affairs Commission (1903–5) that outlined racial and labor relations in the new political dispensation. The Commission's report included a section on 'Christianity and Civilisation' that emphasized the importance of religion in the advance of capitalism, implying that industrial capitalism promised victory in South Africa in the 'great struggle between the powers of good and evil, of light and darkness, of enlightenment and ignorance, of progress and tradition, of Christianity and heathenism.' In these oppositions, the Commission celebrated the worldview of capitalism as a religious worldview in its own right.

Nevertheless, the churches lent their support to the Commission's findings, as the South African Missionary Society concurred with the Commission, observing that 'no more satisfying justification of the missionary work of the churches has ever been penned.' From the beginning of the twentieth century, therefore, English-speaking churches aligned themselves with the rise of industrial capitalism in South Africa. By the same token, they cooperated in the subjugation of black workers to white-controlled capitalist interests. As the official organ of the Methodist Church once declared:

The Native is, we firmly believe, one of the best assets this country possesses. We need him to assist us to develop its vast resources, and he will help us, if we allow him, to make it a country in which an ever-increasing number of Europeans will live in comfort.

(Cochrane, 1987: 63, 114)

By embracing the interests of industrial capitalism, Protestant churches in South Africa became implicated in the racial, class, and gender relations of an industrializing South Africa. Those complex, contradictory relations permeated the character of South African Protestant churches in the twentieth century.

RELIGION AND RACE

Religion rather than racism provided the basic vocabulary used by European colonists for defining differences among people in the emerging Cape society of the seventeenth and eighteenth centuries (MacCrone, 1937; Elphick and Giliomee, 1989b: 526). Differences of language, customs, and even physical traits were often interpreted in religious terms. As used by Dutch colonists, those religious terms were not explicitly Calvinist. Rather, they were drawn from more general notions of 'Christian civilization.' For example, Jacob Hondius reported in 1652 that the Khoisan people in the Cape were 'in every way like animals' because they lacked civilized habits and Christian religion. 'There are no signs of Belief or Religion to be found among them,' Jacob Hondius concluded, 'and it is for this reason they are called Cafres' (Thompson, 1985: 72-3). The precise history of the term is obscure, but it is clear that as early as 1652 a Dutch visitor such as Jacob Hondius interpreted it as a religious term, from the Arabic *kafir*, designating an unbeliever. Since Muslims traditionally used this term to indicate an unbeliever in the religion of Islam, many European commentators drew the unlikely conclusion that blacks in southern Africa were survivors, migrants, outcasts, or refugees from some ancient Islamic civilization.

This conclusion was not only drawn by Dutch observers. The British visitor John Barrow in the 1790s also concluded, on the basis of their practice of circumcision, that blacks in southern Africa exhibited 'remains of Islamisism' (Barrow, 1806, II: 117). The importance of Christian aversion to Islam has often been overlooked as a motive for excluding blacks from full participation in Christian churches and society. Among the many other religious misunderstandings under which European colonists suffered, this identification of blacks with Islam provided a recurring justification for drawing a line of separation between Christians and non-Christians in southern Africa.

As we have seen, the Dutch Reformed Church institutionalized racial divisions in the 1850s, not as a matter of racialist principle, but in deference to 'the weakness of some.' Again, a religious, rather than an explicitly racial classification was used, as the Dutch Reformed Church separated out people it referred to as 'heathens.' At its formation in 1853, however, the Neder-duitsch Hervormde Kerk was more explicit in its exclusion of blacks, writing racial separation into the church's original constitution. Likewise, the Gereformeerde Kerk defined itself as a white church. As a congregation of the 'Dopper' church stated in 1860:

> We did not learn in the Word of God that we had to allow them to share in the same social rights. Given the nations which surround us here, such a policy will lead to the political downfall of whites and the corruption of blacks. Thus we consider it imperative for both us and them that they keep their religion separate and that their spiritual needs be met in a special way.
>
> (Spoelstra, 1963: 61; Villa-Vicencio, 1988: 27)

Racial policies of both churches were consistent with the constitution, or *Grondwet*, of the Boer Republics which required 'no equality between black and white in church or state.' Apparently, however, the 'Dopper' church also justified the religious exclusion of blacks on biblical grounds. According to Andrew Murray, Jr., the identification of blacks as sons of Ham, cursed to be hewers of wood, and drawers of water, was a common argument advanced by members of the Gereformeerde Kerk for the exclusion of blacks (Loubser, 1987: 7).

At the end of the nineteenth century, these two religious motifs – Islamic origins and the biblical curse of Ham – continued occasionally to be repeated. In 1882, the Dutch theologian F. Lion Cachet, who had worked in South Africa from 1858 to 1880 organizing the Dutch Reformed Church in the Transvaal, published a defense of the Transvaal Republic that repeated the theory of an Arabic and Islamic derivation of southern African blacks. 'The most reliable informants agree,' Cachet claimed, 'that the Kaffers are sons of Ishmael who, in relatively recent times, have reached the South coast of Africa over land' (Thompson, 1985: 84). Similarly, in 1899, J. C. Voigt argued that because they practiced circumcision southern African blacks must have recently migrated from Egypt, Syria, Palestine, or Arabia, as refugees from 'aggressive Mahometanism' (Voigt, 1899: I: 147). This fanciful theory of the Islamic origins of southern African blacks was invoked to justify their dispossession and exclusion. By imagining that blacks were recent arrivals from northern, Islamic lands, white colonists could also imagine that blacks did not really belong in southern Africa.

In 1898 the Afrikaner author J. F. van Oordt published another defense of the Kruger regime in the Transvaal Republic that repeated the second religious motif, assigning the 'mark of Cain,' or the 'curse of Ham,' to southern African blacks as a symbol of their inferior place in the world. 'According to the Boer idea,' Van Oordt reported, 'the Kaffer, the Hottentot, the Bushman belong to a lower race than the Whites. They carry, as people once rightly called it, the mark of Cain; God, the Lord, destined them to be "drawers of water and hewers of wood," as *presses* subject to the white race' (Thompson, 1985: 85). While the myth of the Islamic origin of southern African blacks tried to justify their exclusion, the myth of a biblical curse was invoked to legitimize their domination as servants of white interests. The two myths, however, obviously carried contradictory messages. To state this contradiction simply: White interests in justifying the exclusion, separation, or removal of blacks from the land were in conflict with the white practice of dominating and exploiting blacks as labor. This contradiction resurfaced in the 1930s in the doctrine of apartheid.

Whether excluded or dominated, however, blacks were assigned a subhuman status in these contradictory religious myths. As J. F. van Oordt observed, 'I do not believe that I go too far when I express my feeling that the Boers as a whole doubt the existence of a Kaffer- or a Hottentot-soul' (Thompson, 1985: 85). At the end of the nineteenth century, however, denials of humanity gradually came to be formulated in an explicitly racist ideology of white supremacy. Racist ideology was formulated in terms of two European intellectual currents of the nineteenth century – romantic nationalism and scientific racism. Under the influence of these developments, racialist assumptions came to permeate the thinking of Protestant church leaders in South Africa.

Romantic nationalism emerged in nineteenth-century Europe with all the characteristics of a religious movement. Nationalists followed the lead of German philosopher Johann Gottfried von Herder in maintaining that every *Volk* (people or nation) had its own *Klima* (habitat, culture, or way of life) (Manuel, 1983: 166). Romantic nationalists tended to imagine that nations were like living organisms, each having a life of its own. The many peoples, languages, cultures, and religions, therefore, were imagined as separate organic systems. In South Africa, romantic nationalism was evident in the mobilization of British interests, but it was also important in the emergence of an Afrikaner nationalist identity, beginning with the first Afrikaans language movement in 1875. Relations between the Dutch Reformed Church and Afrikaner nationalism were ambivalent at the end of the nineteenth century, illustrated by the fact that Dutch opposition to Afrikaans in the church was one factor in delaying translation of the Bible into Afrikaans until 1932 (Hofmeyr, 1987: 108). Church and nationalism, however, were clearly linked by the 1930s. By that time, the romantic notion of a nation as a living organism, with a distinctive language, culture, and identity, was explicitly defined in racial terms by leaders of Afrikaans-speaking churches.

Racial classifications, however, tended to be shared by leaders in both the Afrikaans and English churches, who owed much of their understanding of race to late nineteenth-century developments in scientific racism. In Britain, a science of race was initiated by the work of Robert Knox, whose *Races of Man*, published in 1850, argued that human races were separate species with different origins, having fixed and unequal physical, intellectual, and moral characteristics. Although Knox's theory of the 'polygenesis' of human races had been dismissed in scientific circles by the 1870s, his science of race had succeeded in divorcing reflection on human differences from the biblical account of a common origin of humanity. In the 1870s, however, British scientific thinking on race was not so much concerned with conflicts between religion and science as with the more practical objective of providing biological explanations for British domination over diverse groups of people throughout the expanding British Empire.

In that political context, scientific racism was dominated by biological theories of the inherent inferiority and submissiveness of people classified as black, brown, or yellow. For example, in 1870 the scientist T. H. Huxley developed a classification of racial types based on measurements of skin color, hair color and texture, eye color, skull shape, and physical stature. Like most scientific racists, however, Huxley linked those physical observations with what he imagined were fixed intellectual and moral characteristics. While he attributed a white race with the traits of beauty and intelligence, Huxley asserted that black people were inherently inferior, as even the shapes of their skulls suggested to Huxley a 'feminine, or child-like character' (Lorimer, 1988: 413). Clearly, for Huxley and other scientific racists, this identification of all blacks as women or children represented a 'natural' subordination of blacks to white, adult male domination. Through the work of Francis Galton, who had formed much of his racialist thinking during a visit to southern Africa, statistical measurement of skulls and other physical traits became more sophisticated (Fabian, 1987). But the underlying impact of scientific racism remained the same, providing biological explanations for human differences in ways that justified white domination of other people.

Like earlier religious myths for explaining human differences, scientific racism implied that people classified as inferior had to be either excluded from society or incorporated as subordinate labor. In South Africa, that choice was stated in terms of scientific racism in 1894 by author Benjamin Kidd, in a book on *Social Evolution*, when he recorded the observation of a 'leading colonist' that 'the natives must go; or they must work as laboriously to develop the land as we are prepared to do' (Kidd, 1894: 46). In 1901 eugenicist Karl Pearson insisted that science required the elimination of blacks from South Africa. Pearson argued that whites had to replace blacks in every sphere of national life, including the fields and mines, while blacks had to be driven out of the country. From the standpoint of science, Pearson concluded, national life had to be 'a *homogeneous* whole, not a mixture of superior and inferior races' (Pearson, 1901: 47–8). These notions of scientific racism at the beginning of the twentieth century were consistent with legal enactments – from the Glen Grey Act of 1894 to the Native Land Act of 1913 – that sought to institutionalize racial segregation in South Africa. In this context, what came to be called 'race relations' emerged as an urgent concern for South African Protestant churches.

The concern for 'race relations' resulted in several church-supported ventures: the Joint Council of Africans and Europeans in the 1920s, a series of European–Bantu Conferences beginning in 1923, and the formation of the South African Institute of Race Relations in 1929. Liberals involved in these projects were concerned with facilitating dialogue, improving social conditions, and influencing government policy. They were heavily dependent on support from churches and the mission network. Although largely supported by the English-speaking churches, these liberal projects also gained some interest in the 1920s from the Dutch Reformed Church, which convened the European–Bantu Conferences that were held in 1923 and 1927. The influence of missionary Christianity on South African liberals between the First and Second World Wars was suggested by the impact of the work of J. H. Oldham, secretary of the International Missionary Conference, on Christian liberals such as Edgar Brookes and J. H. Hofmeyr. In his 1924 book, *Christianity and the Race Problem*, Oldham described the liberal Christian mission of 'establishing harmonious relations between the different peoples of the world and of providing a moral basis for the Great Society' (Oldham, 1924: 6; Brookes, 1930, 1934; Hofmeyr, 1945).

For all their interest in improving 'race relations,' however, liberals tended to operate with segregationist and paternalistic assumptions. C. T. Loram, for example, argued that blacks should not be assimilated into white society, yet should develop industrial skills that would make them useful to white-controlled economic interests (Loram, 1917). South African liberals supported conservative American ideas on 'race relations' associated with the work of Booker T. Washington, stressing the need for industrial education that would train blacks for productive labor. Loram was one of the organizers of the 1921 Phelps-Stokes Commission that brought James Aggrey, an African educator from the Gold Coast who had worked as a teacher in America for 20 years, to promote industrial training in South Africa. Even Aggrey, however, demonstrated a liberal paternalism by arguing that 'we Africans must, like infants, learn to stand before we can walk and walk before we can run' (Smith, 1929: 175; Rich, 1984: 10–32).

During the 1920s and 1930s, liberal ideals of harmonious 'race relations,' based, however, on separate and unequal relations, permeated much of the thinking of English-speaking churches. For many white, liberal Christians, segregation meant the protection of Africans from being infected by the worst aspects of urban, industrial society. In order to prevent Africans from succumbing to urban evils, particularly alcohol, prostitution, and unemployment, liberal segregationists argued that they should return to what was left of traditional life on the reserves. Church leaders who opposed racial segregation, however, still tended to maintain separate and unequal conditions for inclusion. The Anglican Bishop of George, for example, voiced his opposition to segregation in 1924, but only because he advocated the inclusion of the few blacks that he regarded as 'clean, intelligent, well-educated, civilised men.' Even those few, however, would only be integrated on unequal terms, as the Bishop of George insisted that Africans 'must be made fit to be the Junior Partner in this country, but on our conditions.' That partnership in 'race relations' imagined within English-speaking churches between the wars was clearly selective and unequal. Interracial cooperation, as bluntly stated in a Methodist periodical in 1926, was based on the 'combination of white man's brain and organising power, and black men's hands and sweat' (Cochrane, 1987: 139).

During this same period, a black, Christian, educated elite aspired to play a role as cultural mediators. As A. B. Xuma, one of the founders of the African National Congress (ANC), observed at a European–Bantu Conference in 1930, educated black Christians would 'interpret the European to the African, and the African to the European' (Xuma, 1930). By the end of the 1930s, however, educated black Christians were less optimistic about the benefits that might be gained from such involvement with white liberals and English-speaking churches. For example, James Calata became an Anglican priest and rector of St James's Church in Craddock in the Cape. As a member of the African National Congress, Calata advocated Christian principles and defended the liberal tradition in the Cape. When the limited African franchise in the Cape was removed by legislation in 1936, however, Calata concluded that the promises of liberalism had proven to be empty. In 1938, as Secretary-General of the ANC, James Calata observed, 'I do not believe we can any longer look to the South African Britishers for our champion' (Karis and Carter, 1973, II: 136; Butler, 1987: 96). But others had already come to that conclusion. For example, ANC leader James Thaele, in a 1923 essay on 'Christianity, Basis of Native Policy?', argued that the European–Bantu Conference called by the Dutch Reformed Church in 1923 merely supported a system of oppression in South Africa. Thaele attacked black Christian participants as 'good boys' who would not challenge oppression because they were 'beneficiaries of the system.' Instead of race relations, James Thaele and others proposed an analysis of the class position of black workers in the capitalist system of South Africa (Karis and Carter, 1973: II: 214–15).

RELIGION AND CLASS

Dutch Reformed churches and English-speaking churches were not only divided by language, but also by their relations to industrial capitalism in early twentieth-century South Africa. In general, Anglicans and Methodists were heavily dependent for their support on mining capital and foreign funding from Britain. Although their congregations were increasingly black in composition, the English-speaking churches persisted in emphasizing missions, evangelization, and industrial education in the service of the ruling-class interests of mining, industry, and British capitalism. The Dutch Reformed Church, however, depended upon rural, agricultural capital, at least until the 1920s when it aligned itself with a new coalition under the political leadership of J. B. M. Hertzog that linked farming capital, manufacturing capital, and white workers to assume greater national control over the economy.

Pressing black issues of the period – the dispossession of land, migrant labor, and endemic poverty – were not directly addressed by Protestant churches. These issues were only regarded in ways that tended to reinforce social controls over black workers. In practice, Anglican and Methodist leaders used their religious resources to supplement the political program for South Africa that had been outlined in 1899 by Lord Alfred Milner when he declared that 'the ultimate end is a self-governing white community, supported by well-treated and justly governed black labour from Cape Town to Zambesi.' Neither Milner nor the English-speaking churches imagined political, social, or economic equality for blacks. For the most part, they agreed that blacks should be taught 'habits of regular and skilled labour,' while their discipline as workers should be maintained by keeping them 'away from strong drink' (Davenport, 1977: 152).

Regarding black workers, Anglican Bishop Alan Gibson observed that 'it may be God's will that most of them should always remain labourers, herd men, domestic servants, and the like, and that only a few should come to the front' (Cochrane, 1987: 152). When black workers went on strike, however, English-speaking churches tended to call for a mediating Christian spirit on both sides of the labor line that would restore the status quo. Between 1919 and 1921, the largest number of workers went on strike in South African history (Johnstone, 1976: 126). In response, an Anglican newspaper recognized that the cause of the discontent was 'the realisation of the worker of the position that is due to him as a human being' (Cochrane, 1987: 128). Nevertheless, mediating voices in the churches argued that Christians had to stand above industrial conflicts and point out faults on both sides. While the Dutch Reformed Church was forging an alliance with white workers in the 1920s, the English-speaking churches were instructing black workers to be obedient, disciplined, and loyal.

Against the mobilization of black workers in the Industrial and Commercial Workers Union (ICU) during the 1920s, the Methodist Church exhorted its black membership, 'do not be misled by those who would have you believe that your awakening race-consciousness can be satisfied and your true development secured simply by the improvement of political, educational and economic conditions' (Cochrane, 1987: 137). Although churches showed some support for the principle of collective bargaining, Protestant spokesmen consistently advised labor leader Clements Kadalie that his ICU should not attack whites, should be sponsored by white unions, should accept gradual reform, should avoid socialism, should encourage Christian family life, and should cease 'flouting those who have been responsible for the Native's progressive development from the beginning of the missionary enterprise in South Africa' (Cochrane, 1987: 142; Walshe, 1970: 162). Even church opposition to the Hertzog labor control and color-bar bills after 1926 only objected to extending regulations considered appropriate for the mining industry to the entire country.

In this context, the concern of Dr James Henderson of Lovedale, editor of the *South African Outlook*, was exceptional in paying attention to the forced labor, low wages, poor health conditions, and absence of legal bargaining mechanisms, as well as the overcrowding, land depletion, and rural poverty of the reserves. Henderson argued that 'more than ever before it is necessary for [Christians] to concentrate their study and effort on the material life and the economic position of Native people' (Henderson, 1928; Rich, 1987). Instead, however, Christian leaders tended to concentrate on promoting a spiritual life among black workers that would adapt them to their subservient position in the South African class system.

The mining city of Johannesburg became the center of a new Protestant urban mission directed toward black workers on the mines and in the city. In 1912 the General Missionary Conference resolved that conditions on the mines did not present an obstacle to Christianity. In fact, the Missionary Conference stated that strenuous labor on the mines actually improved the character of men, and it thanked De Beers Consolidated Mines for supporting religious work among miners that helped improve the 'morality' and 'loyalty' of black workers (Cochrane, 1987: 113). The mining compound, with its segregated, single-sex hostels, armed guards, and pass system, provided not only a place in which the 'morality' and 'loyalty' of workers could be controlled, but also a relatively captive audience for church missionaries and religious workers. Evidence that the compounds were dehumanizing environments had come before government agencies. A government Health Officer's report to the Secretary of Native Affairs in 1903 had found that food served to miners in the compounds was 'not fit for human consumption.' Another government report in 1908 found that the compounds were 'unfit for human habitation.' Nevertheless, in 1913, when church leaders feared that the 'morality' and 'loyalty' of black workers was being threatened by the illegal liquor trade in the city, the General Missionary Conference called for expanding and tightening the controls of the closed compound system (Callinicos, 1980: 45; Jeeves, 1985: 22).

In response to the labor unrest and strikes of the early 1920s, Protestant religious leaders developed new methods of social control that were directed toward black workers in and around Johannesburg (Couzens, 1982). Taking the lead in this new urban mission were American missionaries, particularly the enthusiastic representative of the American Board, Ray Phillips. Because the mining industry had brought so many people from rural areas to the city, Phillips saw Johannesburg as a strategic center for reaching the whole country. Migrant labor and mine compounds, according to Phillips, were blessed institutions through which 'the Almighty works to bring His will to pass in this great continent!' (Phillips, 1930: 319). As a humanitarian, Phillips saw part of his work as a duty to inform whites about the conditions under which blacks lived in the city, hoping for fairer treatment of black workers. Phillips' more immediate concern, however, was to defuse the discontent among black workers that unfair working and living conditions in the city had produced. In this aim, Ray Phillips obviously served the interests of mining capital in trying to counteract the work of 'agitators,' communists, and labor unionists who were imagined to be fomenting unrest among workers. Phillips' solution to the discontent of black workers was what he proclaimed as a new, urban 'Social Gospel' that would solve 'the whole great problem of moralizing the leisure time of natives in city and country alike' (Phillips, 1930: 58).

Rather than improving working conditions, Phillips and his colleagues implemented their 'Social Gospel' by creating various leisure-time diversions for black workers. They introduced sports, entertainments, and social clubs as ways of defusing discontent and enhancing the spiritual life of black workers in mining compounds and city. In the mining compounds, Phillips argued that the church had to 'capture the physical and mental life of these young men during six days of the week besides preaching the Gospel to them on the seventh' (Phillips, 1930: 139). In the interests of this mission of total social control, Phillips introduced sports and games, such as football, volleyball, 'hunt the thimble,' and 'who's got the ring,' but gained his greatest success by showing films in the mining compounds. Movies did not merely provide entertainment, education, and recreation, however. Phillips even claimed that his film shows prevented unrest on the mines, as he later claimed that he had restored peace during the Great Strike of 1922 at the New Primrose Mine by showing Charlie Chaplin movies. The Chamber of Mines was so impressed by Phillips' success that it financed equipment and operating expenses for his Christian movie mission. During the 1920s, other Protestant churches initiated similar missions to the mining compounds, receiving financial support from the mining companies for their efforts in providing Christian recreation for black workers by showing films that depicted 'scenes and stories of native life and life in other countries as well as nature sketches, educational subjects and humourous pictures of a healthy kind' (Cochrane, 1987: 141; Phillips, 1930: 147–50; Couzens, 1982: 319–22).

In the city, Phillips introduced projects of a different type, but with a similar aim in creating mechanisms of social control over the black working class. During the early 1920s, as Phillips later recalled, he met with 'embittered native leaders' who were frustrated in their attempts to change the system of racial and class oppression. 'Peaceful measures have failed,' these black leaders apparently told Phillips. 'We are being forced to try violence!' (Phillips, 1930: 118–19). In response to this threat, Phillips started a debating and literary society, called the Gamma Sigma Club, where Phillips claimed that even the most radical and embittered urban blacks could have their attitudes changed. Although this club continued into the mid-thirties, after 1924 it became part of a larger social organization, the Bantu Men's Social Centre, that organized films, theater, and concerts, all part of what Phillips regarded as the Christian mission of 'moralizing leisure time' in the city.

Ray Phillips presented his 'Social Gospel' in the interwar liberal idiom of 'race relations.' Significantly, the South African Institute of Race Relations was formed in 1929 as a result of a meeting that took place at Phillips' home. Nevertheless, Phillips' Christian mission clearly represented an intervention in class relations. In the mining compounds, Phillips' mission was aimed at producing a class of docile black workers. In the city, his mission was directed toward producing a class of moderate, black petty bourgeoisie. Overall, Phillips obviously aligned his urban mission with the class interests of mining capital in maintaining a particular order of social control. Despite its intentions and achievements, however, the urban mission, like the frontier missions of the previous century, did not succeed in establishing a social control that was uniform or total. The complicity of churches in a class system that enforced the political, social, and economic oppression of black workers did not go unnoticed by black Christians. Christian leaders of the African National Congress, such as Pixley Seme, John Dube, Zaccheus Mahabane, and A. B. Xuma, argued that white Christians had betrayed Christian principles by invoking them in support of an oppressive racial and class system.

As a result, John Dube concluded, Christianity had 'an offensive smell to a large number of Africans' (Walshe, 1970: 163). Nevertheless, ANC leaders embraced Christianity in their moral appeals for greater political freedom and economic opportunity in South Africa.

Other black Christians, however, more clearly aligned with the class interests of workers, appropriated Christian symbols to represent the condition of oppression under which they suffered. Prior to the mineworker strikes of 1920, the Transvaal Native Congress presented a forum in which black Christians inverted the Protestant symbolism of social control. Methodist local preacher and leader of the Transvaal Native Congress, S. M. Makghato, in particular, was active in this reinterpretation of Christian symbols from a perspective at the bottom of the class system enforced by industrial capitalism. At a meeting in 1918, for example, Makghato identified the situation of black workers with the slavery of the children of Israel in the land of pharaoh (Bonner, 1982: 293). At another meeting, Makghato redefined Christian symbols of heaven and hell in terms of the class relations of South African racial capitalism. 'The God of the white people was Gold,' Makghato observed, 'their heaven money.' The Christian missionaries of this capitalist religion had warned blacks about the fires of hell reserved for sinners against the God of Gold. But 'black people in this land are in hell already,' Makghato observed, 'the owner of the hell, which is the white man, will not allow the blacks to pray.' The impact of this type of Christian religion was not beneficial social control but social oppression, as Makghato concluded that 'the blacks are tormented in this land and the white man does what he likes' (Bonner, 1982: 296). S. M. Makghato's reinterpretation of Christianity in terms of the economic and class relations of a white-controlled industrial capitalism represented a creative, innovative inversion of religious symbols, turning upside down the symbolic and material order that Protestant churches were trying to reinforce in South Africa.

Similarly, black Christians aligned with working-class interests employed two other symbolic strategies for reinterpreting Christianity in the context of industrial capitalism. Although they often overlapped, these two strategies might be distinguished as the 'traditional' and the 'apocalyptic' promises of redemption from class oppression. First, the 'traditional' strategy identified Christian salvation with the power and authority of the ancient gods, ancestors, and chiefs of Africa. For example, at a meeting of the Transvaal Native Congress in 1918, the journalist Selope Thema restated a familiar dissatisfaction with the white Christian promise of a heaven after death. 'The white people teach you about heaven and tell you that after death you will go to a beautiful land in heaven,' Thema noted. However, he continued, white Christians 'don't teach you about this earth on which we live.' The truth about this earth, Thema suggested, was that blacks had been dispossessed and then prevented by law from recovering their possession of any more than the seven per cent of the land that then made up the 'Native Reserves.' Turning the message of the Christian churches upside down, Thema declared that 'if we cannot get land on this earth neither shall we get it in heaven.' In conclusion, however, Selope Thema linked his inversion of the Christian message with a 'traditional' promise of redemption. 'The God of our Chiefs,' Thema declared, 'gave us this part of the world we possess' (Bonner, 1982: 293; Starfield, 1988: 29). In this 'traditional' strategy, therefore, some black Christians symbolized the promise of their redemption from dispossession and oppression in terms of an ancient spiritual entitlement to the land.

While the 'traditional' strategy referred back to the God of the chiefs, the 'apocalyptic' strategy looked forward to anticipate a sudden, dramatic change in class relations in the near future. In that apocalyptic redemption, the first would be last, the last would be first, and blacks would be liberated from an evil system of white oppression. At another meeting of the Transvaal Native Congress in 1920, this 'apocalyptic' symbolism was evident in a speech delivered by a certain Mgoja of Boksburg. Identifying whites as agents of absolute evil, Mgoja declared that the 'black race must know that white people are thieves and devils.' Mgoja identified the resistance of workers to labor oppression, even if it resulted in workers being imprisoned, with divine will. 'God did not want cowards,' Mgoja declared. 'They must look to the gaols as their homes. The mine natives must know they are producers of wealth and must get better pay.' In this conflict between good and evil, Mgoja introduced an apocalyptic theme that would be repeated frequently during the 1920s and 1930s in both the cities and the countryside of South Africa – the Americans were coming. 'America said they would free all natives and they will help,' Mgoja declared. 'America has a black fleet and it is coming' (Bonner, 1982: 305). In this millenarian promise of redemption, some black Christians could anticipate a reversal of class relations through the miraculous intervention of God and Americans in the liberation of blacks in South Africa.

RELIGION AND GENDER

At the turn of the twentieth century, Protestant churches were not only entangled in racial and class conflicts, but also in reinforcing a particular pattern of gender relations in South Africa. Religious, political, and cultural leaders in South African, male-dominated white society were in general agreement in defining a role for women that was based on a glorification of the domestic and an exclusion from the political arena. In circumscribing women within the sphere of home, family, and children, Afrikaans-speaking and English-speaking cultural leaders basically spoke in the same terms. Both enveloped the separate, distinctive roles that they ascribed to men and women in a sacred aura. Cape liberal politician J. X. Merriman opposed the inclusion of women in the qualified Cape franchise in 1892 by declaring that 'God Almighty had made the sexes separate' (Walker, 1990b: 323). The Afrikaans poet C. J. Langenhoven, in 1909, glorified the domestic role of caring for children and husband as 'the divinest duty of "our women" – the duties of the heart' (Walker, 1990b: 339). For their part, leaders of South African Protestant churches tended to adopt this ideological framework that in principle removed women from economic production and political action so they could represent stereotypical domestic virtues of care, frugality, and discipline that were regarded as appropriate to the Christian home (Douglas, 1977).

In the early twentieth century, some women contested this definition of the female domestic role. For example, in 1911, Olive Schreiner was active in calling attention to the exploitation of women in labor and the exclusion of women from politics. According to Schreiner, the oppression of women was only obscured by the Christian doctrine of sacred domesticity. 'At the present day when probably more than half the world's most laborious and ill-paid labour is still performed by women,' Olive Schreiner observed, 'it is somewhat difficult to reply with gravity to the assertion "let women be content to be the divine child bearer and ask no more"' (Walker, 1990b: 319). While Afrikaner nationalists were promoting a myth of the Afrikaner woman as *volksmoeder* – 'mother of the nation' – whose religious devotion, care for husband and children, and sacrifices for liberty had given birth to Afrikaner nationalism, Marie du Toit, sister of the poet Totius, a leader of the second Afrikaans language movement, published a rebuttal in 1921 that attacked this male fantasy. Although Afrikaner nationalists praised women for their 'position of honour,' Marie du Toit observed, it was a 'beast-of-burden position of honour indeed!' (M. Du Toit, 1921: 138–9; Brink, 1990: 282). For the most part, however, even white feminists were oblivious to the gender relations within which black Christian women lived.

During the nineteenth century, Christian missions had directly intervened in relations between African men and women by imposing a particular European pattern of gender relations on converts. Consistent attacks on African marriage, especially polygyny and bridewealth, and African gender divisions of labor figured prominently in Christian missions. Both of these features of African gender relations appeared to the missionaries as signs of female slavery. Bridewealth was misunderstood as a custom of 'buying wives,' resulting in what the missionary James Laing called 'the most revolting slavery,' while the role of women in agricultural production was misunderstood as the enslavement of women by African men who were too lazy to work (Williams, 1959: 306). For most missionaries, therefore,

Christian conversion required the subversion and transformation of African patterns of marriage and gender relations. As the missionary R. Young insisted in 1902, 'One of the works of Christian missions is to change, root and branch, [African] ideas about marriage.' In transforming the concept of marriage, the missionaries tried to redefine the role of women in particular so that 'women's sphere as the helpmeet and no longer the slave of man shall be universally acknowledged' (Young, 1902: 127). In working to change African marriage patterns and gender roles, Christian missionaries celebrated a Protestant 'cult of domesticity' that ritualized the roles of women as wives, mothers, and homemakers within the domestic sphere.

The Protestant 'cult of domesticity' exalted the role of women as agents of religion and civilization. Celebrating what he called 'the female influence' in the 1850s, the missionary Henry Calderwood asked, rhetorically, 'Who is so likely as a pious, judicious, educated and good-tempered woman to create and foster those very amenities which are at once the fruits and the means of civilisation?' (Calderwood, 1858: 206). However, the 'cult of domesticity' required 'the female influence' to be confined within the home, where women were charged with the duty of creating a distinctively Protestant domestic space for their children and husbands. Mission stations and schools concentrated on reinforcing this 'cult of domesticity.' While the missionary and his wife stood as living exemplars of Protestant gender relations, education was divided into what missionaries regarded as appropriate programs of study for males and females. At Christian educational institutions, boys received industrial training in construction work, agriculture, and trades, but girls received a domestic education that would prepare them to be wives in their own Christian homes or to be domestic servants in white homes. Lovedale Girls' School, with its own Industrial Department, taught housekeeping, cooking, sewing, and laundry work. According to its founder and principal, Jane Waterson, the Girls' School was less a school than a home, arguing that 'homes are what are wanted in [this land], and that the young women will never be able to make homes unless they understand and see what a home is' (Shepherd, 1940: 425; 474–6). Similarly, education at Healdtown defined different gender roles, with boys receiving industrial training, while girls were trained in 'various domestic duties' (Hewson, 1959: 169). This nineteenth-century connection between religion and homemaking in the Protestant 'cult of domesticity' continued into the twentieth century to define a separate, subordinate sphere for Christian women that was confined in the household and excluded from the larger society (Cock, 1990).

In the early twentieth century, Protestant churches pursued two basic projects – women's hostels and women's prayer unions – to reinforce the 'cult of domesticity,' particularly in new urban environments, over black Christian women. The General Missionary Conference in 1912, in a report on 'Native Girls in Town,' stressed the importance of 'the establishment of Homes under the management of Christian ladies, assisted by Christian Native women, where Native girls may be received and cared for' (Gaitskell, 1979: 49). The Anglicans, Methodists, and American Board Mission each established Christian hostels for girls in Johannesburg, but similar institutions appeared in other major cities. Like the mining compounds for men, these hostels tried to create a closed, supervised environment, even though their accommodation and recreational facilities were voluntary. The purpose of the hostels was two-fold in promoting Christian purity and Christian domestic education (Gaitskell, 1983). Purity was defined explicitly as sexual chastity, a moral purity that was enforced through supervision, spiritual teaching, and healthy recreation. This objective of sexual purity was consistent with the goals of other women's church movements of the period, such as the Purity League formed in the 1920s in Natal, that tried to teach girls how to 'live clean lives' (Walbridge, 1978; Hughes, 1990: 218). The other purpose of the Christian hostels, domestic education, not only trained girls for female roles as wives and mothers, but also for employment as domestic servants. Within the first 10 years of its founding in 1919, for example, the American Board's Helping Hand Club had placed nearly a thousand girls in jobs as domestic servants for white homes (Gaitskell, 1979: 58).

The first women's prayer unions developed out of the practice of regular devotional meetings held by missionary women or ministers' wives with 'uneducated' adult African churchwomen. Sometimes those meetings combined prayer with sewing classes, since being 'dressed' or 'clothed' was an important outward sign of Christian conversion. In the early twentieth century, more formal prayer unions, often known as *manyanos*, evolved as large-scale women's organizations. Anglican, Methodist, and Congregational American Board prayer unions expanded throughout the country. Prayer unions involved women in a distinctive style of religious devotionalism through weekly meetings for prayer, Bible exposition, and testimony. But they also provided women with scope for evangelism in preaching to 'heathen' women, a base for social work in visiting the sick and denouncing alcohol, and an opportunity for developing organizational skills that in many cases transformed prayer unions into relatively independent religious movements (Gaitskell, 1990: 256).

From the perspective of missionary supervisors, the prayer unions were useful organizations for promoting female chastity, marital fidelity, and domestic responsibilities among black Christian women. The women members, however, seemed to take greater interest in the religious enthusiasm generated by the prayer meetings and the greater independence over their religious lives that the organization of prayer unions made possible. As a result, recurring conflict over the control of women's prayer unions marked their early history.

In the Johannesburg area, the first Methodist prayer union was started in 1907 by Mrs W. Gqosho, wife of a black Methodist minister in Potchefstroom. Under her leadership, the union conducted regular prayer meetings at which women prayed for the protection of their husbands and sons who were working on the mines. But they also prayed in more general terms for the uprooting of witchcraft and superstition, indicating that the women were undertaking independent religious work to advance a Christian symbolic order. Three years later, however, the growing prayer union was placed under the supervision of the white district chairman's wife, Mrs Burnet, who tried to shift the focus of the prayer union to the cultivation of the domestic virtues she regarded as appropriate for a devout wife and mother. At the union's convention in 1915, for example, Mrs Burnet insisted that members had to 'show the power of their religion in the way they care for their husbands – many of whom are not Christian – and in an increased effort to train their children for the Lord' (Gaitskell, 1990: 258).

The Anglican women's prayer union, the Women's Help Society, later linked with the Mothers' Union, was founded by Deaconess Julia Gilpin in 1908 for the purpose of developing regular devotional habits and a Christian standard of life based on 'purity and self-respect.' The Congregationalist American Board women's movement, *Isililo*, which derived its name from a Zulu term for the ritualized 'wailing' of grief, was founded in Natal in 1912 and expanded into the Johannesburg area in the early 1920s (Gaitskell, 1990: 258–9). Like the Methodist *manyanos*, these women's prayer movements were focused by white supervisors into the 'cult of domesticity,' particularly stressing the responsibility of mothers for maintaining the sexual purity of their adolescent daughters. For many black Christian women, this emphasis of the prayer unions did in fact address the central tension in which they lived, the breakdown of family life under conditions of industrialization, migrant labor, and rural and urban poverty. Furthermore, the prayer unions provided spiritual support for Christian women who lived with the conflict between the religious demands of being devout housewives and the economic necessity that forced an increasing number of women out of the home and into wage labor.

Nevertheless, the 'cult of domesticity' imposed by white supervisors, women missionaries, and ministers' wives was to a large extent supplanted in the prayer unions through the independent initiative of black Christian women. As merely one indication of this desire for independence, in 1915 an Anglican prayer union was reported to have been praying to be spared from being assigned a white supervisor (Gaitskell, 1990: 264). Participation in the prayer unions signified a somewhat ambivalent relationship with the 'cult of domesticity.' On the one hand the prayer union uniforms, with their distinctive colors, badges, blouses, and hats, signified conformity to the ideals of Christian domesticity. On the other hand, however, the uniforms signaled a new independence assumed by black Christian women over the direction of their own religious lives. Although most members could not read or write, they could pray, preach, and organize. Between 1915 and 1930, while white women presidents of the prayer unions advocated domestic virtues and restraint, black women Christians assumed an increasingly active role in organizing the prayer unions as relatively independent movements of religious revival.

Regardless of denomination, prayer union meetings developed a pietistic, revival style of worship, an emotional enthusiasm that was distinguished by loud praying, crying, wailing, and lamenting, often continuing through the night. This enthusiastic worship might have been adapted from the preaching and praying styles of touring British and American evangelists, but it was adopted as a distinctive form of worship within the prayer unions (Mills, 1975; Christofersen, 1967: 93–4). Rather than the individual, silent prayer taught by the missionaries, this worship was corporate, vocal, and dynamic. In addition to weekly prayer meetings, prayer union women assumed an active and independent role in preaching, proclaiming their gospel to 'heathens' as well as fellow Christians. As one white Anglican woman supervisor reported in 1916, revealing her reservations about the independent preaching and distinctive styles of worship emerging in the prayer unions:

> There is no need for paid Bible women here, for all the women want to preach, either to the heathen or to each other.... many of them are possessed by the idea that souls can only be won through noisy ranting.
>
> (Gaitskell, 1990: 266)

Although for the most part prayer unions did not become directly involved in politics, the independent organizational abilities of women who expanded the prayer unions created a power base that was occasionally drawn upon in supporting political protest. In the urban context, prayer union members were active in the 1913 anti-pass demonstrations, while in the rural context of the eastern Cape during the 1920s prayer union members organized political protest and action against local government authority (Wells, 1980). Particularly in the Herschel district of the eastern Cape in 1925, large numbers of women of the local Methodist prayer union showed their religious and political independence by leading a desertion from the Methodist Church to the local African Methodist Episcopal Church, whose leader was more supportive of their political opposition to the government (Beinart and Bundy, 1987: 245–7). Even in less dramatic ways, however, women's prayer unions demonstrated religious initiatives by black women Christians to gain greater independence from white control (Brandel-Syrier, 1962). Not merely confined within the 'cult of domesticity,' women's prayer unions became arenas for independent religious action. At the same time, religious independence was also being exercised in the formation of African indigenous or independent churches. Like the women's movements, these new Christian churches rejected the imposition of white authority and developed distinctive styles of religious belief, practice, and organization that directly addressed the situation of many blacks in South Africa.

REFERENCES

Barrow, John (1806). *An Account of Travels into the Interior of Southern Africa, 1797 and 1798, 1804*. 2 vols. 2nd edn. London: Cadell & Davies; New York: Johnson Reprints, 1968.

Beinart, William, and Colin Bundy (1987). *Hidden Struggles in Rural South Africa*. London: James Currey; Berkeley: University of California Press; Cape Town: David Philip.

Bird, John (1888). *The Annals of Natal*. 2 vols. Pietermaritzburg: Davis.

Bonner, Philip (1982). 'The Transvaal Native Congress 1917–1920: The Radicalisation of the Black Petty Bourgeoisie on the Rand.' In: Shula Marks and Richard Rathbone (eds) *Industrialization and Social Change in South Africa*. London: Longman. 270–313.

Brandel-Syrier, Mia (1962). *Black Woman in Search of God*. London: Lutterworth Press.

Briggs, D. R. and J. Wing (1970). *The Harvest and the Hope*. Johannesburg: United Congregational Church of Southern Africa.

Brink, Elsabe (1990). 'Man-Made Women: Gender, Class and the Ideology of the *Volksmoeder*.' In: Cherryl Walker (ed.) *Women and Gender in Southern Africa to 1945*. London: James Currey; Cape Town: David Philip. 273–92.

Brookes, Edgar (1930). 'The Racial Question in the Light of Christian Teaching.' *Christian Students and Modern South Africa: A Report of the Bantu-European Student Christian Conference, Fort Hare, June 27–July 3, 1930*. Fort Hare: Student Christian Association, Christian Union. 185–8.

Brookes, Edgar (1934). *The Colour Problems of South Africa*. Lovedale: Lovedale Press.

Bundy, Colin (1972). 'The Emergence and Decline of a South African Peasantry.' *African Affairs* 71(285): 369–88.

Bundy, Colin (1979). *The Rise and Decline of the South African Peasantry*. Berkeley: University of California Press.

Butler, Jeffrey (1987). 'Interwar Liberalism and Local Activism.' In: Jeffrey Butler, Richard Elphick, and David Welsh (eds) *Democratic Liberalism in South Africa: Its History and Prospect*. Middletown, CT: Wesleyan University Press; Cape Town: David Philip. 81–97.

Butler, Jeffrey, Richard Elphick, and David Welsh (eds) (1987). *Democratic Liberalism in South Africa: Its History and Prospect*. Middletown, CT: Wesleyan University Press; Cape Town: David Philip.

Calderwood, Henry (1858). *Caffres and Caffre Missions*. London: James Nisbet.

Callinicos, Luli (1980). *Gold and Workers*. Johannesburg: Ravan Press.

Carwardine, Richard (1990). 'Religion and Politics in Nineteenth-Century Britain: The Case Against American Exceptionalism.' In: Mark A. Noll (ed.) *Religion and American Politics: From the Colonial Period to the 1890s*. New York and Oxford: Oxford University Press. 225–52.

Christofersen, A. F. (1967). *Adventuring with God: The Story of the American Board Mission in Africa*. R. Sales (ed.). Durban: Robinson.

Cochrane, James R. (1987). *Servants of Power: The Role of English-speaking Churches in South Africa, 1903–1930*. Johannesburg: Ravan Press.

Cock, Jacklyn (1990). 'Domestic Service and Education for Domesticity: The Incorporation of Xhosa Women into Colonial Society.' In: Cherryl Walker (ed.) *Women and Gender in Southern Africa to 1945*. London: James Currey; Cape Town: David Philip. 76–96.

Couzens, Tim (1982). '"Moralizing Leisure Time": The Transatlantic Connection and Black Johannesburg 1918–1936.' In: Shula Marks and Richard Rathbone (eds) *Industrialization and Social Change in South Africa*. London: Longman. 314–37.

Davenport, T. R. H. (1977). *South Africa: A Modern History*. Johannesburg: Macmillan.

De Gruchy, John (1979). *The Church Struggle in South Africa*. Grand Rapids, MI: Eerdmans.

Douglas, Ann (1977). *The Feminization of American Culture*. New York: Alfred A. Knopf.

Du Plessis, J. (1919). *The Life of Andrew Murray in South Africa*. London: Marshall Bros.

Du Toit, André (1985). 'Puritans in Africa? Afrikaner "Calvinism" and Kuyperian Neo-Calvinism in Late Nineteenth-Century South Africa.' *Comparative Studies in History and Society* 27: 209–40.

Du Toit, André (1987). 'The Cape Afrikaners' Failed Liberal Moment.' In: Jeffrey Butler, Richard Elphick, and David Welsh (eds) *Democratic Liberalism in South Africa: Its History and Prospect*. Middletown, CT: Wesleyan University Press; Cape Town: David Philip. 35–63.

Du Toit, Brian (1984). 'Missionaries, Anthropologists, and the Policies of the Dutch Reformed Church.' *The Journal of Modern African Studies* 22: 617–32.

Du Toit, Marie (1921). *Vrou en Feminist: Of Iets oor die Vroue-Vraagstuk*. Bloemfontein: Nasionale Pers.

Elphick, Richard (1987). 'Mission Christianity and Interwar Liberalism.' In: Jeffrey Butler, Richard Elphick, and David Welsh (eds) *Democratic Liberalism in South Africa: Its History and Prospect*. Middletown, CT: Wesleyan University Press; Cape Town: David Philip. 64–80.

Elphick, Richard and Hermann Giliomee (eds) (1989a). *The Shaping of South African Society, 1652–1840*. Cape Town: Maskew Miller Longman.

Elphick, Richard and Hermann Giliomee (1989b). 'The Origins and Entrenchment of European Dominance at the Cape, 1652–c.1840.' In: Richard Elphick and Hermann Giliomee (eds) *The Shaping of South African Society, 1652–1840*. Cape Town: Maskew Miller Longman. 521–66.

England, Frank, and Torquil Paterson (eds) (1989). *Bounty in Bondage: The Anglican Church in Southern Africa*. Johannesburg: Ravan Press.

Fabian, Johannes (1987). 'Hindsight: Thoughts on Anthropology upon Reading Francis Galton's *Narrative of an Explorer in Tropical South Africa* (1853).' *Critique of Anthropology* 7(2): 37–49.

Florin, Hans W. (1967). *Lutherans in South Africa*. Durban: Lutheran Publishing Co.

108 *Religions of South Africa*

Gaitskell, Deborah (1979). '"Christian Compounds for Girls": Church Hostels for African Women in Johannesburg, 1907–1970.' *Journal for Southern African Studies* 6: 44–69.

Gaitskell, Deborah (1982). '"Wailing for Purity": Prayer Unions, African Mothers and Adolescent Daughters 1912–1940.' In: Shula Marks and Richard Rathbone (eds) *Industrialization and Social Change in South Africa*. London: Longman. 338–57.

Gaitskell, Deborah (1983). 'Housewives, Maids or Mothers? Some Contradictions of Domesticity for Christian Women in Johannesburg, 1903–1939.' *Journal of African History* 24: 241–56.

Gaitskell, Deborah (1990). 'Devout Domesticity? A Century of African Women's Christianity in South Africa.' In: Cherryl Walker (ed.) *Women and Gender in Southern Africa to 1945*. London: James Currey; Cape Town: David Philip. 251–72.

Gerdener, G. B. A. (1958). *Recent Developments in the South African Mission Field*. Cape Town: N. G. Kerk-Uitgewers; London: Marshall, Morgan & Scott.

Geyl, Pieter (1958). *The Revolt of the Netherlands, 1555–1609*. London: Ernest Benn.

Geyl, Pieter (1961). *The Netherlands in the Seventeenth Century: Part One, 1609–1648*. London: Ernest Benn.

Goedhals, Mandy (1989a). 'Ungumpriste: A Study of the Life of Peter Masiza, First Black Priest in the Church of the Province of Southern Africa.' *Journal of Theology for Southern Africa* 68: 17–28.

Goedhals, Mandy (1989b). 'From Paternalism to Partnership? The Church of the Province of Southern Africa and Mission 1848–1988.' In: Frank England and Torquil Paterson (eds) *Bounty in Bondage: The Anglican Church in Southern Africa*. Johannesburg: Ravan Press. 104–29.

Guy, Jeff (1983). *The Heretic: A Study of the Life of John William Colenso 1814–1883*. Johannesburg: Ravan Press.

Hempton, David (1987). *Methodism and Politics in British Society 1750–1850*. London: Century Hutchinson.

Henderson, James (1928). 'The Problem of Native Poverty.' In: J. Dexter Taylor (ed.) *Christianity and the Natives of South Africa: A Year-Book of South African Missions*. Lovedale: General Missionary Conference of South Africa: 24–32.

Hewson, Leslie A. (1950). *An Introduction to South African Methodists*. Cape Town: Standard Press.

Hewson, Leslie A. (1959). 'Healdtown: A Study of a Methodist Experiment in African Education.' PhD thesis, Rhodes University.

Hinchliff, Peter (1963). *The Anglican Church in South Africa*. London: Darton, Longman, & Todd.

Hinchliff, Peter (1976). 'The English-speaking Churches and South Africa in the 19th Century.' In: André de Villiers (ed.) *English-Speaking South Africa Today*. Cape Town: Oxford University Press. 171–82.

Hodgson, Janet (1979). 'Zonnebloem College and Cape Town: 1858–1870.' *Studies in the History of Cape Town*. 1: 1–16.

Hodgson, Janet (1987). *Princess Emma*. Johannesburg: Ravan Press.

Hofmeyer, Jan H. (1945). *Christian Principles and Race Problems*. Johannesburg: South African Institute of Race Relations.

Hofmeyr, Isabel (1987). 'Building a Nation from Words: Afrikaans Language, Literature and Ethnic Identity, 1902–1924.' In: Shula Marks and Stanley Trapido (eds) *The Politics of Race, Class and Nationalism in Twentieth Century South Africa*. London: Longman. 95–123.

Hofmeyr, J. W. and K. E. Cross (1986). *History of the Church in Southern Africa. Volume 1: A Select Bibliography of Published Material to 1980*. Pretoria: Union of South Africa.

Hogan, Neville (1980). 'The Posthumous Vindication of Zachariah Gqishela: Reflections on the Politics of Dependence at the Cape in the Nineteenth Century.' In: Shula Marks and Anthony Atmore (eds) *Economy and Society in Pre-Industrial South Africa*. London: Longman. 275–92.

Hudson-Reed, S. (ed.) (1977). *Together for a Century: The History of the Baptist Union, 1877–1977*. Pietermaritzburg: South African Baptist Historical Society.

Hughes, Heather (1990). '"A Lighthouse for African Womanhood": Inanda Seminary, 1869–1945.' In: Cherryl Walker (ed.) *Women and Gender in Southern Africa to 1945*. London: James Currey; Cape Town: David Philip. 197–220.

Jeeves, Alan H. (1985). *Migrant Labour in South Africa's Mining Economy: The Struggle for the Gold Mine's Labour Supply, 1890–1920*. Johannesburg: Witwatersrand University Press.

Johnstone, Frederick A. (1976). *Class, Race, and Gold*. London: Routledge & Kegan Paul.

Karis, Thomas, and Gwendolen M. Carter (eds) (1973). *From Protest to Challenge: A Documentary History of African Politics in South Africa 1882–1964*. 4 vols, published in 1972–7. Stanford: Hoover Institution Press.

Kidd, Benjamin (1894). *Social Evolution*. New York: Macmillan.

Kinghorn, Johann (ed.) (1986). *Die N. G. Kerk en Apartheid*. Johannesburg: Macmillan.

Kinghorn, Johann (1990). 'The Theology of Separate Equality: A Critical Outline of the DRC's Position on Apartheid.' In: Martin Prozesky (ed.) *Christianity Amidst Apartheid*. London: Macmillan; published as *Christianity in South Africa*. Johannesburg: Southern Book Publishers. 57–80.

Langenhoven, C. J. (1909). 'The Female Franchise and the Native Franchise.' *The State* 2(7): 58–65.

Lewis, Cecil, and Gertrude Elizabeth Edwards (1934). *Historical Records of the Church of the Province of South Africa*. London: SPCK.

Lichtenstein, Henry (1930). *Travels in Southern Africa in the Years 1803, 1804, 1805, and 1806*. 2 vols. Trans. A. Plumptre. Cape Town: Van Riebeeck Society (orig. edn 1812–15).

Loram, Charles T. (1917). *The Education of a South African Native*. London: Longmans, Green.

Lorimer, Douglas (1988). 'Theoretical Racism in Late-Victorian Anthropology, 1870–1900.' *Victorian Studies* 31: 405–30.

Loubser, J. A. (1987). *The Apartheid Bible: A Critical Review of Racial Theology in South Africa*. Cape Town: Maskew Miller Longman.

MacCrone, I. D. (1937). *Race Attitudes in South Africa: Historical, Experimental, and Psychological Studies*. London: Oxford University Press.

Manuel, Frank (1983). *The Changing of the Gods*. Hanover, NH: University Press of New England.

Marais, Johannes S. (1957). *The Cape Coloured People 1652–1937*. Johannesburg: Witwatersrand University Press.

Marks, Shula, and Richard Rathbone (eds) (1982). *Industrialization and Social Change in South Africa*. London: Longman.

Marks, Shula, and Stanley Trapido (eds) (1987). *The Politics of Race, Class and Nationalism in Twentieth Century South Africa.* London: Longman.

Mills, Wallace G. (1975). 'The Role of African Clergy in the Reorientation of Xhosa Society to the Plural Society of the Cape Colony, 1850–1915.' Ph.D. thesis, University of California, Los Angeles.

Moorrees, A. (1937). *Die Nederduitse Gereformeerde Kerk in Suid-Afrika, 1652–1873.* Cape Town: S. A. Bybelvereniging.

Noble, John (1877). *South Africa, Past and Present: A Short History of the European Settlements at the Cape.* London: Longman.

Nuttall, M. (1970). *Synodical Government 1870–1970: The Making of a Tradition.* Johannesburg: SPCK.

Oldham, J. H. (1924). *Christianity and the Race Problem.* London: SCM Press.

Pearson, Karl (1901). *National Life from the Standpoint of Science.* London: A & C Black.

Phillips, Ray (1930). *The Bantu Are Coming.* London: SCM Press.

Prozesky, Martin (ed.) (1990). *Christianity Amidst Apartheid.* London: Macmillan; published as *Christianity in South Africa.* Johannesburg: Southern Book Publishers.

Rich, Paul B. (1984). *White Power and the Liberal Conscience: Racial Segregation and South African Liberalism 1921–60.* Johannesburg: Ravan Press.

Rich, Paul B. (1987). 'The Appeals of Tuskegee: James Henderson, Lovedale, and the Fortunes of South African Liberalism, 1906–1930.' *The International Journal of African Historical Studies* 20: 271–92.

Schöffer, I. (1961). 'The Dutch Revolt Anatomized: Some Comments.' *Comparative Studies in Society and History* 3: 470–77.

Schreiner, Olive (1911). *Women and Labour.* London: Fisher & Unwin.

Schutte, Gerrit J. (1987). 'The Netherlands, Cradle of Apartheid?' *Ethnic and Racial Studies* 10: 392–414.

Shepherd, Robert H. W. (1940). *Lovedale, South Africa: The Story of a Century, 1841–1941.* Lovedale: Lovedale Press.

Smith, Edwin (1929). *Aggrey of Africa: A Study in Black and White.* London: SCM Press.

Smith, Edwin (1949). *The Life and Times of Daniel Lindley.* London: Epworth Press.

Spoelstra, B. (1963). *'Die Doppers' in Suid Afrika, 1760–1899.* Cape Town: Nasionale Boekhandel.

Starfield, Jane (1988). '"Not Quite History": The Autobiographies of H. Selby Msimang and R. V. Selope Thema and the Writing of South African History.' *Social Dynamics* 14(2): 16–35.

Taylor, J. Dexter (ed.) (1928). *Christianity and the Natives of South Africa: A Year-Book of South African Missions.* Lovedale: General Missionary Conference of South Africa.

Thompson, E. P. (1968). *The Making of the English Working Class.* London: Gollancz.

Thompson, Leonard (1985). *The Political Mythology of Apartheid.* New Haven: Yale University Press.

Trapido, Stanley (1980). '"The Friends of the Natives": Merchants, Peasants, and the Political and Ideological Structures of Liberalism in the Cape, 1854–1910.' In: Shula Marks and Anthony Atmore (eds) *Economy and Society in Pre-Industrial South Africa.* London: Longman. 247–74.

Turrell, Rob (1982). 'Kimberley: Labour and Compounds, 1871–1888.' In: Shula

Marks and Richard Rathbone (eds) *Industrialization and Social Change in South Africa*. London: Longman: 45–76.

Valentyn, François (1973). *Description of the Cape of Good Hope with the matters concerning it*. Trans. R. Raven-Hart. Cape Town: Van Riebeeck Society (orig. edn 1726).

Villa-Vicencio, Charles (1988). *Trapped in Apartheid*. Maryknoll, NY: Orbis.

Voigt, J. C. (1899). *Fifty Years of the History of the Republic in South Africa 1795–1845*. 2 vols. London: T. Fisher Unwin.

Walbridge, C. K. (ed.) (1978). *Thokozile: The Letters of Margaret Walbridge*. Kansas: Mainline Printing.

Walker, Cherryl (ed.) (1990a). *Women and Gender in Southern Africa to 1945*. London: James Currey; Cape Town: David Philip.

Walker, Cherryl (1990b). 'The Women's Suffrage Movement: The Politics of Gender, Race and Class.' In: Cherryl Walker (ed.) *Women and Gender in Southern Africa to 1945*. London: James Currey; Cape Town: David Philip. 313–45.

Walshe, Peter (1970). *The Rise of African Nationalism: The African National Congress, 1912–1952*. Berkeley, CA: University of California Press.

Warner, Wellman Joel (1930). *The Wesleyan Movement in the Industrial Revolution*. London: Longmans, Green.

Wells, Julie (1980). 'Women's Resistance to Passes in Bloemfontein during the Inter-war Period.' *Africa Perspective* 15: 16–34.

Whiteman, A. (1962). 'The Restoration of the Church of England.' In: G. F. Nuttall and O. Chadwick (eds) *From Uniformity to Unity 1662–1962*. London: SPCK. 19–88.

Willan, Brian (1982). 'An African in Kimberley: Sol T. Plaatje, 1894–1898.' In: Shula Marks and Richard Rathbone (eds) *Industrialization and Social Change in South Africa*. London: Longman. 238–58.

Williams, Donovan (1959). 'The Missionaries on the Eastern Frontier of the Cape Colony, 1799–1853.' PhD thesis, University of the Witwatersrand.

Wilson, Monica, and Leonard Thompson (eds) (1969). *The Oxford History of South Africa*. 2 vols. Oxford: Oxford University Press.

Xuma, A. B. (1930). 'Bridging the Gap between White and Black.' *Christian Students and Modern South Africa*. Fort Hare: Student Christian Association, Christian Union. 189–202.

Young, G. M. (1964). *Victorian England: Portrait of an Age*. New York and Oxford: Oxford University Press.

Young, R. (1902). *African Wastes Reclaimed: The Story of the Lovedale Mission*. London: J. M. Dent.

4   Independent churches

Beginning in the 1880s, a number of black Christian churches were formed, independent of the European mission churches and white control. Since Christian mission work had been aggressively pursued from the early nineteenth century, it might appear that there was a considerable time lag before black Christians began forming separate, independent churches. In most regions of southern Africa, however, independent black Christian initiatives coincided with the first widespread African interest in the Christian missions. As noted in Chapter Two, Christian missions had only limited success in gaining converts until the destruction of relatively independent African polities at the end of the nineteenth century. At the same time that an increasing number of blacks were turning to the mission churches, therefore, a few black ministers in those churches sought to create Christian churches that were independent of white missionary control.

The first independent churches tended to retain the doctrines and practices of the missions, while creating separate organizational structures. Often referred to as 'Ethiopian' churches, independent African churches that emerged at the turn of the twentieth century provided scope for black religious leadership. Religious independence from white control has often been explained as a result of certain features of the Protestant mission churches – such as their denominational divisions, emphasis on the private interpretation of scripture, racial segregation, and reluctance to ordain African ministers – that inspired some black Christians to form their own independent churches (Oosthuizen, 1971). However, these features of the mission churches had been in place since at least the 1830s. For the most part, black Christians in the mission churches showed little interest in becoming ordained ministers or assistants for the simple reason that salaries were so low. The mission churches kept salaries for black religious workers much lower than the income that could be derived from farming, business, or skilled trades. By the 1880s and 1890s, however, colonial governments had introduced policies of land reservation, racial restrictions, and heavy taxation that drastically limited black economic opportunity. Under those conditions, therefore, interest in church leadership appears to have increased as other avenues of advancement were closed (Etherington, 1979: 123).

In forming independent churches, however, black Christian leaders asserted not only leadership but also equality with whites in the religious sphere that particularly addressed the contradiction of their economic incorporation, yet political exclusion in the rise of industrial capitalism in South Africa. In this respect, independent churches had some connection with an emerging African nationalism at the beginning of the twentieth century. Although most of the so-called 'Ethiopian' churches concentrated on a religious mission of preaching, teaching, and industry, some religious leaders were involved in African nationalist political movements. From the perspective of most white missionaries, magistrates, and government officials, however, the very existence of churches independent of white religious control posed a potential threat to white political control. Ironically, most leaders of the 'Ethiopian' movement advocated political moderation, obedience to government, private ownership of property, and equality of blacks and whites in a common society. Nevertheless, many white religious and political leaders argued that 'Ethiopianism' threatened white political domination in South Africa.

One reason South African government officials perceived 'Ethiopian' churches as dangerous was their apparent connections with American religious movements. Some had merged with the African Methodist Episcopal Church, the black American church led in the 1890s by Bishop Henry M. Turner, who occasionally proclaimed a message of African nationalism. But the American connection was much more complex than merely the influence of the African Methodist Episcopal Church. In the early twentieth century, representatives of several new, alternative American Christian movements came to South Africa. Most important were the missionaries of American faith-healing, Pentecostal, and millennial movements who attracted a considerable black and white South African following. Appropriating the religious beliefs and practices of these movements, significant black religious leaders emerged to form independent 'Zionist' or 'Apostolic' churches. Rather than promoting African nationalism, these churches tended to create alternative enclaves of religious authority and power. Nevertheless, 'Zionist' and 'Apostolic' churches did not operate in a political vacuum. In very general terms, churches in the 1920s and 1930s advanced a religious protest to black dispossession by emphasizing land and sacred sites that became alternative centers of symbolic order in a disordered world. After the Second World War, however, under conditions of endemic poverty, particularly among the black, urban working class, 'Zionist' and 'Apostolic' churches flourished by concentrating on spiritual healing to recover a human identity in the midst of dehumanizing economic, social, and political environments.

During the twentieth century, independent churches proliferated in number and expanded in membership. Statistics merely hint at the extent of this religious creativity and involvement: from an estimated 32 independent denominations in 1913, indigenous churches had multiplied to 800 in 1948, 2,000 in 1960, and nearly 5,000 different denominations by 1990 (Oosthuizen, 1987; 1989). By 1990 independent churches accounted for the religious involvement of over 30 per cent of the black population of South Africa. Commentators have tried to organize this religious diversity into characteristic types of African indigenous churches – independent, separatist, syncretist, nativist, prophetic, messianic, and so on. The clearest picture of independent churches, however, emerges from considering the historical process of their religious formation. In that history, African indigenous churches were not only important religious movements, but also significant indicators of conflict, change, and creative innovation in South African society.

ETHIOPIANS

Independent, black Christian initiatives were evident in the nineteenth-century religious work of Ntsikana and his successors in the eastern Cape, in the Uzondelelo movement in Natal, and in the Christian community of Mafolofolo led by Johannes Dinkwanyane in the northern Transvaal. For the most part, however, nineteenth-century, black Christian initiatives remained within the ambit of the white-controlled mission churches. But in the 1880s a black Wesleyan Methodist minister in the eastern Cape, Nehemiah Tile, broke with his mission church to form an independent church, initially known as the Thembu Church, that demonstrated the potential for religious leadership and organization outside of the missionary network. In the next decade, other black religious leaders and organizations looked back to Tile as an inspiration for their own ventures in church building. Preceding that 'Ethiopian' movement, however, Tile's church pursued its own religious and political objectives that distinguished it from later churches.

In the early 1870s, Nehemiah Tile worked for the Methodist mission. Receiving his education in theology at Healdtown, Tile was admitted into the Methodist Church as a minister on probation in 1879. Tile ministered in Thembuland in the eastern Cape, developing a close relation in the early 1880s with the Thembu paramount chief, Ngangelizwe. By 1883, however, Tile came into conflict with his white Methodist supervisors. Tile was dissatisfied with his long period of probation before being ordained, and he resented the fact that church funds were only allowed to be handled by white ministers, but the main source of conflict seemed to have been Tile's increasing involvement in Thembu politics. As a close advisor to the paramount chief, Nehemiah Tile was involved in Thembu political protest against the colonial government rule in the eastern Cape. When his Methodist superior, Theophilus Chubb, accused him of stirring up hostility toward the magistrates in the region, Tile did not refute the charges, but simply resigned from the Methodist Church.

At the great place of the Thembu paramount in October 1884 Nehemiah Tile founded the Thembu National Church. Through that new church Tile was able to pursue protest against the Cape colonial government in both religious and political terms. Tile preserved Methodist forms of worship in his new church, but he spoke against paying hut taxes, against pass laws, against white settlement, and against the network of magistrates that enforced colonial rule over Thembuland. Rather than colonial rule, Tile and the Thembu Church demanded that Thembuland be placed under the direct rule of the British Empire. In 1885 Tile was arrested for this political protest. Although he seems to have fallen out of favor with the Thembu paramount, and his successor Dalindyebo, by November 1890 Tile was once again representing the Thembu chiefdom in calling for independence from the colonial government. The paramount chief Dalindyebo proposed that the Thembu National Church should be the official church of the chiefdom, while Tile aligned his church with Thembu nationalism, pledging Christian allegiance to the authority and sanctity of the Thembu paramount chief. In this alliance of religion and politics, Tile apparently imagined his Thembu Church as a state church, like the Church of England, with the ruling monarch at its head. However, Nehemiah Tile died in 1891 before he could implement plans for constructing a large church building at the great place of the Thembu paramount chief that would have been the center of this state church.

With Tile's death, political protest ended, but his church survived. After three successors failed, the ordained Methodist minister Jonas Goduka was invited by the Thembu Church to assume leadership. From a Gaika Xhosa rather than a Thembu background, however, Goduka led the 'Tilites' during their transition away from an ethnic nationalism to a more broadly based independent Christian church. Even without Tile's leadership in political protest, however, the church continued to be perceived by the Cape colonial government as a threat, described by one government spokesman in 1893 as 'sedition in the disguise of a religious movement' (Saunders, 1970: 565). In rejecting white religious control, Tile's church seemed to the colonial government to be threatening the entire white-dominated political order. Government officials saw Tile's church as a greater threat than the educated black Christian elite because of the church's potential to build a mass following. Unlike the emerging African nationalism embraced by many black Christians, however, Tile's Thembu nationalism was identified with a single chiefdom and ethnic group. The nationalist political program of Tile's church looked back to chiefly rule, rather than looking forward to equal participation in a common colonial society.

Tile's ethnic religious nationalism, however, did not survive for very long after his death. Under pressure from the colonial government, the Thembu paramount Dalindyebo agreed in 1895 to rejoin the Methodists. Church leader Jonas Goduka eventually left Thembuland, founding a new church in the Herschel district in 1898, the African Native Church. Nevertheless, Nehemiah Tile had established a precedent for the independent religious organizations that emerged in the 1890s. Other independent churches, also aligned with a particular chiefdom or ethnic group, also emerged at this time throughout southern Africa: the Native Independent Congregational Church founded in Taung, Bechuanaland in 1885 (Pauw, 1960: 47), the Lutheran Bapedi Church founded in the northern Transvaal in 1889 (Mönnig, 1967: 32), and the Zulu Mbiana Congregational Church, founded in 1890 by Mbiana Ngidi, a relative of William Ngidi, one of the first converts of Bishop J. W. Colenso (Etherington, 1979: 117–19; Sundkler, 1961: 45). Unlike these primarily ethnic Christian churches, however, the 'Ethiopian' churches formed in the 1890s were multi-ethnic, pan-African religious movements. Although they did not share Tile's ethnic political interests, organizers of the 'Ethiopian' churches could nevertheless refer back to Nehemiah Tile as a model of independent religious leadership (Saunders, 1970: 566–7; Léenhardt, 1976: 18). Likewise, as in the case of Tile, these 'Ethiopian' churches were generally perceived by colonial religious and political leaders as a threat to the order of white domination in South Africa.

The 'Ethiopian' movement began in the 1890s in the changing urban environments of Pretoria and Johannesburg during the expansion of the gold-mining industry. In Pretoria, a former Anglican, Joseph Napo Kanyane formed the African Church in 1889, but a few years later he joined forces with the founder of the first independent 'Ethiopian' church, Mangena M. Mokone. Baptized as a Methodist in 1874, Mokone had worked as a carpenter in Pietermaritzburg, but also taught school, studied theology, and was ordained as a Methodist minister. After 2 years as a minister in Natal, Mokone was appointed in 1882 to a position in Pretoria. When a young white missionary was promoted ahead of him, Mokone resigned and launched his own church – the Ethiopian Church – in 1892 (Karis and Carter, 1972, 1: 93; Léenhardt 1976: 21; Sundkler, 1961: 39). Something of his motivation might be suggested by a manifesto Mokone wrote with several colleagues for a conference held in Pretoria in 1899. The manifesto addressed the profound discrepancy between Christian missionary teaching and white missionary attitudes toward Africans. Although they taught converts to be responsible, Mokone observed, white missionaries objected when black converts took responsibility for their own churches. Mokone and his colleagues argued that they intended to practice their Christian faith free of any interference from white church leaders who failed to understand the people with whom they worked (Léenhardt, 1976: 86–7). This motivation for freedom from white religious control must have been present at the beginning of Mokone's Ethiopian Church. Nevertheless, Mokone sought to cooperate with white political authority in the Transvaal, requesting and receiving recognition for his church in 1893 from the government of Paul Kruger. Under the leadership of Mokone, Kanyane, and Samuel J. Brander, the Ethiopian Church quickly emerged as an independent Christian alternative to the mission churches.

Like Mokone, another 'Ethiopian' leader, James Mata Dwane had been an evangelist and minister in the Methodist mission church. Ordained in 1881, Dwane demonstrated leadership and organizational skills by representing the Methodists in England during 1884 and 1885. On his return from England, however, Dwane objected to being excluded from any authority in the distribution of funds that had been raised during his travels. Leaving the Methodists in 1896, James Dwane joined Mokone and became a leader in the Ethiopian Church (Sundkler, 1961: 41–2).

Leaders in the 'Ethiopian' movement elevated 'Ethiopia' to an important symbolic status in Christian faith. This symbol held several layers of significance. First, 'Ethiopia' appeared in the biblical psalm that declared, 'Ethiopia shall stretch forth her hands unto God' (Ps. 68: 31). Occasionally used by missionaries as a metaphor for the Christian conversion of Africa, the biblical reference to 'Ethiopia' was appropriated by the new church to refer to its own independent African Christianity. Second, 'Ethiopia' was to a certain extent identified with the nation of Ethiopia, the Christian kingdom of Abyssinia that had remained independent during the nineteenth-century European colonization of Africa. In this regard, James Dwane even wrote to the Abyssinian King, Menelik, about Christian interests in northern Africa. After the Abyssinian victory over European troops at the battle of Adowa in 1896, Ethiopia rose in prominence as a symbol of African independence (Sundkler, 1961: 57).

Finally, and most importantly for the development of the 'Ethiopian' movement, 'Ethiopia' was employed as a symbol of pan-African unity that was also shared by Afro-Americans. As a common motif in black American preaching, 'Ethiopia' represented a promise of black redemption and liberation. Particularly in the African Methodist Episcopal Church, founded in Philadelphia by the Afro-American Richard Allen, after leaving the Methodist Church in 1787, the symbol of 'Ethiopia' came to represent black unity and liberation from white oppression. Under the leadership of Bishop Henry M. Turner, the African Methodist Episcopal Church aspired to create a 'highway across the Atlantic' that would unify black Christians in America and Africa in human dignity, freedom, and advancement. In South Africa, it was the Ethiopian Church that reached out to make that Afro-American connection (Turner, 1904: 91–2; Redkey, 1969; 1971).

While on a concert tour of America, Mangena Mokone's niece, Charlotte Manye, a singer in the South African Choir, was abandoned by white promoters, but was offered a home by an official of the African Methodist Episcopal Church (AME). Charlotte Manye remained in America to study at the church's Wilberforce University, writing to her uncle in South Africa about the religious and educational work of the African Methodist Episcopal Church (Erlmann, 1988: 346–7). In 1896 Ethiopian Church leaders in Pretoria decided to seek affiliation with the AME and sent James Dwane to America to forge that connection. While in America, Dwane arranged for AME Bishop Henry M. Turner to visit South Africa. During his 5-week visit in 1898, Bishop Turner consecrated Dwane as assistant bishop, ordained 65 ministers, and bought a site for a school in Queenstown (Sundkler, 1961: 41). In 1901 the American L. J. Coppin arrived as the first AME resident bishop in South Africa (Chirenje, 1987: 98; Coan, 1961).

Membership in the AME expanded rapidly. But some of the Ethiopian Church leaders grew dissatisfied with the American connection. After a second visit to America in 1899, James Dwane, having failed to obtain recognition as a full bishop in the AME, arranged with the Church of the Province of Southern Africa for the formation of the 'Order of Ethiopia' in 1900 as a semi-autonomous order within the Anglican Church (Verryn, 1972). The Anglicans informed Dwane that the AME 'could not hand on Episcopal Orders because they had never received them' (Lewis and Edwards, 1934: 214). A few years later, Samuel J. Brander grew dissatisfied with the American control over the AME, complaining that the American church 'took, like the old "Papae Romanorum", all moneys collected for the interests of the church in Africa to America, and there expended them obviously on purely American interests and not on Ethiopic interests' (Sundkler, 1961: 42; Chirenje, 1987: 105). In 1904 Brander left the AME to found his own Ethiopian Catholic Church in Zion, with at least six congregations spread throughout the Transvaal (Lahouel, 1986: 684).

In the Cape, at roughly the same time, another independent church, the Presbyterian Church of Africa, was started by Pambani J. Mzimba. Although Mzimba's church has often been linked with the 'Ethiopian' churches, it emerged in the different context of the religion and politics of the Cape. Ordained in 1875 as a minister in the Free Church of Scotland, Mzimba served as pastor of the Lovedale Native Congregation. As a leader among the educated black Christian elite in the Cape, Mzimba generated controversy by a speech in 1886 to the Lovedale Literary Society in which he declared, 'Let the white man rule, and the South African people be out of politics.' Arguing that involvement in politics had been disastrous for blacks in

America, Mzimba concluded, 'Let us be content to be ruled by the colonist' (Mills, 1978: 58). Not politics, but education and economic advancement, Mzimba insisted, should be the immediate concerns of black Christians. After returning from an 1892 visit to Scotland as a representative of the Free Church, Pambani Mzimba, like James Dwane, was frustrated by being prevented from having any say in the allocation of money that he had raised. In 1898, Mzimba left to found his Presbyterian Church of Africa, taking a large part of the Free Church of Scotland following with him. Within 10 years, Mzimba's church claimed as many as 7,000 full members and 20,000 adherents (Lahouel, 1986: 685; Wells, 1908: 287–99).

Although Pambani Mzimba had rejected direct political involvement, his church could nevertheless be interpreted as a statement of African independence. After Mzimba's death in 1911, for example, one of his eulogies declared that his church had served 'the double purpose of keeping ablaze the fire of Christianity in Africa, and at the same time maintaining and strengthening our national spirit and patriotism' (Chirenje, 1987: 156–7). Similarly, the 'Ethiopian' movement in the Transvaal disavowed political involvement, particularly any political challenge to the authority of the white-controlled government. In an 1897 speech, made while still an assistant bishop in the African Methodist Episcopal Church, James Dwane declared that his church taught 'the most sacred duties to its members notably that every soul is subject to a higher power. For there is no power but from God and the authorities are established by God' (Léenhardt, 1976: 43). Rather than politics, the AME, and the 'Ethiopian' movement in general, proclaimed Booker T. Washington's philosophy of character building, hard work, thrift, and capital accumulation. At the beginning of the twentieth century, the American Board in Natal acknowledged the orthodoxy of the 'Ethiopian' churches, noting that 'in the most important point, moral purity, while there are many individual back-slidings, there is encouragingly little lowering of the standards or careless laxity on the part of the churches' (Lahouel, 1986: 684–5).

In spite of its basically middle-class morals, values, and aspirations, however, the 'Ethiopian' movement was perceived by government as a threat simply by virtue of its independence from white control. In 1902, as Boer and Briton recovered from the South African War to create a united white order in South Africa, both regarded the 'Ethiopian' movement as a dangerous symbol of black political independence. During that same year, the magistrate of Bedford complained that the 'Ethiopian' churches represented 'foreign political agitation in the guise of religion'; the Governor of Natal banned AME missionaries, warning that 'American agitators shall not play the deuce with our natives under the guise of religion'; and Alfred Milner, high commissioner for South Africa, called for an official government inquiry into the 'Ethiopian' movement (Page, 1982: 184–91). Conducted from 1903 to 1905, the South African Native Affairs Commission gathered wide-ranging and disparate evidence on the 'Ethiopian' phenomenon. The commission's interviews with government, tribal, and religious leaders indicated, at the very least, that independent African Christian churches were perceived in many different ways in South Africa at the beginning of the twentieth century.

Representatives of government, chiefdoms, and mission churches expressed strong disapproval of the 'Ethiopian' movement. The principal of Lovedale, Reverend James Stewart recognized that the 'Ethiopian revolt' was only against white control over matters of religion, motivated 'solely from a desire to have control over their own ecclesiastical affairs' (SANAC, 1905, IV: 905). Other white ministers, however, attributed more sinister motives to the 'Ethiopian' churches. Describing the 'Ethiopians' as political agitators, Reverend J. J. McClure testified that 'their main object is to establish a South African native State, or a country purely for South African natives' (SANAC, 1905, II: 174). Similarly, Free Church of Scotland minister D. A. Hunter claimed that the 'Ethiopian' message to fellow blacks was that South Africa was 'our country; these are our farms, and our mines, why are we not working them for ourselves and for our own benefit instead of working them for the white people and giving them all the benefit?' (SANAC, 1905, II: 685). Government officials agreed that the 'Ethiopians' were ready to overthrow white domination, as the chief inspector of the Criminal Investigation Department in Natal testified that his secret agents had found that the 'Ethiopians' preached that they were 'quite capable of running the country without the aid of the white man' (SANAC, 1905, III: 615). Many witnesses blamed Americans for being outside agitators, as the Reverend Scott claimed that 'men from America come in and make our natives imagine they have grievances when there are no grievances' (SANAC, 1905, III: 375).

When the commission interviewed leaders of the 'Ethiopian' movement, however, they heard a very different story. For example, Mangena Mokone testified that the African Methodist Episcopal Church was not a political movement, but a Christian church dedicated to evangelizing, educating, and encouraging its followers in the habits of hard work. The church held no hostility towards whites, Mokone insisted, because it accepted white members and even had a white minister in Cape Town (SANAC, 1905, IV: 474–5). AME Bishop Charles Spencer Smith, who had replaced Coppin in 1904, assured the commission that his church did not necessarily follow the lead of Bishop Henry M. Turner, particularly with regard to Turner's declaration of 'Africa for the Africans.' In fact, Bishop Smith revealed, Henry Turner was regarded in America as 'a national character,' whose pronouncements about Africa 'none of us take seriously' (SANAC, 1905: IV: 962–4).

Partly as a result of testimony by 'Ethiopian' leaders, the South African Native Affairs Commission decided not to recommend banning the movement. In its final report in 1905, the commission regarded the independent churches as an 'outcome of a desire on the part of natives for ecclesiastical self-support and self-control' (SANAC, 1905, I: 64). The next year, however, a rebellion in Natal, known as the Bambatha Rebellion, renewed fears amongst white government and church officials that 'Ethiopian' religious leaders were behind a general uprising against white domination. Contrary to this impression, however, as many 'Ethiopian' Christians stayed out of the 1906 rebellion as participated in it (Marks, 1970: 334; Saunders, 1978: 208). Nevertheless, in the aftermath of the rebellion, the Natal Native Affairs Commission (1906–7) declared that blacks had 'to realize that the presence and predominance of the White race will be preserved at all hazards, and that all attempts to destroy its hegemony, whether overt or covert, such as the Ethiopian propaganda, will be promptly punished, instead of being disdainfully treated, as in the past.' As a result, S. O. Samuelson, the Under-Secretary for Native Affairs, declared that 'Ethiopian' churches, defined as churches 'independent and free from direct and effective European control,' would not be granted registration of marriage officers, nor government recognition of schools, nor any right to address meetings or assemblies of blacks in Natal (Sundkler, 1961: 69–70).

By contrast, in the Cape, Prime Minister J. X. Merriman in 1901 recommended tolerance of independent African churches, largely because he feared that repression would make martyrs out of their leaders and thereby contribute to their growth. Merriman recommended giving recognition to Mzimba's African Presbyterian Church, so that the government would not appear to be discriminating against churches on the basis of race. In practical terms, therefore, Merriman remembered the historian Edward Gibbon's account of the ancient Roman Empire's attitude toward religion, recalling that for the government, 'all religions are equally useful' (Sundkler, 1961: 68). Instead of the repression in Natal, therefore, the Cape Prime Minister advocated tolerance of independent religious movements that seemed to be encouraging Christian beliefs, morals, education, and industry.

With the Union of South Africa in 1910, however, the colonial governments adopted a common policy with regard to the official recognition of churches. In the Union of South Africa, rejection of independent churches became more entrenched, as a Native Affairs Commission reported in 1918 that churches independent of white control were 'a source of serious embarrassment to the Administration, and, what is of infinitely greater importance, a serious hindrance to the spread of true religion among the natives of this country' (Sundkler, 1961: 71). In this context, some of the earliest 'Ethiopian' churches benefited from government recognition, allowing them to buy sites for churches or schools in Native Reserves, appoint ministers as marriage officers, and obtain concessions for travel. Few other churches were approved, however, so that by 1945 only eight out of an estimated 800 independent churches had been granted official government recognition (Sundkler, 1961: 76–7).

Although African indigenous churches consistently claimed to be apolitical, the South African government persisted in limiting their religious scope because it perceived them as political threats to white domination. In some instances, leaders of 'Ethiopian' churches did become involved in opposition politics, particularly in the South African Native National Congress, founded in 1912, the political organization that later changed its name to the African National Congress (ANC). For example, the opening prayer at the founding of the ANC was delivered by an 'Ethiopian' minister. Reverend Henry Reed Ncgayiya, who became president of the Ethiopian Church of South Africa, founded in 1919 and claiming 20,000 members, was a founding member on the national executive committee of the ANC (Walshe, 1970: 240). Charlotte Manye, Mokone's niece who had initiated the first contacts with the African Methodist Episcopal Church, became president of the women's section of the African National Congress (Lahouel, 1986: 686; Chirenje, 1987: 140). By 1935, under her married name, Charlotte Maxeke was introduced at a meeting of the All African Convention as 'the mother of African freedom in this country' (Karis and Carter, 1973, II: 43). Nevertheless, most of the leaders of the African National Congress were Christians who remained affiliated with the mission churches. Rather than concentrating on political action, the 'Ethiopian' churches provided greater scope for an independent religious identity for many black Christians in South Africa.

MILLENARIANS

The American religious connection with independent South African churches was not limited to the influence of the African Methodist Episcopal Church. At the beginning of the twentieth century a variety of recently formed American Baptist, faith-healing, Pentecostal, and millenarian movements entered the South African mission field with dramatic results, but also with unexpected consequences in the proliferation of new independent African churches. All of these movements introduced new symbolic resources of religious meaning and spiritual power. In some cases those resources were mobilized by black Christians in resistance to the political order of white domination in South Africa. For example, the American Reverend Charles S. Morris of the National Baptist Convention, working in Natal at the end of the nineteenth century, established seventeen Baptist congregations. One of his converts, however, a blind man by the name of Johannes Zondi, started his own religious movement, called the Cushites, or the Blind Johannies, which featured open-air baptism and ritual foot-washing, but also apparently included a religious message of political redemption, 'Africa for the Black man.' This religious message of dramatic change in the political order so disturbed Natal local authorities that in 1898 they arrested Johannes Zondi and in 1901 they deported him to a remote part of Zululand. By 1903 the Cushites had split into several different movements, but the religious work of creating an alternative symbolic order in South Africa continued. Much of that work continued to be inspired by American emissaries of alternative Christian churches (Marks, 1970: 65; Chirenje, 1987: 93).

One of the most influential of these American churches was the Christian Catholic Church, later known as the Christian Catholic Apostolic Church in Zion (CCACZ), founded in 1896 by the faith-healer, John Alexander Dowie. Born in Australia, and educated at Edinburgh, Dowie embarked on a faith-healing ministry in America that eventually came to be centered near Chicago, Illinois. As 'First Apostle and General Overseer' of the Christian Catholic Church, Dowie attracted a considerable following by proclaiming divine healing, baptism by triple immersion, and the imminent second-coming of Christ. In 1899, Dowie acquired land on Lake Michigan, 42 miles north of Chicago, where he began construction of Zion City, Illinois, as a new sacred center of religious purity, healing, and divine law. Residents of Zion City, Illinois observed regular daily prayer, healing services, and prohibitions on alcohol, tobacco, pork, and medicines. Like the biblical mountain of God, or the sacred city of Jerusalem, Zion City, Illinois, was imagined as a pure spiritual center in the midst of a dangerous and defiling world (Harlan, 1906; Wacker, 1985). By 1906, a year before his death, Dowie had lost control of his church and religious community, as leadership was assumed by W. G. Voliva, who took the church in an even more millenarian direction by predicting the specific date for Christ's return. As a result of conflicts over leadership, the church split into several different factions in America. In South Africa, however, Dowie's church had an impact that eventually resulted in the formation of thousands of Zionist churches (Sundkler, 1961: 48; Comaroff, 1985: 177–84)

Zionist interest in South Africa began with the 1897 visit to Zion City, Illinois, by Reverend J. U. Buchler, a South African Congregationalist minister, who was placed by Dowie in charge of 'African work.' In 1902, Edgar Mahon, of the Salvation Army, began work on behalf of Dowie's church in the Orange Free State. In 1904, one of the overseers of the Christian Catholic Apostolic Church in Zion, Daniel Bryant, arrived in Johannesburg, baptizing nearly thirty people, mostly black South Africans, into the faith of

Zion. From the beginning, however, the Zionist faith in South Africa was taken in different directions. When the Zionist convert, Lucas Thomas Madhleni Zungu, was refused ordination by Daniel Bryant, he founded in 1907 the African Christian Baptist Church of South Africa. Another convert, Pieter le Roux, a former Dutch Reformed Church minister, and student of Andrew Murray, Jr, was initially very active in promoting the Zionist faith. In 1908, however, Le Roux converted once again, this time to the Pentecostal faith introduced by American missionaries of the Apostolic Faith Mission. Against the CCACZ, the Apostolic Faith Mission argued that they had found baptism and divine healing in South Africa, but not the Pentecostal baptism of the Holy Spirit made evident through speaking in tongues. Serving as president of the Apostolic Faith Mission for nearly thirty years, Pieter le Roux concentrated on Pentecostal work among white South Africans. Many black South Africans, however, embraced the Pentecostal faith of the Apostolic Faith Mission, as well as the faith of another American Pentecostal church, the Assemblies of God (Hollenweger, 1972: 111–75).

Inspired by these Zionist, Pentecostal, and Apostolic innovations from America, independent churches proliferated, appropriating and incorporating elements of their ideology and practice. The names of these new, independent churches displayed their inspiration: the Christian Apostolic Church in Zion, founded by Paulo Mabilitsa, the Christian Catholic Apostolic Holy Spirit Church in Zion, founded by Daniel Nkonyane, and the Holy Catholic Apostolic Church in Zion, founded by J. G. Phillipps (Sundkler, 1961: 49). These churches, and many others, found distinctive ways to combine and recombine the basic elements of baptism by triple immersion, ecstatic spiritual experience, the recovery of an original Christianity, and the expectation of the return of Christ. In very general terms, these churches created vital alternatives of religious meaning and power in the South African context. First, they represented an alternative source of power, the power of the Holy Spirit, regarded as more powerful than the political order upheld by the government and the mission churches. Second, they created an alternative spatial order by establishing new religious centers, 'Zions' of sacred purity, healing, and protection. Third, they created an alternative temporal orientation by referring back to ancient, biblical religious life, but also by looking forward to the imminent return of Christ that would establish a new kingdom on earth. In that millenarian expectation, as it assumed different forms in the 1920s, some alternative African religious movements came into conflict with the South African government.

The most dramatic confrontation between religion and government occurred in 1921 when South African police, armed with rifles, machine guns, and cannon, massacred nearly 200 members of a church in the eastern Cape known as the Israelites. Enoch Mgijima, the leader and prophet of the

Israelites, grew up near Bulhoek, in a place called Ntabelanga, 'the mountain of the rising sun.' While his older brothers were educated at Lovedale and Zonnebloem, Enoch Mgijima became a farmer. But he was also active in the Wesleyan Methodist Church as a lay preacher and evangelist. In 1907, at nearly 40 years of age, Enoch Mgijima experienced a vision in which an angel took him into the heavens and told him that he had a special mission on earth to bring people back to the ancient religion of the Bible. In that vision, Mgijima also heard rumblings in the sky that signaled the coming of a great war that would end the world. Three years later, when Halley's Comet appeared, Enoch Mgijima saw it as a sign of divine anger and a warning to return to Old Testament religion. In 1912 he broke with the Methodists, gathered a following of his own that he called Israelites near his home at Ntabelanga. By the end of that year, Enoch Mgijima had established links with an American church, the Church of God and Saints of Christ, and quickly rose to a position of leadership.

The Church of God and Saints of Christ had been founded by the Afro-American William Saunders Crowdy, a former cook on the Sante Fe railroad, who towards the end of his life had discovered the 'stone of truth' which had revealed to him the origins of black people in the lost tribes of ancient Israel. Crowdy based his church on 'seven keys' of salvation that represented the ritual and ethical commandments of the Church of God and Saints of Christ (Edgar, 1982: 413–14). The church observed Saturday as Sabbath, held daily services four times a day, and celebrated the major annual festival of Passover. These practices were also adopted by followers of the church in South Africa. In 1902 Crowdy had applied to visit South Africa, but was denied entrance to the country. Nevertheless, he sent church representatives, the most important being the American-educated South African, John Msikinya, who preached throughout the eastern Cape. Although occasionally arrested for vagrancy, John Msikinya built a following that in 1912 was joined by Enoch Mgijima and his Israelites. Assuming the title of bishop in the Church of God and Saints of Christ, Enoch Mgijima continued to have violent visions of an impending war, even predicting that the world would end on Christmas 1912. In another vision, Mgijima saw two white goats fighting each other, while a black baboon who was merely looking on emerged victorious. Disturbed by Mgijima's visions, American leaders of the Church of God and Saints of Christ excommunicated him in 1916. Nevertheless, Enoch Mgijima retained a large following that continued to consider themselves as members of the church. They were more commonly known, however, as Israelites.

The center of Israelite religious life was Ntabelanga, the sacred site for the annual Passover festival at which all members gathered for worship and celebration. An impoverished and destitute region, the entire Native Location of Bulhoek around Ntabelanga suffered from scarcity of land, soil erosion, overcrowding, escalating taxation, the deadly influenza epidemic of 1918, and a severe drought during 1919. In that year, Enoch Mgijima issued a call for all Israelites to gather at Ntabelanga to await the return of Christ and the end of the world. As usual, Mgijima applied to the local magistrate for permission to hold the annual Passover festival at Ntabelanga. During 1920, however, the arrival of Israelites, eventually numbering nearly 3,000, indicated that no ordinary festival was being planned. Israelites began building brick houses, streets, and a permanent tabernacle for worship at the center of a growing village, where services were conducted four times a day. The settlement also included a school for Bible study and a court for trying offenses against religious law. The local magistrate, however, insisted that the Israelites were illegally occupying the land. When the magistrate ordered the Israelites to leave, Enoch Mgijima's brother Charles responded:

We are not making war against you; we are your servants living in this place for the purpose of praying and fearing God's wrath which is coming upon the whole world.... We humbly beg you to give us a chance to pray.

(Edgar, 1988: 15)

The local magistrate and the government in Pretoria, however, were determined to evict the Israelites from their village. In December 1920, a police force of 100 men was positioned outside the village, but the police fled when they were approached by a group of Israelites marching out to meet them. At a subsequent meeting, a government representative reminded the Israelites of the New Testament passage (Romans 13: 1–4) that enjoined obedience of government authority upon Christians. But Charles Mgijima replied that 'God sent us to this place. We shall let you know when it is necessary that we go' (Edgar, 1988: 21). In January 1921 the Israelites sealed their defiance of the government by refusing to pay taxes. But their dire situation was acknowledged by the prophet Enoch Mgijima when he welcomed new arrivals to the Israelite community by saying, 'Tell these children that they have come to face their death' (Edgar, 1988: 21). The government moved from negotiation to coercion by organizing a force of 800 policemen, the largest police force ever assembled in peace time in South Africa, to arrest the leader and demolish the houses of the Israelites. When the police threatened attack, Enoch Mgijima observed that the 'whole world is going to sink in blood. I am not the cause of it. The time of Jehovah has now arrived.' Mgijima invited his followers to leave, but they apparently said, 'We are not leaving. If there is death, let us die through our belief' (Edgar, 1988: 26–7).

On 24 May, 1921, the police force attacked, leaving 183 Israelites dead, and nearly 100 wounded, during 20 minutes of rifle and machine-gun fire. During the fighting, Enoch Mgijima entered the tabernacle and prayed to

Jehovah, 'Is the blood required by you enough? Have enough Israelites been sacrificed?' (Edgar, 1988: 33). When the police entered the village, they arrested Enoch Mgijima, along with 150 Israelites, and began demolishing the village. Blaming the victims, the police held Enoch Mgijima responsible for the violence. But the prophet replied, 'You take your orders from the Government. I take mine from Jehovah' (Edgar, 1988: 33). Nevertheless, the government courts sentenced Enoch and Charles Mgijima to 6 years' hard labor and sentenced their followers to prison terms of 12 to 18 months.

Although the Israelite movement survived the destruction at Bulhoek, the massacre in 1921 represented an apocalyptic event that revealed the character of religion in South Africa during the 1920s. In response to the massacre of the Israelites, representatives of African political movements, such as the African National Congress and the Industrial and Commercial Workers Union, defended the Israelites as a religious response to the exclusive land laws and oppressive government tyranny that drove Enoch Mgijima and his followers into a position of desperate defiance. By contrast, moderate black Christians, particularly John Tengo Jabavu, and his son D. D. T. Jabavu, argued that the Israelites had been 'primitives' and 'fanatics' who showed they were 'demented' by stubbornly resisting cooperation with the government. For its part, the government was adamant that the religious independence demonstrated by the Israelites could not be tolerated because it threatened white domination in South Africa. In the House of Assembly, J. B. M. Hertzog declared that no white government could allow blacks to have such a 'consciousness of independence,' while J. X. Merriman agreed that the Israelites had been dangerous because they believed in 'Africa for the Africans, that Africans must combine and sweep the white man out of the country' (Edgar, 1982). While these assessments revealed white fears more than Israelite doctrine, they were embodied in the decision of the judge at the trial of the Israelites who concluded that they had been motivated by the 'crazy notion that the day was coming when the black man would have his freedom' (Edgar, 1988: 38; Lea, 1926: 37).

Although the government, mission churches, and moderate blacks had branded them as crazy, the Israelites had gained a different appreciation of relations between religion and sanity in South Africa. During the year before the massacre, a member of the Israelite Church, Walter Dinca, wrote a letter to the local Queenstown newspaper in which he argued that the government and mission churches had used Christianity as 'an instrument of power for the establishment of European supremacy and domination in the world.' Christian churches, the Israelite argued, had failed to Christianize Europeans, as 'their religion or Christianity spells the exploitation of the blacks in this country. Hence the insane phrase, "South Africa a white man's country."' As a result of this observation, the Israelite Walter Dinca concluded, 'Can any sane black man follow this religion which is out to exterminate the Natives of this country?' (Edgar, 1982: 412). Rather than insanity, therefore, the Israelite movement might better be regarded as a reasonable resistance to religious and political oppression in South Africa.

In the history of religions, millenarian movements have often been explained as responses to poverty, disaster, or oppression. During the 1920s in South Africa, however, religious movements with apocalyptic expectations of sudden redemption responded to the more specific historical conditions of capital penetration, labor exploitation, and white political domination. Although they occasionally drew on 'traditional' symbolic resources, these millenarian movements were not 'primitive.' Rather, religious movements in the 1920s that promised an imminent, instant, collective, and this-worldly redemption were modern, twentieth-century innovations. Particularly in the second half of the decade, millenarian movements captured the imagination of many people, especially in the eastern Cape and Natal, with promises of supernatural intervention by powerful black American liberators. According to this widespread apocalyptic expectation, black Americans were coming in airplanes to liberate South Africa from white, colonial domination and to redeem the land and its wealth for black people. Like many other twentieth-century millenarian movements, in Africa and elsewhere, this South African movement looked for redemption in a capitalist future, symbolized by westernized black Americans, the latest military technology, and the wealth controlled by whites, rather than looking for redemption in the recovery of a precolonial past (Bradford, 1985: 366).

After the First World War, the message of 'Africa for the Africans,' proclaimed by the black Jamaican and American activist, Marcus Garvey, attracted considerable interest amongst black South Africans. Garvey's organization, the Universal Negro Improvement Association, with its official organ, *Negro World*, and its plans for a 'Black Star Line' of ships that would link America and Africa, gained a large following among black political activists, trade unionists, and independent church leaders in South Africa. Many were inspired by accounts of Marcus Garvey's First International Convention of Negro Peoples of the World, held in New York, in August 1920, at which Garvey had predicted an impending world war that would provide 'the Negroes' opportunity to draw the sword for Africa's redemption' (Hill and Pirio, 1987: 212). In South Africa, Garvey's message was often received in ways that fused political liberation and religious salvation into a single promise of African redemption. Increasingly, toward the end of the 1920s, the African nationalism of Marcus Garvey was given a distinctively apocalyptic twist in the popular reception of his promise of liberation from white domination in South Africa.

A political activist such as James Thaele, a leader of the African National

Congress, drew out the political and religious implications of Marcus Garvey's principle of 'Africa for the Africans.' In the political sphere, Thaele argued, blacks had to work out their own liberation, just as in the religious sphere they had to seek their own salvation in churches independent of white control. As James Thaele advised, 'Keep out of white churches as much as you can' (Hill and Pirio, 1987: 232). Other political leaders, however, merged religion, politics, and economics in a single promise of redemption. During the 1920s, the Industrial and Commercial Workers Union, under the leadership of Clements Kadalie, drew heavily on the inspiration of Marcus Garvey. At a meeting near Cape Town, Kadalie described his union as 'a movement which assures every man and woman of his or her salvation. We must therefore unite with racial pride that at least Africans will be redeemed' (Hill and Pirio, 1987: 216). This fusion of religious, political, and economic salvation was also found in some independent churches. In the northern Cape, for example, a church known as the House of Athlyi, or the Afro-Athlican Constructive Gaathly, which based its teachings on *The Holy Piby*, the 'Black Man's Bible,' also used literature from Marcus Garvey in its church services (Hill and Pirio, 1987: 221). In a variety of ways, therefore, during the 1920s, many black South Africans embraced the promise of redemption associated with Marcus Garvey and black Americans.

In the rural eastern Cape, the most prominent prophet of American redemption was the enigmatic Wellington Buthelezi. Although born in Natal, Wellington Buthelezi claimed to have been born in Chicago and trained as a medical doctor in North America. In 1925 he initiated a religious movement based on the promise that American blacks were coming to South Africa as powerful liberators. As he traveled around the region, Wellington Buthelezi rapidly gained a large following that included local chiefs, headmen, ministers, and congregations of both independent and mission churches. In particular, Wellington Buthelezi mobilized the rural poor and migrant laborers who were most responsive to the prospect of liberation. Followers of this millenarian movement were known as Wellingtonites, or 'Americans,' but they were also known by a term that signified their preparation for an imminent apocalyptic war of liberation, *Amafela Ndawonye*, 'those who are prepared to die together' (Beinart and Bundy, 1987: 222–69). At Wellingtonite meetings, hymns, prayers, and sermons celebrated the coming salvation, when black Americans in airplanes would fly over the country, dropping fire from the skies that would destroy all whites and all black non-believers. 'The Americans are coming,' became the rallying cry of Wellington Buthelezi's millenarian movement, as his followers looked to the skies for signs of the American planes. 'Now when these things begin to take place,' Wellington declared, 'look up and raise your heads, because your redemption is drawing near' (Edgar, 1976: 41).

When local government authorities deported Wellington Buthelezi in March 1927, the 'American' movement continued, with its promise of redemption taken up by other leaders, especially by representatives of the Industrial and Commercial Workers Union. One ICU organizer in eastern Pondoland, the American-educated Baptist minister Filbert Mdodana, who had formed his own independent Regular Christian Baptist Church, played a prominent role in preparing people for the arrival of the American planes that was expected in December 1927. Reverend Mdodana, and other leaders of the movement, advocated two ritualized means of preparation. First, people had to purchase membership tickets in the Industrial and Commercial Workers Union. When the American liberators came, holders of the red ICU tickets would be spared from destruction. During 1927, the ICU membership ticket was transformed into a religious icon of salvation, as a minister of the independent African Native Church told his followers, 'You will die if you do not buy the ticket!' (Bradford, 1985: 404). Although ticket holders were also instructed to stop paying taxes, adding practical interest to membership, the ownership of a ticket itself became a religious symbol of redemption from the impending destruction of whites and white rule in South Africa.

Second, people had to protect themselves through other ritual acts, by painting their houses black, by getting rid of needles, but especially by killing their white animals and fowl. If they wanted to avoid being burned to death by the fires descending from the skies, believers in the American redemption had to eliminate animals associated with whites. In particular, believers had to kill pigs. The widespread, ritualized pig slaughters carried out by believers in the 'American' movement during 1927 drew on a complex of religious symbolism that associated pigs with whites, not only because pigs had been introduced by Europeans into southern Africa, but, more importantly, because pig fat was associated with lightning, fire, and witchcraft. Although many people in the eastern Cape believed that lard provided protection from lightning sent by witches, leaders of the 'American' movement argued that pig fat would attract the lightning flames that descended from the American planes. If the believers killed their pigs, then whites and non-believers would be the only ones left in South Africa still owning the pigs that would attract the flames of destruction from the skies (Edgar, 1976: 41; Bradford, 1985: 386–90).

Although the ritual killing of pigs drew on 'traditional' religious resources, it was clearly linked with a 'modern' means of fighting white political domination and economic exploitation, the purchase of a membership ticket in a labor union. Furthermore, both the 'traditional' and the 'modern' aspects of this movement were woven together by adapting a Christian expectation of a final cosmic battle, an Armageddon, in which the forces of good would defeat and eliminate evil from the world. Believers were disappointed in

1927, however, when the millenarian prophecy of black American liberators failed. Nevertheless, the promise of redemption by foreign liberators was occasionally revived. As late as 1939, on the eve of the Second World War, a preacher by the name of Mdindwa Maranqna, still claiming to be an ICU member, even replaced the Americans with German liberators by proclaiming that Germans would soon drive whites out of South Africa (Bradford, 1985: 407). The millenarian promise of a sudden, this-worldly redemption, however, was muted in most independent churches. In most cases, independent churches sought redemption, not in the promise of political liberation, but in the creation of a separate, alternative sacred order that accommodated itself to white political domination in South Africa, yet provided powerful spiritual resources of healing, purity, and protection from a hostile world.

NAZARITES

One of the most prominent independent churches committed to creating a separate order of religious purity, Isonto lamaNazaretha, the Church of the Nazarites, was started in 1911 by the Zulu prophet and healer, Isaiah Shembe. By the time of Shembe's death in 1935, the Church of the Nazarites had a following of nearly 30,000 members, almost completely comprised of Zulu-speaking converts (Sundkler, 1961: 133). Most of his following were initially attracted by Shembe's powers of healing. But many must have also welcomed the security and stability that his church provided in a world that seemed to have been turned upside down by the destruction of the Zulu kingdom, the failed rebellion of 1906, and the widespread dispossession of land that followed the Native Land Act of 1913. In one respect, the Church of the Nazarites provided a base for remobilizing a Zulu ethnic identity after those disruptions, becoming, as more than one commentator has noted, a 'Zulu High Church' (Vilakazi, 1986: 156).

The Bambatha Rebellion of 1906 had inspired some millenarian hopes of redemption. After his arrest and exile, one of the rebel leaders, Meseni, chief of the Qwabe clan, had predicted that a black prophet would arise to save the Zulu nation. Years later, Meseni's widows proclaimed Isaiah Shembe as the fulfillment of that nationalist vision (Sundkler, 1961: 313). In the political and economic displacements that followed the 1913 Native Land Act, Isaiah Shembe provided the stability and security of a land base for his followers (M'timkulu, 1977: 20; Gunner, 1988: 214). Rather than rebelling against white political domination, however, Isaiah Shembe created an alternative social order, anchored in specific sacred sites, that gave new meaning and power to the land. Nevertheless, the Church of the Nazarites was not a movement of political protest, but a community dedicated to creating an alternative domain of religious purity, focusing in particular upon religious healing (Etherington, 1979: 125).

Born some time around 1870, Isaiah Shembe converted to the African Native Baptist Church, an independent church inspired by the missionary work of American Baptist groups in Natal. As a minister of the African Native Baptist Church, Shembe conducted faith-healing services and performed open-air baptisms. In 1911, however, a series of visions compelled Shembe to go to the mountain of Inhlangakazi in Zululand, where he remained in prayer and trance for days. While on the mountain, Shembe apparently had visions of a skeleton informing him that God was going to give him the power to heal and angels who conveyed special sacraments to him (Chirenje, 1987: 158). Following these extraordinary religious experiences, Isaiah Shembe founded his Church of the Nazarites. A few years later, Shembe acquired over 50 acres of land at Ekuphakameni, 18 miles outside of Durban, which became the nucleus of his church.

The village of Ekuphakameni became the sacred center, the 'exalted place,' where a growing community formed around the healing, worship, and discipline of the Church of the Nazarites. In their regular cycle of worship, the Nazarites performed daily morning and evening prayers, observed Saturday as Sabbath, fasted before communion, and practiced ritual foot-washing for purity. Dancing, accompanied by drums, whistles, and hymns, formed an integral part of worship. In addition to daily and weekly worship, the Church of the Nazarites observed a sacred calendar that revolved around two annual festivals: the July festival held in Shembe's village at Ekuphakameni and the January festival at the holy mountain of Inhlangakazi, where worshipers retreated for 2 weeks of prayer. As a sign of religious purity, members of the church observed certain prohibitions, abstaining from pork, beer, and tobacco, but also from any 'traditional' or 'modern' medicines. For all its emphasis on ritual purity, however, the Church of the Nazarites also stressed the value of hard work and condemned laziness as a sin. Purity, discipline, and labor, however, went together in building up the alternative sacred order represented by the church.

The sacred order of the Nazarite church revolved around healing. His followers, Isaiah Shembe observed, 'had taken a sacred oath not to resort to medicine in any shape or form nor submit their bodies to be cut' (Sundkler, 1961: 227). Skepticism about modern, westernized medical practices seems to have been fairly common amongst Zulu speakers in Natal and Zululand. In an interview with a missionary in 1912, for example, a Zulu chief expressed his skepticism about white doctors. 'I have consulted several of them at different times,' he observed. 'The wonder is that they all agree in their nonsense' (Chirenje, 1987: 159). In addition to its limited success, western medical practice also had limited availability. But Isaiah Shembe's healing power, while directed toward the body, created for his followers a total way of life of purity and protection in community. In this respect, healing was not merely addressed to physical symptoms, but to the social relations in which people lived.

In addition to healing, Isaiah Shembe was a prolific composer of hymns, over two hundred of which were collected and written in the Nazarite hymnal, *Izihlabelelo zamaNazaretha* (Ooosthuizen, 1967; Vilakazi, 1986). The hymns employed the styles and rhythms of Zulu praise poetry, the *izibongo*, traditionally directed to royalty, but redirected by Shembe into an ardent Christian worship (Gunner, 1982; 1988). Shembe's hymns celebrated the love and power of God, inviting his followers to join him in calling upon God to 'pour in me the spirit of power *(umoya wamandla)*' (Vilakazi, 1986: 105). Occasionally, however, Shembe's hymns reflected the ambivalent political situation of his followers. On the one hand, his followers could celebrate a Zulu royal heritage with its roots in the kings Senzangakhona and Shaka. That heritage, however, was a mixed blessing, visiting both the glory and the sins of those royal ancestors on their children. On the other hand, therefore, Shembe's followers could assess their current political situation as a loss of former glory and a tragic displacement from ancestral lands. In one hymn, for example, Shembe addressed God: 'Thou has made us leave our land. We are destitute. We have no Saviour but you' (Vilakazi, 1986: 99).

As an independent prophet, Isaiah Shembe was not a product of the European mission or school system. Although Shembe had received no formal education, he claimed to have acquired a kind of sacred literacy through revelation. In 1931, Shembe remarked, 'No, I have not been taught to read and write, but I am able to read the Bible a little bit, and that came to me by revelation and not by learning. It came to me by miracle' (Gunner, 1986: 187). In writing Shembe's biography, a year after the prophet's death, former president of the African National Congress and Christian educator, John Dube, addressed the government and mission churches by observing, 'If you had educated him in your schools you would have taken pride in him. But that God may demonstrate his wisdom, he sent Shembe, a child, so that he may speak like the wise and the educated' (Gunner, 1986: 182). Rather than taking pride in the prophet, however, government and mission authorities in the 1920s and 1930s opposed the work of Isaiah Shembe. Mission church opposition was reflected in the recurring complaints of white missionaries and ministers that Shembe was 'under no European control.' Referring to the prophet as a 'scurrilous fanatic,' a local magistrate insisted that the government should 'deal with this mischievous growth swiftly and destroy the trouble in its inception' (Gunner, 1988: 214–15).

This opposition to Shembe was ironic, however, because the prophet strongly opposed any actions against the white-controlled government. During the 1920s, as support for the Industrial and Commercial Workers Union grew, Shembe instructed his followers not to join the ICU because it fought against the government, the missionaries, and whites in general. Isaiah Shembe dismissed people from his church who spoke against whites, because whites had brought the word of God to Africa. Therefore, Shembe argued, to fight against whites was to stand against God (Becken, 1965: 3–4; Lahouel, 1986: 686).

Not concerned with subverting or overthrowing white domination, therefore, Isaiah Shembe concentrated on building up a sacred, alternative, and separate Nazarite community. At Isaiah Shembe's funeral in 1935, his followers proclaimed, 'He is holy! He is holy!' (Roberts, 1936). Rather than announcing Shembe's messianic status, as many commentators have argued, this acclamation seems to have acknowledged Isaiah Shembe's central role in the community as prophet, healer, and inspired visionary. After the prophet's death, prophetic leadership of the Nazarites was assumed by his son, Johannes Galilee Shembe, who supervised the expansion of the church until his death in 1976. At that time, a controversy over leadership ensued that reflected the challenge of institutionalizing a prophetic church without a recognized living prophet (Oosthuizen, 1981). Although the Church of the Nazarites displayed many unique features, especially in its Zulu ethnic nationalism, the Nazarite concern for creating a separate domain of healing, purity, and protection was shared by many other independent churches that cultivated a 'Zionist' or 'Apostolic' spirituality in South Africa.

ZIONISTS

The Zion Christian Church (ZCC), based in the northern Transvaal, emerged as the largest of the Zionist churches in South Africa. Founded around 1910 by Ignatius Lekganyane, of Pedi background, the ZCC became a pan-ethnic church that expanded dramatically under the leadership of his son and successor, Edward Lekganyane. From less than a thousand followers in 1925, the ZCC grew to nearly 30,000 in the early 1940s, with a membership of around 80,000 in 1960. By 1970, however, the church had an estimated following of 200,000, which multiplied to over a million by 1990 (Sundkler, 1961: 132; West, 1975a: 22; Schoffeleers, 1988: 54). Part of this dramatic expansion can be accounted for by the fact that the ZCC avoided the schisms that divided other churches into many separate, independent churches. Maintaining a centralized, hierarchical organization, the ZCC managed to hold together a network of hundreds of local congregations, operating as franchises of the central church.

At the same time, however, the history of the expansion of the ZCC suggests that the church attracted its large membership during the second half of the twentieth century in a different economic, social, and political context than the one in which independent churches had previously gathered followings. After the 1940s, the ZCC gained its large following from people who lived under the pressures of the more complete penetration of capitalism, the more widespread incorporation of workers in wage labor, and the more totalitarian government policies of racial discrimination and separation. In that context, the ZCC, like other 'Zionist' and 'Apostolic' churches, offered a haven of healing, personal integrity, and spiritual power in a social world in which people were increasingly disempowered. As in other Zionist churches, healing through the spirit became the primary religious practice of the Zion Christian Church.

Unlike most of the other churches that grew after the 1940s by attracting the poor, disenfranchised, and disempowered, particularly from among the urban, working class, the Zion Christian Church maintained the earlier religious emphasis of the 1920s on sacred land. Like the Israelites and Nazarites, the ZCC was a church that was anchored in a specific sacred site, the sacred center of Moria, 25 miles from Pietersburg in the northern Transvaal. Taking a biblical name for Jerusalem, which itself had been taken from the ancient religious center at Mt Moriah in the northern kingdom of Israel, the founder of the ZCC established his Moria as a sacred city (2 Chron. 3: 1; Gen. 12: 6; 22: 2). Moria became a sacred center that stood apart from the political center of Pretoria and the economic center of Johannesburg in the ZCC's spiritual geography of South Africa (Comaroff, 1985: 240). One aspect of the sacred power of Moria was reflected through its symbols of wealth, the opulence of its buildings and the expanse of its productive farmlands and business enterprises. In this respect, the automobile became a symbol of power, as the founder toured in a Rolls Royce and his successor maintained a fleet of 45 cars. Although it stood in contrast with the general poverty of local congregations, the display of these symbols of wealth represented the power and success of the bishop and the sacred center of his church. In a capitalist world, the ZCC was able to demonstrate its power in the idiom of material symbols (Schoffeleers, 1988: 49).

Supported by these material symbols of power, Moria was a center of spiritual power, a sacred site of pilgrimage three times a year, but especially at the annual Easter festival when thousands of ZCC members journeyed to Moria for healing, worship, and celebration. At Moria, spiritual power was focused in the person and office of the bishop, but it was disseminated throughout the country through the ministers and prophets of all the local congregations. When members of those local congregations made pilgrimage to Moria, therefore, the material and spiritual power of the ZCC was dramatically consolidated in a single, sacred center. As donations were collected in 10-gallon oil drums, pilgrims received the healings, blessings, and power that flowed through the leader of the church. The leader of the ZCC, whether the founder Ignatius, his son Edward, or Edward's son and successor, Barnabas Lekganyane, carried the mantle of spiritual power in the church, standing at the center of the center of the ZCC in Moria.

The ZCC leader has often been compared to a traditional African chief or diviner, but those comparisons have merely been metaphors that have tried to represent his spiritual power as if it were peculiarly African. Rather than imitating the authority of a 'traditional' chief, ZCC leadership organized the church along the bureaucratic lines of the colonial government, with a hierarchical division of offices and services, from a centralized administration, down to the local government of congregations, with their prophets, ministers, secretaries, and treasurers (Comaroff, 1985: 241). Furthermore, unlike the 'traditional' African diviner, who drew on ancestral power and practices, ZCC leaders and prophets practiced faith-healing techniques, involving prayer, invocation of spiritual power, and the laying on of hands, sometimes accompanied by water, ash, or blessed objects, that were adapted from basic, Pentecostal faith-healing practices. Rather than a persistence of African 'traditional' religion, therefore, the Lekganyanes, as leaders of the ZCC, represented innovations in material, organizational, and spiritual power in South African religion.

At the same time that many Protestant theologians tried to explain the Lekganyanes as African 'chiefs' or 'diviners,' they also accused them of trying to usurp the position of Jesus in the Christian tradition. From the perspective of many Christian theologians, the leader of the ZCC, who was praised by his followers as 'Emmanuel,' or 'King of Zion,' seemed to have assumed a Christ-like or messianic role. Although ZCC hymns and praises exalted the role of Lekganyane, they might better be understood, not as messianic claims, but as the expression of the religious orientation of the ZCC around an alternative spiritual center in South Africa. In this sense, the ZCC celebrated a world and a worldview that was recentered around a single sacred person in a separate sacred place. Proclaiming Jesus as the cornerstone of that sacred place, the ZCC nevertheless revolved around the material and spiritual power demonstrated by its central prophet.

Like other Zionist churches, the ZCC practiced baptism by immersion and emphasized faith healing, manifestations of the spirit, including speaking in tongues, and the imminent return of Christ. To create a domain of purity and protection, they observed prohibitions against pork, tobacco, and alcohol, but also against medicines, whether derived from 'traditional' or 'modern' medical practice. In these religious beliefs and practices, the ZCC, like other Zionist churches, was not a syncretism of 'traditional' African and Christian worlds, but a modern innovation that opposed the evils that were associated with both. Incorporating dance in worship, the 'Soldiers of Zion' wore khaki uniforms, with large white boots, in rituals of 'praising with the feet.' Besides signaling the strength and solidarity of the community, however, ritual dancing also reinforced the personal purity of Zionists, as the dance was often devoted to 'stamping evil underfoot,' destroying a defiling evil such as tobacco, described in one ZCC publication as 'the most subtle poison known to chemists except the deadly prussic acid' (Werbner, 1986: 154). In this ritual, the dance announced a militant cultural protest, not against political domination, but against the personal pollution represented by the violation of Zionist prohibitions on evil substances.

Maintaining personal and communal purity in a defiling world, members of the church wore the ZCC badge in public. The silver star, inscribed with 'ZCC,' on a black cloth identified members of the church as a people set apart. The extensive membership of the ZCC created a network of social control, but also of mutual support. Although generally drawn from the poorest of the poor in South African townships, ZCC members achieved considerable success in the labor market, preferred by employers who recognized them as hardworking, disciplined, obedient, and sober, but especially as workers who would not go on strike (Schoffeleers, 1988: 48). As the church grew after 1960, during 30 years of recurring violence, political unrest, and labor action in South Africa, the ZCC attracted the religious involvement of people who wanted to stay out of the cycle of violence. In 1985 the ZCC Bishop Barnabas Lekganyane explained the remarkable growth of his church as a result of its commitment to non-violence and obedience to the governing authorities of South Africa. Inviting State President P. W. Botha as special guest at the April 1985 Easter festival at Moria, Bishop Lekganyane preached a message of accommodation to the government, instructing his following that the Bible 'teaches us that a man cannot be a follower of God without rendering due respect to the earthly government which he has ordained.' The Bishop specified the extent of that divinely ordained earthly government by preaching to his followers that the 'President, Prime Minister, Ministers of States, chiefs and all members of administrations are in authority over you' (Werbner, 1986: 154). Rather than political protest, therefore, the Zion Christian Church was committed to creating a separate enclave of spiritual purity in South Africa, a separate cultural order in which hard work, discipline, and obedience were as important as ritual healing in generating spiritual purity and power.

URBAN ZIONISTS

While hundreds of congregations of the Zion Christian Church were forming throughout South Africa, thousands of churches emerged with a similar 'Zionist' or 'Apostolic' commitment to spiritual healing and purity. Often no larger than a congregation of twenty people, these churches of the spirit continued to draw an increasing following after 1960. Although many commentators have tried to explain Zionist religious practice as a syncretism of Christian and pagan religion, these churches actually provided a religious option that was distinct from the practices of either the mission church or ancestral religion. Scholars have often explained Zionist churches as a reaction to white conquest and domination, arguing that Zionists sought to reinforce social barriers against the dominant white society. But the more immediate Zionist concern was to achieve separation from other blacks in the world of the rural reserves or the urban townships. While many Zionist churches flourished in rural areas, the basic outline of Zionist religious life is probably best suggested by considering the practices of small congregations in South African urban environments.

At least from the early 1960s in the township of Langa, near Cape Town, Zionists created a social network that was separate from adherents of ancestral ritual, but also separate from Christians who attended mission churches or other independent churches, as well as from a growing number of people with no religious involvement. However, Zionists were separate not merely in religious terms but also in class terms, as membership in Zionist churches tended to be drawn from the poorest residents of the township. Not aspiring to the middle-class values supported by other churches, the Zionists were for the most part drawn from the poorest of the working class. Christians in the mission churches or 'Ethiopian' churches tended to dismiss the Zionists as 'fake' or 'self-made' churches in contrast to their 'genuine' Christian institutions. This distinction, however, was primarily based, not on any theological or ecclesiastical criteria, but on a general disdain for the poverty and lower-class position of Zionists in Langa. They lacked the full-time clergy, permanent buildings, and substantial funding that supported the so-called 'genuine' churches. Nevertheless, Zionists pursued a religious way of life that gave spiritual content to their difference from other township residents. Rather than symbolically inverting the South African political order of white domination, therefore, the separate, sacred order created by Zionist churches addressed the more immediate social environment of the township. Transforming their social position in the township, Zionists turned the disdain in which they were held by other residents into a sign of their special status as bearers of the spirit (Mafeje, 1975).

Similarly, small Zionist congregations in the township of KwaMashu, near the city of Durban, drew lines of religious and social separation that set them apart from the world of the township. Zionist religious practice required the careful avoidance of certain aspects of township life that were perceived as spiritually dangerous. Zionist men, who were mostly employed as skilled and unskilled laborers, had to avoid social involvements with fellow workers, especially drinking, gambling, and other recreations, because they violated strict religious prohibitions on conduct. As a result, Zionist working men kept to themselves while out of the workplace. Maintaining stricter rules of purity, and regarded as more potent receptacles of spiritual power, men tended to play the major leadership roles in Zionist congregations. Women, however, comprised the majority of members. Although they observed less stringent restrictions on social contact with other women, Zionist women were particularly obligated to avoid any contact with 'traditional' medicine, *umuthi*, or the services of diviners and herbalists. Since those specialists had flourishing practices in the township, the Zionists referred to ordinary township residents as 'eaters of *umuthi*,' people polluted and corrupted by evil medicine. From the Zionist perspective, the township was an arena of evil forces, a dangerous chaos that resulted from the indiscriminate socializing of workers and the indiscriminate use of the powerful medicines and techniques of sorcery. In response to that dangerous chaos of the township, the Zionist congregation created a safe, ordered haven of spiritual power and purity (Kiernan, 1974: 87).

During Sunday services, ritual reinforced the social and spiritual separation of Zionists from the township. The meeting room might have been an ordinary home, but on Sunday it became a center of Zion. A 'gate-keeper' stood at the door, preventing strangers from entering, unless they had received prior permission from the minister, in order to maintain control over who participated in the service that was about to be conducted 'within the gates.' Anything required from outside, such as a bowl of water, was carried in by the gate-keeper, maintaining control over the threshold to the meeting place. Those who entered removed their shoes, thereby leaving outside the dust of the township, while members put on white robes that covered their ordinary clothing. At the opening of the meeting, doors and windows were shut to block out the township and create a self-contained sacred space in which worshipers could build up a reservoir of spiritual power.

To the singing of the hymn, 'Arm yourselves with the weapons, says the Lord of Hosts,' the minister, or sometimes the gate-keeper, distributed to each member a long staff, called an *isikhali*, literally meaning a 'weapon,' that was an important part of the ritual equipment of Zionist worship. Receiving a staff, a Zionist man not only acknowledged his solidarity with the community, but also received a symbolic instrument of power against the evil forces of the township (Kiernan, 1974: 84). Not unlike a fighting stick, the staff was a potent symbol of spiritual power, referred to as *umoya*, a term derived from air, breath, or spirit, but carrying a specific connotation in the context of Zionist worship. Invoked through prayer, both formal prayers such as the Lord's Prayer, as well as more extemporaneous prayer that often included speaking in tongues, *umoya* was built up as a reservoir of spiritual power within the closure of the Zionist place of meeting. The 'weapon' of Zion, therefore, served also as a symbol of the spiritual power, *umoya*, that was generated through prayer during the opening of the Zionist service (Kiernan, 1979; Hammond-Tooke, 1986).

The second phase of the service was devoted to preaching. As the minister opened his Bible, the doors and windows of the meeting room were thrown open so the outside world of the township could hear the minister's sermon. Besides being an act of communication with the outside world, the minister's preaching redirected the spiritual energy that had been generated in the room out into the township, extending the influence of *umoya* against its evils and perhaps seeking converts from its inhabitants. Concentrating primarily on the members seated around him, however, the Zionist minister, referred to as *umfundisi*, or 'teacher,' preached a religious message designed to gain consensus within the congregation. As the sermon was punctuated by responses from the audience, the words of the minister provided an opportunity for members to express their agreement on basic principles of the Zionist religious way of life. Argument and emotion combined in the minister's attempt to achieve consensus. While the congregation expressed its agreement on religious beliefs and moral values, the emotional fervor of interaction between preacher and audience contributed to the highly charged atmosphere in the room. During the third stage of the service, that energy was finally directed into the most important ritual work conducted by the Zionist congregation, spiritual healing.

Once again, as the healing ritual began, the doors and windows of the room were shut, closing out the world of the township. As the service shifted into the primary healing work of Zion, the prophet (*umprofeta*) replaced the minister as leader of the congregation. Although the separate religious functions of minister and prophet were sometimes combined in a single person, the prophet necessarily was a person invested with specialized spiritual powers of discernment and healing. While the minister was concerned with building consensus in the Zionist group, the prophet directed his or her attention toward individuals. Prophets singled out individuals for special recognition, decoration, or reward, but they also singled out individuals for blame if they had violated prohibitions or had allowed themselves to be exposed to evil influences. Shifting from the collective to the personal, therefore, the final stage of Zionist worship was devoted to the healing of individuals in the context of a caring, supportive, and spiritually charged group. Assisted by other members who had been designated as healers, empowered to lay hands on the sick, pray over them, and bless them, the prophet directed the healing work of Zion toward individuals who presented themselves as suffering from some affliction. Standing inside the healing circle, the individual sufferer was treated by the ritual work of Zion.

In determining the cause of any illness, the Zionist prophet dismissed the theoretical framework of scientific medical practice, but he also rejected the practice of traditional diviners and herbalists. Like the traditional medical practitioner, the Zionist prophet determined that illness was caused by evil spiritual agents, whether demons, spirits of disease, ancestral spirits, or the evil acts of a witch or sorcerer. In Zionist practice, however, the prophet discovered that the sufferer had become vulnerable to those evil influences through some moral lapse or lack of spiritual protection that could be corrected by an infusion of the Holy Spirit. In counteracting the evil influences that brought illness, misfortune, and death, the prophet did not resort to ancestral practices or traditional medicines. Rather, the prophet reinforced the moral rules, ritual purity, and spiritual power of the Zionist community. In terms of the Zionist theory of illness, an afflicted person was regarded as either morally or spiritually unfit to be a member of the pure community of the spirit. Returning an afflicted member to health, therefore, was a crucial ritual act for restoring the spiritual integrity of the Zionist community (Kiernan, 1976a: 350–1).

In general, Zionist healing was practiced in three different contexts, the worship service, special rituals of purification, and private consultations with a prophet (West, 1975a: 92). As the culmination of every worship service, healing ritual was orchestrated by prophets, whose charismatic gifts of the spirit were acknowledged by the community. Healing in the worship service consisted of two basic ritual actions: the act of brushing off impure and evil influences from the afflicted person's body and the act of pressing the staves, the ritual 'weapons' of Zion, onto the sufferer's body to infuse the power of the spirit. These ritual acts, however, were accompanied by a noisy, chaotic celebration of spiritual power, through prayer, hymns, speaking in tongues, and ecstatic motion, that involved the whole community in ritual healing. Although focused on the body of a suffering individual, therefore, ritual healing in the Zionist church service reaffirmed the social solidarity of the congregation.

On certain occasions, rituals of healing took the form of purification rites, performed at rivers, lakes, or the ocean, that utilized the spiritual power that Zionists associated with water. Every Zionist had been baptized by triple immersion, in the name of the Father, Son, and Holy Spirit, so water was regarded as a special medium for transmitting spiritual power. Although rituals of purification might have resembled baptism, involving invocation of the spirit and immersion in water, they were specifically addressed toward restoring an individual's purity and health. Furthermore, the spiritual cleansing achieved through rituals of water was connected with the power of water to expel impurity from the body. Drinking ocean water, or water mixed with salt, ash, or vinegar, acted as an expellent, cleaning out the insides of the person by operating on the contents of the stomach, but also by expelling any evil spirits or influences that had caused affliction. Causing a patient to vomit resembled a common treatment in 'traditional' medical practice. Unlike the herbalist's *umuthi*, however, water was regarded by Zionists as a pure substance, not an artificial mixture of ingredients concocted according to a medical formula. Water was a purifying, cleansing, and expelling agent, therefore, that achieved healing when it was ritually infused with the power of the spirit (Kiernan, 1978).

In addition to supervising healing in worship services and purification rituals, Zionist prophets were sometimes available for private consultation. In those cases, the prophet operated in a certain sense like a 'traditional' sacred specialist or a 'modern' medical doctor, consulting with patients as individual clients. Although prophets diagnosed causes and prescribed treatments in that client relationship, however, they ultimately referred their patients back to the moral and ritual order of the Zionist community. Therefore, the client relationship established in private consultations with a Zionist prophet was replaced by the more basic communal relationship established within the Zionist church. Faith-healers did gain personal reputations that attracted clients for private consultations. Some faith-healers even established centers of pilgrimage, as did Ma-Radebe, the 'Mother of Cancele,' who drew hundreds of pilgrims daily to her home in the Transkei for the holy water that carried the power of her blessing (Becken, 1982; 1983). Zionist prophets, however, tended to exercise their personal, charismatic powers of healing in concert with the ministerial, pastoral, and organizational authority that constituted a Zionist congregation. In that co-ordination of prophetic power and ministerial authority, a Zionist church was both empowered and held together as a community (Kiernan, 1976b).

REFERENCES

Barkun, Michael (1974). *Disaster and the Millennium*. New Haven: Yale University Press.

Becken, Hans-Jürgen (1965). 'The Nazareth Baptist Church of Shembe.' In: *Our Approach to the Independent Church Movement in South Africa*. Mapumulo, Natal: Lutheran Theological College.

Becken, Hans-Jürgen (1967–68). 'On the Holy Mountain: A Visit to the New Year's Festival of the Nazaretha Church on Mount Nhlangakazi 14/1/1967.' *Journal of Religion in Africa* 1: 138–49.

Becken, Hans-Jürgen (1978). 'Ekuphakameni Revisited.' *Journal of Religion in Africa* 9(3): 161–72.

Becken, Hans-Jürgen (1982). 'The Mother of Cancele.' *Journal of Religion in Africa* 13: 189–206.

Becken, Hans-Jürgen (1983). '"Give Me Water, Woman of Samaria": The Pilgrimage of Southern African Blacks in the 1980s.' *Journal of Religion in Africa* 14: 115–29.

Beinart, William, and Colin Bundy (1987). *Hidden Struggles in Rural South Africa*. London: James Currey; Berkeley: University of California Press; Cape Town: David Philip.

Bradford, Helen (1985). 'The African Industrial and Commercial Workers' Union in the South African Countryside.' PhD thesis, University of the Witwatersrand.

Burridge, Kenelm (1969). *New Heaven, New Earth*. Oxford: Oxford University Press.

Chirenje, J. Mutero (1976). 'The Afro-American Factor in Southern African Ethiopianism, 1890–1906.' In: David Chanaiwa (ed.) *Profiles of Self Determination*. Northridge: California State University, Northridge. 250–80.

Chirenje, J. Mutero (1987). *Ethiopianism and Afro-Americans in Southern Africa, 1883–1916*. Baton Rouge: Louisiana State University Press.

Coan, Josephus R. (1961). 'The Expansion of Missions of the African Methodist Episcopal Church in South Africa, 1896–1908.' PhD dissertation, Hartford Seminary.

Cohn, Norman (1961). *The Pursuit of the Millennium: Revolutionary Messianism in Medieval and Reformation Europe and its Bearing on Modern Totalitarian Movements*. 2nd edn. New York: Harper and Row (orig. edn 1957).

Comaroff, Jean (1985). *Body of Power, Spirit of Resistance: The Culture and History of a South African People*. Chicago: University of Chicago Press.

Dow, James (1986). 'Universal Aspects of Symbolic Healing: A Theoretical Synthesis.' *American Anthropologist* 18: 56–69.

Du Toit, Brian M. (1980). 'Religion, Ritual, and Healing among Urban Black South Africans.' *Urban Anthropology* 9: 21–49.

Edgar, Robert (1976). 'Garveyism in Africa: Dr. Wellington and the American Movement in the Transkei.' *Ufahamu* 6(3): 31–57.

Edgar, Robert (1982). 'The Prophet Motive: Enoch Mgijima, the Israelites, and the Background to the Bulhoek Massacre.' *International Journal of Historical Studies* 15: 401–22.

Edgar, Robert (1988). *Because They Chose the Plan of God: The Story of the Bulhoek Massacre*. Johannesburg: Ravan Press.

Erlmann, Veit (1988). '"A Feeling of Prejudice": Orpheus M. McAdoo and the Virginia Jubilee Singers in South Africa 1890–1898.' *Journal of Southern African Studies* 14: 331–50.

Etherington, Norman E. (1979). 'The Historical Sociology of Independent Churches in South East Africa.' *Journal of Religion in Africa* 10: 108–26.

Fernandez, James W. (1973). 'The Precincts of the Prophet: A Day with Johannes Galilee Shembe.' *Journal of Religion in Africa* 5: 32–53.

Flanagan, F. (1981). 'African Independent Churches, with special reference to Isaiah Shembe's Zulu Union.' *African Ecclesial Review* 23: 206–14.

Fogelqvist, Andres (1986). *The Red-Dressed Zionists: Symbols of Power in a Swazi Independent Church*. Uppsala: Uppsala Research Reports in Cultural Anthropology.

Gunner, Elizabeth (1982). 'New Wine in Old Bottles: Imagery in the Izibongo of the Zulu Zionist Prophet, Isaiah Shembe.' *Journal of the Anthropological Society of Oxford* 13: 99–108.

Gunner, Elizabeth (1986). 'The Word, the Book and the Zulu Church of Nazareth.' In: Richard Whitaker and Edgaard Sienaert (eds) *Oral Tradition and Literacy: Changing Visions of the World*. Durban: Natal Oral Documentation and Research Centre. 179–88.

Gunner, Elizabeth (1988). 'Power House, Prison House – An Oral Genre and Its Use in Isaiah Shembe's Nazareth Baptist Church.' *Journal of Southern African Studies* 14: 204–27.

Hammond-Tooke, W. D. (1986). 'The Aetiology of the Spirit in Southern Africa.' *African Studies* 45: 157–70.

Hanekom, Christof (1975). *Krisis en Kultus: Geloofsopvattinge en seremonies binne 'n Swart Kerk.* Cape Town: Academica.

Harlan, R. (1906). *John Alexander Dowie and His Christian Catholic Apostolic Church in Zion.* Evansville, WI.: Press of R. M. Antes.

Haselbarth, H. (1965). 'The Zion Christian Church of Edward Lekganyane.' In: *Our Approach to the Independent Church Movement in South Africa.* Mapumulo, Natal: Lutheran Theological College.

Hill, Robert A., and Gregory A. Pirio (1987). '"Africa for the Africans": The Garvey Movement in South Africa, 1920–1940.' In: Shula Marks and Stanley Trapido (eds) *The Politics of Race, Class and Nationalism in Twentieth Century South Africa.* London: Longman. 209–53.

Hollenweger, Walter J. (1972). *The Pentecostals.* Trans. R. A. Wilson. London: SCM Press.

Kamphausen, Erhard (1971). 'Studies on the Early History of the African Independent Church Movement in South Africa.' *Africana Marburgensia* 4: 28–30.

Kamphausen, Erhard (1976). *Anfänge der Kirchlichen Unabhängigkeits-bewegung in Sudafrika: Geschichte und Theologie der Athiopischen Bewegung, 1872–1912.* Frankfort: Herbert Lang, Bern and Peter Lang.

Karis, Thomas, and Gwendolen M. Carter (eds) (1972–77). *From Protest to Challenge: A Documentary History of African Politics in South Africa 1882–1964.* 4 vols. Stanford: Hoover Institution Press.

Kiernan, James P. (1974). 'Where Zionists Draw the Line: A Study of Religious Exclusiveness in an African Township.' *African Studies* 33(2): 79–90.

Kiernan, James P. (1975). 'Old Wine in New Wineskins.' *African Studies* 34(3): 193–201.

Kiernan, James P. (1976a). 'The Work of Zion: An Analysis of an African Zionist Ritual.' *Africa* 46: 340–55.

Kiernan, James P. (1976b). 'Prophet and Preacher: An Essential Partnership in the Work of Zion.' *Man* 11: 356–66.

Kiernan, James P. (1977a). 'Poor and Puritan: An Attempt to View Zionism as a Collective Response to Urban Poverty.' *African Studies* 36(1): 31–41.

Kiernan, James P. (1977b). 'Public Transport and Private Risk: Zionism and the Black Commuter in South Africa.' *Journal of Anthropological Research* 33: 214–26.

Kiernan, James P. (1978). 'Saltwater and Ashes: Instruments of Curing among some Zulu Zionists.' *Journal of Religion in Southern Africa* 9(3): 27–32.

Kiernan, James P. (1979). 'The Weapons of Zion.' *Journal of Religion in Africa* 10(1): 13–21.

Kiernan, James P. (1979). 'Spouses and Partners: Marriage and Career among Zulu Zionists.' *Urban Anthropology* 8: 95–110.

Kiernan, James P. (1980). 'Zionist Communion.' *Journal of Religion in Africa* 11(2): 124–36.

Kiernan, James P. (1982). 'Authority and Enthusiasm: The Organization of Religious Experience in Zulu Zionist Churches.' In: J. Davis (ed.) *Religious Organization and Religious Experience.* London: Academic Press. 169–79.

Kiernan, James P. (1984). 'A Cesspool of Sorcery: How Zionists Visualise and Respond to the City.' *Urban Anthropology* 13: 219–36.

Kiernan, James P. (1985). 'The Social Stuff of Revelation: Pattern and Purpose in Zionist Dreams and Visions.' *Africa* 55: 304–17.

Kiernan, James P. (1986). 'The Management of a Complex Religious Identity: The Case of Zulu Zionism.' *Religion in Southern Africa* 7(2): 3–14.

Kiernan, James P. (1987). 'The Role of the Adversary in Zulu Zionist Churches.' *Religion in Southern Africa* 8(1): 3–14.

Kiernan, James P. (1988). 'The Other Side of the Coin: The Conversion of Money to Religious Purposes in Zulu Zionist Churches.' *Man* 23: 453–68.

Kruss, Glenda (1985). 'Religion, Class and Culture: Indigenous Churches in South Africa, with Special Reference to Zionist-Apostolics.' MA Thesis, University of Cape Town.

Lahouel, Badra (1986). 'Ethiopianism and African Nationalism in South Africa before 1937.' *Cahiers des études africaines* 26: 681–88.

Lanternari, Vittorio (1963). *The Religions of the Oppressed.* New York: Alfred Knopf.

Lea, Alan (1926). *The Native Separatist Church Movement in South Africa.* Cape Town: Juta.

Lea, Alan (1928). 'Native Separatist Churches.' In: J. D. Taylor (ed.) *Christianity and the Natives of South Africa.* Lovedale: Lovedale Press. 73–85.

Léenhardt, Maurice (1976). *Le Mouvement Éthiopien au Sud de l'Afrique de 1896 à 1899.* Paris: Académie des sciences d'outremer (orig. edn 1902).

Lewis, Cecil, and Gertrude Elizabeth Edwards (1934). *Historical Records of the Church of the Province of South Africa.* London: SPCK.

Mafeje, Archie (1975). 'Religion, Class and Ideology in South Africa.' In: M.G. Whisson and Martin West (eds) *Religion and Social Change in Southern Africa.* Cape Town: David Philip. 164–84.

Marks, Shula (1970). *Reluctant Rebellion: The 1906–08 Disturbances in Natal.* Oxford: Clarendon Press.

Martin, M. L. (1964). *The Biblical Concept of Messianism and Messianism in Southern Africa.* Morija: Morija Sesuto Book Depot.

Mills, Wallace G. (1978). 'The Fork in the Road: Religious Separatism versus African Nationalism in the Cape Colony, 1890–1910.' *Journal of Religion in Africa* 9(3): 50–61.

Mönnig, H. O. (1967). *The Pedi.* Pretoria: Van Schaik.

Mosala, Itumeleng (1985). 'African Independent Churches: A Study in Socio-Theological Protest.' In: Charles Villa-Vicencio and John W. de Gruchy (eds) *Resistance and Hope.* Grand Rapids, MI: Eerdmans; Cape Town: David Philip. 103–11.

Mqotsi, L. and N. Mkele (1946). 'A Separatist Church: Ibandla lika-Krestu.' *African Studies* 5: 106–25.

M'timkulu, Donald (1977). 'Some Aspects of Zulu Religion.' In: Newell S. Booth (ed.) *African Religion: A Symposium.* New York: NOK Publishers. 13–30.

Oosthuizen, G. C. (1967). *The Theology of a South African Messiah: An Analysis of the Hymnal of 'The Church of the Nazarites'.* Leiden: E. J. Brill.

Oosthuizen, G. C. (1968). *Post-Christianity in Africa: A Theological and Anthropological Study.* London: Wever.

Oosthuizen, G. C. (1971). 'Causes of Religious Independentism in Africa.' *Ministry* 11: 121–33.

Oosthuizen, G. C. (1981). 'Leadership Struggle within the Church of the Nazarites – iBandla lamaNazaretha.' *Religion in Southern Africa* 2(2): 12–24.

Oosthuizen, G. C. (ed.) (1986). *Religion Alive: Studies in the New Movements and Indigenous Churches in Southern Africa.* Johannesburg: Hodder & Stoughton.

Oosthuizen, G. C. (1987). *The Birth of Christian Zionism in South Africa.* KwaDlangezwa: University of Zululand.

Oosthuizen, G. C. (1989). 'Black Zionism.' *The Condenser.* Tongaat, Natal: The Tongaat-Hulett Group.

Page, Carol (1982). 'Colonial Reaction to AME Missionaries in South Africa, 1898–1910.' In: Sylvia M. Jacobs (ed.) *Black Americans and the Missionary Movement in Africa.* Westport, Conn.: Greenwood Press. 177–96.

Parsons, Q. N. (1970). 'Independency and Ethiopianism among the Tswana in the Late Nineteenth and Early Twentieth Centuries.' *The Societies of Southern Africa in the Nineteenth and Twentieth Centuries.* London: Institute of Commonwealth Studies. I. 56–67.

Pauw, B. A. (1960). *Religion in a Tswana Chiefdom.* Oxford: Oxford University Press.

Pretorius, H. L. (1985). *Sound the Trumpet of Zion: Aspects of a Movement in Transkei.* Pretoria: Iswen.

Redkey, Edwin S. (1969). *Black Exodus: Black Nationalist and Back to Africa Movements, 1890–1910.* New Haven: Yale University Press.

Redkey, Edwin S. (ed.) (1971). *Respect Black: The Writings and Speeches of Henry McNeal Turner.* New York: Arno Press.

Rich, Paul (1978). 'Black Peasants and Ethiopianism in South Africa, 1896–1915.' In: *Conference on the History of Opposition in Southern Africa.* Johannesburg: Development Studies Group, University of the Witwatersrand. 119–41.

Roberts, Esther Lindsay (1936). 'Shembe: The Man and his Work.' MA thesis, University of South Africa.

Saayman, W. A. (1989). 'Tiyo Soga and Nehemiah Tile: Black Pioneers in Mission and Church.' *Missionalia* 17: 95–102.

SANAC (1903–5). *South African Native Affairs Commission.* 5 vols. Cape Town: Government Printers.

Saunders, C. C. (1970). 'Tile and the Thembu Church: Politics and Independency on the Cape Eastern Frontier in the Late Nineteenth Century.' *Journal of African History* 11: 553–70.

Saunders, C. C. (1978). 'African Nationalism and Religious Independency in Cape Colony: A Comment.' *Journal of Religion in Africa* 9: 207–10.

Schlosser, Katesa (1949). *Propheten in Afrika.* Braunschweig: Limbach.

Schlosser, Katesa (1958). *Eingeborenenkirchen in Süd- und Südwestafrika.* Kiel: Mühlau.

Schoffeleers, Matthew (1988). 'The Zion Christian Church and the Apartheid Regime.' *Leidschrift* 3: 42–57.

Shepperson, George (1962). 'The Comparative Study of Millenarian Movements.' In: Sylvia Thrupp (ed.) *Millennial Dreams in Action.* The Hague: Mouton. 44–52.

Shepperson, George (1966). 'Ethiopianism and African Nationalism.' In: Immanuel Wallerstein (ed.) *Social Change: The Colonial Situation.* New York: John Wiley & Sons. 478–88.

Shepperson, George, and Thomas Price (1958). *Independent African: John Chilembwe and the Origins, Setting and Significance of the Nyasaland Rising of 1915.* Edinburgh: Edinburgh University Press.

Smith, Charles S. (1922). *A History of the African Methodist Episcopal Church.* Philadelphia: Book Concern of the AME Church.

Sundkler, Bengt G. M. (1961). *Bantu Prophets in South Africa.* 2nd edn Oxford: Oxford University Press; 1st edn London: Lutterworth Press, 1948.

Sundkler, Bengt G. M. (1965). 'Chief and Prophet in Zululand and Swaziland.' In: Meyer Fortes and Germaine Dieterlen (eds) *African Systems of Thought.* London: Oxford University Press. 276–90.

Sundkler, Bengt G. M. (1976). *Zulu Zion and Some Swazi Zionists.* Oxford: Oxford University Press.

Taylor, J. Dexter (ed.) (1928). *Christianity and the Natives of South Africa.* Lovedale: Lovedale Press.

Turner, Henry M. (1904). 'The Races Must Separate.' In: Willis B. Parks (ed.) *The Possibilities of the Negro: A Symposium.* Atlanta: Franklin.

Van der Merwe, Gerhard (1989). 'The Understanding of Sin among Some Members of the Zion Christian Church.' *Missionalia* 17(3): 199–205.

Verryn, Trevor David (1972). *A History of the Order of Ethiopia.* Pretoria: Ecumenical Research Unit; Cleveland: Central Mission Press.

Vilakazi, Absolom, with Bongani Mthethwa and Mthembeni Mpanza (1986). *Shembe: The Revitalization of African Society.* Johannesburg: Skotaville.

Wacker, Grant (1985). 'Marching to Zion.' *Church History* 54: 496–511.

Walshe, Peter (1970). *The Rise of African Nationalism in South Africa: The African National Congress, 1912–1952.* Berkeley: University of California Press.

Wells, James (1908). *Stewart of Lovedale: The Life of James Stewart.* London: Hodder and Stoughton.

Werbner, Richard P. (1985). 'The Argument of Images: From Zion to the Wilderness in African Churches.' In: Wim van Binsbergen and Matthew Schoffeleers (eds) *Theoretical Explorations in African Religion.* London: Routledge & Kegan Paul. 253–86.

Werbner, Richard P. (1986). 'Review Article: The Political Economy of Bricolage.' *Journal of Southern African Studies* 13: 151–56.

West, Martin (1975a). *Bishops and Prophets in a Black City: African Independent Churches in Soweto, Johannesburg.* Cape Town: David Philip.

West, Martin (1975b). 'The Shades Come to Town: Ancestors and Urban Independent Churches.' In: M.G. Whisson and Martin West (eds) *Religion and Social Change in Southern Africa.* Cape Town: David Philip. 185–206.

Whisson, M. G. and Martin West (eds) (1975). *Religion and Social Change in Southern Africa.* Cape Town: David Philip.

Whitaker, Richard, and Edgaard Sienart (eds) (1986). *Oral Tradition and Literacy: Changing Visions of the World.* Durban: Natal Oral Documentation and Research Centre.

Williams, Charles S. (1982). 'Ritual Healing and Holistic Medicine among the Zulu Zionists.' PhD thesis, American University, Washington, DC.

Worsley, Peter (1968). *The Trumpet Shall Sound: A Study of 'Cargo' Cults in Melanesia.* 2nd edn New York: Schocken Books (orig. edn 1957).

5 Religious pluralism

The religious traditions considered in previous chapters – ancestral religion, Protestant denominations, and independent churches – have all been inherently plural. In addition, however, South Africa has also been home for nearly every religious tradition that has made up what has often been referred to as 'world religions.' By 1980 religious traditions that were not Protestant, but were also not indigenous to Africa, had large followings. Roman Catholics accounted for nearly 10 per cent of the population, while Muslims, Hindus, and Jews, along with other religious traditions, including Buddhists, Confucians, and Parsees (or Zoroastrians), made up almost 5 per cent of the population of South Africa. Obviously, South Africa has been a religiously plural place.

Ignoring the reality of religious pluralism, however, the National Party government's constitution of 1983 persisted in declaring that South Africa was a Christian country, underwritten by a particular Protestant, national understanding of Christianity. But the histories of other religious traditions – the Christian tradition of Roman Catholics, but also the Muslim, Hindu, and Jewish religious traditions – provide useful reminders that South Africa has not been an exclusively Protestant Christian country. Rather, as should already be obvious from previous chapters, South Africa has been a religiously plural country. Religious traditions with sacred centers outside of the geographical boundaries of southern Africa have struggled to establish a place in the region. Originally identified with what the anthropologist Victor Turner called 'centers out there,' whether in Rome, Mecca, Benares, or Jerusalem, these religious traditions recentered themselves in the South African context. However, their efforts to find a place in South Africa have often come into conflict with the laws of the land. An important part of the story of religious pluralism in South Africa, therefore, has been the history of legal conflicts in which religious pluralism has been suppressed by the force of law.

During the period of Dutch East India Company rule in the Cape, from

1652 to 1795, legal controls over religion were exercised directly by the Company. Under the direction of the Amsterdam Classis, the Company government established the Dutch Reformed Church as the only legally recognized form of public worship in the Cape Colony. Although Lutherans, Catholics, Muslims, and others lived in the colony, they were prohibited by law from practicing their religions in public. Through this denial of religious pluralism, the government of the Cape tried to reinforce uniformity in matters of religion throughout the colony. However, as the Dutch Reformed Church was established in the Cape as an extension of government, religion inevitably coincided with politics. Especially in the case of Catholics and Muslims, legal restrictions on religion carried definite political overtones. Political motives for restricting the religious practices of Catholics and Muslims lingered from two international arenas of conflict, one in Europe, the other in South-east Asia, in which Dutch military and economic interests were involved.

On one front, Dutch Calvinists in the Netherlands had emerged from decades of war against Spanish Catholic political domination with strong anti-Catholic sentiments. Those sentiments were only strengthened in 1688 with the arrival in the Cape of Huguenot refugees, French Calvinists who had escaped Catholic persecutions in Europe. The exclusion of Catholics from the Cape Colony, therefore, had as much to do with European politics as it did with a principled denial of religious toleration. Nevertheless, European political and religious conflict became the basis for legal prohibition of Catholic forms of worship in the Cape Colony. In 1660, a French Catholic bishop, shipwrecked in Table Bay, was forbidden to perform the ritual of the Mass on shore. Similarly, in 1685, six Jesuit astronomers, stopping in the Cape on their way to Asia, were also prevented from performing Mass in the colony. In both cases, any Catholics who happened to be living in the Cape Colony were forbidden to board the visiting ships for the purpose of religious worship. Although Portuguese Catholics had pioneered European explorations of southern Africa during the previous century, all Catholics were denied any legal right to practice their religion throughout the period of Dutch rule in the Cape Colony.

On a second front, the Dutch East India Company was involved in a military struggle in the Indonesian islands for control over their lucrative trade. In that struggle for control, resistance against Dutch interests was often mounted by Muslim leaders. During the seventeenth-century wars of resistance against the Dutch, Muslims were among the captives and political prisoners who were taken out of the field of conflict to be enslaved, imprisoned, or exiled in the Cape Colony. Colonial restrictions on the public practice of Islam, therefore, reflected a political interest in containing Muslim resistance to the Dutch East India Company. As in the case of Catholics, however, the Cape colonial government tried to further its political interests by directly targeting religious practices. In 1657, Cape Governor John Maetsuycker issued an edict forbidding Muslims to practice Islam in public or to convert the local population, whether heathen or Christian. Punishment for violating this order was specified as death. This ordinance was consistent with Dutch East India Company policy, contained in the Statutes of India, in prohibiting Muslims from worshiping, preaching, or seeking to gain converts in public. Although these religious practices were defined as capital crimes, there is no evidence of executions of Muslims for practicing their religion in public. However, legal prohibition certainly discouraged Cape Muslims from establishing any places of public worship until 1798, under the first British occupation (1795–1803), when a mosque was allowed to be built in Cape Town.

The possibility of a more liberal Dutch approach to religious pluralism, however, had already been indicated in 1778 when the Cape Colony granted Lutherans permission to worship in public. That promise of religious toleration was written into law in the Cape Colony during the brief restoration of Dutch rule between 1803 and 1806. Under the rule of the Batavian Republic in 1804 Commissioner-General Jacob Abraham de Mist issued an edict of religious toleration. According to De Mist's *Kerkenordre*, 'All religious societies, which for the furtherance of virtue and good morals worshiped an Almighty Being, are to enjoy in this colony equal protection from the laws.' In this new spirit of toleration, three Catholic priests from the Netherlands were permitted to perform Mass in the colony. When the British resumed control of the Cape in 1806, Governor David Baird agreed to uphold this declaration of religious toleration. Baird's agreement was remarkable, since this extension of the right of public worship to Catholics in the Cape predated the full legal toleration of Catholics in Britain by nearly 25 years. Almost immediately, however, Governor Baird ordered the three Catholic priests to leave the colony.

Perhaps Governor Baird expelled the Dutch priests because he saw them as agents of the Batavian government. But he also seems to have been enforcing a policy of religious intolerance in practice, because during the same year the British administrator rejected a petition from a group of Cape Catholics for permission to build a church at their own expense. Subsequent British governors also agreed to uphold the principle of religious toleration. The Earl of Caledon in 1806 and Sir John Craddock in 1811 were both given instructions from London:

to permit liberty of conscience and the free exercise of religious worship to all persons who inhabit or frequent the settlement provided they be contented with a peaceful enjoyment of the said, without giving offence or scandal to the government.

(Theal, 1897–1905: VI: 14; VIII: 37)

In spite of this expressed commitment to religious toleration, however, permission for building a church was not granted to the Catholic community in the Cape until 1822.

Like the building of the first Muslim mosque in 1798, the erection of a Catholic church in 1822 was a landmark in the history of religious pluralism in South Africa. Other religious communities would also build foundations for their religious worlds on the southern tip of Africa. Although there were Jews living in the Cape during the seventeenth century, the first synagogue was not consecrated until 1849. Although many of the indentured laborers from India had performed Hindu devotions, making wattle and daub shrines, while working on the Natal sugar plantations in the 1860s, the first iron and wood Hindu temple was built in 1869 in Durban by Indian immigrants. Religious pluralism, therefore, has been an important facet of South African religious life. A brief outline of the histories of Catholics, Muslims, Hindus, and Jews in South Africa can only underscore the facet that South Africa has been a plural religious world.

CATHOLICS

Although the first Catholic Mass in southern Africa might have been performed as early as 1488, the practice of Catholic worship, as we have seen, was severely limited during the seventeenth and eighteenth centuries by legal enactments of the Cape Colony government. Without a church, a bishop, or even a priest, the few Catholics in the Cape Colony in 1814, many of whom were Irish troops serving in the colonial army, petitioned the Colonial Office in London for the appointment of Catholic clergy. In response to that request, London agreed to allow a priest, but no bishop, to preside over Catholic worship in the Cape. When the English Benedictine priest, Dom Edward Bede Slater, was appointed, however, his appointment did little to benefit the Catholics in the Cape, since he was assigned to residence on the island of Mauritius. But a member of his party, Father Patrick Scully, did arrive in Cape Town in 1819 to serve as chaplain for the Catholic community. It was Father Scully who organized the construction of the first Catholic Church in Cape Town, on Harrington Street, in 1822. Plagued by problems in financing the church, however, Father Scully returned to England 2 years later. Although the building was constructed, and other priests served briefly as chaplains, the first Catholic church was destroyed in 1837 by storms, bringing to an end the first stage in Catholic attempts to establish a place in South Africa.

During that same year, the Roman Catholic Church consecrated the Irish Dominican, Patrick Raymond Griffith, as the first Vicar Apostolic of the Cape of Good Hope. After the long voyage from London, Griffith arrived in Table Bay in 1838, accompanied by two priests. Over the next few years, Bishop Griffith and his priests supervised the development of Catholic churches based in Cape Town and Grahamstown. Unlike many of his predecessors, Bishop Griffith did not suffer religious persecution from the government, which even granted him the normal annual stipend of £200 as a recognized chaplain in the colony. In Cape Town Griffith sold the Harrington Street property and purchased land for a new church. Although its foundation stone was laid in 1841, that church, St Mary of the Flight into Egypt, was not completed until 1851. During those years, Bishop Griffith devoted much of his time to raising funds (Brain, 1988: 198). At the same time, however, Bishop Griffith anticipated projects in interfaith relations, missions, and education that would later be developed by the Catholic Church in South Africa.

On a tour of the Cape, shortly after his arrival, Bishop Griffith observed the limited success of Protestant missions in the region. Although they had converted a considerable number of displaced Khoisan people by the end of the 1830s, the Protestant missionaries that he encountered had not converted them to what Bishop Griffith regarded as legitimate religion. 'They teach the Hottentots to sing psalms,' Bishop Griffith complained, 'but teach them *no* religion.' Although he granted that Protestant missionaries might one day be seen as 'Pioneers to Truth,' Bishop Griffith concluded that 'the time of the Conversion of the said Hottentots, as well as the rest of the barbarous tribes on the borders of the Colony has not yet come' (Brain, 1988: 130). In these remarks, Bishop Griffith not only recognized the failure of Protestant missions, but also argued that even their successes had failed to extend what he regarded as genuine religion.

Dismissing the authenticity of Protestant conversions, Bishop Griffith's observation reflected a tension in interfaith relations between Catholics and Protestants that occasionally resurfaced during the nineteenth century. In 1840, for example, Bishop Griffith became the target of Protestant anti-Catholic attacks in Cape Town newspapers. Griffith noted that there was 'great writing just now in the Papers against our Religion.' Apparently, Protestant opposition to the Catholic Church was widespread in the Cape Colony. Griffith's Anglican counterpart, Bishop Robert Gray, observed that 'there were strong feelings of antipathy towards the Romanists.' Betraying his own prejudices against Roman Catholics, as well as Dutch Protestants, the Anglican Bishop Gray claimed that the Dutch colonists were 'so credulous and ignorant that they would fall easy victims to the [Catholic] Church's teachings were it not for their wholesome fear of it' (Brain, 1988: 202). As a result of Protestant dominance in the settler communities of the Cape and Natal, Bishop Griffith and his successors had to adapt to minority status in South Africa.

Perhaps that minority status made Bishop Griffith more sensitive to the importance of another minority faith in the Cape, Islam. On his tour of the Cape in 1839, for example, Griffith visited the tomb of Shaykh Yusuf, the Muslim leader who had died at the Cape in 1699, while being held there in exile from his home in the Indonesian archipelago. Many Muslims regarded Shaykh Yusuf as a saint and his tomb as a holy place. Bishop Griffith recognized the importance of the tomb for Muslims, as a place for religious devotions, a pilgrimage site, and a burial ground. Nevertheless, Bishop Griffith rendered its religious significance in his own terms. The tomb of Shaykh Yusuf, Griffith concluded, 'proves great respect for the Dead and indicated a further State – may be implicitly – Purgatory' (Brain, 1988: 189–90). Although he translated its significance into terms of Catholic doctrine, Bishop Griffith, perhaps ironically, seemed to display more sympathy for this Muslim ritual site than he did for the Protestant missions. Later, in Cape Town, Bishop Griffith also recognized that Islam was gaining more converts than the Protestants among former slaves. Even slaves who had been raised as Protestants, Bishop Griffith noted, 'as soon as they get free they join their own people (Blacks, Yellows and Brown, as may be) in Mahometanism' (Brain, 1988: 204).

Aware of the failures of Protestant missions, Bishop Griffith argued for an extension of Catholic missions in South Africa. Initially, during his 1838 tour of the Cape, Griffith had expressed skepticism about the possibility of converting the indigenous people of the country. Lumping them all together, Bishop Griffith wrote in his journal that the people he encountered in the Cape 'are a sad race – Boschmen, Fingoes, Caffers, Hottentots – they are all base and barbarous' (Brain, 1988: 130). Certainly, there was some irony in this Irish Dominican labeling people 'barbarians' when Irish Catholics had suffered a long history of being labeled 'barbarians' by English Protestants (Fredrickson, 1981: 13–16). Nevertheless, after a few months in the Cape, Bishop Griffith had resolved his attitude toward the indigenous people on biblical grounds by concluding that all people had a common origin, '*one* common father and one common mother for *all* the human, black or white, Beings' (Brain, 1988: 186–7). Based on this recognition of a common humanity, Bishop Griffith advocated Catholic missions and Catholic education for blacks in the Cape. In 1839 Bishop Griffith argued that the expansion of the Catholic religion would come through education. 'The Boorish Dutch will not allow the children of colour to be educated with them in the same schools,' Griffith wrote. By contrast, Bishop Griffith argued that Catholic schools should be established and staffed by teachers who would 'receive the children with joy, educate them with feeling, teach them the true character of our Holy religion, that they are as dear and dearer even, than the Whites' (Brain, 1988: 201). Although his dreams of schools and seminaries were not fully realized during his lifetime, Bishop Patrick Raymond Griffith anticipated the basic connection between religion and education that would eventually be central to the expansion of the Catholic Church in South Africa.

When Bishop Griffith died in 1862, the Catholic population, which had numbered only about 700 at his arrival, had expanded to nearly 30,000. By that time, however, the expanding frontier of the Catholic Church had shifted to the colony of Natal, where missionaries of the French Oblates of Mary Immaculate (OMI) had initiated mission work. The founder and superior of the OMI, Bishop of Marseilles, Eugène de Mazenod, became interested in a southern African mission in the early 1850s. He sent Bishop Jean François Allard, who at the time was serving in Canada, to be the first Apostolic Vicar of Natal. Arriving in Durban in March 1852, Bishop Allard rented a house for the purpose of Catholic worship. Like Bishop Griffith in the Cape, Allard encountered Protestant resistance among the settler community in Natal against the Roman Catholic Church. 'All the ministers of the different denominations took considerable trouble to insult our Holy Religion in their sermons,' Bishop Allard reported, several months after his arrival. One Protestant minister in particular, Allard complained, 'enticed his congregation to assault us, even throw us into the sea so as to drown us' (Brain, 1975: 42). By the next year, Protestant ministers in Natal had apparently organized to stop the spread of the Catholic Church.

Gradually, however, this interfaith conflict subsided. By the 1880s tensions between Protestants and Catholics in Natal had basically been forgotten (Brain, 1982: 9). White leadership of both Protestant and Catholic churches combined forces in Natal to defend the colonial government. By contrast, anti-Catholic sentiment persisted in the Voortrekker colonies of the Transvaal and Orange Free State. In both republics, Catholics were excluded by law from positions in the civil service or education departments (Brown, 1960: 188).

Initially, during the early 1850s, Catholic priests of the OMI concentrated on building churches in Pietermaritzburg and Natal. But the priests soon turned to missions among the Zulu-speaking population of the region. After their request to obtain refugee children from the government failed, the OMI missionaries petitioned for a land grant that would provide a base for a mission station. Although the Natal government seemed reluctant to allocate land for a Catholic mission, a second OMI request for land was granted by setting aside 500 acres in a remote part of Zululand. The chapel for the mission station of St Michaels was finally completed in 1859. As Bishop Allard wrote to the founder of his religious order, a typical service was simple, with hymns in Zulu, a sermon, and the litany of the Blessed Virgin Mary. The Mass was not celebrated in front of the Zulu-speaking people, however, as Allard explained, because 'they understand nothing of its heavenly function.' Religious services at the Catholic mission, however, attracted as little interest as the Protestant. In 1860 Allard reported that the people 'constantly remained in a state of opposition to the teaching of the Gospel.' Although they did respond 'to certain material advantages' brought by the mission station, the people showed so little interest in the mission that it was closed by the end of 1861. Explaining this failure, Bishop Allard complained about the worldliness of the people, their close relations with their chiefs, and their attachment to what he called 'evil customs.' Most revealing, however, was Allard's admission that the people in Zululand lacked interest in the mission because of 'their prosperity.' Like the Protestant missions, the Catholic missions did not attract large numbers of African converts until their political, social, and economic worlds had been destroyed (Brain, 1975: 57–63). Although the French Catholics of the OMI did achieve considerable success among the Basuto of Chief Moshoeshoe, largely because they provided support for the chief in territorial conflicts, they were just as unsuccessful as the Protestant missionaries in Natal and Zululand until the 1880s (Brain, 1975: 80–99).

In 1871 Father J. D. Ricards was appointed as Bishop in the Cape, devoting much of his attention to establishing schools and seminaries for the training of black priests (Ricards, 1879). While Ricards supervised the Catholic Church in the Cape, Bishop Allard's successor in Natal, Charles Constant Jolivet, who arrived in 1875, initiated churches and schools in Bloemfontein, Pretoria, the diamond fields of Kimberley, and eventually the gold-mining region of Johannesburg. Although this expansion of Christian institutions primarily served a white population, Catholic bishops persisted in mission work (Brown, 1960: 166–9). Hearing of the recent success of Trappist monks in advancing Catholic missions in Algeria, Bishop Ricards arranged for a group of Trappists, under the direction of Father Franz Pfanner, to come to southern Africa in 1880.

After some time in the eastern Cape, the Trappist monks finally settled in 1885 on a 12,000 acre farm in Natal that became the mission center of Mariannhill. The heart of this Catholic mission was agricultural education. Although credit for this educational innovation has been given to the young A. T. Bryant, who later became a Catholic priest, Zulu linguist, and historian, the Trappists had already based their success in Algeria on an agricultural mission (Schimlek, 1953: 67–9). Whatever its inspiration, however, the devastations of the recent Anglo-Zulu war had made many people in the region more receptive to this type of religious education through agriculture and industry. After lessons in the morning, students at Mariannhill spent their afternoons working with skilled artisans or laboring in the fields. By 1887 the Mariannhill agricultural mission had become so successful that it provided a home for more people than any other Catholic abbey in the world (Brain, 1975: 173). Celebrating this missionary success, Bishop Jolivet suggested that the Catholic monks had been better at instilling the 'Protestant work ethic' than the Protestants. In 1890, Bishop Jolivet declared that the Trappists 'give the best lesson of all to the Negroes, that of work.' As a result of its success in converting people to that gospel of work, Bishop Jolivet concluded, 'Mariannhill is the envy of every Protestant' (Brain, 1975: 173; Brown, 1960: 236–7). Like the Protestant missions in Natal and Zululand, however, this Catholic mission only attracted people after the Anglo-Zulu war. The war had brought about, not only the destruction of the Zulu kingdom, but also the displacement, widespread poverty, and increasing vulnerability of people to government exactions of land, labor, and taxes. For converts of the Catholic mission, therefore, Mariannhill provided a shelter from these political, social, and economic storms.

By 1909 the Mariannhill missionaries had founded twenty-five similar mission stations throug᷉ ᷉ut Natal and the eastern Cape as bases for religious, agricultural, and industrial training (Dischl, 1982: 96). In addition to the work of the Trappist monks, Catholic missions expanded through the efforts of nuns from various religious orders who staffed a growing number of convent schools throughout the country. The Trappist mission, for example, relied heavily on the work of nuns in the religious order of the Sisters of the Precious Blood. The earliest arrivals, however, the Sisters of the Congregation of the Religious of the Assumption, were led by Mother M. Gertrude de Hennigsen. Coming to Natal from Paris in 1850, these sisters played a crucial role in the expansion of education, health care, and religious life in the Catholic Church (Young, 1989). Similarly, in the Transkeian Territories of the eastern Cape, the religious order of the Holy Cross Sisters, founded in Switzerland, was instrumental in the expansion of Catholic convents, schools, and orphanages (Dischl, 1982: 72–83). Providing staff for the mission schools, the teaching nuns of various religious orders assumed the primary responsibility for academic education.

Linked with agricultural and industrial training, this focus on education was largely responsible for the remarkable growth of the Catholic Church during the first half of the twentieth century. Catholic mission initiatives in southern Africa received strong support during that period from the Pope in Rome. In an Apostolic Letter in 1919, Pope Benedict urged Catholic missions all over the world to develop missions, schools, and seminaries for training local clergy. Those instructions were restated by Pope Pius XI in an encyclical letter of 1926. In South Africa, one of the most ardent proponents of Catholic mission education between 1920 and 1940 was Father Bernard Huss. Working in the eastern Cape and Natal, Father Huss proclaimed a Catholic message that was particularly adapted to the social and economic changes of the times. Born in Germany, Father Huss became a Trappist monk in Natal in 1895. He immediately devoted himself to the agricultural mission of the Trappists, teaching ploughing, soil conservation, and the dipping of livestock to prevent East Coast fever. So successful was Father Huss in convincing people to dip their livestock, against widespread objection to this practice, that a local magistrate told him, 'I am sorry that you are a priest, I would like to have you as a stock inspector' (Dischl, 1982: 175; Beinart and Bundy, 1987: 191–221).

In 1915 Father Huss became principal of the school at Mariannhill. Besides serving as administrator, Father Huss taught courses in religion (with separate classes for Catholics and Protestants), psychology, and agriculture. A prolific author, Father Huss published a series of textbooks in various fields, but each designed specifically for African students: *Psychology for Everyday Life for African Students* (1920), *Textbook on Agriculture* (1920), and *Elementary Economics for Native Students* (1924). Clearly, Father Huss perceived his religious and educational mission as also embracing the personal, social, and economic life of African converts. In an attempt to counteract the popularity of the Industrial and Commercial Workers Union in Natal and the eastern Cape during the 1920s, Father Huss in 1923 founded the Catholic African Economic and Social Organisation, which by 1927 was reorganized and renamed as the Catholic African Organisation. Bearing the motto – 'better homes, better fields, better hearts' – this Catholic society sponsored agricultural and industrial education, but also initiated cooperative credit unions in support of African farmers. Under increasingly difficult circumstances, Father Huss persisted throughout the 1930s in this religious and economic mission. In addition to his Christian gospel, Father Huss proclaimed a message of economic hope that he called the 'eight P's' – 'Poor People Proceed from Poverty to Power and Prosperity because they Paid the Price' (Schimlek, 1949: 98). In spite of his efforts, however, poor people became poorer in the African reserves. In 1948, the year that Father Bernard Huss died, the National Party government assumed power and embarked on policies that would contribute to the further impoverishment of those African reserves, which were eventually renamed homelands, in an apartheid South Africa.

Catholic education also suffered under the new National Party government. By 1948, the Catholic Church controlled 740 schools with over 85,000 pupils. In 1953, when the Catholic Church operated 15 per cent of all black schools, with over 111,000 pupils, the National Party government enacted legislation that drastically curtailed the operation of Catholic and other mission schools. The Bantu Education Act of 1953 legislated the government's educational policy of separate education for students classified into different racial groups. In addition, however, the Bantu Education Act cut off state subsidies to mission schools in order that the government might assume greater national control over education. On a mission of its own, the National Party government sought to capture the schools for its own program of Christian-National education. Expressly Protestant, Calvinist, and Afrikaner nationalist, the program of Christian-National education set out to convert all South African schools. But it placed a particular burden on Catholic schools and educators, many of whom perceived Christian-National education as a specifically anti-Catholic intervention by the government. Afrikaner nationalists, who had argued in the 1930s that communism and Catholicism posed greater threats than fascism or dictatorship, were by the 1950s in a position to express anti-Catholic sentiments as public policy. The National Party government's capture of schools for its own particular brand of Protestant religion, therefore, was only one dramatic instance of a religious agenda that after 1948 affected many other areas of South African public life (Abraham, 1989: 62–85).

MUSLIMS

Although Islam was restricted by law during the period of Dutch East India Company rule, the religion was nevertheless practiced by Muslim slaves, prisoners, and political exiles in the Cape. The most prominent political exile during the seventeenth century, the Indonesian religious and military leader, Shaykh Yusuf, arrived in the Cape in 1694 with a large escort, including perhaps as many as twelve other *imams*, or Muslim religious leaders. Shaykh Yusuf was an Indonesian nobleman, from Makassar, who had supported the Sultan Ageng in the 1650s in efforts to maintain political independence by breaking the Dutch monopoly on trade in Indonesia. In 1682 Shaykh Yusuf had led the Sultan's troops against the Dutch and their allies. Following Sultan Ageng's surrender in 1683, Shaykh Yusuf continued a campaign of guerrilla warfare against the Dutch until he was captured in 1686. After periods of imprisonment in Batavia and Ceylon, Shaykh Yusuf was exiled to the Cape, where he and forty-eight followers were kept on a farm called Zandvliet, which was owned by a Dutch Reformed Church minister, in an isolated area near the False Bay coast (Greyling, 1980; Dangor, 1982).

In spite of its remote location, the farm apparently became a meeting place for Muslim slaves and exiles in the colony. Since he had been the head of a Sufi order in Makassar, Shaykh Yusuf probably led his followers in the esoteric Islamic practices of Sufism (*tassawwuf*). Shaykh Yusuf's Sufi order, the *Khalwatiyyah* order, originally founded in Persia during the fourteenth century, was noted for performing mystical practices in seclusion. In common with other Sufi orders, Shaykh Yusuf would have led his followers in the practice of chanting the names and praises of Allah, a mystical practice known as *dhikr*, as a ritual for building up spiritual power. To the extent that Islam spread in the Cape during the seventeenth century, and most of the eighteenth century, it might have assumed the form of small, secret Sufi schools, or *tariqas*, that gathered around individual shaykhs (Bradlow, 1988). Evidence for such schools, however, is scarce. The influence of Shaykh Yusuf on the development of Islam in the Cape was extremely limited, not only by his isolation, but also by the fact that after his death in 1699 all but three of his followers were permitted to return to Indonesia. Initially entombed at Faure, near the Zandvliet farm, the body of Shaykh Yusuf was transported back to Indonesia for reburial at the request of the King of Goa in 1705.

Nevertheless, as the Catholic Bishop Griffith discovered in the 1830s, the tomb of Shaykh Yusuf became a popular Muslim pilgrimage site. By that time, however, Muslims in the Cape had been organized into a viable community. Although Shaykh Yusuf was not in any direct sense a founder of that community, Muslims in the Cape regarded his tomb as one of the holy places of an emerging Islamic sacred geography. By the 1800s, that holy place, like other sacred burial sites that would be located in the Cape, was referred to as a *karamat*, meaning a 'divine grace' in Arabic, but signifying a holy place of spiritual power in the Islamic world of South Africa (Jeffreys, 1934-39).

A large percentage of the growing Muslim community at the turn of the nineteenth century had experienced the bondage of slavery in the Cape. Although historians once assumed that Islam was transplanted from Indonesia to the Cape by slaves, the history of the rise of Islam depended on more complex local circumstances of conversion and community formation in the Cape. Although slaves and convicts played an important role in that process, an Islamic community in the Cape was not merely imported from Indonesia. Many, but not all, of the slaves taken from Indonesia and Malaya were Muslims. The Indonesian archipelago, however, supplied only about 15 per cent of the slaves in the Cape, with only about 1 per cent taken from Malaya. Since the rest of the slaves were brought from Bengal, the southern coast of India, Ceylon, Madagascar, and the east African coast, the religion of Cape slaves reflected the diversity of their different backgrounds (Bradlow and Cairns, 1978: 92; Ross, 1983). Perhaps of greater importance to the growth of Islam than the geographical point of origin of slaves was the 1770 law in the Cape that prevented Christian slaves from being bought or sold (Theal, 1897-1905, IX: 131-2). Reacting to this legislation, slaveowners tended to prevent their slaves from converting to Christianity. As a result, within a few years the benches reserved for slaves in the Groote Kerk in Cape Town were nearly empty (Marais, 1957: 168). Although some slaves were already Muslims, and others were attracted to the alternative offered by the Islamic faith, many apparently turned to Islam because they were prevented from becoming Christian. As the British government official William Wilberforce Bird noted concerning the slave in the Cape, 'some religion he must have and he is not allowed to turn Christian' (Bird, 1966: 349). By the time the law preventing buying and selling Christian slaves was repealed in 1812 it had created among the slave population of the Cape an interest in Islam that would contribute to the growth of a Muslim community in the early nineteenth century (Shell, 1974; Elphick and Shell, 1989: 191–4).

In addition to political exiles and slaves, convicts of the Dutch East India Company formed a third source of support for the growth of Islam. Company convicts, numbering about 1,000 from Indonesia between 1653 and 1767, accounted for an important avenue of entry for Muslims into the Cape. After serving their sentences, convicts were regarded by the Company government as 'free blacks.' Among those former convicts, some were Muslims who apparently organized secret meetings in private homes for religious worship. A visitor to the Cape in the 1770s observed that 'free blacks' and slaves 'weekly meet in a private house belonging to a free Mohammedan in order to read, or rather chant, several prayers and chapters from the Koran' (Forster, 1777, I: 60–1). At least one of these former convicts, the Imam Said Alochie, later known as Tuan Said, was a Muslim religious leader from Arabia. After serving eleven years imprisonment on Robben Island, off the Cape coast, Tuan Said ironically found employment as a policeman in Cape Town. Apparently, Imam Said took advantage of the freedom of movement offered by his position as a policeman to enter slave quarters for the purpose of preaching his Islamic faith.

The convict who played the most important role in the development of a Muslim community in the Cape was the Imam Abdullah Kadi Abdus Salaam, who came to be known as Tuan Guru (Lubbe, 1986a). Son of an Islamic Kadi, or judge, Tuan Guru grew up under the Dutch rule that had been established on the Indonesian island of Tidore since 1667. He was arrested by the Dutch East India Company, perhaps for conspiring to trade with the British, and imprisoned on Robben Island in 1780. Thirteen years later, in 1793, Tuan Guru was released. Almost immediately, the 81-year-old imam provided religious leadership for Muslims in the Cape, conducting open-air services in a stone quarry in Cape Town. By 1798, however, Tuan Guru had succeeded in founding the first mosque in South Africa, the Auwal Mosque in Cape Town, as the institutional center for an emerging Muslim community. But the mosque was also a new sacred axis of the world, as Tuan Guru declared that it 'must remain as long as the world stands' (Davids, 1980: 93–4). If there was a founder of Islam in South Africa, therefore, it was Tuan Guru, the organizer of the first Muslim community in Cape Town. Before Tuan Guru, Muslims might have organized in small *tariqas* around individual shaykhs; through his efforts, however, Muslims organized as an *'ummah*, a community of the faithful, around the institution of the mosque.

In addition to founding the first mosque, Tuan Guru also established the first Islamic school, or *madrassah*, as a base for conducting Muslim education in the Cape. So successful was the Muslim education initiated by Tuan Guru that by 1832 at least twelve schools were operating in Cape Town (Davids, 1989: 2). The foundation for Muslim religion and education was provided by the sacred text of the Qur'an. Tuan Guru had written several copies of the Qur'an from memory while imprisoned on Robben Island. Tuan Guru not only reproduced the Qur'an, but also provided guidance for its interpretation and application. As a follower of one of the four Islamic schools of law, the Shafi'i school, Tuan Guru wrote an authoritative text in Islamic jurisprudence, *Fiqa Kitaab*, that served as a guide for the ethical life and ritual practice of the emerging Islamic community in the Cape. As a result, Muslims in the Cape followed the Shafi'i school of Islamic law during the early nineteenth century. In addition to interpreting legal, ethical, and ritual rules of Islam, however, Tuan Guru's textbook of Islamic jurisprudence also included instruction in ritual formulas for mystical divination, for spiritual protection, and, most important, for ritual healing. Ritual formulas for healing, including the use of *Azeemats*, or amulets containing passages from the Qur'an to be worn on the body, formed an important part of the popular Islam practiced at the Cape under the inspiration of Tuan Guru.

When Tuan Guru died at the age of 95 in 1807, he left a legacy of religious worship, legal guidance, and spiritual healing that formed the foundation of Muslim life in the Cape. According to legend, Tuan Guru promised his Muslim community a spiritual protection, and a promise of political liberation, that was specific to its location in the Cape. Apparently, Tuan Guru instructed his followers:

> Be of good heart my children and serve your masters; for one day your liberty will be restored to you and your descendants will live within a circle of karamats safe from fire, famine and plague, earthquake and tidal wave.
>
> (Du Plessis, 1972: 33)

Buried on Signal Hill above Cape Town, Tuan Guru himself became an essential link in that 'circle of karamats' that constituted a Muslim community in the Cape during the nineteenth century.

By the time slavery was abolished in the Cape in 1838, as much as two-thirds of Cape Town's 'Non-European' population was Muslim (Shell, 1984: 32). In 1842, as that Islamic community continued to grow, there were 6,435 Muslims in Cape Town, accounting for over one-third of the total population of the city. Although by mid-century, Muslims in the Cape were referred to as 'Malays,' this was not by any means a racial or ethnic designation. In the 1860s, for example, an aristocratic English visitor to the Cape, Lucy Duff Gordon, noted that the term 'Malay' simply meant Muslim in the Cape. Rather than designating a racial or ethnic group, Lucy Duff Gordon observed, the term 'Malays' signified the Muslims of the Cape who 'embrace every shade, from the blackest [African] to the most blooming Englishwoman.' Lady Gordon reported that emigrant English girls in the Cape often married Muslims, thereby turning 'Malay,' in order to obtain husbands 'who know not billiards or brandy – the two diseases of Capetown.' Some European Christians, however, were horrified by what they perceived as illicit religious and racial mixing in the Cape. A leading expert on Islam in the 1870s, John Meuhleisen Arnold, declared that he found it 'a terrible sight to see a European face now and then in the streets of the metropolis dressed up as a Moslem.' Whatever racial considerations might have been at stake, however, many Christian leaders in Cape Town endeavored to limit the expansion of Islam in the middle of the nineteenth century (Shell, 1984: 5).

A Muslim festival in the Cape that attracted the attention of Christian municipal authorities in the middle of the nineteenth century was the ritual of Khalifa, also known as Ratiep, an annual celebration, perhaps of Hindu origin, that became associated with the birthday of Abu Bakr, the successor of the Prophet Muhammad. During that annual festival, Muslim devotees enacted a dramatic pageant that included ordeals of self-torture. In the Khalifa celebration, Muslim participants stuck sharp skewers or swords through their bodies, demonstrating an extraordinary spiritual endurance and power, but also, perhaps, providing an opportunity for Muslim slaves to exercise a power over their own bodies that had been denied in the slave system (Davids, 1980: 33). Municipal authorities in Cape Town, however, perceived this festival as a danger to public health. Accordingly, in 1856, the municipality of Cape Town banned the annual religious festival of Khalifa as 'dangerous to the law and peace of the community.' Arguing against the Khalifa festival, however, a writer in the *Cape Monthly Magazine* betrayed a Christian motive behind the restriction of a Muslim ceremony by arguing that the annual festival had been responsible for 'luring away potential converts from the pure and rational faith of Christians' (Shell, 1974: 38). The banning of the Khalifa festival in the 1850s initiated a new era of government interference in the religious practices of the Islamic community in the Cape. In the name of new municipal religious commitments to public health, law, and order, the Christian leadership of the city tried to contain the expansion of Islam in Cape Town.

In the arena of law and order, the growing number of Cape Town mosques occasionally became involved in controversies over leadership succession. In the 1860s, the Cape Colony government tried to settle those disputes by bringing in an expert in Islamic law from outside of South Africa. Contacting the Ottoman Empire, then under British rule, the Cape Colony found a Turkish Islamic legal expert who was willing to come to Cape Town and settle the disputes over the leadership of the various mosques in the city. In 1863, that Islamic legalist, Abubakr Effendi, arrived in Cape Town. Although expert in Islamic jurisprudence, Abubakr Effendi represented a different legal school, the Hanafii school, than the Shafi'i school of Islamic law that had been established in the Cape by Tuan Guru. Rather than resolving disputes, therefore, the introduction of Abubakr Effendi into the Cape Muslim community created a new conflict between two different schools of Islamic jurisprudence. Although he was established in a local mosque, gathered a following, and produced a new textbook in Islamic legal theory, the *Bayannuddin* (1873), financed by the Ottoman Empire, Abubakr Effendi's promotion of the Hanafii school of Islamic law created more problems than it solved in the Cape Muslim community. As only one instance of conflict, crayfish, providing not only a food source, but also an important business in the Cape, was declared *haram*, or ritually impure, by the Hanafi jurist. In addition to previous conflicts, therefore, the division between the Shafi'i majority and this new, powerful Hanafii minority between 1866 and 1900 resulted in as many as twenty internal Muslim conflicts over leadership of mosques becoming legal cases before the Cape Supreme Court (Davids, 1980: 52–4).

Public health measures taken by the municipality of Cape Town represented a second type of government intervention into the religious practices of Muslims. In particular, the Public Health Act of 1883 was applied by the city to close the Muslim cemetery in Cape Town. The municipal closing of a Muslim sacred site resulted in a mass demonstration of protest in January 1886 that was subdued by police action. Described as the 'riot of the Malays' in the local press, this protest was the culmination of years of conflict between the Muslim community and the Cape Town municipal authorities over issues of religion, law, and public health. The religious, legal, and medical dimensions of this conflict were clearly intertwined. Religion, law, and health had been connected in the work of the founder of the Cape Muslim community, Tuan Guru. The founder of the first mosque had left copies of the Qur'an, the religious foundation of the community. But he had also left a text of Islamic law and spiritual healing that suggested that religion, law, and medicine were interwoven in Muslim life. Likewise, municipal authorities in Cape Town also tried to create a community in which religion, law, and medicine were part of the same fabric of public order. Operating with a different image of public order, however, the municipality of Cape Town tried to enforce its definitions of religion, law, and health over Muslims living within its jurisdiction. As a result, a basic religious conflict in Cape Town during the nineteenth century appeared in terms of sanitation programs, medical care, and public health measures instituted by the municipality to enact its own religious worldview.

The city had developed various public health measures in the early 1800s to combat epidemics of smallpox. Vaccinations, isolation hospitals, and sanitation measures, including the use of limewash, chlorine, and vinegar for sanitizing houses, were introduced by the municipality to control the spread of disease. While medical practice remained rudimentary, these public health measures achieved some success in containing the spread of smallpox in the city. They were used in reaction to outbreaks of smallpox in 1834, 1840, and 1858, but not employed in disease prevention. Furthermore, they were not widely available in the sections of the city where people suffered from the poverty and overcrowding that made them more vulnerable to the spread of disease. In any event, most Muslims living in those areas resisted conforming to these alien methods of health care. Even when public health services were made available to them, most Muslims refused to have their bodies punctured by vaccination or to be confined in an isolation hospital, cut off from family, visits by religious leaders, access to the pure, Halal food required by Muslim law, or permission to perform Muslim burial rites for the deceased. Conflict over health care, therefore, was entangled in a conflict between two different religious ways of life. That religious conflict was suggested by the Anglican Dean of Cape Town, addressing a meeting of the Relief Committee for Smallpox Patients in 1858, when he advocated extending health care to Muslims as 'a means of softening their minds towards Christianity' (Davids, 1984: 69).

Conflict intensified, however, when the municipality enacted legal controls over religious rituals of death in the name of public health. In 1857 the Cape Town Cemeteries Bill was proposed that would have removed burial sites in the city from the control of religious organizations. But the objections of religious groups in the city defeated the proposed legislation. In response to the smallpox epidemic of the 1880s, however, a similar law was introduced. By that time, an ideology of sanitation had come to pervade the imaginations of Cape Town municipal authorities and the middle class, much as it had operated in Britain, Europe, and America. Sanitation represented the promise of a new urban world, cleansing the city of those twin evils – disease and crime – that threatened urban purity, law, and order. Revealing the religious content behind the ideology of sanitation, the editor of a local

Cape Town newspaper in 1882 declared: 'The Smallpox has come! The Angel of Vengeance of outraged Sanitation hangs over the city' (Davids, 1984: 59). However exaggerated, this vision of an avenging angel of sanitation suggested that a religious imagination was at work in the Public Health Act of 1883. Conflicting religious commitments were at stake in Muslim resistance to the Public Health Act.

Muslims resisted the Act's provision for closing their local cemetery, the Tana Baru. Not only did the Act violate a sacred site, but it in effect prevented Muslim funerals, which required carrying the body of the deceased from the home through the streets to the nearby burial ground. In response, the leader of the Muslim resistance, Abdol Burns, declared, 'religion is superior to the law' (Davids, 1984: 63). The Mayor of Cape Town, however, replied that he would not allow Muslims to dictate matters of law and public health in the city. Abdol Burns organized a Muslim political movement, the Malay Cemetery Committee, against the closure of the cemetery and the proposed relocation of a Muslim burial ground at some distance from the city. For several years, this movement tried without success to influence the policy of Cape Town through petitions, delegations, and demonstrations. Two days after the final closure of the Muslim cemetery in Cape Town, as many as 3,000 Muslims walked through the streets in a funeral procession in defiance of the government. When police arrived to exercise control, stone-throwing and violence ensued.

Muslims perceived police action not only as an act of provocation, but also as the desecration of a religious ritual and a sacred site. Over the days that followed, the police and army were called into action to contain violence but also to prevent Muslim burials. Finally, Abdol Burns and other Muslim leaders were arrested and sentenced to 2 months' imprisonment. Without the leadership of Abdol Burns, the Muslim community accepted a burial site outside of the city. But as the city expanded that site was also closed by municipal authorities on a similar pretext of public health in 1894. Clearly, the Muslim cemetery controversy during the second half of the nineteenth century involved the contending sides in conflicts over religion, law, and health. By the end of the century, however, municipal authorities had also begun to combat Muslims on racial grounds. As a Cape Town newspaper declared in 1882, 'the sooner the Malays are made to reside in a separate district the better for all concerned' (Davids, 1984: 73). The exclusion of the Muslim dead from the city, therefore, anticipated subsequent government policies that would enforce the residential separation of the Muslim living. During the second half of the twentieth century the segregation of Muslims living in the city, although justified along racial lines by the National Party government, would also invoke the municipal religious themes of sanitation, purity, and public health that had been important elements of the nineteenth-century Muslim cemetery controversy (Davids, 1980: 62–84; Bickford-Smith, 1981: 50–2).

By the beginning of the twentieth century, Muslims from India had established themselves as merchants and traders in Natal. This growing Muslim community, with its roots in India, distinguished itself from the large number of indentured laborers, who were mostly Hindu, that made up an Indian working class in Natal. To set themselves apart from Indian workers, Indian Muslim merchants and traders in Natal identified themselves as 'Arabs' (Ginwala, 1974: 136; Bhana and Brain, 1990: 66). This designation only contributed to the compounding ironies of racial classification in South Africa, particularly as those classifications affected Muslims. While 'Malays' in Cape Town were not from Malaysia, the 'Arabs' in Natal were not from Arabia. Further complicating the matter, former slaves from northern Mozambique, known as Zanzibaris, comprised Muslims, Roman Catholics, and adherents of ancestral African religion. Remaining an anomaly for government classification, most Zanzibaris were eventually labeled 'Other Asiatics,' while some found themselves arbitrarily classified as 'Coloured' or 'African' in the government's system of racial classification (Oosthuizen, 1985). Nevertheless, these new 'ethnic' identities became political realities in the twentieth century. Not only influencing the way local, provincial, and national government treated these 'ethnic' communities, new 'ethnic' identities provided rallying points for Muslim political organization.

In Natal, Muslim merchants and traders were instrumental in the formation of the Natal Indian Congress, a political movement initially deriving its support from and reflecting the economic interests of the 'Arabs.' In the Cape, in 1903, the short-lived South African Muslim's Association was founded. Twenty years later, the Cape Malay Association was formed, primarily as a welfare organization, but also as a political base for mobilizing Muslims. In addition to forming Muslim or Malay organizations, Muslim leaders played prominent roles in political movements in the so-called 'Coloured' politics in the Cape. For years, Dr Abdullah Abdurahman served as leader of the African Political (later, People's) Organization that provided a base for mobilizing people around the 'ethnic' designation of 'Coloured' (Davids, 1981; Goldin, 1987; Lewis, 1987).

For the most part, these political organizations sought cooperation with the government. In terms of Muslim religious interests, however, this cooperation required an accommodation to minority status in South Africa. Since they did not live in an Islamic state, Muslims in South Africa lived in what many regarded as an alien environment, a *Dar al Harb*, or 'House of War.' During the 1920s and 1930s, Muslim leaders generally recommended acceptance of this situation. Muslims were advised not to resist the government, as long as they were allowed to perform the basic requirements of their faith –

daily prayer, the poor tax, fasting, and pilgrimage to Mecca. Those who opposed the government should not fight against it but should emigrate to an Islamic country within the *Dar al Islam*, the 'House of Peace.' If they remained in South Africa, however, Muslims should obey the laws of the land and adapt their faith to a minority religious status.

This spirit of accommodation reached a high point in the widespread participation of Muslims in the Cape Malay Choir Board, formed in 1937 by the Afrikaner nationalist, I. D. Du Plessis. Although no Muslim leaders participated in the Board, the involvement of Muslims resulted in the formation of twenty-six choirs by 1945 competing in an annual 'Malay' festival. In addition to serving as President for Life of the Choir Board, I. D. Du Plessis published books and articles on the 'Cape Malay', even lobbying the University of Cape Town for the creation of a 'Department of Malay Studies'. As an 'expert' on the language, religion, and culture of the 'Cape Malay', Du Plessis contributed heavily to the redefinition of 'Malay' as an ethnic designation in terms of the larger racialist scheme of apartheid (Du Plessis, 1944; 1953).

As a member of the secret society, the Afrikaner Broederbond, I. D. Du Plessis directed his ideological and organizational work toward reinforcing a separate ethnic identity for Cape Muslims. In 1952, however, the Cape Malay Choir Board lost community support when Du Plessis planned to involve the choirs in government celebrations for the three-hundredth anniversary of the arrival of Jan van Riebeeck. Nevertheless, I. D. Du Plessis continued to exercise an influence over the Muslim community. Under the National Party government's scheme for residential apartheid, Du Plessis in 1950 succeeded in having the section of Cape Town in which most Muslims lived, the BoKaap, declared a 'Group Area for the Malays.' Three years later, as an administrator of the 'Coloured Affairs Department,' Du Plessis insisted that an area near False Bay, the site of Shaykh Yusuf's tomb, should also become a group area for the 'Malays.' Although he admitted that the land was 'sandy, bushy, [and] partly waterlogged,' Du Plessis declared that 'Malays' should live there because it was the original home of the 'founder of Islam in South Africa' (Jeppe, 1988: 24). Reinterpreting the history of Islam in South Africa in ethnic terms, I. D. Du Plessis appropriated that history to serve the National Party government's design for racial apartheid.

Muslim organizations, however, did advance a moderate resistance to this government policy of cooptation. In 1945, the Muslim Judicial Council was formed in the interests of Muslim unity, but also to voice a protest against oppressive laws and government policies. According to its original statement of purpose, the Muslim Judicial Council was founded 'in the interests of all Non Europeans, who should at all times, irrespective of race or creed, join forces against the oppressive forces which are endeavouring to retard their progress in all spheres in this country' (*Cape Standard* 3 April 1945). The Muslim Judicial Council played an important role in Muslim religious and social life. However, political opposition to the government assumed stronger forms in other organizations, particularly in the emergence of militant Islamic movements in the 1980s that rejected the legitimacy of the National Party government. In response to the apartheid 'pluralism' of separate groups, based on separate ethnic, cultural, or religious identities, many Muslims joined with Protestants, Catholics, Hindus, Jews, and others during the 1980s in forming a plural religious front against the enforced, divisive 'pluralism' of apartheid (Davids, 1985).

HINDUS

Nineteenth-century immigrants from India entered southern Africa either as indentured laborers or as free British subjects looking for economic opportunity. Between 1860 and 1866, over 6,000 people from India entered the country to serve as indentured laborers on the expanding sugar plantations in Natal. The majority of indentured workers were low-caste Hindus, primarily Tamil or Telegu speakers from southern India. But they did not all come from a common background. Some came from northern or central India, speaking Gujarati or Hindi as their home languages. Although over 80 per cent were Hindu, Muslims made up 12 per cent and Christians 5 per cent of the first Indian immigrants in Natal. About one-quarter of these indentured immigrants were women. By the time recruitment of indentured labor from India had stopped in 1911, a total of about 150,000 Indian workers had entered the country. Two-thirds of this population were Tamil- or Telegu-speaking Hindus from southern India. Having served their contracted period of labor, many of these workers decided to remain in South Africa, settling primarily in Natal, but also in other urban centers throughout the country (Thompson, 1952).

Evidence of Hindu religious practices among Indian workers in the nineteenth century is scarce. But an 1874 article on the Indian way of life among workers on the diamond mines, published in the Kimberley *Diamond Field Advertiser*, suggested that at least some of the workers practiced forms of Hindu devotion. As the Christian author of this article noted, with transparent disdain, some workers on the mines could be heard 'chanting their devotions in the whine of primitive piety' (Bhana and Brain, 1990: 101). Although the author of this article failed to appreciate the practice of Hindu prayer, he nevertheless noted that it was not uncommon. Probably, therefore, many of the Hindu workers, during and after their periods of indenture, found ways to perform some of the prayers, offerings, and services that represented the popular devotional practices they had known in southern India. However, the workers lacked the financial resources to support households, temples, or priests that would have provided their devotional religion with a visible organization.

Initial financial support was largely provided by a second group of immigrants from India who came as traders, merchants, or entrepreneurs. As a distinct social class, often further distinguished from the class of indentured laborers by language and religion, free British subjects who immigrated to southern Africa were known as 'passenger' Indians. Most of the free immigrants were Gujarati Muslims, but there were also Hindus among this population of 'passengers.' They tended to be higher-caste Hindus, including some of the priestly class, who spoke Gujarati or Hindi as home languages (Palmer, 1957). Beginning with the first Hindu temple in 1869, Indian immigrants gradually were able to acquire land and build a growing number of temples in Durban, Pietermaritzburg, Port Elizabeth, Johannesburg, and Pretoria. By the turn of the century, Hindu religious life had thereby established a more secure base in South Africa.

Due to the divisions of social class, home language, and region of origin, the Hindu religion in South Africa remained extremely diverse. If regarded as a single religion, Hinduism has often been characterized by diversity, apparently embracing many gods, many religious practices, and many different forms of organization. Scholars have often insisted that the only thing that has unified the diversity of Hindu religion has been the caste system, the complex traditional system of social classes and inter-group relations. In its basic division of social classes, this system drew a line that separated priestly, ruling, and householding classes from a subordinate class of workers. According to priestly authority, embodied in the texts of the *Dharmashastra*, especially the *Laws of Manu*, only the upper three classes could participate fully in religious ritual. But the caste system has not featured prominently in the lives of South African Hindus. Obviously, lower-caste Hindus who arrived as indentured laborers had no interest in perpetuating a system of social classes that excluded them. Furthermore, the effects of immigrating into new urban environments dramatically changed the class relations of all Hindus. Therefore, not even the traditional class or caste system unified Hinduism as a single religion in South Africa (Rambiritch and van den Berghe, 1961).

Arguably, however, the very notion of Hinduism as a single religion was a nineteenth-century invention that emerged under the pressures of European colonialism, the scrutiny of European scholars, and the creative innovations of leaders of what came to be called Neo-Hinduism. Originating in nineteenth-century India, several important Neo-Hindu movements had a definite impact on Hindu religion in South Africa.

For example, the religious movement, Ārya Samaj, formed in Bombay,

India in 1875 by Swami Dayanand Saraswati, proclaimed Hinduism as a single religion that was based on the ancient collection of sacred texts, the Vedas. Calling all Hindus 'back to the Vedas,' which Swami Dayanand Saraswati understood as a single authoritative text, analogous to the Christian Bible, the Ārya Samaj reform movement eliminated all of the religious images and most of the rituals that had been important to religious practices in India. Instead, Ārya Samaj developed a system of belief, worship, and ethics that was based on the existence of one deity, the creator and sustainer of the universe. Introduced from India, this Hindu reform movement inspired the formation of several Ārya Samaj organizations in South Africa. In 1925, most of these organizations came under the centralized coordination of a national Ārya Samaj association, the Ārya Pratinidhi Sabhā, which was established in Durban. As a Neo-Hindu monotheism, therefore, Ārya Samaj defined what Hinduism meant to many Hindus in South Africa (Naidoo, 1985).

Likewise, another Neo-Hindu movement that stressed monotheism, the Śaiva Siddanta Sangum of South Africa, was founded in 1937 by Guru Swamigal. Although it referred back to ancient religious practices devoted to Lord Shiva, which were forms of worship primarily based in the traditions of Tamil- and Telegu-speaking people in southern India, the Saiva Siddanta Sangum was a Neo-Hindu movement that proclaimed Shiva as the single, Supreme God of all religions. In this movement as well, Hinduism was understood by Hindu devotees as a single, monotheistic religion (Pillay *et al.*, 1989: 156).

By contrast, other Neo-Hindu religious movements drew their primary inspiration not from the Vedas but from the Upanishads, a collection of ancient texts that supported the religious insight that every human being is divine. These movements were known as Vedantic, a term meaning 'after the Vedas,' indicating that they were grounded in the post-Vedic texts of the Upanishads and their central religious claim that the self (*atman*) can be recognized as equivalent to the sacred power that pervades the universe (*brahman*). As a Vedantic Neo-Hindu movement, the Ramakrishna Mission of Swami Vivekananda built a following in South Africa. Based in Durban, the Ramakrishna Centre of South Africa, founded in 1942, promoted the recognition of the divinity of every human being as a basis for both personal spirituality and social responsibility (Sooklal, 1988).

With a similar purpose, a center for the Vedantic movement known as the Divine Life Society, founded in India by Swami Śivananda, was formed in 1949 in Durban (Singh, 1986). Unlike the monotheism of the Ārya Samaj, these Vedantic Neo-Hindu movements supported what might be called a monism, recognizing that all life, including every human being, was one with the divine. They also tended to argue for the unity of all religions, with each religion representing a different path to the one goal of God-realization. In either case, whether monotheist or monist, Neo-Hindu movements in South Africa relied on sacred texts and religious education that distinguished them from the more broadly based, popular forms of religion in which most South African Hindus participated.

In contrast to the Neo-Hindu movements, most Hindus in South Africa participated in a religious life that revolved around rituals in the home, the temple, and the annual festivals of a sacred calendar. In South Africa, this basic form of Hindu religious practice has been called Sanatanist, a term derived from the *sanatana dharma*, or 'eternal way.' Drawing inspiration from the myths, legends, and stories of the gods collected in the popular Hindu texts of the Puranas, Sanatanists practiced a religious way of life that they regarded as traditional. Although it was most visible in the temples devoted to various deities, such as Vishnu, Shiva, or the many forms of the Mother Goddess, and especially in annual public festivals, this form of religion was most intimately integrated into the daily life of the Hindu household (Kuppusami, 1983).

Based in the home, this Hindu religious practice required prayers, offerings, and other domestic rituals to be performed by the head of every household. A fire ritual, with prayers and offerings, and the daily lighting of a sacred lamp were important rites of Hindu worship in the home. But other domestic rituals were practiced, such as the *katha* (legend) or *jhanda* (flag-pole) rite, which required the erection of a flag on a bamboo pole and the recitation of stories illustrating the victory of good over evil, usually in fulfillment of a vow undertaken to obtain blessing or healing. Although supervised by a priest, this ritual was performed for the benefit of a specific household. At its most basic level, therefore, this form of Hindu religion was interwoven in the relations of marriage, children, and daily rituals that constituted a household.

In the early twentieth century, however, this religion of the home was threatened by a South African judicial system that refused to recognize the legality of Hindu marriage. By ruling Hindu marriages illegal, South African courts intervened in Hindu religious life based in the household. The position of South African courts in the early twentieth century had been anticipated by earlier legislation, such as Cape Act 16 of 1860 and Natal Act 19 of 1881, that had appointed marriage officers for Jews and Muslims, but had made no provision for Hindus. Although the Indian Immigration Act of 1891 recognized the marriages of indentured and free Indians who entered the country, the legality of Hindu marriages performed in Natal remained open to question. That question was settled by a series of court cases in 1912 and 1913. In 1912 a South African court ruled that all polygynous marriages, permitted in both Hindu and Muslim practice, were illegal in South Africa. More decisively, during the following year a South African court ruled that only marriages performed by Christian rites or by a civil marriage officer were legal. In the eyes of the law, therefore, the marriage relation that formed the basis for the religious life of a Hindu household was illegal in South Africa. As a result, the issue of marriage, an essentially religious issue, propelled many Hindus, especially large numbers of Hindu women, into an organized movement of resistance in 1913 against the discriminatory laws of the South African government (Ginwala, 1974: 196–8).

In addition to the household, the Sanatanist religious practices of most South African Hindus were anchored in the sacred sites of temples (Mikula *et al.*, 1982). Devoted to specific deities, Hindu temples were built not only in Natal but also in cities all over South Africa. Temples provided sacred sites for the priests and devotees of various Hindu deities, but they also tended to attract support from different segments of the Hindu population. For example, in Pietermaritzburg, Shiva temples were supported by a primarily Tamil-speaking constituency, while Vishnu temples were primarily supported by Hindi speakers. Divisions based on language, therefore, persisted in the formation of religious congregations. Nevertheless, there were forms of temple worship that cut across linguistic divisions, such as the widespread appeal of the Mother Goddess, particularly in the form of the Mother Mariamma (Mariyammai), who received the prayers, offerings, and pilgrimages of many Hindu devotees (Buijs, 1980).

The temples were less bases for congregations than they were sites for annual ceremonies that celebrated a sacred calendar of Hindu festivals. Although the Tamil and Telegu sacred calendar differed from the Gujarati and Hindi, all Hindus who identified with temples celebrated annual festivals, such as the Deepavali or Diwali (festival of lights), the Krishna Jayanti (birthday of Krishna), and the Shivarathri (night of Shiva). One of the most dramatic annual festivals, known as Kavadi, involved dramatic displays of spiritual power. Going into trance, participants demonstrated their devotion and power, some by piercing their tongues with sharp skewers, others by carrying pictures of deities through the streets, many by dancing, singing, and chanting the names and praises of God in a state of ecstasy. Celebrated in Durban, the Kavadi festival drew thousands of Hindu celebrants every year (Kuper, 1959; Naidoo, 1981).

Temples and annual festivals, therefore, represented Hindu resources of alternative spiritual power in South Africa. In the early twentieth century, however, these alternative sites of Hindu religious power occasionally came into conflict with the South African government. For example, a group of prosperous Hindus in 1900 applied to the Cape Colony for permission to purchase land for the purpose of building a temple. Their spokesman, K. Samy, informed the colonial government that the Hindus required ownership of the land, rather than a temporary lease, if they were to build a temple. Once the temple was consecrated, it had to remain as a permanent sacred site in the possession of the Hindu community. 'According to our religious rites,' Samy wrote, 'all buildings which are erected for places of worship cannot be disposed of or pass from us, as would be the case on the termination of the present lease.' Struggling against the reluctance of the Cape government to grant land to Indians, Samy entered into a conflict over legal entitlement to land that would persist throughout the twentieth century.

Although the Cape, like other colonial governments in South Africa, tended to regard Indians as resident aliens, K. Samy spoke on behalf of most Hindus in the country by proclaiming loyalty to the British Empire. 'What the Hindoo community wants,' Samy declared, 'is a piece of ground which they could hold as long as the English flag waves in this town.' Denied permission to purchase the land they wanted, Samy and his Hindu constituency finally settled on another site for their temple in Port Elizabeth. Others, like the British Hindoo Mauritian Society, in 1902, were simply denied permission to purchase land and build temples (Bhana and Brain, 1990: 113). Nevertheless, like K. Samy, many Hindus in early twentieth-century South Africa continued to argue that they were citizens of the British Empire and persisted in appealing to what they regarded as British ideals of social justice in support of their religion.

In 1900, K. Samy might have thought that the British flag would fly over his town of Port Elizabeth forever. But 10 years later a different flag flew over Hindus and everyone else in the new Union of South Africa. Another Hindu, however, Mohandas K. Gandhi, continued to appeal to what he regarded as the eternal ideals of British Empire – citizenship, and justice – until he finally rejected them for new ideals of God and India (Wilson, 1986).

While studying law in London between 1888 and 1891, Gandhi was exposed to aspects of Neo-Hinduism that became important in the formation of his religious worldview. First, he joined the London Vegetarian Society, demonstrating a commitment to the principle of *ahimsa*, or harmlessness, in human relations with animal life. In his later political work, Gandhi adapted that principle of harmlessness as a principled non-violence in the struggle for social change. Second, he attended lectures of the Theosophical Society, a society that might be regarded as a Neo-Hindu movement because it relied on the Vedantic insight that every soul is divine. From the lectures of the leader of the Theosophical Society in London, Annie Besant, Gandhi was introduced to the notion of a spiritual 'Truth' that revealed the divine power of the soul. In his later political work, Gandhi defined that truth as *satyagraha*, the 'truth force,' or 'soul power,' that could be mobilized through spiritual discipline and utilized in the political arena. Finally, while in London, Gandhi read widely in popular English translations of Hindu and Buddhist sacred texts. Particularly in the versions provided by the translator, Edwin Arnold, Gandhi became familiar with the *Bhagavad Gita*, the life of the Buddha, and selections from the Upanishads. Arguably, therefore, Gandhi became a Hindu in London, incorporating aspects of Neo-Hinduism – the principle of non-violence, the divinity of the soul, and the unity of all religions – into his own religious worldview (Hay, 1989).

From 1893 to 1914, Gandhi practiced law in South Africa. But he also played an active role in political campaigns against the governments of Natal, the Transvaal, and, after 1910, the Union of South Africa (Huttenback, 1971). Initially, Gandhi based his political action on moral appeals to principles of British justice, claiming civil rights for Indians in South Africa as free subjects of the British Empire. In this respect, he had much in common with black Christian leaders of the early African National Congress, who appealed to 'Christianity and Civilization' as the foundation of British justice. However, Gandhi saw no common ground with black political struggles in South Africa, even noting in 1909 regarding blacks that 'there is no common ground between them and us in the daily affairs of life' (Gandhi, 1958, IX: 149). Gandhi's appeals for civil rights and the removal of discriminatory legislation, therefore, were made solely on behalf of the Indian community.

Furthermore, within the class divisions of that community, Gandhi was clearly aligned with the economic interests of the successful traders and merchants represented by the Natal Indian Congress. Since the commercial elite was mostly Muslim, with a few, higher-caste Hindus from northern India, Gandhi's ideology of the unity of all religions supported Hindus and Muslims joining in a common cause, even if that common ground did not necessarily include the majority of Indian workers in Natal. Representing the legal and economic interests of the commercial elite from the 1890s, Gandhi gradually replaced British nationalism with Indian nationalism as a unifying religious ideology. With the loss of support from Indian merchants in 1908, however, Gandhi began to formulate and promote a new unifying ideology that transcended religious and social divisions.

By 1907 Gandhi had become convinced of the failure of his appeals to British nationalism to exact concessions from government, as well as the failure of his appeals to Indian nationalism to mobilize the merchant class, unless it served its self-interest. In place of nationalism, Gandhi formulated a new religious ideology for his campaign by proclaiming 'the strength of Truth, otherwise spelt God' (Gandhi, 1958, VIII: 52). In place of self-interest, Gandhi proclaimed a spiritual truth of self-sacrifice. Small numbers of passive resisters were inspired by this new religious ideology to defy discriminatory laws and face arrest. Mass resistance, however, was only mobilized in 1913 when a major grievance of workers – the £3 poll tax – was finally made part of the passive resistance campaign. The strikes and protests of 1913, therefore, were largely responsible for the government's Act 22 of 1914, known as the 'Indian Relief Bill.' The act abolished the poll tax and extended legal recognition to Indian marriages. However, the 'Relief Bill' did not satisfy the merchants because it did nothing to remove the restrictions on residence, travel, and commerce that had been the major grievances of the commercial elite (Swan, 1985; 1987). Nevertheless, Gandhi interpreted the act as a victory for the spiritual power of Truth or God that was made possible by the disciplined non-violence, self-sacrifice, and 'soul power' of thousands of people during the passive resistance campaign (Gandhi, 1928).

Leaving South Africa a few weeks after the Indian Relief Bill became law, Gandhi embarked on his successful religious and nationalist campaign in India. In South Africa, however, subsequent attempts at passive resistance organized by the Natal Indian Congress and the Transvaal Indian Congress during the 1930s and 1940s failed to produce results (Mesthrie, 1989). But during the early 1950s the Defiance Campaign sponsored by the African National Congress did draw widespread support for passive resistance. Although not directly inspired by Gandhi, the Defiance Campaign nevertheless employed Gandhian strategies of resistance in which protesters intentionally violated unjust laws, faced imprisonment, and maintained a disciplined non-violence. Unlike Gandhi's political program, the Defiance Campaign found Hindus in a common cause with blacks in resisting oppression. Among the leaders of the campaign, Hindus were represented by the pacifist philosopher Nana Sita and by Manilal Gandhi, the son of Mahatma Gandhi. By the time the Defiance Campaign was launched in 1952, therefore, new alliances were being drawn across religious lines in opposition to the apartheid government of South Africa (Kuper, 1957).

JEWS

Because of the small number of Jews living in the Cape at the beginning of the nineteenth century, De Mist's *Kerkenordre* of 1804 did not immediately affect Jewish public worship. Not until 1841 was the first Jewish congregation assembled in Cape Town. During the 1840s, attendance for Friday evening and Saturday Sabbath services remained small. The synagogue was finally consecrated and opened for worship in 1849. A Jewish community of about sixty families was initially ministered to by Rabbi Isaac Pulver, and after 1859 by Rabbi Joel Rabinowitz, both coming from London. In English, the congregation was called 'The Society of the Jewish Community of Cape Town, Cape of Good Hope.' Perhaps as a pun on its location, however, its Hebrew name was *Tikvath Israel*, 'Hope of Israel.' Although small in membership, the synagogue in Cape Town represented a religious center for the people of Israel in the Cape of Good Hope (Herrman, 1930: 114–46; 191).

As a result of immigration from 1880 to 1914, centers of Jewish life rapidly expanded. The Jewish population in South Africa increased from 4,000 to 40,000 in less than 35 years. In Cape Town expansion was supervised by A. P. Bender, who served the Cape Town synagogue for 42 years (Geffen, 1955: 47). Opposing international efforts to establish a Jewish homeland led by the Zionist movement, Bender concentrated on building up a community that was firmly based in the Cape. But other centers of Jewish life also emerged in South Africa. During the boom in the ostrich feather industry, serving the tastes of the European fashion market at the end of the nineteenth century, the town of Oudtshoorn became a center of Jewish settlement, even known as the 'Jerusalem of South Africa.' An Oudtshoorn synagogue was built in 1888, but the Jewish community was large, prosperous, and divided enough to build another synagogue in 1896. With changes in European fashion, however, the ostrich feather industry and the Jewish community at Oudtshoorn both declined at the beginning of the twentieth century (Hellig, 1987: 6; Aschman, 1955). But the largest center of Jewish life emerged in and around the gold-mining city of Johannesburg. During the large-scale immigration between 1880 and 1914, about 50 per cent of the Jews who arrived in South Africa settled in Johannesburg. By 1980 Johannesburg still accounted for about half of the 125,000 Jews in the country, with 25 per cent in Cape Town and the rest primarily based in other urban areas. The history of Jews in Johannesburg, therefore, best illustrates the process of Jewish community formation in South Africa. As elsewhere in the diaspora, Jewish religious life in South Africa was based on the authority of the Torah, or written law, the guidance of the oral law, and the observance of the ritual and ethical duties that comprised the halakha. Beginning in the 1880s, the small number of Jews from English, German, or Dutch backgrounds were joined in South Africa by immigrants from Lithuania (Gershater, 1955). One hundred years later, most of the Jewish population in South Africa was descended from these Lithuanian immigrants. Not merely attracted to economic opportunity in Africa, Lithuanian immigrants fled the political domination and antisemitic persecutions under which they had suffered in Russian-controlled Lithuania. Many brought with them forms of religious learning and piety that produced a distinctive character of orthodoxy in South Africa. In addition, however, Lithuanian Jews had lived in the midst of political and economic turmoil in eastern Europe that had produced a number of important social movements. In particular, many Lithuanian immigrants were aligned with either the labor movement or the political movement for a Jewish state that was known as Zionism. With different agendas, these movements focused basic divisions in the Jewish community in South Africa.

At the turn of the century in Johannesburg, the most basic factor that divided Jews was social class. As the city expanded from 3,000 prospectors in the 1880s to 250,000 residents by 1913, Jews represented about 10 per cent of the population. They were highly visible in the two most extreme positions of social class in the city. Among the highest class, Jews held prominent positions in the Johannesburg elite of mining capitalists, successful merchants, and civic leaders. At the lower reaches of the social scale, however, most Lithuanian immigrants suffered from extreme poverty. Within the poor underclass of the city, Lithuanian Jews were noted for their involvement in illegal liquor trading and prostitution, even acquiring an 'ethnic' designation in Johannesburg as 'Peruvians.' Just as there were 'Malays' in Cape Town who were not from Malaysia, and 'Arabs' in Natal who were not from Arabia, Johannesburg at the turn of the century had nearly 7,000 'Peruvians' who were not from Peru. Victims of poverty, these Jewish immigrants, as the historian Charles van Onselen has noted, were also 'the unhappy recipients of the most vicious class and race prejudice that society could muster' (Van Onselen, 1982: I: 74). In Johannesburg, Jewish community formation was aimed directly at redeeming this lower class of 'Peruvians' from poverty and crime.

After the South African War (1899–1902), the Jewish Board of Deputies of the Transvaal was formed to address the problem of community formation. Founded in 1903 by middle-class Jewish civic leaders, the Jewish Board of Deputies set out to redefine the role of Jews in the reconstruction of Johannesburg society. As an indication that the middle-class leaders of the Board of Deputies identified with British rule in South Africa, they invited imperial governor Lord Alfred Milner to speak at the board's opening. Milner was a significant choice as a speaker. In 1899 Milner had complained about the 'low class of Jews known as "Peruvians."' He had argued that Jewish immigrants from eastern Europe were 'wholly undesirable... [a] danger to the health, as well as to the resources of good order of British South Africa' (Cammack, 1982: 248). A year before the founding of the Jewish Board of Deputies, Milner had been instrumental in the drafting of the 1902 Alien Immigration Act that was targeted at restricting the entry of these 'Peruvians' (Shain, 1980; 1984). In his address at the launch of the Jewish Board of Deputies, speaking to a gathering that represented Jews affiliated with the four, major Johannesburg congregations, Milner restated his aversion to the immigrants. In principle, he argued, Judaism was not incompatible with British patriotism, but only if Jews abandoned the lifestyles associated with Russia, Poland, or Lithuania. If they abandoned the ways of eastern Europe, Lord Milner promised the Jews of Johannesburg that they would be admitted to what he regarded as 'the greatest benefit of all, the high privileges of British citizenship' (Saron, 1955a: 240–1; Krut, 1987: 147).

Clearly, the leadership of the Jewish Board of Deputies agreed that

Judaism should be aligned with British citizenship. Accepting Milner's terms, the Board of Deputies conducted a campaign against the 'Peruvians' on two fronts. First, supporters of the board, such as the *South African Jewish Chronicle*, waged a public relations campaign to identify a Jewish community that was aligned with white supremacy in South Africa. A 1905 editorial in the *Chronicle*, for example, declared that the 'Jews of the Transvaal, if they wish to live up to their name, are pledged to maintain the superiority of the white man in this country.' Since Lithuanian immigrants, as the editorial argued, stood 'on the border-line between white and coloured,' the 'Peruvians' posed a problem in the formation of a totally white Jewish community (Krut, 1987: 150). Through its publications, however, the Jewish Board of Deputies argued that the 'Peruvians' were capable of 'assimilation' into a completely white Jewish community in Johannesburg within the next generation. Second, therefore, to assist that assimilation, the Jewish Board of Deputies set up committees to provide patronage and support for immigrants and to police those who were involved in illegal liquor trading, prostitution, or other criminal activity. For their part, Lithuanian immigrants tended to respond to this intervention, with its promises of self-improvement, stable family life, and a supportive community. By 1912, when a national organization, the South African Jewish Board of Deputies, was formed, the basic pattern for a mainstream Jewish community in South Africa had been set. By suppressing elements of its immigrant heritage, that mainstream Jewish community could be characterized as white, English-speaking, middle-class, urban, and upwardly mobile (Shimoni, 1980: 8; Krut, 1987: 137). On those terms, the Jewish Board of Deputies continued to defend a place for Jews in South Africa.

Alternatives to this definition of a Jewish community, however, were provided by two political movements, Zionism and socialism. Led by Theodor Herzl, and by his successor, David Wolffsohn, following Herzl's death in 1904, Zionism was an international movement that mobilized support for a Jewish homeland in Palestine. Although the movement evoked a Jewish nationalism, it also drew on religious motives by appealing to a perennial Jewish theme of redemption through returning to Israel. In South Africa, that redemptive aspect of Jewish Zionism was stressed by the movement's most important leader, Samuel Goldreich (Shimoni, 1980: 21–4). Arguing that Zionism was Judaism at its best, Goldreich was instrumental in forming several Zionist associations in South Africa that were committed to the political and religious goal of achieving a Jewish state in Palestine. Samuel Goldreich adhered to Herzl's approach to Zionism, often called 'political Zionism,' that insisted that the purpose of the movement was to obtain a legal charter for a Jewish state before beginning large-scale settlement. This political line, however, conflicted with the objectives of the Jewish Board of

Deputies in establishing a community that was firmly settled in South Africa. Therefore, the Jewish Board of Deputies, in its ongoing attempts to create a Jewish community that was aligned with South African nationalism, tried to undercut the political implication of Jewish Zionism. Instead of the 'political Zionism' that advocated the ultimate emigration of all Jews to a Jewish state, implying thereby that Jews were only temporary residents in South Africa, the Board of Deputies promoted a 'practical Zionism' designed to build and defend a Jewish community that was firmly grounded in South Africa (Krut, 1987: 148).

Although this conflict between the 'political' and the 'practical' was not entirely resolved, Zionism, in one form or another, continued to be an integral part of Jewish religious life in South Africa. The most vocal opposition to Zionism among Jews, however, came from the socialist movement. During the 1920s and 1930s, Jewish socialist organizations attracted a considerable number of eastern European immigrants. Although they were Jewish, they did not fit the mainstream image of a Jewish community that was being cultivated by the Jewish Board of Deputies. Rather than English-speaking, middle-class, and upwardly mobile, the membership of Jewish socialist organizations tended to be Yiddish-speaking, working class, and exploited by the harsh working conditions in Johannesburg. In particular, the Johannesburg Jewish Workers' Club provided an organizational base for workers, but also an association for celebrating the Yiddish culture of the Jewish working class. In response to Zionism, the Jewish Workers' Club argued that the creation of a Jewish state would be controlled by capitalist and imperialist interests that could only be expected to continue exploiting workers. Against the 'political Zionists' who argued that the problems of Jews could only be solved by the creation of a Jewish state, the Jewish Workers' Club insisted that their problems could only be solved by a socialist reorganization of South African society. Since that proposal also conflicted with the 'practical Zionism' of the Jewish Board of Deputies, which was middle-class, capitalist, and South African nationalist, the Jewish Workers' Club clearly stood outside of the mainstream Jewish community that the Board was trying to build (Adler, 1979).

Jews in South Africa, therefore, were obviously divided. But those divisions were blurred in the racialist imaginations of South Africans who adhered to the quasi-religious ideology of antisemitism. Occasionally surfacing in the press and public discourse, the antisemitic imagination depicted Jews in terms of negative stereotypes, whether as international capitalists, subversive socialists, or undesirable immigrants. Nevertheless, those antisemitic sentiments were rarely given the force of law. Like Roman Catholics, Jews in the Transvaal Republic under Paul Kruger had been denied civil rights and access to positions in civil service or education. Under the Union government formed in 1910, however, those civil disabilities were removed. Legislation against Jews, however, took the form of immigration restrictions and quotas, particularly targeted against eastern European immigrants. The restriction of Jewish immigrants was especially advocated in the 1930s and 1940s by Afrikaner nationalists of the National Party.

As we will see in the next chapter, some Afrikaner nationalists in the 1930s adopted racialist ideas and policies that were current in Nazi Germany. During the 1930s and 1940s, antisemitism formed part of an Afrikaner nationalist ideology that promised power and purity to a white, Christian, Afrikaans-speaking nation. For example, in 1930 Minister of the Interior D. F. Malan, later to become Prime Minister of South Africa in 1948, introduced a new immigration quota act that was primarily targeted at restricting the entry of eastern European Jews. In defending this act, D. F. Malan argued that limiting eastern European immigrants was required by three nationalist principles. First, he claimed that every nation desired to maintain its basic racial composition. Second, indicating that his understanding of racial composition did not allow for diversity, Malan insisted that every nation should be 'homogeneous.' On that basis, only immigrants who could demonstrate 'assimilability' ought to be admitted. Third, Malan declared that South Africa had to maintain its distinctive 'type' of 'civilization,' which was, he claimed, western, not eastern European. The Quota Act of 1930 had the effect of reducing the number of Jewish immigrants into South Africa (Saron, 1955b: 378–9).

German Jews, not from a country restricted under the Act, were still able to enter South Africa in the mid–1930s. In 1937, however, the antisemitic motive behind immigration restrictions was made transparent with the repeal of the Quota Act and the passage of the Aliens Act, which clearly specified 'assimilability' as a qualification for immigrants. Under the Aliens Act, Jewish immigration was further reduced. But there were Afrikaner nationalists who felt that restrictions on Jews were not sufficiently strict. Even when most European Jews became trapped in Europe by the Second World War, D. F. Malan's National Party called for a total ban on Jewish immigration. The National Party election manifesto of 1938, adopted again by the Federal Council of the National Party in 1941, bluntly advocated the 'immediate cessation of all further immigration of Jews.' In the name of 'Christian Civilization,' the National Party labeled Jews a 'dangerous alien element which must be subjected to strict control' (Ngcokovane, 1989: 57–8). Further underscoring this antisemitic undercurrent in Afrikaner nationalism, the Transvaal National Party in 1943 banned Jews from membership in the party, even though it courted their votes during elections (Saron, 1955b: 387). Although more extreme antisemitic sentiments were expressed by radical right-wing movements, such as the 'Greyshirts,' the 'Brownshirts,' and the militant Afrikaner nationalist movement, the *Ossewa Brandwag* ('Oxwagon Sentinels'), the National Party led by D. F. Malan clearly combined racialism with antisemitism in formulating its policy positions.

In the apartheid ideology proclaimed by Malan's National Party, every racially or ethnically defined group required its own, separate homeland. In the early 1940s, D. F. Malan argued that antisemitism in South Africa had been caused by the fact that 'the Jewish people have no national home' (Saron, 1955b: 380). When the modern state of Israel was founded in 1948, many Afrikaner nationalists proclaimed it as a model for the separate, ethnic homelands that they wanted to create in southern Africa (Shimoni, 1980: 217–18). As the National Party in power established relations with the state of Israel, antisemitic rhetoric in the party gradually disappeared. In 1951 the ban on Jewish membership in the Transvaal National Party was lifted. By 1955 D. F. Malan, echoed by the new Prime Minister, J. G. Strijdom, assured Jews that they had an important role to play in building up a new, 'multi-racial' South Africa. Abandoning his earlier antisemitic rhetoric, D. F. Malan declared that every Jew could be 'a good South African as well as a true son of Israel' (Saron, 1955b: 400).

In spite of the policies of Christian nationalism promoted by the National Party government, Jewish religious life flourished in South Africa. By the 1980s, most Jews were affiliated with an Orthodox synagogue, under the jurisdiction after 1986 of the Union of Orthodox Synagogues of South Africa. About 20 per cent of Jews were affiliated with the Reformed or Progressive movement that had been introduced in South Africa in 1933 under the leadership of Rabbi Moses Cyrus Weiler. Conflict between Orthodox and Reform Judaism in South Africa resulted in an agreement, signed by the chief rabbis of the two movements, which acknowledged that from 'the religious point of view there is an unbridgeable gulf between Orthodoxy and Reform' (Hellig, 1987: 11). Jewish diversity was further underscored by the emergence of several ultra-orthodox groups in the Johannesburg area during the 1970s.

The history of Jews in South Africa, therefore, like the histories of Roman Catholics, Muslims, and Hindus, does not only prove that South Africa has been religiously plural. History also reinforces the fact that every single religious tradition has been plural. The National Party government that came to power in 1948 tried to enforce a racial, cultural, and religious 'pluralism' in its doctrine of 'separate development.' But it ignored the fact that its basic categories, whether a race, a culture, or a religion, were not permanent, stable things. As the history of religious traditions in South Africa has suggested, they were diverse, changing, and inherently plural. In any case, apartheid, or 'separate development,' as implemented by the National Party government, was not pluralism but the domination of the many by one nationalism that claimed a privileged religious legitimacy.

REFERENCES

Abraham, Garth (1989). *The Catholic Church and Apartheid: The Response of the Catholic Church to the First Decade of National Party Rule 1948–1957.* Johannesburg: Ravan Press.

Adler, Taffy (1979). 'Lithuania's Diaspora: The Johannesburg Jewish Workers' Club, 1928–1948.' *Journal of Southern African Studies* 6: 70–92.

Aschman, George (1955). 'Oudtshoorn in the Early Days.' In: Gustav Saron and Louis Hotz (eds) *The Jews in South Africa: A History.* Cape Town: Oxford University Press. 121–37.

Beinart, William, and Colin Bundy (1987). *Hidden Struggles in Rural South Africa.* London: James Currey; Berkeley: University of California Press; Johannesburg: Ravan Press.

Bhana, Surendra and Joy B. Brain (1990). *Setting Down Roots: Indian Migrants in South Africa, 1860–1911.* Johannesburg: Witwatersrand University Press.

Bickford-Smith, Vivian (1981). 'Dangerous Cape Town: Middle Class Attitudes to Poverty in Cape Town in the Late 19th Century.' *Studies in the History of Cape Town* 4: 29–65.

Bird, W. W. (1966). *The State of the Cape of Good Hope in 1822.* Cape Town: Struik (orig. edn 1823).

Brain, J. B. (1975). *Catholic Beginnings in Natal and Beyond.* Durban: T. W. Griggs.

Brain, J. B. (1982). *Catholics in Natal II, 1886–1925.* Durban: Archdiocese of Durban.

Brain, J. B. (ed.) (1988). *The Cape Diary of Bishop Patrick Raymond Griffith for the Years 1837 to 1839.* Cape Town: Mariannhill Mission Press.

Bradlow, Frank R. and Margaret Cairns (1978). *The Early Cape Muslims.* Cape Town: A. A. Balkema.

Bradlow, Muhammad 'Adil (1988). 'Imperialism, State Formation and the Establishment of a Muslim Community at the Cape of Good Hope, 1770–1840: A Study in Urban Resistance.' MA thesis, University of Cape Town.

Brandel-Syrier, Mia (1960). *The Religious Duties of Islam as Explained by Abu Bakr Effendi.* Leiden: E. J. Brill.

Brown, W. E. (1960). *The Catholic Church in South Africa.* London: Burns & Oates.

Buijs, Georgina C. (1980). 'The Role of the Mother-Goddess Mariamma in Natal.' *Religion in Southern Africa* 1(1): 1–8.

Cammack, Diana (1982). 'The Politics of Discontent: The Grievances of Uitlander Refugees, 1899–1902.' *Journal of Southern African Studies* 8: 243–70.

Dangor, Suliman Essop (1982). *A Critical Biography of Shaykh Yusuf.* Durban: University of Durban-Westville, Centre for Research in Islamic Studies.

Davids, Achmat (1978). 'A Social History of the Bo-Kaap.' *Arabic Studies* 2: 21–55.

Davids, Achmat (1980). *The Mosques of Bo-Kaap: A Social History of Islam at the Cape.* Cape Town: South African Institute of Arabic and Islamic Research.

Davids, Achmat (1981). 'Politics and the Muslims of Cape Town: A Historical Survey.' *Studies in the History of Cape Town* 4: 174–220.

Davids, Achmat (1984). 'The Revolt of the Malays: A Study of the Reactions of the

Cape Muslims to the Smallpox Epidemics of Nineteenth Century Cape Town.' *Studies in the History of Cape Town* 5: 55–87.

Davids, Achmat (1985). 'From Complacency to Activism: The Changing Political Mood of the Cape Muslims from 1940–1985.' Unpublished paper, Workshop on the History of Cape Town, University of Cape Town.

Davids, Achmat (1989). 'The Words the Slaves Made: A Study of the Culture, Languages, Schools and Literacy of the Slaves in Cape Town and their Influence on the Development of Arabic-Afrikaans.' Unpublished paper, University of Cape Town, Centre for African Studies.

Dischl, Marcel (1982). *Transkei for Christ: A History of the Catholic Church in the Transkeian Territories.* Umtata: Queenstown Printing Company.

Du Plessis, I. D. (1972). (2nd edn) *The Cape Malays.* (1st edn 1944), Cape Town: A.A. Balkema.

Du Plessis, I. D. (1953). *The Malay Quarter and its Peoples.* Cape Town: A. A. Balkema.

Elphick, Richard and Robert Shell (1989). 'Intergroup Relations: Khoikhoi, Settlers, Slaves, and Free Blacks, 1652–1795.' In: Richard Elphick and Hermann Giliomee (eds) *The Shaping of South African Society 1652–1820.* Cape Town: Maskew Miller Longman.

Forster, George (1777). *A Voyage Round the World.* 2 vols. London.

Fredrickson, George M. (1981). *White Supremacy: A Comparative Study in American and South African History.* Oxford: Oxford University Press.

Gandhi, M. K. (1928). *Satyagraha in South Africa.* Trans. Valji Govidji Desai. Ahmedabad: Navajivan Publishing House.

Gandhi, M. K. (1958). *The Collected Works of Mahatma Gandhi.* New Delhi: Government of India.

Geffen, Max (1955). 'Cape Town Jewry, 1902–10.' In: Gustav Saron and Louis Hotz (eds) *The Jews in South Africa: A History.* Cape Town: Oxford University Press. 45–58.

Gershater, Chaim (1955). 'From Lithuania to South Africa.' In: Gustav Saron and Louis Hotz (eds) *The Jews in South Africa: A History.* Cape Town: Oxford University Press. 59–84.

Ginwala, Frene N. (1974). 'Class, Consciousness and Control: Indian South Africans, 1860–1946.' PhD thesis, Oxford University.

Goldin, Ian (1987). *Making Race: The Politics and Economics of Coloured Identity in South Africa.* Cape Town: Maskew Miller Longman.

Greyling, Chris (1980). 'Schech Yusuf, The Founder of Islam in South Africa.' *Religion in Southern Africa* 1: 9–22.

Haron, Muhammed (1986). 'Imam 'Abdullah Haron: Life, Ideas, and Impact.' MA thesis, University of Cape Town.

Hay, Stephen (1989). 'The Making of a Late-Victorian Hindu: M. K. Gandhi in London, 1888–91.' *Victorian Studies* 33: 75–98.

Hellig, Jocelyn (1984). 'The Religious Expression.' In: M. Arkin (ed.) *South African Jewry: A Contemporary Survey.* Cape Town: Oxford University Press. 95–116.

Hellig, Jocelyn (1986). 'South African Judaism: An Expression of Conservative Traditionalism.' *Judaism 35:* 232–42.

Hellig, Jocelyn (1987). 'The Religious Expression of South African Jewry.' *Religion in Southern Africa* 8(2): 3–17.

Herrman, Louis (1930). *A History of the Jews in South Africa from the Earliest Times to 1895.* London: Victor Gollancz.

Huttenback, Robert A. (1971). *Gandhi in South Africa*. Ithaca: Cornell University Press.

Jeffreys, Kathleen M. (1934–39). 'The Malay Tombs of the Holy Circle.' *The Cape Naturalist* 1: 15–17, 41–3, 89–91, 119–21, 157–63, 195–9.

Jeppe, Shamil (1988). 'I. D. du Plessis and the "Reinvention" of the "Malay", c.1935–1952.' Unpublished paper, University of Cape Town, Centre for African Studies.

Krut, Riva (1987). 'The Making of a South African Jewish Community in Johannesburg, 1886–1914.' In: Belinda Bozzoli (ed.) *Class, Community, and Conflict: South African Perspectives*. Johannesburg: Ravan Press. 135–59.

Kuper, Hilda (1959). 'An Ethnographic Description of Kavady, A Hindu Ceremony in South Africa.' *African Studies* 18: 118–32.

Kuper, Hilda (1960). *Indian People in Natal*. Durban: Natal University Press.

Kuper, Leo (1957). *Passive Resistance in South Africa 1899–1907*. Oxford: Oxford University Press.

Kuppusami, C. (1983). *Religions, Practices and Customs of South African Indians*. Durban: Sunray.

Lewis, David (1949). 'Cape Muslims.' In: Ellen Hellmann and Leah Abrahams (eds) *Handbook on Race Relations in South Africa*. London: Oxford University Press. 586–98.

Lewis, Gavin (1987). *Between the Wire and the Wall: A History of South African 'Coloured' Politics*. Cape Town: David Philip.

Lubbe, Gerrie (1986a). 'Tuan Guru: Prince, Prisoner, Pioneer.' *Religion in Southern Africa* 7(1): 25–37.

Lubbe, Gerrie (1986b). 'Christians, Muslims and Liberation in South Africa.' *Journal of Theology for Southern Africa* 56: 24–33.

Marais, Johannes S. (1957). *The Cape Coloured People, 1652–1937*. (orig. edn 1939), London: Longmans, Green.

Mayson, John S. (1861). *The Malays of Cape Town*. Manchester: J. Galt; rprt Cape Town: Africana Conoisseurs Press, 1963; rprt Pretoria: The State Library, 1970.

Mesthrie, Uma Shashikant (1989). 'Indian National Honour versus Trader Ideology: Three Unsuccessful Attempts at Passive Resistance in the Transvaal, 1932, 1939 and 1941.' *South African Historical Journal* 21: 39–54.

Mikula, Paul, Brian Kearney, and Rodney Harber (1982). *Traditional Hindu Temples in South Africa*. Durban: Hindu Temple Publications.

Naidoo, Thillayvel (1981). 'Kavadi: Worship through Ceremonial Festival.' *Religion in Southern Africa* 2(2): 3–11.

Naidoo, Thillayvel (1985). 'Arya Samaj in South Africa.' *Religion in Southern Africa* 6(2): 3–10.

Ngcokovane, Cecil (1989). *Demons of Apartheid: A Moral and Ethical Analysis of the N. G. K., N. P. and Broederbond's Justification of Apartheid*. Johannesburg: Skotaville.

Oosthuizen, G. C. (1985). 'The Zanzibaris of South Africa.' *Religion in Southern Africa* 6(1): 3–27.

Palmer, Mabel (1957). *The History of Indians in Natal*. Cape Town: Oxford University Press.

Pillay, Gerald J., Thillayvel Naidoo, and Suliman Dangor (1989). 'Religious Profile.' In: A. J. Arkin, K. P. Magyar, and G. J. Pillay (eds) *Indian South Africans: A Contemporary Profile*. Pinetown: Owen Burgess. 145–70.

Prior, Andrew (ed.) (1982) *Catholics in Apartheid Society*. Cape Town: David Philip.

Rambiritch, Birbal, and Pierre L. van den Berghe (1961). 'Caste in a Natal Indian Community.' *African Studies* 20: 217–25.

Republic of South Africa (1990). *White Paper on the Organisation and Functions of the South African Police*. Pretoria: Government Printers.

Ricards, James (1879). *The Catholic Church and the Kaffer: A Brief Sketch of the Progress of Catholicity in South Africa*. London: Burns & Oates.

Ross, Robert (1983). *Cape of Torments: Slavery and Resistance in South Africa*. London: Routledge & Kegan Paul.

Saron, Gustav (1955a). 'The Long Road to Unity.' In: Gustav Saron and Louis Hotz (eds) *The Jews in South Africa: A History*. Cape Town: Oxford University Press: 226–69.

Saron, Gustav (1955b). 'Epilogue, 1910–1948.' In: Gustav Saron and Louis Hotz (eds) *The Jews in South Africa: A History*. Cape Town: Oxford University Press: 370–400.

Saron, Gustav and Louis Hotz (eds) (1955). *The Jews in South Africa: A History*. Cape Town: Oxford University Press.

Schimlek, Francis (1949). *Against the Stream: Life of Fr Bernard Huss, the Social Apostle of the Bantu*. Mariannhill: Mariannhill Mission Press.

Schimlek, Francis (1953). *Mariannhill: A Study in Bantu Life and Missionary Effort*. Mariannhill: Mariannhill Mission Press.

Shain, Milton (1980). 'Diamonds, Pogroms and Undesirables: Anti-alienism and Legislation in the Cape Colony, 1890–1906.' *South African Historical Journal* 12: 13–28.

Shain, Milton (1983). *Jewry and Cape Society: The Origins and Activities of the Jewish Board of Deputies for the Cape Colony*. Cape Town: Historical Publications Society

Shain, Milton (1984). 'From Pariah to Parvenu: The Anti-Jewish Stereotype in South Africa, 1880–1910.' *Jewish Journal of Sociology* 26: 111–27.

Shell, Robert C-H. (1974). 'The Establishment and Spread of Islam at the Cape from the Beginning of Company Rule to 1838.' BA (Hons) dissertation, University of Cape Town.

Shell, Robert C-H. (1984). 'Rites and Rebellion: Islamic Conversion at the Cape, 1808–1915.' *Studies in the History of Cape Town* 5: 1–45.

Shell, Robert C-H. (1986). 'Slavery at the Cape of Good Hope, 1680–1831.' PhD dissertation, Yale University.

Shimoni, Gideon (1980). *Jews and Zionism: The South African Experience, 1910–1967*. Cape Town: Oxford University Press.

Singh, N. (1986). *A Study of the Divine Life Society with special reference to its Socio-Religious Implications in South Africa*. Durban: University of Durban-Westville.

Sooklal, Anil (1988). *The Ramakrishna Movement with special emphasis on the South African Context since 1965*. Durban: University of Durban-Westville.

Swan, Maureen (1985). *Gandhi: The South African Experience*. Johannesburg: Ravan Press.

Swan, Maureen (1987). 'Ideology in Organised Indian Politics, 1891–1948.' In: Shula Marks and Stanley Trapido (eds) *The Politics of Race, Class and Nationalism in Twentieth Century South Africa*. London: Longman. 182–208.

Theal, George McCall (ed.) (1897–1905). *Records of the Cape Colony from February 1793 to April 1831*. 36 vols. London: William Clowes.

Thompson, Leonard M. (1952). 'Indian Immigration into Natal 1860–1872.' *South African Archives Year Book*. Pretoria: Government Printers.

Van Onselen, Charles (1982). *Studies in the Social and Economic Transformation of the Witwatersrand, 1886–1914*. Vol. 1: *New Babylon*. Vol 2: *New Ninevah*. Johannesburg: Ravan Press.

Wilson, Jim (1986). 'Gandhi's God – A Substitute for the British Empire?' *Religion* 16: 343–57.

Worden, Nigel (1985). *Slavery in Dutch South Africa*. Cambridge: Cambridge University Press.

Young, Margaret (ed.) (1989). *Reminiscences of Amelia de Hennigsen*. Cape Town: Maskew Miller Longman.

6   Religious legitimation

Throughout South African history, religion has provided an open set of resources for justifying various economic, social, or political interests. By drawing on religious resources – symbol, myth, ritual, and tradition – cultural workers have been able to give those interests a sacred aura of legitimacy. In particular, religious legitimation has been drawn into justifying political power, the power to dominate, control, and exploit human and material resources. The National Party government that came to power in 1948 was particularly successful in drawing religious legitimation into the service of its domination of the political, social, and economic order of South Africa. Certainly, that religious legitimacy was not unquestioned. Critics noted that the National Party government derived its mandate from a small, racially defined minority; it pursued policies of institutionalized injustice to promote the interests of that minority at the expense of the majority of the population; it repressed legitimate forms of protest against its unjust policies; and eventually it was condemned by nearly every state and by most religious organizations in the world. Nevertheless, the National Party government, supported by the Dutch Reformed Church, persisted into the 1980s in trying to advance religious justifications for its legitimacy in South Africa.

This religious justification of political power, however, was produced through a long, discontinuous, and fragmented history of ideological redefinition that created various types of what came to be known as Afrikaner nationalism. The creation of an Afrikaner nationalism involved the production of a language, a culture, a history, and an ethnicity. Although many Afrikaner nationalists claimed that these things were given by God, the history of their production suggests that they were in fact constructed by cultural brokers or cultural entrepreneurs who tried to mobilize support for their political projects. Furthermore, the history of Afrikaner nationalism also reveals that it did not receive a single construction. Rather, Afrikaner nationalism was a site for competing definitions of what it meant to be an Afrikaner. Although religion featured prominently in those definitions, the entire complex of nationalism operated like a religion, with its own sacred symbols, myths, rituals, and traditions. If regarded as a religion, nationalism, arguably, has been the dominant world religion of the nineteenth and twentieth centuries. Likewise, nationalism has dominated the religious arena of South Africa, particularly in the varied forms and constructions of Afrikaner nationalism.

The fact that Afrikaner nationalism, like all nationalisms, was constructed, however, does not mean that it was not real. Besides providing different religious resources for imagining the solidarity of an Afrikaner nation, Afrikaner nationalists created organizations, institutions, and alliances across class lines that provided this 'imagined community' with a material base. After 1948, that material base extended throughout the political, military, and legal order of South Africa. In the name of a Christian nationalism, the National Party government set out to legislate its utopian vision of an exclusively white South Africa. That utopian vision assumed the name, apartheid. Signifying racial separation, or 'apartness,' apartheid became slogan, symbol, and public policy for a total reorganization of South Africa. Apartheid legislation enforced not only racial segregation but also white supremacy, with its implicit domination and exploitation of the vast majority of the population. In principle, apartheid was logically separable from Afrikaner nationalism, since the development of a national identity might not necessarily entail the exclusion or domination of others. During the 1940s, however, the ideology of apartheid became intertwined with Afrikaner nationalism to the extent that racialist exclusion and domination seemed to define the identity, purity, and power of an Afrikaner nation in South Africa. Although there were those who defined themselves as Afrikaners who dissented from this totalizing vision of apartheid, the National Party government was largely successful by the 1950s in mobilizing Afrikaner nationalist support for its racialist policy.

Ultimately, the racialist policy of apartheid required the creation of separate states, or nations, or what came to be called 'homelands' for the black population of South Africa. Under the policy of 'separate development,' apartheid ideologues of the National Party set out to remove all black people from the nation of South Africa. On the one hand, that project of removal was symbolic, because it symbolically excluded black people from South African citizenship by declaring them citizens of new ethnic homelands, even if they lived and worked within the geographical boundaries of South Africa. On the other hand, removal was quite literally implemented, as the forced relocation of large numbers of people was required to realize the apartheid goal of an all-white South Africa. The symbolic and material were interwoven, however, in this massive project of social engineering, causing the real suffering of dehumanization, displacement, and dispossession for the majority of the people of South Africa.

Obviously, the policy of 'separate development' served the religious interests of Afrikaner nationalists. But it also resulted in the creation of new religious nationalisms that were promoted in the black homelands. Constructed along new ethnic lines, such as 'Xhosa,' 'Zulu,' or 'Tswana' ethnicity, those nationalisms sought to provide religious legitimation for 'nations' that remained unrecognized by any other nation in the world except the Republic of South Africa. Religious nationalism, therefore, assumed unexpected forms in the 1970s and 1980s as a result of the program of 'separate development' undertaken by Afrikaner nationalists. Like Afrikaner nationalism itself, however, these new religious nationalisms can be located in a history of their ideological construction, material reinforcement, and religious legitimation during the twentieth century. Although claiming ancient, even primordial authority, these religious nationalisms were modern inventions in South Africa.

AFRIKANER NATIONALISM

Afrikaner nationalist movements emerged at three different junctures in South African history prior to the National Party coming to power in 1948. First, during the 1870s and 1880s, a cultural movement was formed in the Cape to promote Afrikaans as a language, particularly as a written language in competition with English. Resisting the dominance of British language and culture in Parliament, courts, schools, and churches, this first language movement worked to elevate the status of Afrikaans by linking it to a distinctive culture, history, and religious way of life. The first language movement drew support from those who resisted recent religious developments associated with English liberalism, such as the removal of Christian instruction from state schools after 1865 and the 'voluntary system' that ended state funding for ministers and churches in 1875. Although led by teachers and clergy, financial support for this cultural movement was largely drawn from Cape wine farmers who resisted British control over the economy. In 1875 these interests combined to form the Genootskap van Regte Afrikaners (Fellowship of True Afrikaners) in the Paarl wine-farming region of the Cape. According to one of its founders, the Dutch Reformed Church minister S. J. Du Toit, the white population of South Africa was divided amongst those with English, Dutch, and Afrikaner hearts. For those with Afrikaner hearts, the Afrikaans language would express their unique character as a people, or *volk*, with its own culture, history, and religion, since no nationality could be created without its own language (Giliomee, 1989: 34).

The question of who owned the Afrikaans language, however, was problematic. As a spoken language, Afrikaans was used by people of Khoisan, European, and slave descent who came to be classified as 'Coloureds.' Furthermore, as a written language, it had been used by Muslims in the Cape to produce Afrikaans texts in Arabic script. Nevertheless, the leaders of the Genootskap van Regte Afrikaners claimed Afrikaans as the authentic language of white, Dutch-Afrikaners, producing a grammar, a newspaper, and a history in hopes of mobilizing an Afrikaner identity. This language movement was met with some derision in the English press. The *Cape Argus* in 1876, for example, complained that an 'attempt is being made by a number of jokers near Cape Town to reduce the 'plat Hollands' of the street and the kitchen to a written language and to perpetuate it' (Davids, 1989: 20). Furthermore, this attempt to construct an Afrikaner identity around a language was in competition with other white South African nationalists who were trying to create a broader definition of an 'Afrikaner' that would encompass both Dutch and English.

When S. J. du Toit founded the Afrikaner Bond in 1880, as an organization that would coordinate the language movement, the cultural movement, and the economic interests of wine farmers, it was soon taken over by a different contingent of South African nationalists, led by 'Onze' Jan Hofmeyr, who defined 'Afrikaner' as anyone committed to maintaining white 'civilization' in Africa, regardless of language, history, or religious background. Although this definition of 'Afrikaner' made the Afrikaner Bond more congenial to the administration of Cecil Rhodes in the Cape, it frustrated the designs of S. J. du Toit for a more narrow, exclusive Afrikaner nationalism. Inspired by the successful 1881 revolt against British authority by the Transvaal Republic in the north, however, Du Toit left the Afrikaner Bond, the Dutch Reformed Church, and the Cape to align himself with the Transvaal nationalism of Paul Kruger. Defining Afrikaner nationalism specifically as loyalty to the Transvaal Republic, Paul Kruger clearly enveloped his nationalism in the religious aura of a sacred calling and destiny. A product of the small Gereformeerde Kerk, or 'Dopper' church, Kruger proclaimed an ardent Christian nationalism for the Transvaal South African Republic. Even as that republic faced defeat in the Anglo-Boer war, Paul Kruger declared that his army served the 'supreme commander of heaven and earth, Jesus Christ' (Moodie, 1975: 32).

Second, after the Anglo-Boer War (1899–1902), a different coalition of school teachers and clergy in the Dutch Reformed churches worked to define a new religious nationalism in resistance to British cultural dominance. This second language movement, like the first, asserted Afrikaans as the spoken and written language of a particular people, once again proclaiming a white nation with its own, unique history, culture, and religion in Africa. But the religious character of this new nationalism was even more pronounced, as much of its inspiration was drawn from the Neo-Calvinist Christian nationalism promoted by Abraham Kuyper in the Netherlands. Centered in Potchefstroom, leaders of the Gereformeerde Kerk, or 'Doppers,' worked to articulate this religious nationalism. The son of the leader of the first language movement, J. D. du Toit, served as minister and Professor of Theology for the Gereformeerde Kerk in Potchefstroom. Assuming the pen name Totius, he published poetry that celebrated a uniquely sacred Afrikaner history. Not only declaring a divine providence in that history, Totius and other poets worked to inspire an Afrikaner recovery from defeat in war. They reworked the history of the Voortrekkers, the Boer Republics, and the Anglo-Boer War as the salvation history of a chosen people. In particular, the history of the 1830s – the Great Trek, the 1838 Battle of Blood River, and the roots of Boer Republics – was rewritten as a sacred narrative of a chosen people in covenant with God. By 1918 the Gerformeerde Kerk minister and theologian Willem Postma could declare that Afrikaners were 'God's chosen people, [who] were brought to this land with the commission to establish and spread the kingdom of God' (Hexham, 1981: 48; A. Du Toit, 1983).

As an indication that the influence of this new sacred history extended beyond the Gerformeerde Kerk in Potchefstroom, J. D. Kestell, a prominent Dutch Reformed Church minister, and editor of its monthly magazine, *Die Kerkbode*, argued that Postma's religious nationalism applied to all Afrikaners (Hexham, 1981: 46). Another minister in the Dutch Reformed Church, D. F. Malan, who returned from studies in the Netherlands in 1905, also played an active role in promoting this new religious nationalism. In 1908, Malan embraced the Afrikaans language movement as a vehicle for national upliftment. 'Raise the Afrikaans language to a written language,' Malan declared in 1908, 'let it become the vehicle for our culture, our history, our national ideals, and you will raise the people who speak it' (Giliomee, 1989: 43). At a religious conference in the Cape in 1911, Reverend Malan promoted the sacred history of Afrikaner nationalism as evidence of a divine calling from God. God had 'a unique calling for our People with its own ethnic nature,' Malan declared. 'My feeling of nationality thus rests finally upon a religious foundation' (Moodie, 1975: 71).

Obviously, religion and ethnicity merged in this Afrikaner nationalism. Its religious and ethnic foundation, however, also required material support. From 1905 to 1915 the ministers, teachers, and poets who worked to create this ethnic religious nationalism drew support largely from wealthy farmers who were opposed to the control over the economy exercised by British merchants and mining capitalists. That cultural and economic alliance was tested and reinforced by the 1914 rebellion against the pro-British government of the Union of South Africa. Led by Boer generals, the rebellion directly challenged the imperialist and capitalist order in South Africa. At a special council of the Dutch Reformed Church in 1915, clergy refused to condemn the rebels. Rather, they adopted a statement drafted by D. F. Malan that aligned the church with the Afrikaner resistance to British nationalism. Defining the Dutch Reformed Church as an Afrikaner *volkskerk*, or national church, the statement announced:

> The church has a special calling with regard to the Afrikaner people. The church sees it as its duty to be nationalistic, to guard the specific national interests, and to teach the people to see the hand of God in its own history and to keep alive an awareness of its national calling and purpose.
>
> (Loubser, 1987: 22)

In solidarity with the rebels, D. F. Malan was among the clergy who pleaded with Prime Minister Jan Smuts to reprieve one of the rebel leaders, Jopie Fourie, who faced a firing squad for his part in the rebellion. As Jopie Fourie became a martyr for Afrikaner nationalism, the Dutch Reformed Church increasingly provided that nationalism with religious legitimation. Like the Great Trek, the covenant at Blood River, and the redemptive suffering of the Anglo-Boer war, the rebellion of 1914 became absorbed into Afrikaner sacred history, a history that D. F. Malan described as 'the greatest master-piece of the centuries.' According to Malan, Afrikaner national identity had been designed by the 'Architect of the Universe.' It was 'not the work of men but the creation of God' (Pienaar, 1964: 235–6). Clearly, however, Afrikaner nationalism was also the product of new institutions and shifting alliances. After the rebellion, the church forged an alliance with the National Party of J. B. M. Hertzog, which had supported the rebels, against the ruling government of Jan Smuts' South African Party. Between 1924 and 1933, Hertzog's National Party held a majority in parliament. When Hertzog joined with Jan Smuts to form a government under the United Party in 1933, however, D. F. Malan and other Afrikaner nationalists saw that fusion government as a betrayal of their nationalist interests. Forming a 'Purified' National Party, D. F. Malan played a prominent leadership role in a third historical emergence of Afrikaner nationalism.

During the 1930s, the cultural work of the Afrikaans language movements was claimed by several different nationalist factions. The Calvinist nationalism of the Potchefstroom 'Doppers,' with its strict theology, sacred history, and program for Christian-National education, represented only one version of Afrikaner nationalism. Potchefstroom academics, such as J. C. van Rooy, L. J. Du Plessis, H. G. Stoker, and C. Coetzee, continued to promote a Calvinist politics, drawing on Abraham Kuyper's theology of 'sphere sovereignty' to argue that every sphere of society – church, state, schools, and households – had to conform to what they regarded as divine law. With respect to nationalism, Neo-Calvinism in the 1930s was drawn upon to provide religious legitimation for a separate, independent Afrikaner nation.

According to Neo-Calvinism, as D. G. S. van der Merwe wrote in 1934, the 'separate people or nation is also a peculiar cosmic phenomenon with a law of its own, an own essence and task, with an own area and in that area an own freedom' (Loubser, 1987: 47). By implication, therefore, the Neo-Calvinist doctrine of sphere sovereignty required the creation of an Afrikaner nation with its own essence, area, and freedom in South Africa.

Although this Calvinist nationalism continued to exert considerable influence, it competed with two other approaches to Afrikaner nationalism that emerged in the 1930s. A second nationalist ideology drew inspiration from the romantic German nationalism of the early nineteenth century that had imagined each separate nation as a 'volk' with its own unique cultural identity. Depicting national identity as if it were a living organism, romantic nationalists imagined that a nation had a life of its own in which individuals were absorbed as parts of a greater national whole. Of more immediate influence on the development of romantic nationalism in South Africa, however, was the rise of Nazism in Germany during the 1930s. Many of the leaders of romantic nationalism in South Africa had been educated in Germany. Nico J. Diederichs, Piet J. Meyer, and Geoff Cronjé returned from studies in Germany to promote this nationalist ideology through meetings and publications sponsored in the 1930s by the Afrikaans-Nasionale Studentebond. After 1937, a version of this Afrikaner nationalism was promoted by H. F. Verwoerd, editor of *Die Transvaler*. Under the influence of the racialist ideology of Hitler's National Socialist Party, these romantic nationalists promoted an Afrikaner nationalism that echoed many of the themes of Nazism.

Romantic nationalists celebrated the rise of National Socialism in Germany. Piet J. Meyer, for example, who later became chairman of the South African Broadcasting Company, declared that 'National Socialism would determine the nature of the ages to come' (Loubser, 1987: 50). In South Africa, according to Meyer, that form of nationalism demanded that the 'Afrikaner accepts his national task as a divine task, in which his individual life-task, and his personal service to God has been absorbed in a wider, organic context' (Thompson, 1985: 43). The absorption of each individual in the organic totality of the nation was perhaps most clearly stated by Nico J. Diederichs, professor of political philosophy, who served as an important nationalist organizer in the 1930s and 1940s. 'Only in the nation as the most total, most inclusive human community can man realize himself to the full,' Diederichs wrote. 'The nation is the fulfillment of individual life' (Moodie, 1975: 157). In the formulations of these romantic nationalists, therefore, the Afrikaner nation was defined as a pure, ideal, and divinely ordained totality.

By contrast to the Calvinist and romantic nationalists of the 1930s, a third Afrikaner nationalism advocated more practical measures to secure power in

South Africa. Adopting what might be called a pragmatic nationalism, D. F. Malan emerged as the main political leader in efforts to forge a power base that could succeed in electoral politics. Although based in the Dutch Reformed Church, drawing support from church leaders such as J. D. Kestell and William Nicol, this pragmatic nationalism worked through other organizations and alliances to mobilize an Afrikaner nationalism along rather generally defined ethnic lines (O'Meara, 1977: 175). In support of Malan's 'Purified' National Party, Afrikaner nationalists forged alliances between farming and manufacturing capital, white workers, and a class of people referred to as 'poor whites,' estimated at 300,000 in 1930. In particular, pragmatic nationalists made ethnic appeals to white workers threatened by competition from black workers over jobs. In addition to redefining the ideology of Afrikaner nationalism, therefore, nationalists formed class alliances by organizing trade unions and financial institutions that promised to protect, support, and uplift white workers.

These economic projects initiated by Afrikaner nationalists assumed the form of a *volkskapitalisme* (O'Meara, 1983). Merging economics with religious nationalism, nationalist organizations and institutions promised a comprehensive Afrikaner salvation. As Nico Diederichs declared in 1941, while serving as head of a financial institution called the Reddingsdaadbond ('Society of the Saving Deed'), his institution was a 'great ethnic organization, Christian National in principle' (Moodie, 1975: 205). It promised economic, political, and even an essentially religious salvation for Afrikaners through an ethnic mobilization of human and material resources. Much of that ethnic mobilization was orchestrated during the 1930s and 1940s by a secret society, the Afrikaner Broederbond. Formed in 1918 as a cultural organization, the Broederbond became a secret Afrikaner society in 1924, dedicated to serving Afrikaner educational, social, economic, and nationalist interests. By the 1930s the Broederbond had become more militant in advancing those interests. As a secret circular declared in 1934, 'Afrikanerdom will reach its ultimate destiny of domination in South Africa... [when] the Afrikaner Broederbond shall govern South Africa' (Ngcokovane, 1989: 61).

In its quest for power, the Broederbond established a network of affiliated organizations. Besides the Reddingsdaadbond, it formed a cultural organization (the Federation of Afrikaans Culture), an educational organization (the Institute for Christian National Education), and a labor organization (the White Workers' Protection Society). Although small in membership, the Broederbond exerted remarkable influence through these organizations, as well as through Malan's National Party and the Dutch Reformed Church. Representatives of all three versions of Afrikaner nationalism – Calvinist, romantic, and pragmatic – were members of the Broederbond. While this suggests some ideological differences in the secret society, there does seem to have been general agreement that Afrikaner nationalism, however defined, was not merely the product of organizations and alliances but a sacred work of God. Reaffirming this religious legitimation in 1944, chairman of the Broederbond, J. C. van Rooy, asserted that 'God created the Afrikaner People with a unique language, a unique philosophy of life, and their own history and tradition in order that they might fulfill a particular calling and destiny here in the southern corner of Africa' (Moodie, 1975: 110–11; Thompson, 1985: 29).

All of this work in ideological redefinition, building institutions, and forging alliances, however, would not have been effective if it had not mobilized large numbers of people to identify themselves as Afrikaner nationalists. In 1938 an Afrikaner ritual drama seemed to provide the occasion for that mass mobilization of support. Celebrating the centenary of the Battle of Blood River, Afrikaner religious, cultural, and political organizations staged a ritual reenactment of the Great Trek. On 8 August 1938 two ox-wagons set off from the statue of Jan van Riebeeck in Cape Town for Pretoria, symbolically recreating the journey of the Voortrekkers from the Cape to the Transvaal. Popular enthusiasm for the ox-wagons was so great, however, that eventually nine wagons were outfitted to trek around the country, visiting nearly 500 locations throughout South Africa. Dressing up as Voortrekkers, Afrikaners welcomed the wagons with great enthusiasm. The wagons were regarded with a kind of religious fervor as Afrikaner sacred symbols. People flocked to touch them, to obtain grease from their wheels, and even in some cases to baptize babies and perform marriages next to one of the ceremonial Voortrekker ox-wagons (MacCrone, 1938; Grundlingh and Sapire, 1989: 26). Wherever the wagons stopped was declared holy ground. Local organizations in towns and villages sprang up to organize festivities when the wagons arrived. When the wagons reached their destinations – at Monument Hill in Pretoria and Blood River in Natal – they were welcomed by torch processions, camp meetings, and an intensely religious enthusiasm.

On 16 December 1938, the Day of the Covenant, celebrating the vow to God that was said to have been made by Voortrekkers at the Battle of Blood River, over 200,000 Afrikaners gathered at the two ceremonial sites to hear patriotic speeches by Afrikaner nationalists. The content of those speeches suggested that the appeal of this Afrikaner nationalist ritual was based on its promise of dissolving class divisions in a common ethnic and religious culture. In particular, the economic protection and upliftment of white workers was a recurring theme in the ceremonial rhetoric. That theme had been anticipated at the launching of the first ox-wagons from Cape Town, as administrator of the Cape Province, J. H. Conradie, announced that the wagons 'should not only honour the descendants of Voortrekkers, but should also bring a message of hope to the poor and discouraged' (Grundlingh and Sapire, 1989: 23). That message of hope for white workers and poor whites was reinforced on 16 December 1938 by D. F. Malan.

Speaking at the site of the 1838 battle in which Voortrekkers killed 3,000 Zulus, D. F. Malan told his large Afrikaner audience, 'Here at Blood River you stand on holy ground.' Certainly, Malan honored the Voortrekkers. 'They received their task from God's hand,' Malan declared. 'They gave their answer. They made their sacrifices. There is still a white race.' But he shifted quickly from 1838 to 1938 to argue that Afrikaners had embarked on a 'second Great Trek' into new urban environments. Just like the Voortrekkers, however, Afrikaners moving into the labor markets of South African cities faced black and British enemies. In particular, white, Afrikaans-speaking workers found themselves in competition with black workers. 'Today,' as Malan observed, 'black and white jostle together in the same labor market.' Standing on holy ground in the Natal countryside, Malan urged his audience: 'Your Blood River is not here. Your Blood River lies in the city.' The ritual rhetoric of the Blood River centenary, therefore, promised to support the economic advancement of white workers in the urban labor market. Over the next 10 years, Afrikaner nationalist initiatives in labor unions and financial institutions made that promise of support a reality.

In exchange, white workers were drawn into giving their support to the political program of Afrikaner nationalists. The celebration of the Voortrekkers was not only an occasion for mobilizing an Afrikaner ethnic identity but also for reaffirming a political program that was explicitly racist. At Blood River, D. F. Malan called for a common Afrikaner commitment to white supremacy which could only be achieved if his audience realized that the sacred calling of the Voortrekkers 'to make South Africa a white man's land' was also their calling. Drawing on the sacred power represented by the Voortrekker celebration, Malan promised a single salvation that was simultaneously religious, political, and racial. 'Unite that power purposely in a mighty salvation-deed,' Malan urged, 'and then the future of Afrikanerdom will be assured and white civilization will be saved' (Pienaar, 1964: 128–9; Moodie, 1975: 199–201).

Merging with Afrikaner nationalism, the racialism celebrated by D. F. Malan at the Blood River centenary became the hallmark of National Party rule when it came to power 10 years later. That racialism was captured under the single slogan of apartheid. But that simple slogan covered a complex network of racial separation, exclusion, and domination under National Party rule. Furthermore, it derived religious legitimation from the Dutch Reformed Church. Through the development of a theology of apartheid, the Dutch Reformed Church proclaimed a racialist gospel of salvation in South Africa that attempted to justify the political policies of the National Party.

APARTHEID

During the 1940s apartheid meant different things to the Afrikaner nationalists who adopted it as a racialist symbol of salvation. First, some Afrikaner nationalists advocated what came to be called 'pure' apartheid. Arguing that the 'purity' of a white, Afrikaner nation had to be protected, nationalists such as Nico J. Diederichs, Piet J. Meyer, Gerhardus Eloff, and Geoff Cronjé insisted on a total separation from black South Africans. Proponents of 'pure' apartheid insisted that even black workers who served white economic interests ultimately had to be removed from any contact with whites. Insisting on apartheid as a defence of racial 'purity,' Gerhardus Eloff, in a 1942 pamphlet entitled *Rasse en Rasvermenging* (*Race and Race-mixing*), hinted at the religious motives that were interwoven in this obsession with purity. Eloff declared:

> The preservation of the pure race of the *Boerevolk* must be protected at all costs in all possible ways as a holy pledge entrusted to us by our ancestors as part of God's plan with our People. Any movement, school, or individual who sins against this must be dealt with as a racial criminal by the effective authorities.

Three years later, the sociologist Geoff Cronjé published a book that became a standard text of apartheid ideology – *'n Tuiste vir die Nageslag: Die Blywende Oplossing van Suid-Afrika se Rassevraagstukke* (*A Home for Posterity: The Permanent Solution of South Africa's Racial Questions*) – that insisted on the application of 'pure' apartheid. 'The more consistently the policy of apartheid could be applied,' Cronjé argued, 'the greater would be the security for the purity of our blood and the surer our unadulterated European racial survival.' Hoping that it would protect what he imagined as racial 'purity,' Cronjé concluded that 'total racial separation... is the most consistent application of the Afrikaner idea of racial apartheid' (Thompson, 1985: 43–4).

The National Party clearly played on this theme of racial 'purity,' declaring its commitment to 'preserving and safeguarding the White race' (Bunting, 1964: 114). But it also invoked a second understanding of apartheid by linking it with what it claimed as a Christian religious duty to exercise trusteeship or guardianship over blacks in South Africa. Second, therefore, apartheid signified what the National Party announced in 1947 as 'the maintenance and protection of the indigenous racial groups as separate ethnological groups with possibilities to develop in their own territories into self-reliant national units' (Bunting, 1964: 118). In this sense, apartheid implied not only the separation of white and black South Africans, but also the division of black South Africans into ethnically defined groups that would be confined to territorial areas delimited by the National Party. Under National Party rule, this definition of apartheid, often referred to as 'separate development,' resulted in the brutal, costly, and ultimately futile attempt to relocate all black South Africans in ethnic homelands. Under the slogan of racial separation, however, these homelands actually provided reserves of migrant labor that served white-controlled farming, mining, and industry. Even separated in artificial homelands, therefore, black workers would remain an integral part of the South African economy.

The contradiction between dreams of purity and desires for economic power produced a third definition of apartheid – 'practical' apartheid. Advocates of practical apartheid recognized that their economic power depended upon cheap, exploitable black labor. While they might dream of separation, Afrikaner nationalists who defended practical apartheid settled for domination. For example, the journal of the Afrikaanse Handelsinstituut, an organization formed by the Broederbond in 1942 to promote Afrikaner economic interests, defended a policy of practical apartheid:

> No, a person must be practical. It must be acknowledged that the non-white worker already constitutes an integral part of our economic structure, that he is now so enmeshed in the spheres of our economic life that for the first fifty to one hundred years (if not even longer), total segregation is pure wishful thinking. Any government which disregards this irrefutable fact will soon discover that it is no longer in a position to govern.
>
> (Posel, 1987a: 130)

The implementation of practical apartheid, therefore, allowed for some compromise in the matter of total racial separation, as long as compromise served the economic and political interests of white, Afrikaner domination in South Africa. In this sense, apartheid was less about purity than about power, the power to rule South Africa. This understanding of apartheid as political domination was clearly stated before the 1948 election by the minister, politician, and later prime minister of South Africa, J. G. Strijdom. 'Our policy is that the Europeans must stand their ground and must remain *baas* [master] in South Africa,' Strijdom declared. 'Our view is that in every sphere the European must retain the right to rule the country and to keep it a white man's country' (Bunting, 1964: 118).

Although these commitments to a symbolic purity, order, and power in the world already suggested that a religious worldview was at work in apartheid, the doctrine of apartheid received even more explicit religious legitimation from the Dutch Reformed Church. As noted in Chapter Three, a new generation of clergy was active in the church and mission councils of the Dutch Reformed Church in the 1930s. In 1942 the church formed a

Federal Mission Council that coordinated work on racial matters. That same year the executives of the Federal Mission Council met with the Minister of Native Affairs for the United Party government to argue that church policies on race, particularly those prohibiting interracial sex, interracial marriage, and integrated residential areas, should be made law. Arguing for this racial legislation, church spokesmen declared: 'It is the conviction of the majority of Afrikaans-speaking South Africans and the majority of the Dutch Reformed Church that the only way of insuring the continued survival of the nation is by observing the principles of racial separation (Strassburger, 1974: 190). After the National Party came to power in 1948, those principles of racial separation supported by the Dutch Reformed Church were legislated in the Mixed Marriages Act (1949), the Population Registration Act (1950), the Group Areas Act (1950), and the Immorality Amendment Act (1950). From the beginning, therefore, the church placed its religious authority behind the proliferation of apartheid laws of racial discrimination and separation.

After 1948 the Dutch Reformed Church seemed even more militant than the government in demanding total racial separation. A conference of the Federal Mission Council brought 600 white, Afrikaans-speaking delegates to Bloemfontein in 1950 to work out the church's position on what the council called the 'native problem.' In its official statement, the 1950 conference advocated separate churches, schools, residential areas, and territories for racially defined groups. Defending racially separated churches, the council pointed to the emergence of African independent churches in support of its own religious policy of 'distinctive' or 'separate' development of churches. Moving from religion to politics, the council argued that only the 'distinctive development' of racially defined groups in separate territories was consistent with 'divine Purpose and Destiny.' The council insisted that the pattern set by the Dutch Reformed Church in creating separate churches for racially defined groups had to be extended in South Africa to a 'total territorial separation.' In conclusion, the Federal Mission Council called on Malan's National Party government to implement 'total segregation' immediately in all aspects of South African life.

In response to the church's call for total racial separation, D. F. Malan restated his policy of 'practical' apartheid. He agreed with the church that total and complete territorial separation of races would be an 'ideal state of affairs.' Against the 'pure' apartheid advocated by the church, however, Malan argued that 'total separation was impractical under present circumstances in South Africa, where our whole economic structure is to a large extent based on Native labour.' The 'practical' policy of apartheid, advocated and implemented by the National Party government, was a mixture of racial separation and white racist domination of black labor. By 1952 the Dutch

Reformed Church seems also to have adopted this policy of 'practical' apartheid for South Africa. A statement issued in 1952 by the Federal Mission Council still held to 'the ideal of separation,' but argued that the policy of racial separation did not exclude the employment of 'Native labour for the economic machine of the whites for a long time to come' (Strassburger, 1974: 203). The 'practical' racist policy of apartheid proclaimed by the Dutch Reformed Church, therefore, seems to have been worked out in negotiations over racial purity and economic power with the National Party government. Nevertheless, the Dutch Reformed Church continued to advance its ideal of total racial separation.

At the same time, the Dutch Reformed Church developed and promoted a theology of apartheid. Elements of that theology were already in place by the end of the 1930s. Theologians had begun to argue that the separation of peoples, races, or nations was based on the Bible. In a 1938 Gereformeerde Kerk journal, for example, Reverend J. G. Strijdom published an article – 'Apartheid, a Matter of Faith' – in which he claimed that the Bible supported racial separation. 'There are people who falsely maintain on biblical grounds that apartheid is wrong,' Strijdom complained. 'We, however, believe on the basis of God's Word that He had willed nations to be apart' (Loubser, 1987: 53). A council of the Dutch Reformed Church in 1943 lent its support to apartheid nationalism by resolving that 'according to the Bible God actually called nations into existence.' But the elaboration of a racialist apartheid theology, drawing its religious legitimation from the Bible, was not fully worked out in the Dutch Reformed Church until 1947. During that year, councils of the church considered a report drawn up by the theologian Evert P. Groenewald which argued that 'the policy of apartheid was not only born of circumstances but has its basis in the Holy Scripture' (Geldenhuys, 1982: 27–30).

Groenewald's report was published the following year as part of an influential manual on apartheid. Drawing on selected texts from the Bible, Groenewald tried to justify apartheid in three spheres: religion, society, and politics. First, a kind of spiritual apartheid was demonstrated in the total, ultimate separation promised in the afterlife for the saved and the damned. Spiritual separations – the sheep from the goats, the wheat from the tares, the light from the dark – provided a model for 'religious apartheid' (Mt 15: 25). Second, social apartheid was defended by referring to the biblical instruction that the people of Israel were not to have fellowship with neighboring peoples (Deut 7). Following that precedent, racially defined groups had to avoid social relations with each other in South Africa. Third, texts from the Bible were drawn upon to justify a political division of nations. The report insisted that God had willed that there should be separate peoples, races, and nations

(Gen 11; Acts 2). Therefore, they should remain separate (Loubser, 1987: 61; Cronjé and Nicol, 1948).

By the time the National Party came to power in 1948, theologians in the Dutch Reformed Church were intent upon defending an apartheid theology that drew its religious legitimation from the Bible. In 1953 the Federal Mission Council of the Dutch Reformed Church convened a 3-day conference on 'Christian Principles in a Multi-Racial South Africa.' Although the conference was open to a discussion of various options, it seems to have been part of a concerted effort by the Dutch Reformed Church and the Federal Mission Council during the early 1950s to promote an apartheid theology. Inviting representatives from both English-speaking and Afrikaans-speaking Protestant churches, the Federal Mission Council encountered some resistance to its biblical justification of apartheid. The conference report noted that three positions emerged during debate: Some church leaders advocated what the report called a 'righteous racial separation' based on the Bible. Others advocated racial separation, but did not base their position on the Bible. Finally, some representatives, for the most part drawn from English-speaking churches, argued that racial separation was actually contrary to the Bible.

At this conference, the strongest statement of an apartheid theology based on the Bible was produced by C. B. Brink, the moderator of the Transvaal synod of the Dutch Reformed Church. Brink announced that it was necessary for theologians to discredit 'the equalitarian idea.' In his effort to undermine racial equality in church or state, Brink proposed a comprehensive apartheid theology which insisted that racial separation, from creation to the last judgment, was the will of God. In the creation of the world, according to Brink, God was the 'Maker of Separations.' In the beginning, God created separations – light/darkness, waters above/waters below, land/sea, males/females – that established a basic divine pattern of making divisions in the world. Following this principle of division, Brink insisted that when the Bible recorded God instructing Noah to 'be fruitful and multiply,' the text should be read as commanding human beings to be fruitful and divide into separate groups, tribes, or nations (Gen 9: 1). Furthermore, Brink read the biblical story of the Tower of Babel as revealing 'the intention of the Lord that mankind should live in separate nations and peoples' (Gen 11: 6–8). In the end, as Brink read the Book of Revelation, even the last judgment would maintain the separation of 'all nations, and kindreds, and peoples, and tongues' (Rev 7: 8; Brink, 1953: 33–4).

By 1953, therefore, the Dutch Reformed Church had not only produced an apartheid theology but had in effect rewritten the Bible as an apartheid Bible. Into the 1970s, the Dutch Reformed Church continued to draw this Bible into a religious legitimation of racial separation. As the General Synod of the Dutch Reformed Church maintained in 1974, 'Under certain circumstances and conditions the New Testament does leave room for organizing the co-existence of different nations in one country through the policy of separate development' (Ngcokovane, 1989: 155).

At the same time, however, there were a few dissenting voices in the Dutch Reformed Church. While most Afrikaner theologians during the 1940s and 1950s were intent upon underwriting apartheid with a biblical foundation, the Dutch Reformed Church theologians B. B. Keet and Ben Marais opposed this effort to link apartheid to the Bible. Drawing on the evangelical and pietist tradition of the church, Keet and Marais argued that the Bible was not a blueprint for society but a history of sin and salvation. Although they disagreed strongly with their church's attempt to provide theological or scriptural justification for apartheid, both Keet and Marais maintained that racial segregation might in some instances be acceptable. Nevertheless, they warned that a theological adherence to racial separation would lead to disaster by reinforcing conflict between whites and blacks in South Africa. Instead of preserving the values of western civilization, B. B. Keet warned, the apartheid theology of racial separation threatened to destroy them. 'The more one examines the case for complete, permanent apartheid,' he concluded, 'the less can one avoid the conclusion that its supporters are labouring under a delusion that belongs to a world of make-believe' (Keet, 1956: 85; Marais, 1953). Despite these occasional theological objections, however, the fantasy of apartheid continued to become a reality in South Africa.

The violent reality of apartheid received international attention on 21 March 1960 when police responded to a peaceful protest march by opening fire on black men, women, and children, killing sixty-nine and wounding 186 in the small Transvaal town of Sharpeville. Later that year, a church conference under the auspices of the World Council of Churches that included representatives from English-speaking and Afrikaans-speaking churches met at Cottesloe, in Johannesburg, to draft a statement rejecting racism. The Cottesloe statement was signed by delegates representing most churches in South Africa, including leaders of the Transvaal and Cape synods of the Dutch Reformed Church. Although its condemnation of racism would later appear fairly moderate, the Cottesloe resolutions marked a departure from apartheid theology for the delegates of the Dutch Reformed Church. Almost immediately, however, the Cottesloe statement was condemned by South African Prime Minister H. F. Verwoerd. In concert with the government, apartheid theologians ensured that all four synods of the Dutch Reformed Church formally rejected the Cottesloe statement against racism in South Africa.

One Dutch Reformed Church leader who stood by the Cottesloe resolutions, however, was the acting moderator of the Transvaal synod, Beyers Naudé. As son of a founding member of the Broederbond, Naudé had impeccable Afrikaner nationalist credentials. After 1960, however, Naudé resigned from the Broederbond, denounced the theology of apartheid, and founded the Christian Institute in 1963 as an ecumenical organization opposed to apartheid in South Africa. Drawing inspiration from the 'Confessing Church' movement that had opposed Hitler in Nazi Germany, the Christian Institute tried to counter apartheid racial separation by promoting 'one-ness' in church and society (De Gruchy, 1985: 17). Although the Dutch Reformed Church responded by removing him from its role of ministers, Naudé continued to pursue an alternative ministry through the various study projects, conferences, and publications of the Christian Institute. After years of official persecution by the security police, the Christian Institute was finally closed by the government in 1977. While many on the staff of the Institute were arrested, or fled into exile, Beyers Naudé was silenced under a banning order, forbidden by the government to write, publish, or be in the presence of more than one other person at a time.

As the Dutch Reformed Church continued to proclaim its theology of apartheid throughout the 1970s, it became increasingly isolated from the international Christian community. Withdrawing from the World Council of Churches in 1961 over the Cottesloe statement, the Dutch Reformed Church remained a member of the World Alliance of Reformed Churches. In August 1982, however, the general council of that organization issued a statement on 'Racism and South Africa' that condemned both the theology and the political policy of apartheid. In its analysis of racism in South Africa, the World Alliance of Reformed Churches found that apartheid was a 'sin' for three reasons: it was based on an anti-Christian premise that human beings were irreconcilable; it was applied through racialist structures that provided exclusive privileges for whites at the expense of blacks; and it created injustice, oppression, deportations, and suffering for millions of people in South Africa. Following upon this analysis of apartheid, the World Alliance of Reformed Churches concluded that any religious legitimation for such a system that claimed to be Christian or based on the Bible was not only false, but was a 'pseudo-religious ideology' that had to be condemned as a heresy. Therefore, the World Alliance of Reformed Churches declared that 'Apartheid' ('separate development') is a sin, and that the moral and theological justification of it is a travesty of the Gospel and, in its persistent disobedience to the Word of God, a theological heresy' (De Gruchy and Villa-Vicencio, 1983: 170). For its adherence to the heresy of apartheid, the Dutch Reformed Church was suspended from this international organization of Reformed churches.

SEPARATE DEVELOPMENTS

Apartheid was condemned by churches, international religious organizations, and the General Assembly of the United Nations, which declared in 1973 that apartheid was a 'crime against humanity.' Nevertheless, the Dutch Reformed Church and the National Party government defended apartheid as if it were a moral Christian policy for South Africa. Consistently, spokesmen for apartheid complained that the world misunderstood its moral basis. As the public relations officer for the Dutch Reformed Church, W. A. Landman, tried to argue in 1968, neither church nor state in South Africa defended a theology of racism; rather, they practiced a 'theology of differentiation.' This subtle distinction was certainly lost on most of the people who suffered under church and government policies of racial discrimination, exclusion, and domination. Consistently, however, the Dutch Reformed Church and the National Party government defended those policies as the extension of a moral plan called 'separate development.'

In the early 1960s, South African Prime Minister H. F. Verwoerd argued that his government's racial policies were 'following the moral course of trying to bring about human equality through the creation of separate nations' (Landman, 1968: 146–7). If the world would only leave South Africa alone, Verwoerd frequently declared, 'we shall in a just way such as behooves a Christian nation, work out solutions in the finest detail and carry them out' (De Klerk, 1975: 247). Verwoerd's detailed Christian plan for South Africa was 'separate development.' Although disguised under different terminology – 'multinational development,' 'plural democracy,' 'a confederation of independent nations,' or even 'good neighborliness' – the basic project of the apartheid policy of separate development was the creation of ten artificial black nations out of the territories that had been designated as Native Reserves in the 1913 and 1936 Land Acts. Relegating 80 per cent of the population to about 13 per cent of the land, the architects of separate development hoped to create an entirely white Republic of South Africa. As Minister of Bantu Administration Connie Mulder announced in 1978, 'If our policy is taken to its logical conclusion as far as the Bantu people are concerned, there will be not one Black with South African citizenship' (Ngcokovane, 1989: 187). Obviously, therefore, the National Party government in the 1970s regarded separate development as the logical conclusion of the 'pure' apartheid of racial separation advocated by Afrikaner nationalists in the 1940s.

In a parliamentary debate before the 1948 election, the Minister of Native Affairs, E. G. Jansen, declared his allegiance to 'a nation, an Afrikaner nation, with its own language and culture, with interests of its own' (Ngcokovane, 1989: 87). Once the National Party was in power, E. G. Jansen briefly retained the portfolio of Minister of Native Affairs, embarking on a government policy of creating more nations with languages, cultures, and interests of their own. As the Tomlinson Commission, established by the new government in 1948, was studying the Native Reserves to determine how they could be developed into independent nations, the National Party set out to restore tribal life and the local authority of chiefs in those reserves. 'We are of the opinion that the solidarity of the tribes should be preserved,' Jansen announced in 1950, 'and that they should develop along the lines of their own national character and tradition' (Jansen, 1950: 4–8).

Tribal authority in the reserves could not simply be preserved, however. It had to be recreated. The National Party replaced Jansen with an even more ardent proponent of apartheid, H. F. Verwoerd. The Bantu Authorities Act of 1953, designed by Verwoerd, attempted to implement the 'retribalization' of the reserves by designating chiefs, expanding their powers of tax collection, and organizing them in local regional authorities under the jurisdiction of the Bantu Administration. As a new version of the old British system of 'indirect rule,' the government hoped to establish a system of tribal authorities that would cooperate with the apartheid program of separate development.

From its inception, the policy of separate development drew support from the Dutch Reformed Church. At a church conference at Bloemfontein in 1950, the Dutch Reformed Church resolved that 'total separation' and 'separate economic development' could only be achieved by the 'gradual movement towards total territorial separation between whites and Bantu' (Ngcokovane, 1989: 46). In an effort to mobilize support for the separate development of black nations, the Dutch Reformed Church convened a series of conferences during 1951 and 1952. In keeping with the National Party government's policy of 'retribalization,' the Dutch Reformed Church invited representatives to separate 'ethnic' conferences. A conference for 'Sotho' was held in 1951, one for 'Xhosa' in 1952, and another for 'Zulu' during the same year. Since separate development required the creation of new ethnic and national identities, the Dutch Reformed conferences represented early experiments in the building of black ethnic nationalisms.

In August 1952, at a joint, 'multi-ethnic' conference, the Dutch Reformed Church issued a resolution that lent its religious and moral support to the program of separate development. 'The present urban areas are to be kept as far as possible solely for Europeans,' the church concluded, 'seeing that the Reserves are to become the national home of the Bantu.' Claiming that it was not merely based on economic, social, or political considerations, the Dutch Reformed Church asserted that the separation of South African blacks into 'national homelands also rests on moral grounds' (DRC, 1953: 15). In short, the Dutch Reformed Church wished to confer on black South Africans what it regarded as its own greatest blessing – nationalism. But blacks would have to exercise that blessing in their own, separate nations that would be carved out of the territory of South Africa.

In 1955 the results of the Tomlinson Commission's investigation into the Native Reserves were published. The commission's report reinforced the racism of Afrikaner nationalists and proponents of separate development by stating bluntly that blacks and whites in South Africa were 'culturally and racially alien to each other' (Tomlinson, 1955: 10). But the report also suggested that it was unlikely that the Native Reserves, with their overcrowding, land depletion, and endemic poverty, could be easily transformed into viable independent nations. Undaunted, however, apartheid ideologues called another conference to respond to the Tomlinson Report. In 1956 the Dutch Reformed Church was joined by the Afrikaner cultural organization (FAK) and the Afrikaner Bureau of Race Relations (SABRA) in organizing a *Volkskongress*, or 'Peoples Congress,' in Bloemfontein to formulate a position on separate development. Ironically, this 'Peoples Congress' was convened a year after the 1955 'Congress of the People' in which political movements opposed to the government's racial policies had drafted a Freedom Charter. The Freedom Charter declared that 'South Africa belongs to all who live in it, black and white.' But the Dutch Reformed Church and the *Volkskongress* a year later insisted that 'in South Africa it is not possible for whites and Bantu to grow together into one community.' Furthermore, the *Volkskongress* resolved:

> A policy of integration will inevitably give rise to increasing racial tension and racial conflict and will eventually lead to the annihilation of the national existence of one or both of the groups.... The Congress is convinced that the only acceptable policy, and a policy which is also practically possible, is a policy which is based on the principle of separate development, which must provide for the existence of separate communities in their own territories where each community will have the opportunity of full self expression and development, and will be assured of a free existence and of the right of self-determination.
>
> (SABRA, 1956: 137; Ngcokovane, 1989: 155)

The National Party government set out to implement the relocation of black South Africans to the Native Reserves through pass laws, resettlement acts, amendments to land acts, and even the forced removal of large populations. The government forcibly relocated an estimated 3.5 million people between 1960 and 1983 in the interest of separate development (Platsky and Walker, 1985).

In 1970 the National Party government symbolically eliminated all blacks from the Republic of South Africa through the Bantu Homelands Citizenship

Act. As a result, every black South African became a citizen of one of the ten mythical homelands created by separate development. In 1976 the first of those homelands, the ethnically defined 'Xhosa' nation of the Republic of Transkei, was declared independent. Transkei was followed into independence by the 'Tswana' nation of the Republic of Bophuthatswana in 1977, the 'Venda' nation of the Republic of Venda in 1979, and another 'Xhosa' nation, the Republic of Ciskei, in 1981. The six remaining ethnically defined territories continued to be designated as self-governing homelands, but they refused to accept a national independence that would not be recognized by the world anymore than the independence of Transkei, Bophuthatswana, Venda, or Ciskei was recognized. Nevertheless, the leaders of these artificial nations and homelands tried to mobilize support for their new ethnic nationalisms. Frequently, they drew on resources of religious legitimation to reinforce their own claims to political power within the larger apartheid system of separate development.

The architects of the homeland system sought to create the appearance of political legitimacy through a combination of 'democratic' and 'tribal' politics. In the Transkei, for example, an election held in 1963 leading up to 'self-government' for the homeland produced what appeared as a mandate for the homeland system, but only because the majority of the seats in the Transkei legislature were reserved for 'chiefs' employed by the South African government. Although nearly 75 per cent of the popular vote opposed the homeland system, the 'chiefs' had a sufficient number of seats in the legislature to provide the system with a 'democratic' mandate. If the 'democratic' process was illusory, the 'tribal' politics was also artificial in the homeland system. The leading 'chief' in the Transkei, Kaiser Matanzima, was originally the head of a small clan under the authority of the Paramount Chief of the Thembu. When conflict arose in the 1960s over 'tribal' authority, the South African government declared Kaiser Matanzima the 'Paramount Chief of the Emigrant Thembu,' providing him with a 'tribal' status equal to the Paramount Chief. By 1979, after independence, Kaiser Matanzima was in a position to have the Paramount Chief arrested and stripped of his 'tribal' authority.

Since the political legitimacy of the homelands was extremely tenuous, their leaders occasionally tried to create ethnic or religious nationalisms to confer legitimacy on their new nations. In the Transkei, for example, an ethnic nationalism was difficult to create. Not everyone who lived in the ethnically defined 'Xhosa' nation was 'Xhosa.' A large number of people classified as 'Zulu' or 'southern Sotho' had also been encompassed in the new nation. Furthermore, not everyone classified as 'Xhosa' lived in the new 'Xhosa' nation. Besides the vast number of people living and working in the Republic of South Africa, half a million people classified as 'Xhosa' lived in the neighboring homeland of Ciskei. These factors made the mobilization of an ethnic nationalism difficult, but not impossible. In the 1960s, Kaiser Matanzima tried to mobilize an ethnic nationalism along the lines of the 'Grand Apartheid' policy of H. F. Verwoerd. 'We believe in the sincerity of Dr Verwoerd's policy,' Matanzima declared at a Transkei celebration in 1968. 'The Transkei should cling to its ideals and continue building its nationhood as a separate entity' (Matanzima, 1976: 99). Achieving nominal independence as a separate nation in 1976, Matanzima insisted that 'the only evolution possible is within the framework of separate development' (Matanzima, 1976: 76). Working within the ethnic system of separate nations, Kaiser Matanzima embraced and promoted a new ethnic nationalism.

That new nationalism was not only manufactured within the apartheid system, but it was also built following the example set by Afrikaner nationalism. In a collection of his speeches, titled *Independence My Way*, Kaiser Matanzima revealed that his 'model' had been the Afrikaner nationalist J. B. M. Hertzog (Matanzima, 1976: 137). As a logical extension of this new 'Xhosa' nationalism, Matanzima even demanded annexation of the neighboring 'Xhosa' homeland of the Ciskei on the pretext of creating a unified ethnic nation. In the Ciskei, however, a more obviously religious, ethnic nationalism was created by its president, Lennox Sebe. Perhaps because ethnicity had already been claimed by the 'Xhosa' Republic of Transkei as the basis for its nationalism, Lennox Sebe worked to generate explicitly religious symbols of national legitimacy for the 'Xhosa' Republic of Ciskei. In a speech in 1979, for example, Sebe argued that the 'three pillars' of his nation were politics, education, and 'the religious category' (Sebe, 1980: 40). The 'religious category' that imputed legitimacy to the Ciskei nation, however, drew together elements of 'tradition,' Christianity, and religious nationalism in a new combination that reinforced the system of separate development.

In the matter of 'tradition,' Lennox Sebe argued that the separate development of nations had always been a feature of 'traditional' African life. Addressing an audience in the United States in 1977, for example, Sebe claimed that in ancient times Ciskei was 'our homeland where we lived as a proudly independent and free nation, quite separate and distinctly different from the other black nations of Southern Africa' (Sebe, 1980: 221–2). Rather than acknowledging that Ciskei nationality was a historical product of the Native Reserves and the homeland system, Sebe argued that his nation was not being created but was being restored to its former glory. In religious terms, that restoration of nationality permitted the revival of 'traditional' religion. At a national Ciskei Day of Prayer in 1976, celebrated on December 16 to coincide with the Afrikaner nationalist 'Day of the Covenant,' Lennox Sebe declared that the 'homeland concept, as far as the majority of black

South Africans are concerned, opens the door to the re-establishment of their own cherished national traditions and customs' (Sebe, 1980: 179). Religious and political 'tradition,' according to Sebe, converged in the person of the chief. Of commoner origin, however, Lennox Sebe had to arrange for his own installation as a chief in 1977 to legitimate his claims on 'traditional' religious and political power. At that installation, Sebe declared that the chief was the central symbol of national honor and pride, the 'custodian of all those tribal and national customs and practices that are dear and sacred to the tribe' (Sebe, 1980: 238).

Clearly, Lennox Sebe, like other homeland leaders, tried to manipulate 'traditional' and 'tribal' religious resources in a project of nation-building. As a prominent layman in the Congregational Church, however, Lennox Sebe required a religious nationalism that fused the 'traditional' with Christianity. In 1975, for example, Sebe announced that both a 'traditional' and a Christian religious legitimacy supported his nation. 'We desire to establish, cherish and safeguard our own individual national identity,' Sebe declared, 'to observe our own traditional way of life and seek to live our lives according to Christian principles' (Sebe, 1980: 211). As an indication of what he understood by 'Christian principles,' Sebe told an audience at the South African Defence College in Pretoria, in 1979, that the people of his nation only desired to 'safeguard their Christian democratic and capitalist way of life against the ever aggressive Communistic threat' (Sebe, 1980: 19). In this sense, Lennox Sebe professed a version of Christianity that was particularly congenial to the economic and military interests of the South African government. Interweaving the 'traditional' and the 'Christian,' however, Sebe tried to create a religious nationalism that would mobilize support within his own new nation.

In 1975, Lennox Sebe celebrated the new nationalisms that were emerging in the homeland system: 'The individual indigenous black nations of Southern Africa have established their nationality; they have identified and accepted their national heritage; they have their own language, flag, anthems, mottoes and established constitutional governments' (Sebe, 1980: 210). What made Ciskei unique among these new nationalisms, according to Sebe, was its remarkable parallel with the biblical nation of ancient Israel. At a 1979 convention of his political party, Lennox Sebe declared, 'I am drawing a parallel between the nation of Israel and the nation of Ciskei' (Sebe, 1980: 14). Instructing his audience to read the Book of Exodus, Sebe compared himself to Moses, leading the Ciskei people to their promised land. Anticipating the independence that would be declared for his Ciskei nation in 1981, Sebe concluded: 'I say to the pharaohs of South Africa: 'Let my people go so that they may move on to the promised land and serve Almighty God with joy and thanksgiving' (Sebe, 1980: 18).

Lennox Sebe was even able to draw this parallel between Ciskei and the children of Israel while on visits to the modern state of Israel. Speaking in Tel Aviv in 1979 to the Israel Chamber of Commerce, Sebe referred back to the ancient 'prophets' and 'warriors' of a Ciskei national heritage. Ciskei had its Abraham, the nineteenth-century Chief Ngqika, whom Sebe described as the 'father of us all'; it had its Joshua, the warrior Maqoma; and it had its own prophet, Ntisikana, who had served the political interests of Ngqika's chiefdom with his Christian teachings against the rebel prophet Nxele. In addition to all these appeals to a sacred history, however, Lennox Sebe also compared the Ciskei to the modern state of Israel, claiming that both had achieved a national consensus and the total commitment of every citizen (Sebe, 1980: 141). On one visit to Israel, Sebe was impressed by the monument to ancient Israeli heroism on the mountain of Masada. Returning to Ciskei, he established a national Ciskei shrine, *Ntaba kaNdoda*, the holy mountain. There, Sebe proclaimed, all citizens of Ciskei 'will swear their oaths and allegiance to the nation before this National Shrine' (Hodgson, 1987: 30). The religious nationalism of Lennox Sebe, therefore, had not only a mythic history, but also a sacred ritual center where a Ciskei national identity could be reinforced.

Although he was 'President' for life of that Ciskei nation, Lennox Sebe, like Kaiser Matanzima in the Transkei, had been deposed by 1990. In the Republic of Bophuthatswana, President Lucas Mangope continued to preside over an 'independent' nation. Like Lennox Sebe, Mangope occasionally tried to justify the existence of his nation with reference to Israel. At a symposium in Germany in 1986, for example, Lucas Mangope argued that the word 'homeland' should be used in referring to his nation 'in the same sense that the Jewish people use it when they refer to Israel; that is, as the ancestral land of their forefathers; the forefathers of my people, the Tswanas, were buried in Bophuthatswana' (Mangope, n.d.b: 72). When his nation was declared independent in 1977, Mangope described the moment as a 'turning point in history.' In the rhetoric of religious nationalism, Mangope declared that 'the hallowed ground of our forefathers trembled beneath our feet' at the moment of independence (Mangope, n.d.a: 35–43).

Ten years later, however, still unrecognized by the world as an independent nation, Mangope's government continued to invoke a religious nationalism by proclaiming that 'in this divine origin the Batswana claim equality of status with other nations of the world' (Republic of Bophuthatswana, 1987: 18). Although not everyone living in this 'Tswana' nation was classified as 'Tswana,' Mangope persisted in trying to mobilize a religious nationalism in the idiom of ethnicity. Like Sebe in the Ciskei, Lucas Mangope built a ritual shrine, in this case a shrine that recreated a 'traditional' Tswana village. Ironically, the sacred specialist employed by the Bophuthatswana government to design that shrine was not a 'Tswana' but a 'Zulu' witchdoctor, Credo Mutwa, a popularizer of 'traditional' religious beliefs and customs who had formerly been employed in Soweto by the South African government as a tourist attraction (Lelyveld, 1985: 249–56). Paying tribute to Lucas Mangope, the self-proclaimed 'Zulu witchdoctor' Credo Mutwa declared, 'Anyone who gives me the opportunity to rebuild the African past knows what he is doing' (Republic of Bophuthatswana, 1987: 19).

Building an imagined sacred past, however, was a significant project of religious legitimation undertaken by leaders of many of the new homelands. Perhaps the most successful homeland leader in this respect was Chief Minister of KwaZulu, Mangosuthu Gatsha Buthelezi. Presiding over a 'Zulu' homeland made up of over forty disconnected pieces of land, Chief Buthelezi worked to mobilize an ethnic nationalism. Although he refused to accept national independence, Buthelezi exercised political power – as president, as leader of the only political party, and as head of his own police force – in the 'self-governing' homeland of KwaZulu. In 1975 Buthelezi founded a cultural organization, known as Inkatha. The name was derived from the nineteenth-century symbol of Zulu royalty, but it also revived the name of a Zulu cultural movement in the 1920s that had tried to gain government recognition for the Zulu king. In the 1920s, this ethnic Zulu organization drew support from government officials in Natal, such as G. N. Heaton Nicholls, who argued that 'If we do not get back to communalism we will most certainly arrive very soon at communism' (Marks, 1989: 217). Similarly, Buthelezi's Inkatha movement was encouraged by support from the National Party government for its revival of a 'tribal' or 'ethnic' Zulu nationalism.

Ethnic nationalism was proclaimed by Inkatha from its inception. In 1975 Buthelezi declared 'all members of the Zulu nation are automatically members of Inkatha if they are Zulus. There may be inactive members as no one escapes being a member as long as he or she is a member of the Zulu nation' (Maré and Hamilton, 1987: 57). By that ethnic definition, therefore, at its founding, Inkatha had an instant membership, whether they liked it or not, of over 5 million people. Like other ethnic nationalisms in the homelands, Buthelezi's Inkatha movement also tried to mobilize 'traditional' religious symbols. In 1954, the year after he was installed as a chief under the system of Native Administration, Buthelezi arranged the first 'Shaka Day' celebration, initiating a ritual occasion that became an annual event in a new Zulu ceremonial calendar. To mark the occasion, Buthelezi convinced the Zulu King Cyprian and the royal family to wear 'traditional' costumes of leather loin coverings, leopard skin, feathers, and beads. Ironically, this was the first time that King Cyprian had ever worn 'traditional' Zulu dress. Neither had his father, King Solomon, ever worn such a costume. In the ritual revival of Zulu royalty, however, a new form of ceremonial costume was displayed to symbolize the authenticity of 'Zulu' religious and political power. As leader of the KwaZulu homeland and Inkatha, Buthelezi, with the support of King Goodwill Zwelethini, continued to draw on such 'traditional' religious and political symbols of 'Zuluness' for legitimation (Klopper, 1989).

Although royal symbols referred back to what were imagined as ancient models, they represented the assertion of a modern 'Zulu renaissance' within the context of the new ethnic nationalisms supported by the government policy of separate development. While Buthelezi proclaimed his organization as a black liberation movement, Inkatha was nevertheless entangled in the coercive structures of the homeland system. During the 1980s, Inkatha's ethnic 'Zulu' nationalism increasingly came into conflict with black liberation movements that were working to overcome the ethnic divisions that had been reinforced by apartheid. In response, Buthelezi tried to secure his power base, not only by alleged tactics of coercion and intimidation, but also through renewed appeals to the unifying power of an ethnic nationalism. At a Shaka Day celebration in 1988, Buthelezi declared: 'It is in times of national stress that Zulu nationalism rises to its greatest heights. Our nationalism is a weapon we pick up whenever we are threatened' (Maré, 1989: 4). Threatened by declining support during the 1980s, Inkatha exercised the weapon of ethnic nationalism in ongoing conflicts against supporters of alternative political and labor movements. Not only like a weapon, however, Inkatha's ethnic nationalism also operated like a religion in its efforts to provide sacred symbols, myths, and rituals of national identity that would underwrite the legitimacy of a 'Zulu' nation.

THE NEW RELIGIOUS RIGHT

At its General Synod of 1986, the Dutch Reformed Church undermined some of the religious legitimation that it had provided for apartheid by announcing that racial separation could no longer be justified by the Bible. The church resolved that 'a forced separation and division of peoples cannot be considered a biblical imperative. The attempt to justify such an injunction as derived from the Bible must be recognized as an error and be rejected' (Villa-Vicencio, 1988: 147–8). The Dutch Reformed Church did not go so far as to declare apartheid a 'pseudo-religious ideology,' a 'heresy,' a 'sin,' or even an inherently unjust political system. But it did try to divorce apartheid from any religious legitimation that might have been provided by the Bible or by a church that claimed adherence to the Bible. The General Synod of 1986, therefore, seemed to be withdrawing its religious support from the National Party government. But the relation between church and state was more complex. As the government under P. W. Botha since 1979 had moved away from the rhetoric of apartheid, the Dutch Reformed Church did not have to defend apartheid to continue lending religious legitimation to the government. With new slogans of 'reform' and 'power sharing' being promoted by the National Party government, the Dutch Reformed Church arguably supported the government by abandoning its own religious commitment to apartheid (Posel, 1987b).

At the same time, however, P. W. Botha's regime had created alternative symbols, myths, and rituals of religious legitimacy that stood independent of any support that might have been given by the Dutch Reformed Church. Institutionalized in the South African Defence Force, the South African Police, the public school system, and other agencies of the state, a new religious nationalism took on a life of its own in South Africa under the rule of P. W. Botha. For example, the Defence Force was placed in the service of a 'total strategy,' described by P. W. Botha, while still Minister of Defence in 1977, as comprehensive warfare in all fields – 'military, psychological, economic, political, sociological, technological, diplomatic, ideological, cultural' – including 'religious-cultural action' (Republic of South Africa, 1977). That 'total strategy' was necessary, P. W. Botha and his government argued, to protect South Africa militarily, but also spiritually from the 'total onslaught' of communism. Mandatory military service for all adult white males reinforced this religious nationalism.

Likewise, this new religious nationalism tried to envelop the South African Police in a sacred aura. Despite its obvious and often brutal involvement in maintaining apartheid laws, the South African Police, according to Minister of Law and Order Adriaan Vlok, had 'always maintained Christian norms and civilized standards' (Steytler, 1990: 121). Its official historian even insisted that the South African Police had made a vital contribution 'to the maintenance and expansion of the nation's common spiritual concerns' (Dippenaar, 1988: 246). Drawing on more conventional religious resources, the South African Police maintained a Protestant chaplaincy that reinforced its 'spiritual armament' (Republic of South Africa, 1990: 64–5). But P. W. Botha's government attributed a religious legitimacy to the South African Police in its own right as the force that maintained a sacred law and order. For example, when P. W. Botha's advisory council needed expert testimony in 1987 on what the Christian gospel in South Africa should be, it turned to the South African Police (South African President's Council, 1987: 60). Like the military, therefore, the police force was invested with its own religious legitimacy in this new nationalism.

Finally, the Christian National Education that had captured the South African public school system in the 1950s was increasingly adapted to embrace the new religious nationalism of anticommunism, militarism, and spiritual law and order. For children, the public school was the established church of this religious nationalism. Various school programs, such as

'Youth Preparedness,' mandatory cadet training, and occasional youth camps, tried to instill in every pupil the ability 'to withstand the onslaught against his spiritual and physical integrity' (Evans, 1989). In addition to receiving Christian and biblical instruction in the public schools, children were indoctrinated in the spiritual training and discipline of this new South African religious nationalism.

Therefore, P. W. Botha's government was less dependent upon religious legitimation from the Dutch Reformed Church than were previous regimes. In any case, P. W. Botha consistently warned religious leaders to stay out of politics, which was somewhat ironic considering the extent to which religion pervaded the institutions of his government. Nevertheless, P. W. Botha's attempt to forge a new religious nationalism was widely perceived as merely a pretext for a greater militarization of South African society. Even his policy of 'power-sharing,' including the creation in 1984 of a 'tricameral' parliament with separate houses for so-called 'Coloureds,' 'Indians,' and 'Whites,' was designed to maintain power in the hands of the National Party.

However, extremely conservative Afrikaner nationalists objected to any modification of the apartheid system. Feeling betrayed by P. W. Botha, a group of Afrikaner nationalists left the National Party in 1982 to form their own Conservative Party. Holding to the old apartheid line, the Conservative Party was led by Andries Treurnicht. As a former Dutch Reformed Church minister, and former chairman of the Broederbond, Treurnicht had played a significant role in the religious and political life of Afrikaner nationalism. In 1960 he had been instrumental in getting the Dutch Reformed Church to reject the Cottesloe statement against racism. In 1975 Treurnicht had published his 'Credo of an Afrikaner,' insisting that there was 'no other policy as moral, as responsible to Scripture, as the policy of separate development' (Treurnicht, 1975: 13, 20). After the 1986 resolution by the Dutch Reformed Church on apartheid and the Bible, a group of conservative ministers of the church broke away to form their own Afrikaans Protestante Kerk, providing religious support for the apartheid policy of the Conservative Party. By 1987, adherence to these racialist, political, and religious commitments had drawn enough support among the white electorate in South Africa to make Andries Treurnicht the leader of the official opposition in parliament.

More dramatically than the Conservative Party, however, Afrikaner nationalist sentiments were mobilized in the 1980s by the Afrikaner Werstandsbewegeng (Afrikaner Resistance Movement), known as the AWB, under the charismatic leadership of former policeman Eugene Terre'Blanche. Founded in 1973, the AWB first achieved national prominence in 1979 when about forty of its members broke up a history conference in Pretoria, assaulted the speaker, the Afrikaner historian Floors van Jaarsveld, and tarred and feathered him. 'We as young Afrikaners,' Terre'Blanche declared, 'are tired of seeing spiritual traditions and everything that is sacred to the Afrikaner desecrated and degraded by liberal politicians, dissipated academics and false prophets who hide under the mantle of learning and a false faith' (Thompson, 1985: 213–14). The following year, Terre'Blanche formed a political party, the Blanke Volkstaat Party, based on the single-minded policy of establishing an all-white state. But the AWB remained by self-definition a cultural organization dedicated to defending a Christian Afrikaner nationalism. Highly militant, the AWB developed several affiliated paramilitary divisions to discipline and train followers so they would be ready for a new Battle of Blood River. On 16 December 1980, Terre'Blanche announced to a large and enthusiastic audience that the AWB would triumph because they were 'bound to the guns of Blood River' (*Cape Times* 13 December 1982). During the 1980s, therefore, while the National Party was proposing 'reform' and 'power sharing,' the AWB claimed to be the authentic inheritors of the sacred tradition of Afrikaner nationalism.

Claiming Afrikaner sacred history as its own, the AWB also insisted on the religious legitimacy of its claims on land in South Africa. In a statement of his political platform in 1986, Eugene Terre'Blanche argued that the land for an all-white state in South Africa had been given to Afrikaner nationalists by God. 'I am asking for, demanding, my fatherland and my ground,' Terre'Blanche declared. 'And I will get my land back and I will restore the Boer Republics. I will get it back because I am entitled to it, because my *volk* entered into a contract with my God that this land would be retained for His glory' (*Argus* 17 May 1986). Terre'Blanche justified his militant demands for land on which to establish an all-white state, therefore, as a renewal of an Afrikaner covenant with God.

The AWB flag, which placed three centered sevens on a white, red, and black background, might have born a striking resemblance to a Nazi swastika. But Terre'Blanche insisted that it displayed the central Christian and Afrikaner symbols of his movement. Rather than recalling a swastika, the three sevens in the flag, according to Terre'Blanche, represented 'numbers from the Bible which are used to counter the 'mark of the Beast' – 666.' In this respect, he argued, the AWB flag was 'the only flag or political emblem which exists anywhere today that is based entirely on the Bible.' As some indication of how Terre'Blanche understood the Christian symbols of '666,' the 'mark of the Beast,' or the 'Antichrist,' however, he once declared that the inclusion of so-called 'Coloureds' and 'Indians' in Parliament was 'praying with the anti-Christ.' In addition to representing the biblical apocalypse, however, the three sevens in the AWB flag also recalled the most sacred event in Afrikaner nationalist history: the vow, covenant, and victory of the Boer Voortrekkers at the Battle of Blood River. 'The Boers prayed for seven days in a row,' Terre'Blanche explained, 'then on a Sunday, the seventh day, the battle took place, the miracle battle.' The AWB flag, therefore, represented a potent combination of Christian and Afrikaner symbols, signifying, as Eugene Terre'Blanche insisted, 'the undying faith of the Boer *volk* in their God' (*Argus* 17 May 1986).

Right-wing Afrikaner nationalists, like the supporters of the AWB, felt that the *volk* had been betrayed by the National Party government of P. W. Botha. From their perspective, betrayal had not only taken the form of proposed political 'reform' and 'power sharing,' but also through the relaxation of pass laws, influx controls, and job reservation for whites that had protected white workers from competition with black workers over employment. Arguably, the removal of these measures that had protected the privileged position of white workers had been motivated by the National Party's recognition that these laws had become unenforceable. In any event, white workers, farmers, and civil servants who were drawn into the right-wing religious nationalism of a movement like the AWB felt threatened by the apparent erosion of their racially privileged position in South Africa. Furthermore, the rise of the AWB coincided with the worst economic crisis for white workers and farmers since the depression of 1930. Although not coming close to the extent of unemployment, poverty, and deprivation suffered by black South Africans, unemployment among white South Africans rose from 6,000 in 1981 to 25,000 by 1985. White unemployment had reached over 32,000 by the middle of 1986. As in the 1930s, therefore, Afrikaner nationalism in the 1980s promised protection and upliftment for 'poor whites' through a salvation that was simultaneously religious, political, and economic. Reviving the familiar themes of an Afrikaner calling, covenant, and destiny in South Africa, right-wing Afrikaner nationalists in the 1980s drew a considerable following to their gospel of racist salvation.

During the 1980s, Afrikaner nationalists engaged in competitions over religious legitimation. As the unqualified support from the Dutch Reformed Church appeared to weaken, P. W. Botha's government occasionally looked to fundamentalist or evangelical Christians of the New Religious Right in the United States and Germany for religious legitimation. In particular, right-wing Christian organizations in the United States offered ideological support for P. W. Botha's 'total strategy' against communism in the region of southern Africa. South Africa seemed to be serving the special interests of right-wing Christian fundamentalism (Green, 1987). American fundamentalist Jerry Falwell, for example, not only defended the South African government's anticommunism, but also its law prohibiting abortion. From Falwell's perspective, South Africa was a Christian nation, upholding human rights – or, more precisely, the rights of the unborn – because abortion was illegal in South Africa. A number of small right-wing religious movements emerged in the 1980s, drawing on evangelical or fundamentalist religious resources to defend the legitimacy of the South African state under P. W. Botha (Gifford, 1988; Arendse, 1989). While these efforts at religious legitimation were unconvincing to the black majority of South Africa, they were also rejected by right-wing Afrikaner nationalists who argued that the National Party government of P. W. Botha was illegitimate because it had betrayed the white supremacy of the Afrikaner nation.

As Afrikanerdom became divided in the 1980s, the sacred times and places of Afrikaner nationalism turned into sites of struggle over religious legitimacy. In particular, the sacred time of 16 December and the sacred place of the Voortrekker Monument in Pretoria, both representing the sacred power of the Battle of Blood River, became sites of ritual conflict over competing claims on Afrikaner authenticity. On 16 December 1983, for example, the cultural organization of the National Party conducted a ceremony inside the Voortrekker Monument for only 500 invited guests. Members of the AWB were prevented from entry into that sacred space. In response to this ritual exclusion, one AWB member was recorded as complaining, 'Why must we stand outside the gate like blacks?' (*Sunday Tribune* 18 December 1983). Obviously, the AWB assumed that black South Africans should be outside the center of ritual power, but not authentic Afrikaner nationalists. For the 'Day of the Covenant' celebrations of 16 December 1985, the Dutch Reformed Church minister, Nico Smith, proposed drafting a new, nonracial vow that could include all South Africans. In response, Eugene Terre'Blanche branded this proposal a 'sacrilege' and threatened Reverend Smith that he would 'suffer the consequences of tampering with a day regarded as sacred by the *volk*' (*Argus* 12 December 1985).

By the time Afrikaner nationalists celebrated the 150th anniversary of the Battle of Blood River in 1988, right-wing Afrikaner nationalists were able to stage their own ox-wagon trek. Mobilizing a more fervent, enthusiastic response than the government's official ox-wagon trek, the right-wing celebrations of 1988 revived some of the Afrikaner nationalist enthusiasm that had been aroused in 1938. On 16 December, while P. W. Botha spoke at the Voortrekker Monument, right-wing Afrikaner nationalists were far away at Donkerhoek, dressed in Voortrekker costume, listening to patriotic hymns, sermons, and speeches, and even participating in a reenactment of the Battle of Blood River, complete with prerecorded sounds of rifle fire and Zulu war cries. After recreating the battle, Eugene Terre'Blanche took the stage to retell the sacred history of the Afrikaner nation. That history, according to Terre'Blanche, belonged to the right-wing Afrikaner nationalists gathered at Donkerhoek, not to the nationalists with P. W. Botha at the Voortrekker Monument. Although the National Party had betrayed their sacred history, Eugene Terre'Blanche promised his audience that they would once again achieve victory and ethnic redemption in a new Afrikaner nation (Grundlingh and Sapire, 1989: 36).

In the battle over Afrikaner sacred symbols, therefore, right-wing nationalists advanced militant claims on a special religious legitimacy. Framed in terms of ethnicity, however, their religious nationalism not only recalled earlier Afrikaner nationalisms, but also the varied forms of 'Xhosa,' 'Tswana,' and 'Zulu' nationalism that had been produced under the historical conditions of separate development. Defending the apartheid system, the Conservative Party, the AWB, and other right-wing movements drew on religious resources to legitimize white supremacy within a system of ethnically defined nations. Others, however, had struggled throughout the twentieth century for liberation from the oppression that ethnic nationalisms had legitimated in South Africa.

REFERENCES

Anonymous (1989). 'Ethnicity and Pseudo-Ethnicity in the Ciskei.' In: Leroy Vail (ed.) *The Creation of Tribalism in Southern Africa*. London: James Currey; Berkeley: University of California Press; Cape Town: David Philip. 395–413.

Arendse, Roger A. (1989). 'The Gospel Defence League: A Critical Analysis of a Right Wing Group in South Africa.' *Journal of Theology for Southern Africa* 69: 95–105.

Brink, C. B. (1953). 'The Fundamental Principles of the Mission Policy of the Dutch Reformed Churches in South Africa.' In: *Christian Principles in Multi-Racial South Africa: A Report of the Dutch Reformed Conference of Church Leaders*. Pretoria: NGK. 28–40.

Bunting, Brian (1964). *The Rise of the South African Reich*. London: Cox & Wyman.

Butler, Jeffrey, Robert I. Rotberg, and John Adams (1977). *The Black Homelands of South Africa*. Berkeley: University of California Press.

Cronjé, Geoff (1945). *'n Tuiste vir die Nageslag: Die Blywende Oplossing van Suid-Afrika se Rassevraagstukke*. Cape Town: Pro Publicite.

Cronjé, Geoff, and William Nicol (eds) (1948). *Regverdige Rasse-apartheid*. Stellenbosch: Christen-Studentevereniging – Maatskappy van Suid-Afrika.

Davids, Achmat (1989). 'The Words the Slaves Made: A Study of the Culture, Languages, Schools and Literacy of the Slaves in Cape Town and their Influence on the Development of Arabic-Afrikaans.' Unpublished paper. Cape Town: University of Cape Town, Centre for African Studies.

De Gruchy, John (1985). 'A Short History of the Christian Institute.' In: Charles Villa-Vicencio and John De Gruchy (eds) *Resistance and Hope: South African Essays in Honour of Beyers Naudé*. Cape Town: David Philip. 14–26.

De Gruchy, John, and Charles Villa-Vicencio (eds) (1983). *Apartheid is a Heresy*. Grand Rapids, MI: Eerdmans.

De Klerk, W. A. (1975). *Puritans in Africa*. Harmondsworth: Penguin.

Dippenaar, M. D. (1988). *Die Geskiedenis van die Suid Afrikaanse Polisie*. Silverton: Promedia.

DRC (1953). *The Racial Issue in South Africa: The Native Problem*. Bloemfontein: Dutch Reformed Press.

Du Toit, André (1975). 'Ideological Change, Afrikaner Nationalism and Pragmatic Racial Domination in South Africa.' In: Leonard Thompson and Jeffrey Butler (eds) *Change in Contemporary South Africa*. Berkeley: University of California Press.

Du Toit, André (1983). 'No Chosen People: The Myth of the Calvinist Origins of Afrikaner Nationalism and Racial Ideology.' *American Historical Review* 88: 920–52.

Du Toit, André (1984). 'Captive to the Nationalist Paradigm: Prof. F. A. Van Jaarsveld and the Historical Evidence for the Afrikaner's Ideas on his Calling and Mission.' *South African Historical Journal* 16: 49–80.

Du Toit, André (1985). 'Puritans in Africa? Afrikaner "Calvinism" and Kuyperian Neo-Calvinism in Late Nineteenth-Century South Africa.' *Comparative Studies in History and Society* 27: 209–40.

Eloff, Gerhardus (1942). *Rasse en Rasvermenging: Die Boerevolk gesien van die Standpunt van Rasseleer*. Bloemfontein: Nasionale Pers.

Evans, Gavin (1989). 'Classrooms of War: The Militarisation of White South African Schooling.' In: Jacklyn Cock and Laurie Nathan (eds) *War and Society: The Militarisation of South Africa*. Cape Town: David Philip. 283–97.

Geldenhuys, F. E. O'Brien (1982). *In die Stroomversnellings: 50 Jaar van die N. G. Kerk*. Cape Town: Tafelberg.

Gifford, Paul (1988). *The Religious Right in Southern Africa*. Harare: University of Zimbabwe.

Giliomee, Hermann (1983). 'Constructing Afrikaner Nationalism.' *Journal of Asian and African Studies* 18: 83–98.

Giliomee, Hermann (1984). 'Reinterpreting Afrikaner Nationalism.' In: *The Societies of Southern Africa in the Nineteenth and Twentieth Centuries*, vol. 13. London: Institute of Commonwealth Studies. 1–10.

Giliomee, Hermann (1987a). 'The Beginnings of Afrikaner Nationalism, 1870–1915.' *South African Historical Journal* 19: 115–42.

Giliomee, Hermann (1987b). 'Western Cape Farmers and the Beginnings of Afrikaner Nationalism.' *Journal of Southern African Studies* 14: 38–63.

Giliomee, Hermann (1989). 'The Beginning of Afrikaner Ethnic Consciousness, 1850–1915.' In: Leroy Vail (ed.) *The Creation of Tribalism in Southern Africa*. London: James Currey; Berkeley: University of California Press; Cape Town: David Philip. 21–54.

Green, Pippa (1987). 'Apartheid and the Religious Right.' *Christianity and Crisis* 47(14): 326–8.

Greenberg, Stanley B. (1987). *Legitimating the Illegitimate: State, Markets, and Resistance in South Africa*. Berkeley: University of California Press.

Grundlingh, Albert, and Hilary Sapire (1989). 'From Feverish Festival to Repetitive Ritual? The Changing Fortunes of Great Trek Mythology in an Industrializing South Africa, 1938–1988.' *South African Historical Journal* 21: 19–37.

Hexham, Irving (1981). *The Irony of Apartheid*. New York: Edwin Mellen.

Hodgson, Janet (1987). '*Ntaba kaNdoda*: Orchestrating Symbols for National Unity in Ciskei.' *Journal of Theology for Southern Africa* 58: 18–31.

Jansen, E. G. (1950). *Native Policy of the Union of South Africa*. Pretoria: State Information Office of the Union of South Africa.

Keet, B. B. (1956). *Suid-Afrika, Waarheen?* Stellenbosch: University Publishers and Book Sellers.

Klopper, Sandra (1989). 'Mobilizing Cultural Symbols in Twentieth Century

Zululand.' Unpublished paper. University of Cape Town, Centre for African Studies.

Landman, W. A. (1968). *A Plea for Understanding: A Reply to the Reformed Church in America*. Cape Town: Information Bureau of the Dutch Reformed Church.

Lelyveld, Joseph (1985). *Move Your Shadow: South Africa, Black and White*. New York: Random House.

Loubser, J. A. (1987). *The Apartheid Bible: A Critical Review of Racial Theology in South Africa*. Cape Town: Maskew Miller Longman.

MacCrone, I.D. (1938). 'The Great Trek and its Centenary Celebration in the Light of Group Psychology.' *Race Relations* 4: 81–4.

Mangope, Lucas M. (n.d.a). *A Place for All*. Cape Town: Via Afrika.

Mangope, Lucas M. (n.d.b). *Mandatory Sanctions: Bophuthatswana and Frontline OAU Nations*. Lagos, Nigeria: Emmcon Books.

Marais, Ben (1953). *Colour: The Unsolved Problem of the West*. Cape Town: Timmins (orig. edn 1952).

Maré, Gerhard (1989). 'The Past, the Present, and Negotiation Politics: The Role of Inkatha.' Unpublished paper. University of Cape Town, Centre for African Studies.

Maré, Gerhard, and Georgina Hamilton (1987). *An Appetite for Power: Buthelezi's Inkatha and the Politics of 'Loyal Resistance'*. Johannesburg: Ravan Press.

Marks, Shula (1989). 'Patriotism, Patriarchy and Purity: Natal and the Politics of Zulu Ethnic Consciousness.' In: Leroy Vail (ed.) *The Creation of Tribalism in Southern Africa*. London: James Currey; Berkeley: University of California Press; Cape Town: David Philip. 215–40.

Matanzima, Kaiser D. (1976). *Independence My Way*. Pretoria: Foreign Affairs Association.

Moodie, T. Dunbar (1975). *The Rise of Afrikanerdom: Power, Apartheid and Afrikaner Civil Religion*. Berkeley: University of California Press.

Ngcokovane, Cecil (1989). *Demons of Apartheid: A Moral and Ethical Analysis of the N. G. K., N. P. and Broederbond's Justification of Apartheid*. Johannesburg: Skotaville.

O'Meara, Dan (1977). 'The Afrikaner Broederbond, 1927–1948: Class Vanguard of Afrikaner Nationalism.' *Journal of Southern African Studies* 3: 156–86.

O'Meara, Dan (1983). *Volkskapitalisme: Class, Capital and Ideology in the Development of Afrikaner Nationalism, 1934–1948*. Cambridge: Cambridge University Press.

Pienaar, S. W. (1964). *Believe in Your People: D. F. Malan as Orator, 1908–1954*. Cape Town: Tafelberg.

Platsky, Laurine, and Cherryl Walker (1985). *The Surplus People*. Johannesburg: Ravan Press.

Posel, Deborah (1987a). 'The Meaning of Apartheid before 1948: Conflicting Interests and Forces within the Afrikaner Nationalist Alliance.' *Journal of Southern African Studies* 14: 123–39.

Posel, Deborah (1987b). 'The Language of Domination, 1978–1983.' In: Shula Marks and Stanley Trapido (eds) *The Politics of Race, Class and Nationalism in Twentieth Century South Africa*. London: Longman. 419–43.

Republic of Bophuthatswana (1987). *A Nation on the March*. Melville: Hans Strydom Publishers.

Republic of South Africa (1977). *White Paper on Defence, 1977*. Pretoria: Government Printers.

Republic of South Africa (1990). *White Paper on the Organisation and Functions of the South African Police*. Pretoria: Government Printers.

Ritner, Susan Rennie (1967). 'The Dutch Reformed Church and Apartheid.' *Journal of Contemporary History* 2(4): 17–37.

Ritner, Susan Rennie (1977). 'Salvation through Separation: The Role of the Dutch Reformed Church in South Africa in the Formulation of Afrikaner Race Ideology.' PhD dissertation, Columbia University.

SABRA (1956). *Volkskongres oor die Toekoms van die Bantoe*. Stellenbosch: South African Bureau of Racial Affairs.

Sebe, L. L. W. (1980). *Challenges*. Cape Town: Via Afrika.

Serfontein, J. H. P. (1979). *Brotherhood of Power: An Exposé of the Secret Afrikaner Broederbond*. London: Rex Collings.

Serfontein, J. H. P. (1982). *Apartheid, Change and the N. G. Kerk*. Emmarentia: Taurus.

Smart, Ninian (1984). 'Christianity and Nationalism.' *The Scottish Journal of Religious Studies* 5: 37–50.

South African President's Council (1987). *Report of the Committee for Social Affairs on the Youth of South Africa*. Cape Town: Government Printers.

Steytler, Nico (1990). 'Policing Political Opponents: Death Squads and Cop Culture.' In: Desirée Hansson and Dirk van Zyl Smit (eds) *Towards Justice: Crime and State Control in South Africa*. Cape Town: Oxford University Press. 106–34.

Strassburger, Elfriede (1974). *Ecumenism in South Africa, 1936–1960*. Johannesburg: South African Council of Churches.

Thompson, Leonard (1985). *The Political Mythology of Apartheid*. New Haven: Yale University Press.

Tomlinson Commission (1955). *Summary of the Report of the Commission for the Socio-Economic Development of the Bantu Areas within the Union of South Africa*. Pretoria: Government Printers.

Treurnicht, Andries P. (1975). *Credo van 'n Afrikaner*. Cape Town: Tafelberg.

Vail, Leroy (ed.) (1989). *The Creation of Tribalism in Southern Africa*. London: James Currey; Berkeley: University of California Press; Cape Town: David Philip.

Villa-Vicencio, Charles (1988). *Trapped in Apartheid*. Maryknoll, NY: Orbis; Cape Town: David Philip.

Villa-Vicencio, Charles, and John De Gruchy (eds) (1985). *Resistance and Hope: South African Essays in Honour of Beyers Naudé*. Cape Town: David Philip.

Welsh, David (1988). 'South Africa's Ultra-Right: Part One.' *Patterns of Prejudice* 22(4): 13–23.

Welsh, David (1989). 'South Africa's Ultra-Right: Part Two.' *Patterns of Prejudice* 23(1): 3–15.

Wilkins, Ivor, and Hans Strydom (1978). *The Super-Afrikaners*. Johannesburg: Jonathan Ball.

7   Religious liberation

The vast majority of South Africans experienced the political projects of white supremacy, apartheid, and separate development as policies of systematic oppression. During the twentieth century, resistance to oppression took many forms, including political movements, labor organization, and mass mobilization. Frequently, the varied forms of resistance were reinforced by religion. As religion had been drawn into the legitimation of an oppressive system in South Africa, religious resources were also drawn upon, often in new, unexpected ways, in the struggle for liberation. The political history of resistance in South Africa has been well documented, with particular attention to the social and economic forces at work in both the system of oppression and the struggles for liberation (Lodge, 1983). At the same time, however, religion was an important dimension of liberation. Religious instruments of power – symbols, myths, rituals, and traditions – were frequently deployed in the struggle for economic, social, and political liberation. In an important sense, liberation required a recovery of humanity from the dehumanizing relations of power that had become established in South Africa. Religious liberation, therefore, was evident in the different ways in which that recovery of humanity could be articulated and realized in a new spirit of freedom.

In the modern era, political resistance to white domination was organized in 1912 in the formation of the South African Native National Congress, renamed in 1923 as the African National Congress (ANC). Initially formed to oppose the Land Act that had been proposed by the new Union of South Africa, the Congress provided a platform for airing a wide range of African grievances. Since the founders of the Congress were mainly educated professional men, they tended to focus on racial policies that excluded them from full participation in South African society. In this respect, the political disfranchisement of Africans was a particular concern of the ANC during its early years. But the Congress also tried to speak on behalf of the dispossessed peasants and the exploited workers who suffered under discriminatory land

and labor laws. As ministers and church leaders were strongly represented among its founders, however, the ANC tended to address all of these issues with religious appeals to Christian morality. Not only affirming their own religious commitment, ANC leaders indicted the government for violating its professed religious affiliation with Christianity. For the early leaders of the ANC, therefore, political resistance required a reaffirmation of basic religious and moral principles of the Christian religion. Through meetings, deputations, and petitions, the ANC tried to advance its resistance based on Christian appeals to the government of South Africa.

During the 1940s, however, this strategy of Christian appeals was supplemented by the emergence of a younger generation in the ANC committed to new African assertions of identity, meaning, and power. As leaders of the older generation continued to appeal to Christian morality, the ANC Youth League that was formed in 1944 asserted a more militant African Nationalism, or 'Africanism,' as a new ideology of liberation. Drawing on both traditional and Christian resources, the Congress Youth League proclaimed this new Africanism as a religious commitment in the present that promised political liberation in the future. The Youth League also called for a more vigorous political strategy that would replace the tactics of petition with mass action, resulting in the sustained civil disobedience of unjust laws in the 1952 Defiance Campaign. Out of that campaign, however, a split emerged between 'Africanists,' who adhered to an orthodox African nationalism, and 'Charterists,' who embraced the multiracial cooperation that in 1955 produced the Freedom Charter, with its declaration that 'South Africa belongs to all who live in it, black and white.' As the 'Charterists' controlled the ANC in the 1950s, 'Africanists' were forced out of the organization, eventually forming their own, alternative liberation movement in 1959, the Pan-Africanist Congress (PAC). By 1960, however, both the ANC and PAC had been declared unlawful by the South African government, with their leaders either imprisoned or forced into exile. Nevertheless, the ideological and religious commitments associated with these movements persisted.

Out of the political struggles of the 1940s and 1950s, a particular type of theology – African theology – emerged in South Africa. Although not necessarily tied to any of the political movements of the time, African theology continued to work out a Christianity that was deeply embedded in traditional African religion and culture. By contrast, another younger generation, growing up under the repression of the 1960s, and coming of age in the 1970s, proclaimed a new theology of liberation – Black Theology. Inspired to a certain extent by the Black Power movement in the United States, a Black Consciousness movement emerged in South Africa during the early 1970s to invest blackness with a new symbolic potency. Not essentially a racial category, black was redefined to represent both the condition of oppression and the potential for the recovery of a free, powerful humanity. Growing out of the Black Consciousness movement, Black Theology was a critical reflection on the practical conditions within which black humanity had been denied and the practices in and through which it could be fully realized. Although actively repressed by the government, particularly after the student uprisings that began in Soweto in 1976, the Black Consciousness movement and Black Theology persisted as vital options in the struggle for liberation in South Africa.

Black Theology had much in common with the liberation theologies that were being developed in Latin America, particularly when black theologians incorporated Marxist class analysis into their critical reflections on oppression and liberation. But during the 1970s South African Black Theology was not directly influenced by Latin American liberation theology. A more direct engagement with international developments in liberation theology, however, did emerge in religious responses to the popular uprising and state repression of the 1980s in South Africa. Particularly after 1984, South African theologians drew upon the resources of liberation theology to advance a critique of the relations among church, state, and popular aspirations for freedom. Perceiving the 1980s as a crucial time, even as a *kairos*, or sacred time of divine revelation, theologians in opposition to the state advanced an ongoing critique of the religious legitimation upon which the state had relied. At the same time, however, opposition theologians in South Africa responded to the initiatives that had been taken by the political liberation movements, even in matters of religion. Toward the end of the twentieth century, therefore, a shift occurred in the relations between religion and politics in the struggle for a religious liberation from oppression in South Africa. To suggest this shift in simple, slightly exaggerated terms: In 1912 the movement of political liberation that was led by the African National Congress worked to conform its political protest to Christian principles. By the 1980s, however, Christian theologians who identified with the struggle for liberation worked to conform their religious principles and practice to the requirements of political, social, and economic liberation in South Africa.

AFRICAN NATIONALISM

In 1911 Pixley ka Isaka Seme returned from his studies at Cornell University in the United States to open a law practice in Johannesburg. While in America, Pixley Seme had delivered an address at Columbia University that celebrated the 'regeneration of Africa' that he saw occurring at the beginning of the twentieth century. In prophetic tones, Seme declared that economic, social, educational, and religious developments in Africa were producing 'a new and unique civilization... thoroughly spiritual and humanistic – indeed a regeneration moral and eternal' (Ferris, 1913, I: 437–9). Shortly after his return to South Africa, Seme proposed the formation of a political organization that would serve this regeneration of Africa.

In a statement of purpose for the new organization, Pixley Seme invoked principles of Christian morality and African unity that would come to characterize the emergence of a new African nationalism in South Africa. Proclaiming a new spirit of progress and cooperation, Seme identified that spirit as essentially Christian. 'This spirit is due no doubt to the great triumph of Christianity,' Seme declared, 'which teaches men everywhere that in this world they have a common duty to perform both towards God and towards one another.' A Christian regeneration of Africa, however, required a new unity. For the sake of unity, 'tribal' divisions, Seme insisted, 'must be buried and forgotten; it has shed among us sufficient blood! We are one people' (Karis and Carter, 1972, I: 72). On 8 January 1912, Seme organized the first meeting of the new political movement in Bloemfontein, gathering several hundred of South Africa's most prominent African ministers, professionals, businessmen, and chiefs. Opening the meeting with Tiyo Soga's hymn, 'Fulfill thy promise, God of truth,' the gathering resolved to found the South African Native National Congress (Lodge, 1983: 1).

During the first decade of its existence, the Congress protested the policies of the government of the new Union of South Africa, primarily the 1913 Land Act, the denial of voting rights, and pass laws for Africans. The Land Act that designated about 7 per cent of South Africa as Native Reserves, barring Africans from purchasing land outside those areas, had caused considerable suffering that the Congress tried to bring to international attention (Plaatje, 1982). The Christian educator John Dube, first president-general of the Congress, argued that the Congress should have 'no protest against the principle of separation so far as it can be fairly and practically carried out' (Karis and Carter, 1972, I: 63). Dube's acceptance of the principle of racial segregation that was embodied in the Land Act, however, was rejected by the Congress. Defeated in the Congress elections of 1917, Dube was replaced as president by the Transvaal leader, S. M. Makgatho.

Rejecting the principle of racial segregation, the Congress pressed for inclusion in a common civil society. For the educated, middle-class founders of the Congress, the denial of voting rights in the Transvaal, Orange Free State, and Natal was particularly disturbing. The qualified franchise in the Cape, which gave the vote to Africans who passed educational and property tests, was upheld in the constitution of the Union of South Africa. Encouraged by this small concession, leaders of the Congress hoped to see that policy of limited inclusion in electoral politics extended throughout the country. They frequently cited the maxim of Cecil Rhodes – 'Equal rights for all civilized men from the Cape to the Zambesi' – as the principle that justified their access to voting rights. While leaders of the Congress called for their inclusion in the franchise, however, mass protest mobilized against the pass laws that restricted freedom of movement, residence, and employment for all Africans in the country. Although the Congress supported demonstrations against pass laws in 1919, it continued for the most part to concentrate on petitioning to gain access to voting rights in the Union of South Africa.

During the 1920s, however, as the Congress changed its name to the African National Congress (ANC), the most pressing political issue in the country was the exploitation of African labor. The realignment in white politics that produced the coalition government in 1924 of Hertzog's National Party and the primarily white, English-speaking socialist Labor Party resulted in a series of labor laws that further entrenched discrimination against black workers. Under the so-called 'civilized labor policy,' South African law denied black workers the jobs, wages, and labor representation that were reserved for white workers. Although the ANC made some effort in the 1920s to protest the 'color bar' in labor, other organizations, particularly the Industrial and Commercial Workers Union (founded in 1919) and the South African Communist Party (founded in 1921) were more aggressive in organizing workers and protesting discriminatory labor laws (Bradford, 1987; Lerumo, 1971; Legassick, 1973).

Leaders of the ANC continued into the 1930s to concentrate on petitioning the government to repeal the 1913 Land Act and to extend the qualified Cape franchise to the rest of the Union of South Africa. In 1936, however, the coalition government of Smuts and Hertzog destroyed the hopes of ANC leadership on both counts. While the Land Act of 1936 further entrenched the African reserve system, the 1936 Native Representation Act dissolved the Cape franchise and replaced it with an impotent Native Representatives Council. Although some of its leaders participated in that council, the ANC went into a period of decline during the 1930s. Other organizations, however, continued its tradition of protest through meetings, petitions, and Christian prayer. The All African Convention, for example, held its first meeting in December 1935 to protest the impending land and representation laws. Led by ANC president-general Pixley Seme and D. D. T. Jabavu, the All African Convention combined protest with prayer by calling for a 'day of universal humiliation and intercession' during which 'prayers must be offered up for the Almighty's guidance and intervention in the dark cloud of the pending disfranchisement of the Cape Natives by the Parliament of South Africa' (Karis and Carter, 1973, II: 33). Although some delegates called for more militant action through mass protest meetings, the All African Convention and the ANC persisted in registering their protests by means of Christian moral appeals to the governments of South Africa and Great Britain.

Without discounting the political, social, and economic history of African political resistance, it is possible to outline the basic themes of a religious ideology of African nationalism that emerged in and through that history between 1912 and 1940 in South Africa. First, this emergent African nationalism was intentionally based on Christian principles. The first president of the ANC, John Dube, an American-educated Congregational minister, and director of the Christian Ohlange Institute for industrial education in Natal, was particularly adamant in his appeals to Christianity. In a pamphlet published in 1892, for example, John Dube had already declared the Christian foundation of his African nationalism. 'Christianity will usher in a new civilization,' Dube had written, 'and the 'Dark Continent' will be transformed into a land of commerce and Christian institutions' (Karis and Carter, 1972, I: 69). In his political work on behalf of the ANC, John Dube consistently called upon Africans to realize the potential of this Christian transformation. 'Onward! Upward!' Dube exhorted, 'into the higher places of civilisation and Christianity – not backwards into the slump of darkness nor downward into the abyss of antiquated tribal systems' (Walshe, 1970: 38).

While calling upon Africans to embrace Christian morality, civilization, and progress, John Dube also had to recognize that the government failed to live up to its own claims on Christian legitimation. Accordingly, Dube's political rhetoric often indicated the failure of South African government policy to conform to Christian morality. In particular, Dube pointed to the 1913 Land Act as 'saddening proof of the utter failure, the inability of Christianity, in spite of all its vaunts to raise even the most enlightened race above the lowest levels of selfishness and greed and godless persecution' (Walshe, 1970: 46). Nevertheless, John Dube persisted in trying to register protests against unjust legislation by appealing to the Christian conscience of the white public and government of South Africa. 'How can a government policy proclaiming itself Christian perpetrate such cruelties on the inarticulate poor?' Dube asked. 'How can a professedly Christian people permit such persecution in their midst and look on unmoved?' (Marks, 1975: 176).

Such appeals to Christian moral conscience remained a prominent feature of the political discourse of the ANC. Dube's successor as president of the ANC, S. M. Makgatho, as noted in Chapter Three, had little confidence in appeals to the Christian moral conscience of whites in South Africa, because the 'God of the white people was Gold, their heaven money' (Bonner, 1982: 296). But other ANC presidents renewed the basic appeal to Christian moral principles. The American and European trained medical doctor, A. B. Xuma, for example, who later served as ANC president during the 1940s, consistently appealed to the ideals of 'Christianity, human decency, and democracy' (Walshe, 1970: 341). Since he claimed that these values were shared by both whites and blacks in South Africa, Xuma tried to gain ideological leverage on a self-professed Christian government in the 1930s by asking, 'Would Christ, whose followers and messengers we profess to be, approve of our Native Policy in practice?' (Karis and Carter, 1972, I: 219). These Christian appeals by the ANC, however, remained largely ignored by both church and state in South Africa.

Outside of the ANC, the most concerted appeals to Christian moral principles as a basis for political protest were made by John Tengo Jabavu, and later by his son, D. D. T. Jabavu. Based in the Cape, both defended the limited Cape franchise on Christian grounds. In 1927, for example, John Tengo Jabavu argued before a government commission that the inclusion of Africans in the Cape franchise had been based on 'the essential Christian ethic, namely: "Do unto others as you would have them do unto you."' The Cape franchise, he declared, was 'the noblest monument of the white man's rule, emblematic of his genuineness in practising the precepts of Holy Scripture towards the subject races.' Optimistic that the limited voting rights granted in the Cape would be gradually extended to the rest of South Africa, John Tengo Jabavu anticipated a future of cooperation and mutual understanding in a common Christian society that would be ruled under this 'obvious Christian policy' (Karis and Carter, 1972, I: 202, 208; Ngcongco, 1979). D. D. T. Jabavu, as well, was convinced that the extension of voting rights would become a reality in South Africa because it was a Christian imperative (Gerhart, 1978: 35; Jabavu, 1928). In the 1930s, however, anticipating the legislation that would remove even the limited voting rights in the Cape, D. D. T. Jabavu apparently despaired at the government's failure to adhere to Christian morality. 'Are we to become Christian,' he asked, 'while our White mentors turn pagan?' (Karis and Carter, 1972, I: 290).

While the ANC and the All African Convention made frequent appeals to Christian principles, other political leaders had no confidence at all in the liberating potential of Christianity for African nationalism. Influenced by the African nationalism of Marcus Garvey while in America, James Thaele returned to express grave doubts about the usefulness of Christian appeals in the political arena. In 1923, Thaele noted that Christianity was 'a doctrine good in all its essentials,' but 'politics rule the world not religion.' Although he rejected appeals to Christian morality, James Thaele did argue that religious resources might support a politics of confrontation. 'The Blacks have got to be told by students of theological thought,' Thaele insisted, 'that in the cosmogonies of Moses, or of Biblical history, we find the Prophet Isaiah breathing politics' (Karis and Carter, 1972, I: 216). Rather than Christian morality, therefore, Thaele saw some value in the biblical model of a prophetic politics that challenged unjust authority. Nevertheless, on behalf of the Industrial and Commercial Workers Union (ICU), James Thaele called for the organization of black labor power, rather than Christian morality, as the basis for economic and political liberation in South Africa. Similarly, the charismatic leader of the ICU, Clements Kadalie, rejected appeals to Christian principles because, as he argued in 1928, history demonstrated that the Christian church has been, 'thoroughly reactionary and drifting from Christ's teaching, [and] has sided with the rich against the poor, opposing every effort towards social and economic freedom for the masses' (Walshe, 1970: 162).

Next to Christian principles, the founding leaders of the ANC appealed most frequently to Britain. A second feature of an emergent African nationalism, therefore, was comprised of what ANC leaders perceived as fundamental British ideals of justice, citizenship, and human rights. Claiming British citizenship under the Empire, the founding leaders of the ANC sent petitions to the British King, the Imperial Parliament, and the public of Great Britain. In particular, John Dube made constant appeals to 'England's duty' to see that South Africa adhered to principles of British justice. At a conference in 1927, Sol Plaatje, who had remained on an ANC deputation to Britain during the First World War, continued to demand the application of British standards of civil rights in South Africa. Africans tended to be 'regarded more as a British object than a British subject,' Plaatje wryly noted, 'but they claimed the enjoyment of all the rights and privileges possessed by British people of every colour in all parts of the Empire' (Karis and Carter, 1972, I: 257).

Similarly, the Anglican priest and ANC leader James Calata reminded a conference in 1931 that British policy in the Cape had allowed voting rights and ownership of land for African citizens. Since 1910, however, the government of South Africa had not followed the policy of Britain but 'the policy of the sjambok' (Karis and Carter, 1972, I: 276). Symbolizing the government policy of white domination by the image of the leather whip, James Calata hoped that the sjambok would be replaced by British standards of citizenship in South Africa. In 1935, another ANC leader, Reverend Z. R. Mahabane noted that British justice required that government adhere to two principles: equal rights for all 'civilized men,' irrespective of color, and no government without the consent of the governed. Hinting at the revolutionary potential of these principles, Reverend Mahabane concluded that if the South African government continued to demand taxes without granting voting rights, 'the Natives would have to raise the cry of the American colonists: 'No taxation without representation' (Karis and Carter, 1973, II: 43). After the removal of the limited Cape franchise in 1936, however, this rhetoric of British justice largely disappeared from the political discourse of the ANC, although it was arguably revived after the 1940s in terms of a new commitment to human rights associated with the United Nations.

Third, the emergent African nationalism of the ANC appealed for African unity. In order to mobilize a unified African opposition to government policies of white domination, the ANC insisted that the divisions associated with 'tribal' politics had to be dissolved. For John Dube, Christianity provided a basis for an African unity that would overcome 'tribal' differences. 'The system of tribal segregation may have suited very well a period when barbarism and darkness reigned supreme,' Dube noted, 'but it had the fatal defect of being essentially opposed to all enlightenment and Christianity' (Marks, 1984: 53–4). Noting that Christianity itself was divided, however, the ANC proposed in its constitution adopted in 1919 that a union of African churches should be formed, 'free from all sectional and denominational anomalies' (Walshe, 1970: 39). Neither Christianity nor a church union, however, provided the basis for an African unity that completely bridged differences of social class or 'tribal' politics. Ironically, John Dube himself seems to have retreated from his commitment to African unity by promoting the narrower ethnic interests of a Zulu nationalism in the late 1920s.

Although Christianity might have provided ideological terms for African unity, the incorporation of Africans in a single economy had greater potential for dissolving 'tribal' divisions. Recognizing the futility of a government policy of racial segregation based on a system of 'tribal reserves,' D. D. T. Jabavu was among those who argued that the incorporation of Africans in a single economy had changed everything, including ways of thinking. In a 1932 pamphlet, Jabavu wrote:

> The basic policy of our present masters is that the African should be precluded from civilisation, forced to develop along his primitive lines, stopped where he presently is, and pushed back to where he was a century ago. Now, the African mind once moved from its old anchorage by European money, machinery, bicycles, clothes, gramophones, cannot be moved back to where it formerly was.
>
> (Karis and Carter, 1972, I: 288)

Jabavu insisted that this economic reality had to be acknowledged by investing Africans with political rights in a common South African society. By 1936, however, disillusioned after years of political, social, and economic exclusion, D. D. T. Jabavu exhorted a conference of the All African Convention to only do business with Africans 'out of a patriotic spirit of African nationalism' (Karis and Carter, 1973, II: 52). If achieved at all, therefore, a unified African front was forged because all Africans found themselves under the same political, social, and economic domination that enforced white supremacy in South Africa.

Fourth, the religious resources of an emerging African nationalism were drawn into fashioning a sustained critique of white supremacy. One of the strongest critics of white supremacy as a false religion was Reverend Z. R.

Mahabane (Mahabane, 1966). As president of the ANC in the Cape Province in 1921, Reverend Mahabane attacked the presumptions of white supremacists who classified blacks as a 'child race.' That dehumanizing classification and its consequences, Reverend Mahabane argued, had to be resisted. 'God forbid,' he declared, 'that we, as human beings, made in the image and after the likeness of Himself, should permit other human beings, made in like manner, to arrogate to themselves a position of superiority over us.' Although he contested white supremacy on this biblical basis, Reverend Mahabane also exposed its absurdity through a simple twist of logic. At an ANC conference in 1926, he noted again that white supremacists in the government persisted in classifying blacks as children and in claiming the right to exercise guardianship or trusteeship over them. Although the government used this logic to justify depriving blacks of voting rights, Reverend Mahabane suggested that a different conclusion might be drawn. 'If the Natives must be regarded as children,' he proposed, somewhat sarcastically, 'then they should not be taxed, but clothed, fed and educated as children.' Otherwise, Reverend Mahabane concluded, there must be 'no taxation without representation' (Karis and Carter, 1972, I: 296, 299).

Having exposed the doctrine of Christian trusteeship as transparent oppression, Reverend Mahabane continued for decades to argue that white supremacy was a false religion. 'By what right did the White man claim to rule the Native,' he demanded in 1935, 'unless it was by the out-of-date doctrine of the divine right of kings reincarnated as the divine right of the White man?' (Karis and Carter, 1973, II: 43). During the 1930s, as white supremacy was amplified by Afrikaner nationalists and the Dutch Reformed Church, African Christians in the ANC occasionally revived the nineteenth-century critique of the missions by observing that there were actually two gods being proclaimed in South Africa. At a conference of the European and Bantu Christian Student Association in 1930, for example, ANC leader Charlotte Maxeke noted that Africans not only observed that laws for black and white were different, 'but we even find some of them convinced that there are two Gods, one for the White and one for the Black.' Referring to an old woman of her acquaintance, Charlotte Maxeke noted that 'she could not be convinced that the same God watched over and cared for us all, but felt that the God who gave the Europeans their life of comparative comfort and ease, could not possibly be the same God who allowed his poor Bantu to suffer' (Karis and Carter, 1972, I: 346). The doctrines and practices of white supremacy, as Charlotte Maxeke suggested, had not only caused human suffering but had also introduced a false religion into South Africa.

For its part in promoting a theology of white supremacy, the Dutch Reformed Church in particular came in for censure by African nationalists. At a 1930 conference, for example, the Cape provincial branch of the ANC proposed a 'declaration of war' against the Dutch Reformed Church. Identifying the ministers and missionaries of that church as enemies of the people, this 'declaration of war' stipulated that every black person affiliated with one of the mission churches of the Dutch Reformed Church should leave this 'unchristian church' within 3 months. Those who remained affiliated after 3 months, would be ostracized and boycotted. Finally, the 'declaration of war' called for communication with other African countries in which the Dutch Reformed Church was conducting missionary work to call upon them 'to expel all missionaries and emissaries of this Church who are in their midst not to enlighten and evangelise them, but to enslave them' (Karis and Carter, 1972, I: 270). During the 1930s, therefore, African Christians attacked white supremacy in church and state as an anti-Christian, dehumanizing, and false religion. Although white supremacists claimed to uphold Christian civilization, as D. D. T. Jabavu noted in 1936, the events of the 1930s had 'scratched this European veneer and revealed the White savage hidden beneath.' By worshiping idols of self-interest and self-preservation, as Jabavu concluded with some irony, white supremacists had replaced Christianity with 'the Law of the Jungle' (Karis and Carter, 1973, II: 48).

Finally, African nationalists began to advance stronger assertions of African humanity in the face of the dehumanizing racist legislation, social conditions, and economic exploitation in South Africa. These new assertions of African humanity were clearly multidimensional, as they redefined a comprehensive recognition of African humanity on religious, political, social, and psychological grounds. In religious terms, for example, Reverend Z. R. Mahabane argued that the divine right of freedom had been granted to all human beings by God in the Garden of Eden. 'Why should we now have to submit,' Mahabane asked, 'to a condition of things which does not give us this God-given right, the inalienable right of self-determination and self-government?' (Karis and Carter, 1972, I: 295).

In political terms, many argued that it was white supremacists in South Africa who had forced Africans into a position in which they had to assert their humanity exclusively as Africans. In 1922, for example, journalist R. V. Selope Thema observed that the 'policy of "White South Africa" has naturally given rise on this side of the colour line to a cry of "Africa for the Africans"' (Karis and Carter, 1972, I: 214). Although often inspired by Marcus Garvey, this political assertion of African humanity directly responded to the local circumstances of white domination in South Africa.

In social terms, a reassertion of African humanity obviously required a transformation of the social and economic relations of power under which Africans had been dehumanized. Occasionally, that social change was imagined as a recovery of important aspects of 'traditional' African society that had been lost under the impact of capitalist penetration and expansion in

South Africa. For example, D. D. T. Jabavu, in his 1936 presidential address to the All African Convention called for an end to racial segregation and economic repression, but he attributed both to capitalist social relations that encouraged a 'selfishness' that was foreign to African society. For contrast, Jabavu looked back to African tradition:

> In our primitive African tradition we used to smell out and destroy all abnormally acquisitive individuals as a danger to society. By this crude method we guaranteed all men a chance to have food, shelter and clothing without prejudice. This is a lesson we Africans can teach Christendom, for Christendom still needs a change of heart from selfishness.
>
> (Karis and Carter, 1973, II: 53)

In psychological terms, some political leaders began to argue that a reassertion of African humanity required a spiritual transformation throughout South Africa. As A. B. Xuma declared in 1930, 'What we need most is a revolution of the people's thoughts, their ideas, their ideals, and their spirit to recognize the African as a human being with human desires and aspirations which must be satisfied' (Karis and Carter, 1972, I: 227). More specifically, however, the recovery of an African humanity required a psychological liberation from a sense of inferiority and impotence under white domination in South Africa. In 1936, the political leader and trade union organizer Selby Msimang argued that African liberation depended upon the deployment of a basic, human psychological weapon. 'That weapon is a power in itself,' Msimang declared:

> in that it is the power of the soul, the indestructible something that is in man – the Sword of God. It is the will and determination to be free, the ineradicable craving of human nature, without which we certainly must agree to perish or be made slaves.
>
> (Karis and Carter, 1972, II: 59)

Despite this psychological power, however, Selby Msimang despaired at achieving liberation from white domination in South Africa. If segregation and color bars were to continue, Msimang proposed a partition of South Africa between black and white 'on a fifty-fifty basis' (Karis and Carter, 1972: II: 59). In the 1940s, however, African nationalists revived these themes of religious, political, social, and psychological liberation with a new intensity that demanded the liberation of the whole of South Africa.

AFRICAN THEOLOGY

The decade of the 1940s marked a period of revival for the African National Congress. Elected president-general in 1940, A. B. Xuma introduced a new constitution and supervised the reorganization of the movement. The most important development in the ANC during this period, however, was the formation of the Congress Youth League in 1944. Inspired by the African Nationalism, or 'Africanism,' of its founding president, Anton Lembede, the Youth League injected a new militancy into the political program of the ANC. Lembede explicitly called upon the ANC to pursue African nationalism with all the fervor of a religious commitment. The Africanism of Anton Lembede, therefore, represented one important option in an emerging African theology in South Africa that drew together African and Christian resources for religious liberation. At the same time, the theology of Africanism required new strategies and tactics in the struggle for political liberation. Accordingly, by 1949, under the influence of the Congress Youth League, the ANC had adopted a new 'Programme of Action' that proposed boycotts, strikes, and civil disobedience as tactics to be deployed in 'the struggle for national liberation' (Karis and Carter, 1973, II: 338). In the early 1950s, finally drawing a larger, mass following, the ANC deployed those tactics in a sustained 'Defiance Campaign' of civil disobedience that openly defied unjust laws in South Africa.

Although not all ANC leaders or supporters subscribed to this new African theology, the religious ideology of African nationalism, particularly as it was articulated by Anton Lembede, clearly contributed during the 1940s to the intensification of the struggle for religious and political liberation. ANC leaders of the older generation continued to make occasional appeals to more conventional Christian principles. Reverend James Calata, for example, who served as Secretary-General of the ANC from 1936 to 1949, urged the ANC in 1943 to 'adopt Christianity and follow Christ as our national leader.' In conventional Christian terms, Calata argued that the ANC should dedicate itself to bringing about the Kingdom of God on earth (Walshe, 1970: 343). After the National Party election victory in 1948, Reverend Calata persisted in appealing to basic Christian principles. Noting that D. F. Malan had promised that his government would act in accordance with the sovereignty of God, James Calata challenged Malan to live up to the demands of Christianity. 'I am one of those who have been preaching that Christianity is a world brotherhood,' Reverend Calata observed, 'but I am beginning to wonder if my European brethren preach a similar doctrine to their people. Well there is your chance Reverend Dr Malan. Prove to the world that you stand by the principles of Christianity which involve the Fatherhood of God and brotherhood of man' (Karis and Carter, 1973, II: 284). A similar adherence to conventional Christianity continued into the Defiance Campaign of the 1950s, particularly evident in the moral and religious leadership provided by Albert Luthuli, even though the National Party government remained intransigent to such Christian appeals.

At the same time, however, innovations in African theology tended to be somewhat foreign to the older generation of Christian leaders in the ANC. Clearly, the independent churches had developed new types of African theology that occasionally surfaced in the ANC. As noted in Chapter Four, ANC leader Charlotte Maxeke had been instrumental in the 'Ethiopian' movement, while ANC leader John Dube had celebrated the ministry of Isaiah Shembe by writing the prophet's biography. For the most part, however, the older generation of Christians in the ANC adhered during the 1940s to the more conventional Christianity of the mission churches.

A conflict that arose in the mid–1940s over government restrictions on African beer brewing revealed the gap between the older generation of ANC Christians and new innovations in African theology. The law restricting the brewing of beer was only one political issue that disturbed the squatters occupying vacant land outside of Johannesburg who were led by James Mpanza, later known as 'the man who founded Soweto' (French, 1983). While in prison, James Mpanza had converted to Christianity, but it was a Christianity that embraced and adapted African beliefs and customs. As leader of the squatter movement, Mpanza declared: 'The position of the chieftainship is given to me like Jesus. Many people thought I was arrested, and yet I was not. The same as with Jesus. Many thought he was dead, and yet he was not.' On the issue of beer brewing, a spokesman for the ANC supported the government restriction. 'We hear much about [African] beer forming part of our "native customs,"' ANC spokesman P. Q. Vundla observed, 'but we do not want these "native customs" because our township being part and parcel of the town we have to follow the white way of living.' In response, James Mpanza dared representatives of the ANC to defend the law against beer brewing in a public meeting. If they did, he suggested, 'they would certainly be stoned to death.' The freedom to brew beer was not only demanded by public sentiment, but also by a religious way of life that Mpanza suggested was simultaneously African and Christian. 'The African when he supplicates his gods, slaughters a goat or sheep,' Mpanza noted, 'brews his traditional beverage' (Lodge, 1983: 16–17). Although largely unappreciated by ANC Christians in the 1940s, this interweaving of Christian and African religious resources remained one vital option in an African theology in South Africa.

Another option within African theology was powerfully articulated by Anton Lembede in the formation of the Congress Youth League. The founders of the Youth League in 1944 were mainly teachers, law students, or medical students who came from middle-class backgrounds similar to those of the original founders of the ANC. By contrast to the 1912 founders, however, none of the leaders of the Youth League were professional ministers of religion. Nevertheless, most had religious backgrounds that in different ways influenced their political development. Walter Sisulu grew up in the midst of the American movement of Wellington Buthelezi in the eastern Cape; Oliver Tambo was a devout Anglican, often described as a puritanical Christian; and Nelson Mandela received a Christian education while growing up in the Thembu royal family. As the most important religious innovator among the founders of the Youth League, however, Anton Lembede drew upon his Roman Catholic background to work out a new theology of Africanism. Pursuing African nationalism as a religion, Lembede articulated a new worldview of religious liberation. Although it drew together many of the themes of the African nationalism of the previous generation, Lembede's Africanism proclaimed the liberation of a new, young Africa.

Working as a legal clerk in the office of ANC founder Pixley Seme, Anton Lembede earned his law degree and became a full partner in the firm of Seme and Lembede. As evidence of his philosophical and theological disposition, Lembede completed an MA thesis on 'The Conception of God as Expounded By or as It Emerges from the Writings of Philosophers from Descartes to the Present Day' (1945). Along with teacher Peter Mda and journalist Jordan Ngubane, Lembede formulated a constitution, a manifesto, and even a statement of 'Our Creed' for the launch of the Congress Youth League in April 1944. In that creed, the Youth League announced, 'We believe in the divine destiny of nations' (Karis and Carter, 1973, II: 308). To achieve a divine national destiny in South Africa, Lembede argued that Africans had to reject foreign leaders and ideologies on the one hand, and 'tribal' divisions on the other, by embracing a new gospel of Africanism or African National-ism. Proclaiming this new promise of religious liberation in 1945, Lembede wrote:

> The African natives then live and move and have their being in the spirit of Africa; in short, they are one with Africa.... So that all Africans must be converted from tribalism into African Nationalism, which is a higher step or degree of the self-expression and self-realization of the African spirit, Africa through her spirit is using us to develop that higher quality of Africanism. We have then to go out as apostles to preach the new gospel of Africanism and to hasten and bring about the birth of a new nation.
>
> (Gerhart, 1978: 61)

Africanism, therefore, promised to remake the world of South Africa, with a new spirit, a new gospel, and a new nation in the process of being born. Although he argued that practical consequences would follow in the birth of a new, unified African nation, Lembede also suggested that a new spiritual nationalism was already born whenever Africanism was 'pursued with the fanaticism and bigotry of religion, for it is the only creed that will dispel and disperse the inferiority complex which blurs our sight and darkens our horizon' (Gerhart, 1978: 62). Liberated from feelings of inferiority, Africans inspired by this new religion were charged with the divine mission of unifying and liberating Africa as a national spiritual force not only in South Africa but in the entire world. 'Although we are physically unarmed yet we are spiritually fortified,' Lembede wrote in 1946. 'We must remember that in all spheres of human activity it is the spiritual forces that lead the W O R L D' (Karis and Carter, 1973, II: 319).

In February 1945, Anton Lembede outlined the basic principles of this religion of Africanism or African Nationalism. First, he identified its philosophical basis as the conviction that humans were not merely biological or economic animals, but human beings of 'body, mind and spirit' moving toward 'complete self-realization.' Second, Lembede argued that the scientific basis of Africanism was found in the natural law of variation, which, with respect to nations, allowed each nation to make its own particular contribution to the progress and welfare of humanity. 'In other words,' he argued, investing natural variation with religious significance, 'each nation has its own divine mission.' Third, Lembede claimed that the historical basis of Africanism was the recovery of a heroic African past. Citing the aphorism of Paul Kruger – 'One who wants to create the future must not forget the past' – Lembede called for the erection of monuments to the great heroes of African history. Significantly, Lembede rejected the recovery of narrowly defined 'ethnic' or 'tribal' histories by suggesting that the heroes of all 'tribal' histories were the common possession of Africa.

Fourth, Lembede proposed socialism as the economic basis for Africanism. Recalling the socialism of traditional African society, particularly evident in the communal ownership of land, Lembede linked Africanism with a socialist economic program that was both old and new. 'Socialism then is our valuable legacy from our ancestors,' Lembede declared. 'Our task is to develop this socialism by the infusion of new and modern socialistic ideas.' Fifth, he argued that the democratic basis of Africanism could also be found in a recovery of African social values and political practices. 'In ancient Bantu society,' Lembede recalled, 'the worth of a man was not assessed by wealth.' Rather, a person's moral worth and spiritual qualities were demonstrated through courage, ability, and participation in the public life of the community. Since any man could participate in the councils that governed the community, Lembede concluded that democratic participation was fundamental to the spirit of Africanism. Sixth, Lembede argued that the ethical basis of Africanism was essential in building a new nation. Observing that morality is the soul of society, Lembede called for an African theological ethics that merged ancestral and Christian religion. 'We must retain and preserve the belief in the immortality of our ancestors,' he argued, 'but our ethical system today has to be based on Christian morals since there is nothing better anywhere in the world.'

Taken together, as formulated by Anton Lembede, these basic principles of Africanism promised a comprehensive salvation and national liberation. 'It is only African Nationalism or Africanism,' he declared, 'that can save the African people. Long live African Nationalism!' (Karis and Carter, 1973, II: 316). In 1946 Lembede restated these Africanist principles in outlining the 'Policy of the Congress Youth League' for publication. Lembede concluded that statement of policy by invoking the motto of the Youth League, 'Freedom in Our Life Time.' Anton Lembede died the following year at the age of 33. His legacy continued, however, in the commitment of the Youth League to 'Africa for Africans, Africans for humanity, and humanity for God and Africa.'

Succeeding Lembede as president of the Congress Youth League, Peter Mda worked to clarify two basic differences between African Nationalism and other ethnic or religious nationalisms in South Africa. First, African Nationalism was not an instrument of oppression, as was 'the imperialistic and neo-Fascist Nationalism of the Afrikaners (the Malanite type).' Unlike a nationalism drawing on religion to justify political domination, African Nationalism, according to Peter Mda, was 'the pure Nationalism of an oppressed people, seeking freedom from foreign oppression.' Not religious legitimation, therefore, but religious liberation was the claim of this African Nationalism. Second, African Nationalism was not an instrument of racial, ethnic, or tribal division. African Nationalism not only rejected the divisive ethnic 'retribalization' of Africans under government policy, but also rejected any form of racism. 'We have no racial hatred,' Peter Mda was adamant to assert, 'we only hate white oppression and white domination, and not the white people themselves!' (Karis and Carter, 1973, II: 321).

The national liberation promised by African Nationalism, according to Peter Mda, required a 'People's Democracy' in which all human beings would enjoy rights and freedoms by virtue of their humanity. However, disagreement within the Congress Youth League over the viability of alliances with people of other racial groups in the struggle for national liberation had by the end of the decade produced 'two streams' of African Nationalism. According to the 'Basic Policy of the Congress Youth League' of 1948, one stream adhered to the Garveyite slogan of 'Africa for the Africans,' while the other, more prominent stream in the Youth League accepted that the various racial groups had come to South Africa to stay (Karis and Carter, 1973, II: 328–9). As the ANC tried to translate policy into practice in the 1950s, however, this disagreement about the character of African Nationalism resulted in a basic split in the movement for national liberation.

Influenced by the Youth League, the ANC in 1949 pledged itself to a new

'Programme of Action' that would adopt the tactics of civil disobedience 'under the banner of African Nationalism.' The leadership continued to make Christian appeals, calling for an annual ANC 'Day of Prayer' so the liberation movement would not 'forget Christ who is the Champion of Freedom' (Walshe, 1970: 344). But even leaders of the older generation seem to have adopted a more militant nationalism. For example, on 16 December 1949, Reverend James Calata introduced a new practice, adapted from the Youth League, of raising the right thumb while singing the national anthem, *Nkosi Sikelel' iAfrika* ('God Bless Africa'). While the first four fingers of the raised fist signified 'Unity, Determination, Solidarity, and Militancy,' Reverend Calata explained, the extended thumb represented a call for 'Africa to come back to us' (Karis and Carter, 1973, II: 291). Besides indicating a new militancy, this innovation in African nationalist ritual coincided with a new activism, as the ANC worked to build a larger, popular mass following that could be mobilized in its campaign of civil disobedience against unjust laws.

Although embarking on a campaign of mass action, the ANC president James Moroka and Walter Sisulu began the campaign by sending a letter to South African Prime Minister D. F. Malan that outlined six unjust laws and requested their immediate repeal. Returning once more to the tactic of protest through petition, the ANC identified some of the more oppressive laws that restricted the freedom of movement, residence, livelihood, political organization, and civil rights of Africans in South Africa. When this appeal was rejected by Prime Minister Malan, however, the ANC initiated its 'Defiance Campaign' under the general leadership of its newly elected president, Albert Luthuli. On 26 June 1952, fifty Africans and Indians, headed by Nana Sita, a veteran of Gandhi's passive resistance campaign, were immediately arrested when they entered an African location near Johannesburg without the necessary passes or permits. Over the following 12 months, volunteers performed similar organized acts of defiance by entering other African areas without permits, ignoring pass laws and curfew regulations, and using facilities reserved for whites in post offices, railway stations, or on trains. More than 8,000 volunteers were arrested, most serving 2 to 3 months in jail, while younger protesters were flogged (Lodge, 1983: 42–3).

In the midst of the campaign, ANC president Albert Luthuli was banned, prevented from attending public meetings, and eventually confined to his home in Natal. During a campaign that mobilized not only mass support but also strong religious sentiments, Luthuli was most committed to providing a Christian interpretation of the Defiance Campaign. Son of a Methodist evangelist, Albert Luthuli had been a teacher, lay preacher, and chief before becoming a leader in the ANC. Forced to relinquish his chiefship under the Bantu Administration, Luthuli devoted both his political leadership and religious vision to the liberation movement. In a 1952 speech, 'The Road to

Freedom is via the Cross,' Albert Luthuli explained his recourse to civil disobedience. 'Who will deny,' Luthuli asked, 'that thirty years of my life have been spent knocking in vain, patiently, moderately and modestly at a closed and barred door.' With his petitions rejected, he observed that moderation had only been met by further repressive legislation and the entrenchment of white supremacy. 'I have joined my people in the new spirit which moves them today,' Luthuli therefore concluded, 'the spirit that revolts openly and boldly against injustice and expresses itself in a determined and non-violent manner' (Luthuli, 1962: 235ff; Woodson, 1982: 41–9; 1986).

Spending most of the rest of his life under arrest, banning orders, or restrictions imposed by the government, Albert Luthuli was awarded the Nobel Peace Prize for his efforts in 1961. Although the ANC achieved minimal political success, Luthuli claimed that his involvement in the liberation movement had been based on a religious commitment. 'For myself,' he wrote in his autobiography, 'I am in Congress precisely because I am a Christian. My Christian belief about human society must find expression here and now, and Congress is the spearhead of the real struggle' (Luthuli, 1962: 138). In 1952, Albert Luthuli found expression for his Christian convictions in the non-violent defiance of unjust laws. But as many commentators have noted, a mood of religious enthusiasm infused the entire Defiance Campaign. Volunteers observed days of prayer and fasting, attended prayer meetings to pledge their allegiance to a code of love, discipline, and cleanliness, sang hymns led by women from *manyano* organizations, and listened to political oratory from ANC leaders that stressed sacrifice, martyrdom, and the ultimate triumph of justice (Lodge, 1983: 43). Frequently, political discourse during the Defiance Campaign emphasized the relation between non-violent resistance and Christian ethics (Kuper, 1957: 117). The Defiance Campaign certainly resembled Gandhi's strategy of *satyagraha*, but ANC leaders tended to interpret non-violence either as a tactical expedient or as an expression of explicitly Christian principles of love in practice.

Even South African communists, however, occasionally used Christian symbols to represent the significance of the Defiance Campaign. J. B. Marks, for example, in a speech delivered before the launch of the campaign, proclaimed the ANC as the genuine 'Noah's Ark.' By making that speech, however, J. B. Marks had broken the banning order that prevented him from attending public meetings. Anticipating arrest, Marks announced: 'This is the hour now. I am being crucified and I feel the weight of the cross' (Lodge, 1983: 44). Christian symbols, however, not only provided terms for representing self-sacrifice for the cause of liberation, but also for once again distinguishing between two Christian gods operating in South Africa. For example, another communist, Moses Kotane, who was outraged by the violent official repression of non-violent protest, declared that government authorities 'are Christians but they eat people.... If they represent God then they represent a false God. And if God is like that, then God is no good for Africa' (Kuper, 1957: 117). In effect, therefore, participants could interpret the Defiance Campaign as revealing two gods – one of legitimation, the other of liberation – locked in confrontation during the campaign of civil disobedience to unjust laws.

During the Defiance Campaign the ANC forged alliances with political organizations that represented constituencies drawn from other racially defined groups working for liberation in South Africa. That interracial, populist cooperation culminated in the drafting and adoption of the Freedom Charter in June 1955. After months of preparation, 3,000 delegates met in Kliptown, near Johannesburg, in a 'Congress of the People' to vote their acceptance of each clause of the document. Outlining basic human rights and freedoms, the Freedom Charter represented a general blueprint for a civil, multiracial society in South Africa. On the second day of the congress, however, armed police raided the meeting, confiscated all documents, and dispersed the delegates. Although agents of the government declared the Congress of the People an act of treason, and eventually banned the Freedom Charter, the event and the document assumed a sacred status in the history of the ANC. While the Congress of the People was often perceived as a time of prophetic revelation, the Freedom Charter became a canonical text, operating in the later history of the ANC as a sacred charter for a nonracial, democratic, and just South Africa.

In the 1950s, however, the text of the Freedom Charter intensified divisions within the ANC between 'Charterists,' who adopted the multiracial cooperation embodied in the document, and 'Africanists,' who adhered to a more rigorous African nationalism. Entitlement to the land of South Africa was a particularly divisive issue. The Freedom Charter announced that 'South Africa belongs to all who live in it, black and white.' Africanists, however, recalling that South African history had been a history of white conquest of African land, insisted that the 'African people have an inalienable claim on every inch of the African soil' (Gerhart, 1978: 147). As Africanists were forced out of the ANC and the Congress Youth League, they began laying the groundwork for an alternative liberation movement. An important element in the reorganization of Africanists after 1955 was the elevation of Anton Lembede to the status of a mythic hero. On the anniversary of Lembede's death in 1955, Africanist leader Peter Mda introduced the first annual celebration of the 'Lembede Memorial Service.' This annual ritual occasion provided an opportunity for Africanists to reaffirm the spiritual power and the promise of salvation associated with Lembede's African Nationalism. Besides Peter Mda, who claimed the spiritual mantle of Lembede during the 1950s, Africanists such as Potlako Leballo, Josias Madzunya, and Victor Sifora used the memorial service to restate the basic principle of Africanism. In the words of Sifora at the Lembede Memorial Service in 1956, Africans 'hold the key to our salvation, to our progress and glory, whether the whiteman, his law, his government, his church are with us or not' (Gerhart, 1978: 161–2).

In August 1959, the Lembede Memorial Service became 'National Heroes' Day.' By that time, however, Africanists had formed a new organization, the Pan-Africanist Congress, led by the Methodist lay preacher Robert Sobukwe. At the inaugural conference of the Pan-Africanist Congress (PAC) in April 1959, Robert Sobukwe was elected president over Josias Madzunya, who had lost support when he referred to 'Africa for the Africans' as 'God's Apartheid' (Lodge, 1983: 84). Sobukwe had been an ardent African nationalist as a member of the Congress Youth League in the late 1940s. At a speech in 1949 at the University of Fort Hare, for example, Robert Sobukwe had proclaimed 'the vision of a new Africa, an Africa re-born, an Africa rejuvenated, an Africa re-created, young AFRICA.' Like Anton Lembede, Sobukwe saw African liberation as a universal salvation. 'On the liberation of the African,' he declared, 'depends the liberation of the whole world' (Karis and Carter, 1973, II: 335). In this spirit of universal salvation, Robert Sobukwe argued at the first convention of the PAC in 1959 that liberation ultimately required the elimination of the racial classifications that had divided people into separate groups in South Africa. 'We guarantee no minority rights,' Sobukwe insisted, 'because we think in terms of individuals, not groups' (Gerhart, 1978: 195). In this sense, therefore, the PAC anticipated an African liberation that would free all South Africans from divisive, oppressive, and dehumanizing racial or ethnic classifications.

An African theology played a prominent role in the Pan-Africanist Congress. In 1949, for example, Robert Sobukwe had framed his vision of African liberation in explicitly theological terms. 'We are what we are,' he declared, 'because the God of Africa made us so' (Karis and Carter, 1973, II: 335–6). At the first convention of the PAC, the opening prayer and sermon was delivered by Bishop Walter M. Dimba, leader of an organization of independent churches, who proclaimed an African theology that was distinct from the theology of 'the hooligans of Europe who killed our God and have never been convicted.' Referring to 'the legend of Christ's education in Africa,' and to the important role played by 'a black man, Simon of Arabia, who carried Jesus from the Cross,' Bishop Dimba argued that Christianity actually belonged to Africa (Gerhart, 1978: 203). Later during the convention, Josias Madzunya called for the establishment of a new African national church. As the PAC mobilized popular support over the following year, an African theology was apparently a significant feature in revitalizing African nationalism. PAC organizers invoked the gods and ancestors of Africa in mobilizing a mass following. Particularly in the Cape, PAC supporters often believed that the militant nineteenth-century prophet, Nxele, was spiritually present in their struggle (Gerhart, 1978: 203–4). Drawing on Christian and African religious resources, the PAC prepared for a sudden, imminent liberation.

The apocalyptic character of this African theology became particularly evident as the PAC launched its protest campaign against the pass system. Under Sobukwe's leadership, the anti-pass campaign was set to begin on 21 March 1960. Demanding nonviolence and discipline from its supporters, the PAC pledged to lead 'the vital, breathing and dynamic youth of our land... not to death, but to the life abundant' (Phillips, 1960: 60). At a press conference before the campaign, Robert Sobukwe promised that protest marches would be conducted 'in a spirit of absolute nonviolence.' If the government insisted, Sobukwe also noted, 'we will provide them with an opportunity to demonstrate to the world how brutal they can be. We are ready to die for our cause' (Karis and Carter, 1977, III: 566–7). As about 7,000 demonstrators assembled for a peaceful protest march in the township of Sharpeville, near Johannesburg, police opened fire, killing 69 men, women, and children, mostly shot in the back, and wounding nearly 200 (Reeves, 1960). During the following week in Cape Town, the young PAC leader Phillip Kgosana, invoking the 'gods of Africa,' led a march of 30,000 people to the city police station. Negotiating with the police, Kgosana agreed to lead the marchers back to the townships, a turn of events that police colonel Terry Terreblanche described as 'a real miracle.' The next day, however, Phillip Kgosana was arrested, while the police cordoned off the townships before embarking on their own campaign of brutalizing the residents with whips and batons over a 4-day period (Gerhart, 1978: 204; Wilson and Mafeje, 1963: 112).

Under a national state of emergency, the government passed its Unlawful Organisations Act that banned the PAC, as well as the ANC, which had planned to launch its own anti-pass campaign. The leaders of the organizations, including PAC president Robert Sobukwe and ANC president Albert Luthuli, were arrested and imprisoned. Although declared illegal, both liberation movements formed underground organizations. After years of commitment to non-violent petition and protest, ANC leaders formed a military wing, *Umkhonto we Sizwe* ('Spear of the Nation'), to undertake acts of sabotage against the government. In April 1961 Nelson Mandela went underground to plan a campaign of bombing government buildings and installations. Arrested, Mandela was convicted for sabotage, and later, in 1964, for treason against the government of South Africa. Along with other ANC leaders, Nelson Mandela was sentenced to life imprisonment.

During those trials, Nelson Mandela explained three basic reasons for the

ANC's decision to form a military wing and embark on an armed struggle for liberation. First, Mandela argued that military organization and leadership had been necessary to channel the anger of the people into controlled, disciplined acts of resistance after the banning of their political organizations. Second, Mandela observed that the government had made counterviolence necessary by relying solely on violence in its response to political protest. Third, Mandela noted that the banning of legitimate, organized, peaceful protest left the ANC no other choice. 'It was only when all else had failed, when all channels of peaceful protest had been barred to us,' Nelson Mandela concluded, 'that the decision was made to embark upon violent forms of political struggle' (Karis and Carter, 1977, III: 777). In launching its sabotage campaign, however, Umkhonto we Sizwe seemed to be continuing the ANC tradition of addressing protest to the government, although now with a more forceful voice, to demand fundamental changes in government policy. As Mandela explained, the ANC embarked on violent protest in the hope that it would 'bring the government and its supporters to its senses before its is too late, so that the government and its policies can be changed before matters reach the desperate state of civil war' (Karis and Carter, 1977, III: 717). Recourse to violence by Umkhonto we Sizwe, therefore, was originally conceived by ANC leaders as the only means left to communicate with the government.

While the ANC justified the use of violence as a rational means to achieve legitimate political ends, the PAC formed a military wing that resorted to violence in the hope of an immediate, sudden, and even apocalyptic redemption. Between 1961 and 1963, the PAC's military wing – *Poqo*, a name meaning 'alone' or 'pure' – was the largest underground political organization in South Africa. For the first time, in the formation of Poqo, political tactics were proposed that required killing people. As its exiled leader Potlako Leballo announced, Poqo supporters on the appointed day would indiscriminately kill white people for a period of 4 hours. Any whites who survived, however, would be invited to lend their support to the formation of a new Pan-Africanist government. Although Poqo launched a few attacks on black collaborators and whites, the plan for a mass insurrection never materialized. The police succeeded in arresting its leadership and thousands of followers, forcing the military wing of the PAC, like that of the ANC, to reorganize resistance to the government in exile.

In addition to planning a violent rebellion, Poqo mobilized potent religious symbols of redemption. Its very name, which had been used by African independent churches in the eastern Cape during the 1930s, signified not only religious independence but also a purity that recalled the ritual, sacrificial killing of animals for purification. Poqo had its own church, which it called *Qamatha*, using a name for God that was common to both Xhosa-speaking

Christians and adherents of ancestral religion. It also engaged in various ritual practices, including ceremonial initiations, war-doctoring for immunity from bullets, and prayers to the ancestors and gods of Africa. These Christian and African religious resources, however, were woven together in the prospect of a single, apocalyptic battle that promised to redeem South Africa from what Potlako Leballo called the white 'forces of darkness' (Lodge, 1977; 1984). In this respect, Poqo had much in common with militant religious and political movements in other colonial situations that have been called 'primary resistance' or 'revitalization' movements (Adas, 1979). Like Poqo, those movements drew upon both local, indigenous religion and Christianity to work toward an apocalyptic overthrow of colonial domination. Although Poqo's apocalypse clearly failed, the movement in the early 1960s represented a new, violent innovation in African theology that was born under the brutal repression and outlawing of African political organizations.

BLACK THEOLOGY

Prior to the 1970s, different forms of African theology had emerged in the context of political struggles for liberation in South Africa. In different ways, those African theologies, whether the eclectic African Christianity of James Mpanza, the Africanism of Anton Lembede, or the apocalyptic vision of redemption promised by Poqo, drew together ancestral and Christian religious resources. In church and university circles as well, however, an African Theology emerged that emphasized an intrinsic relationship between Christianity and 'traditional' African religion and culture. While Lembede was working out his Africanism in the 1940s, the Belgian missionary in Central Africa, Father Placide Tempels, published his influential study of an African religious worldview, *Bantu Philosophy*. In his understanding of African religion and culture, Placide Tempels discerned a common ground between paganism and Christianity in Africa. 'Bantu paganism,' Father Tempels wrote, 'the ancient wisdom of the Bantu, reaches out from the depths of its Bantu soul towards the very soul of Christian spirituality' (Tempels, 1959). In South Africa, a search for common ground between African and Christian theology was explored in a collection of essays, *African Ideas of God*, published in 1950 (Smith, 1950). Inspired by this recovery of 'traditional' African concepts of God, African Christian theologians could argue that African religion was essentially compatible with Christianity.

In some cases, African theologians argued that African religion was not only compatible with but actually superior to western Christianity, particularly in its understanding of the nature of God and human personality. Concerning the doctrine of God, for example, African theologian Gabriel Setiloane chided western Christian theologians by observing that their God 'could easily die because he is so small and human.' The African God, however, 'could never die because it has no human limitations and is so immense, incomprehensible, wide, tremendous, and unique' (Setiloane, 1979: 60; 1973). With respect to the human personality, African theologians argued that the 'traditional' African concept of a person was based in social and ethical relations of mutual recognition that built up the life of a community. Rejecting a self-centered, western individualism, African theologians stressed the importance of the 'corporate personality' which they found in both African society and the biblical society of ancient Israel (Goba, 1974). This African Theology, therefore, celebrated a Christianity that recovered and embraced certain values associated with the rural, village-based, peasant societies of Africa (Schoffeleers, 1988).

At the same time, however, a different theological movement, more directly addressed to the conditions of oppression suffered by blacks in a modern, capitalist, industrialized, and urbanized South Africa, emerged in Black Theology. Drawing a comparison between African and Black Theology, the African theologian John Mbiti suggested in 1974 that African Theology 'grows out of our joy in the experience of the Christian faith, whereas Black Theology emerges from the pains of oppression' (Mbiti, 1979: 481). South African Black Theology drew considerable inspiration from religious developments in the United States. It was inspired by the civil rights movement led by Martin Luther King, Jr., the religious militancy of Malcolm X, and the emergence of Black Power as the symbol of a new resistance to racist oppression. More specifically, however, black theologians in South Africa recognized themselves in the work of American theologian James Cone. Beginning in 1969, James Cone, professor of theology at Union Theological Seminary in New York, produced a series of books that outlined a Black Theology of liberation. 'Black Theology', Cone argued, had 'to analyze the gospel of Jesus Christ in the light of the oppressed black people so they will see the gospel as inseparable from their humiliated condition, bestowing on them the necessary power to break the chains of oppression' (Cone, 1970: 23). Identifying God with the oppressed – which in America, as in South Africa, meant racially oppressed black people – James Cone advanced a Black Theology of religious empowerment in the interest of economic, social, and political liberation.

Although obviously influenced by American developments in Black Theology, the movement of Black Theology in South Africa was more immediately grounded in the local circumstances of resistance to apartheid. Not merely a foreign import, Black Theology developed in South Africa as a religious innovation within new organizations. In December 1968 thirty black representatives of the National Union of South African Students met at Mariannhill, in Natal, to lay the groundwork for the formation of a new black student organization. Holding its first conference in July 1969, the South African Students Association (SASO) was formed as an all-black society. Under the leadership of its first president, Steve Biko, SASO was dedicated to the liberating potential of a new, emergent ideology of Black Consciousness. As Steve Biko explained, the essence of Black Consciousness was:

> the realization by the black man of the need to rally together with his brothers around the cause of their oppression – the blackness of their skin – and to operate as a group in order to rid themselves of the shackles that bind them to perpetual servitude.
>
> (Biko, 1986: 91–2)

By 1971 SASO had drawn up a manifesto that outlined the ideological program of the Black Consciousness Movement. Defining 'black,' not as a racial term, but as the designation for people who were oppressed and exploited, the Black Consciousness Movement sought to create solidarity among all blacks – whether they were classified as 'African,' 'Coloured,' or 'Indian' under the apartheid system – in resistance to the racism of white society in South Africa. The liberation sought by the Black Consciousness Movement, as stated in the SASO manifesto, was 'the liberation of the Black man first from psychological oppression by themselves through inferiority complex and secondly from physical oppression occurring out of living in a White racist society' (Fatton, 1986: 70). Black Consciousness, therefore, promised liberation for both mind and body entangled in the oppression of apartheid. Originating among university students, Black Consciousness was extended through affiliated organizations – the Black People's Convention, the Black Community Program, and the Association for the Educational, Social, and Cultural Advancement of African Peoples – that took Black Consciousness outside the university to the larger black public of South Africa.

Black Consciousness was also extended through its integral connections with Black Theology. The first conference on Black Theology was organized in 1971 by the University Christian Movement. Founded in 1966, the University Christian Movement (UCM) was a nonracial, ecumenical group of students that in 1968 had published a Christian attack on apartheid, *The Message to the People of South Africa*. Some of the SASO leaders, particularly Steve Biko and Barney Pityana, were active in the UCM until they became convinced of the futility of working within liberal, multiracial, but white-controlled organizations or institutions. In 1971, the UCM-sponsored conference on Black Theology provided a public occasion that redefined theology in South Africa. Besides gathering leading innovators in South African Black Consciousness and Black Theology, the conference also invited the American theologian, James Cone. Denied a visa by the South African government, James Cone was nevertheless present in spirit as his tape-recorded address was played at the conference (Kretzchmar, 1986: 59). A collection of papers from the Black Theology seminars was published in 1972, but immediately banned by the government. Nevertheless, the conference and its publication demonstrated that the Black Consciousness Movement and Black Theology had succeeded in redefining 'black' as a religious symbol that threatened the system of psychological, social, and political domination in South Africa.

Defining 'black' as a potent symbol with new, multiple meanings, Black Theology identified 'blackness' as the key to religious liberation. First, black was defined as a symbol that meant different things depending upon whether it was invoked by the oppressor or the oppressed. For example, the Lutheran theologian Manas Buthelezi, who became a leading exponent of Black Theology, as well as the first black bishop of his church, during the early 1970s, observed that the meaning of the symbol 'black' depended upon who spoke it.

> As long as somebody else says to you, 'You are black, you are black', blackness as a concept remains a symbol of oppression and of something that conjures up feelings of inferiority. But when the black man himself says, 'I am black, I am black', blackness assumes a different meaning altogether. It then becomes a symbol of liberation and self-articulation.
>
> (Buthelezi, 1976: 7)

As a symbol, black was part of a relational discourse that operated in the context of specific, unequal social relations. Second, therefore, the social context of racial classification and racist oppression in South Africa inspired Black Theology to redefine black as a symbol that in principle had nothing to do with race. Rather, black designated the oppressed people of South Africa, blackness the condition of being oppressed. Black Theology, therefore, addressed itself directly to the oppressed and their condition of oppression. The implication of this redefinition of blackness for Christian ministers was drawn out by Sabelo Ntwasa. 'Our life as ministers of Christ,' Ntwasa insisted, 'ought to be one of identification with the wretched of the earth' (Ntwasa, 1974: 145). Third, Black Theology redefined black as a symbol of hope for the oppressed. Since 'black' was not a racial term, its opposite was not the 'white race.' Its opposite was the despair, denial, and exclusion that white racism had enforced on blacks in South Africa. Refusing to surrender to nihilism, Black Theology redefined black as a symbol of hope for liberation from racist oppression (Small, 1974).

Like Black Consciousness, Black Theology suggested that the hope of liberation began with the liberation of the consciousness of the oppressed.

As Steve Biko declared at the Black Theology conference in 1971, 'the most potent weapon in the hands of the oppressor is the mind of the oppressed' (Biko, 1986: 92). The 'slave mentality' reinforced by apartheid had prevented blacks from being conscious of a full, free humanity. Fourth, therefore, Black Theology redefined black as a fully human being. To affirm black humanity, Black Theology had to begin with a psychological recovery of the consciousness of the oppressed from the mental shackles of inferiority. In this respect, as Barney Pityana noted, 'Black Theology is a study of black consciousness or self-awareness' (Pityana, 1974: 58). But Black Theology did not stop at psychological liberation. The recovery of black humanity required solidarity in opposition to white racism and capitalism. 'Capitalistic exploitative tendencies, coupled with the overt arrogance of white racism,' Steve Biko observed in 1971, 'have conspired against us' (Biko, 1986: 96). That conspiracy, which had denied black humanity in principle and in practice, had to be resisted. As Biko noted, the God of Black Theology was not a passive but a fighting God. Only by fighting to change the psychological, social, and economic conditions under which black humanity had been denied in South Africa, as Steve Biko concluded, could Black Theology effectively fulfill its mission in 'once more uniting the black man with his God' (Biko, 1986: 94).

Ultimately, that theological mission of rehumanization promised to liberate not only the oppressed but also the oppressor from entanglement in an inhuman system. Fifth, therefore, Black Theology redefined black as a symbol of humanity that had the potential for humanizing even the oppressor. As Manas Buthelezi declared in 1973, 'It is now time for the black man to evangelise and humanise the white man' (Buthelezi, 1973: 55–6). At the Black Theology conference in 1971, Steve Biko concluded his remarks by exhorting blacks in South Africa to pursue the 'quest for a true humanity.' That genuine humanity promised to liberate both black and white in South Africa. Black Consciousness and Black Theology, Biko predicted, would one day be in a position 'to bestow upon South Africa the greatest gift possible – a more human face' (Biko, 1986: 98).

During the early 1970s, however, the National Party government remained committed to foreclosing the possibility of that new humanity emerging in South Africa. In 1972 Prime Minister John Vorster set up a commission to investigate certain organizations, including the National Union of South African Students, the University Christian Movement, and the Christian Institute, that had begun to embrace aspects of the Black Consciousness Movement. In particular, the Christian Institute, still under the direction of Beyers Naudé, had refocused its work in the early 1970s by undertaking a more critical analysis of the socioeconomic conditions under which blacks lived in South Africa. Attracting greater black support and participation, the Christian Institute increasingly identified itself with the aims of Black Theology. By 1976, the Christian Institute had undertaken a more militant opposition to apartheid. One of the institute's directors, the theologian Cedric Mayson, editor of its publication, *Pro Veritate*, urged Christians to enter 'the real battle for Christ: with oppressed and oppressors, with prisoners and jailers, politicians and strikers, revolutionaries and propagandists, soldiers and conscientious objectors, trade unionists and students, people blown up by landmines and victims of indoctrination.' Drawing on the liberating potential of Black Theology, Cedric Mayson called for a non-violent 'Christian revolution' in South Africa (Walshe, 1983: 205). At the same time, Anglican Bishop Desmond Tutu, serving as general secretary of the South African Council of Churches, wrote an open letter to Prime Minister Vorster urging that measures be taken 'to work out an orderly evolution of SA into a nonracial, open and just society' (Tutu, 1984: 28–36). Whether faced with nonviolent revolution or orderly evolution, however, the South African government remained intransigent to Christian appeals for change in the system of apartheid.

One of the dehumanizing aspects of that system that particularly drew the attention of the Black Consciousness Movement and Black Theology was the state policy of Bantu Education. Not only creating a separate school system for blacks, the state had established a philosophy of education designed to entrench black inferiority in South Africa. H. F. Verwoerd had defended that inferior education explicitly in terms of the apartheid model of separate spheres for racially defined groups. 'Education must train and teach people in accordance with their opportunities in life, according to the sphere in which they live,' Verwoerd had insisted. 'There is no place for [blacks] in the European community above the level of certain forms of labour' (Karis and Carter, 1977, III: 29). In 1976 the government introduced a new policy that required that subjects be taught in the medium of Afrikaans in black schools. Parents and students rejected this requirement. During May 1976, high school students in Soweto began boycotting lessons that were taught in Afrikaans. Under some influence from the Black Consciousness Movement, students refused to be educated in the language that they associated with their oppression. On 16 June 1976, about 20,000 children gathered in the Orlando West section of Soweto for a peaceful protest against Bantu Education. Police opened fire, killing seven and wounding seventeen. Over the following months, as protests spread throughout the country, hundreds of people were killed and thousands injured by police action (Lodge, 1983: 328–39; Molteno, 1979).

In repressing the student revolt that began in Soweto, the government banned all Black Consciousness organizations. Black Consciousness leader, Steve Biko, had been under a banning order since 1973, periodically arrested and detained for allegedly violating its restrictions. Arrested in August 1977, Steve Biko died as a result of being tortured while in police custody on 12 September 1977. The official government response, delivered by Minister of Police James Kruger at a National Party congress, was that his death 'leaves me cold.' Mourning Biko's death, however, an editorial in the journal of the Christian Institute described Steve Biko's life as a quest 'for that fullness of humanity and liberation which Christ proclaimed.' Biko's life and death, the editorial insisted, had clarified and intensified a Christian commitment to see 'that this ungodly and revolting society will be destroyed' (Walshe, 1983: 221). In October 1977, however, as police raided its offices, and arrested its leaders, the government destroyed the Christian Institute. Leaders and followers of the Black Consciousness Movement, who were not killed, detained, or imprisoned, fled into exile, many joining the political movements committed to armed struggle against the South African state. After Soweto, the death of Steve Biko, and the repression of the Black Consciousness Movement, Black Theology, as well as other religious movements opposed to apartheid, increasingly had to confront the possibility that violent resistance was justified in bringing about a change in the unjust order in South Africa.

LIBERATION THEOLOGY

In the early 1970s, South African churches confronted the issue of violence in the context of growing international attention to the injustices of apartheid. In 1970 the World Council of Churches, meeting in Uppsala, resolved to provide humanitarian aid to the banned South African liberation movements in exile. Prime Minister John Vorster, echoed by his brother, Reverend J. D. Vorster, moderator of the Dutch Reformed Church, condemned the World Council of Churches as a revolutionary communist front organization. Both demanded that South African churches sever all ties with the World Council of Churches (Walshe, 1983: 113).

Accepting the challenge posed by the World Council of Churches, however, the South African Council of Churches engaged in several years of debate that finally produced a resolution on the relation between the church and violence in 1974. The Hammanskraal Resolution invoked a biblical basis for liberation in the Christian promise to 'set at liberty those who are oppressed' (Luke 4: 18). Calling on member churches to 'identify with the oppressed,' the South African Council of Churches distinguished between the institutionalized violence of apartheid oppression and the counter-violence exercised by the oppressed in the armed struggle of the liberation movements. Since it was hypocritical to deplore guerrilla warfare that aimed to overthrow an unjust system, while defending that unjust system by violent means, the resolution encouraged Christians to analyze violence in South

Africa in the light of the long-standing theological tradition of the 'just war' (Walshe, 1983: 120). Concerned that Christians following this line of theological thought would have religious grounds for refusing to serve in the South African Defence Force, the government quickly amended the Defence Act to make it a crime, punishable by 5 years imprisonment, to encourage conscientious objection to military service.

After the brutal government repression associated with Soweto 1976, however, many Christians saw militant opposition to apartheid as not only a 'just war,' but even as a 'holy war' against racist oppression. In December 1976, for example, the All African Conference of Churches, meeting in Zambia, issued a statement declaring that the liberation movement against the South African state was a 'holy war because its aim is to free both the oppressed and the oppressor in order to bring justice, freedom, progress and stability to the people irrespective of their race' (Cuthbertson, 1985: 53). Based in Lusaka, Zambia, the National Executive Committee of the ANC embarked upon an intensified campaign of guerrilla warfare and sabotage after 1976. Receiving many recruits from a generation of exiles from Soweto, the ANC's military wing, Umkhonto we Sizwe, was considerably expanded. Umkhonto's guerrilla activity within South Africa was initially fairly limited, however, accounting for an average of about 20 attacks or acts of sabotage annually during the years between 1977 and 1981 (Lodge, 1988: 230). During the 1980s, however, which the ANC declared 'the Decade of Liberation,' the ANC intensified its campaign of 'armed propaganda' that called for diplomatic pressure, economic sanctions, and armed intervention to overthrow the South African regime.

In this increasingly violent context, Christian theologians opposed to apartheid had to come to terms with the ANC's recourse to an armed struggle against the government of South Africa. One option was to identify with the political aims of the ANC, but not with the violent means it had embarked upon to achieve those aims. In May 1983, for example, Bishop Desmond Tutu affirmed a Christian commitment to non-violence by condemning an Umkhonto attack on the South African Air Force headquarters in Pretoria. 'The South African Council of Churches,' Bishop Tutu announced, 'expresses its horror and condemns this act of naked terrorism' (*ECUNEWS*, vol.5: 3, June 1983). When the South African Air Force retaliated with a bombing raid into Mozambique, killing a number of innocent civilians, Tutu issued a similar statement condemning violence. 'As I condemned the bomb outrage in Pretoria last Friday,' Bishop Tutu observed, 'I do so relating to the retaliatory strike into Mozambique.' Although dedicated to the principle of non-violence, Desmond Tutu concluded, 'I fear more and more that change, real change in South Africa to a just, democratic, non-racial society will only come violently and with bloodshed' (*ECUNEWS*, vol. 6: 4, July 1983).

A second option, however, was to draw a qualitative distinction between the violence of the oppressor and the violence of the oppressed. In 1983, for example, Reverend Allan Boesak, a minister in the separate Dutch Reformed church for people classified as 'Coloured,' called for an understanding of the conditions under which oppressed people resorted to violence. 'I do not think theology can ever justify any kind of violence,' Reverend Boesak observed, 'although there is the understanding of the Church as to why people out of their helplessness and powerlessness are driven to a situation in which they become so desperate that the taking up of the gun is the only answer. In that respect, the Church has a clear pastoral responsibility to those people' (Novicki, 1983: 8). Beginning in September 1984, the black townships of South Africa erupted into a sustained period of unrest. During this 'uprising' from 1984 to 1986, protest, strikes, and school boycotts mobilized widespread, popular support. In response, the government of P. W. Botha placed the country under a repressive state of emergency, deploying the police and military in the townships, detaining thousands of people without trial, and restricting the activities of popular political organizations (Murray, 1987). In the context of the violent state repression of protest, therefore, Christian theologians opposed to apartheid felt that a qualitative distinction between the violence of the oppressor and the violence of the oppressed had become even more urgent in South Africa.

Theological resources for making that distinction could be found in Latin American liberation theology. Defining the Christian gospel as a promise of liberation for the poor and oppressed from economic, social, and political systems of oppression, Latin American liberation theology had much in common with Black Theology in South Africa. But Latin American liberation theology had more directly addressed the role of violence in the struggle for liberation. At a 1968 church conference in Medellin, Columbia, leaders in the movement had advanced a critique of 'institutionalized violence,' the structural or systemic violence exercised over people by an oppressive state. Although not all liberation theologians condoned violent resistance to oppressive states, they could nevertheless understand resistance as a counter-force against institutionalized state violence (Germond, 1987). In South Africa, similar reflections on violence prompted a group of theologians in 1985 to produce the *Kairos Document*, which represented a turning point in relations between Christian churches and the armed struggle of the ANC.

In the midst of the general 'uprising' in South Africa, the Kairos theologians declared 'the present crisis or KAIROS as indeed a divine visitation' (Villa-Vicencio, 1986: 269). In response to recent events of popular resistance and state repression during that critical, sacred time, the Kairos theologians proposed a rethinking of Christianity in the South African context. The *Kairos Document* distinguished between three types of theology in South Africa: state, church, and prophetic theology. First, state theology supported and legitimated the current regime. Second, church theology, by professing personal piety, neutrality, and non-violence, actually supported the current regime in effect by withdrawing Christianity from the political arena. By contrast, however, the Kairos theologians advocated a third option by proclaiming a prophetic theology that directly challenged the unjust rule of the South African government. In this prophetic stance, the Kairos theologians argued that the moral illegitimacy of the South African state required any truly Christian church 'to confront and to disobey the State in order to obey God' (Villa-Vicencio, 1986: 268).

Committing a prophetic church to non-violent civil disobedience against an unjust state, the Kairos theologians also advanced a redefinition of violence in the armed resistance to the South African government. The document asked: 'Is it legitimate, especially in our circumstances, to use the same word violence in a blanket condemnation to cover the ruthless and repressive activities of the State and the desperate attempts of people to defend themselves?' (Villa-Vicencio, 1986: 259). Distinguishing between violence and force, the Kairos theologians referred to what they regarded as a biblical distinction between the illegitimate violence of oppressors and the legitimate force necessary for self-defense against aggression or injustice. Under extreme conditions, they concluded, recourse to armed force by oppressed people might not only be understandable but also supported by a Christian theological ethics. The *Kairos Document*, therefore, refocused Christian debates on the role of violence in the struggle for liberation.

Although proposed with considerable caution, this apparent justification for violence nevertheless met with a strong reaction. At its general synod in 1986, for example, the Dutch Reformed Church rejected the *Kairos Document* for allegedly advocating violence. Countering the Kairos theologians, the Dutch Reformed Church urged Christians not to participate in anything that would cause 'polarisation, violence, anarchy and "revolutionary" disobedience to the legitimate authority of the state' (Durand and Smit, 1987: 47–8). In the terms set by the *Kairos Document*, however, the Dutch Reformed Church had merely reasserted its allegiance to a church and state theology that supported the South African regime. Christians opposed to the state argued that the times called for a stronger prophetic intervention.

In 1987 a meeting of church leaders in Lusaka, sponsored by the World Council of Churches, produced an even stronger statement of Christian support for the liberation struggle led by the African National Congress. Pledging themselves to the liberation of the poor and oppressed in South Africa, church leaders who signed the *Lusaka Statement* declared that the moral illegitimacy of the South African government required the church 'to work for the removal of the present rulers who persistently usurp the stewardship of God's authority.' Obedience to God, therefore, required civil disobedience to the South African state. But the *Lusaka Statement* also acknowledged that the use of force could also be justified. 'While remaining committed to peaceful change,' the statement concluded, 'we recognize that the nature of the South African regime, which wages war against its own inhabitants and neighbours, compels the movements to use force along with other means to end oppression' (Lamola, 1987: 21–3). In this commitment to change, the *Lusaka Statement* called upon all Christian churches to support the political movements struggling for liberation.

In February 1988, support from church leaders became more crucial within South Africa, as the government banned 18 anti-apartheid organizations. By restricting organizations within South Africa that were committed to non-violent protest, the government placed opponents of apartheid in a position similar to that of the ANC and PAC in the 1960s. As Reverend Frank Chikane noted, the government had, in effect, announced: 'No peaceful, non-violent political activity and resistance against apartheid is going to be allowed. Instead, we want you on the battlefield.' Under those conditions, religious leaders such as Archbishop Desmond Tutu, Reverend Allan Boesak, and Reverend Frank Chikane played prominent roles in carrying on political protest. With respect to the issue of violence, many Christians found it increasingly difficult, as Reverend Chikane noted, to 'still accuse the liberation movement of violence if the government has itself openly resorted to violence' (Chikane, 1988; 1987).

During the second half of the ANC's 'Decade of Liberation,' therefore, significant church leaders had mobilized support for the objectives of the ANC within South Africa. In January 1985, ANC President Oliver Tambo had exhorted the South African religious community to assume a greater responsibility in the struggle for liberation. 'The religious community has an immense and urgent responsibility,' Tambo urged, 'to act in defence of life itself, and accordingly, to fight for justice and peace' (Tambo, 1985: 5). By January 1990, however, Oliver Tambo was able to acknowledge the religious support that had been given to the liberation movement. 'Prominent religious figures have played an outstanding role in the fight against injustice,' Tambo observed. 'We salute these great patriots' (Tambo, 1990: 11).

Nevertheless, as theologians within the 'religious committee' of the exiled African National Congress welcomed this religious support, they also advanced a critique of the relation between church and liberation movement. ANC theologian John Lamola, for example, argued that the new, radical Christianity of liberation theology might create the illusion that the church was leading the struggle for liberation. Even a radicalized church, Reverend

Lamola warned, should not be misunderstood as if it were the 'ANC at prayer.' Reverend Lamola worried that if people thought that the church was leading the struggle for liberation, then they might conclude that they could support liberation by supporting the church. According to John Lamola, however, the church was not a force in the struggle, but a site of struggle, like schools or factories, a gathering point for people and a target to be captured and liberated. Reinforcing this point, ANC theologian Cedric Mayson observed that the 'Church is not an army but a battlefield. It is one of the places where the struggle is being waged, and it is necessary to analyze the forces involved in that conflict in relation to the revolution' (Mayson, 1987a: 54). From the perspective of these theologians within the ANC, therefore, Christian churches were not agents of liberation but institutions to be liberated. In that respect, Reverend John Lamola insisted that the Christian church was not called to lead the revolution but to become a 'servant of the revolution.'

Furthermore, theologians within the ANC were acutely aware that Christian churches represented only one religious constituency that served the liberation movement. Recognizing the vitality of religious pluralism in South Africa, Reverend John Lamola argued that the spiritual politics of the liberation movement had to be based broadly enough to 'draw people from all religious persuasions,' to maintain 'multi-faith' religious support, and to protect 'freedom of religion.' A liberated South Africa, Reverend Lamola concluded, would not be a Christian state, but 'a state that will take into account Christian values, just as it will those of other religions' (Lamola, 1988: 7–11). In particular, theologians within the ANC had to recognize the religious support for the liberation movement that had been given by Muslims. The Natal and Transvaal Indian Congress, for example, with a strong representation of Muslims, had issued a joint statement with the ANC declaring that 'all religions are fundamentally opposed to the apartheid system' (*Sechaba* November 1988: 10). Even the South African Communist Party, however, banned since 1950, had committed itself to the principles of religious freedom and pluralism. 'The ideology of the South African Communist Party is based on scientific materialism,' the party noted. 'But we recognize the right of all people to adopt and practice religious beliefs of their choice' (Mayson, 1987b: 29). Liberation, therefore, could not be tied to an explicitly Christian theology, even a Christian liberation theology that identified itself with the political struggle of the oppressed in South Africa.

On 2 February 1990, P. W. Botha's successor as State President, F. W. de Klerk, delivered a speech in Parliament that promised fundamental changes in the racialist political order of South Africa. Although P. W. Botha had often promised 'reform,' President De Klerk demonstrated a new approach by unbanning political organizations. The African National Congress, the

Pan-Africanist Congress, and the South African Communist Party were reinstated as legal political movements after decades of suppression. On Sunday, 11 February 1990, ANC leader Nelson Mandela was finally released after 26 years of imprisonment. At a welcome in Cape Town, Mandela told 100,000 people gathered in the streets:

> I stand here before you not as a prophet, but as a humble servant of you, the people. Your tireless and heroic sacrifices have made it possible for me to be here today. I therefore place the remaining years of my life in your hands.
>
> (*Argus* 12 February 1990)

Nelson Mandela's release had been anticipated by many people as a signal of liberation. However, instead of a sudden, apocalyptic redemption, the unbanning of political organizations and the release of political prisoners only began a difficult, contested process of negotiation over the future of South Africa. That future, therefore, seemed to depend upon neither religious legitimation nor religious liberation; it depended upon the negotiation of a new world.

REFERENCES

Adas, Michael (1979). *Prophets of Rebellion: Millenarian Protest Movements against the European Colonial Order*. Chapel Hill: University of North Carolina Press.

Appiah-Kubi, Kofi, and Sergio Torres (eds) (1979). *African Theology en route*. Maryknoll, NY: Orbis Books.

Biko, Steve (1974). 'Black Consciousness and the Quest for a True Humanity.' In: Basil Moore (ed.) *The Challenge of Black Theology in South Africa*. 2nd edn: 36–47. Atlanta: George Knox Press; 1st edn London: Hunt, 1973 (orig. edn Mokgethi Motlhabi (ed.) *Essays in Black Theology*. Johannesburg: Ravan Press, 1972.)

Biko, Steve (1986). *Steve Biko – I Write What I Like: A Selection of His Writings*. San Francisco: Harper & Row (orig. edn 1978).

Bonner, Philip (1982). 'The Transvaal Native Congress, 1917–1920: The Radicalisation of the Black Petty Bourgeoisie on the Rand.' In: Shula Marks and Richard Rathbone (eds) *Industrialization and Social Change in South Africa*. London: Longman. 270–313.

Bradford, Helen (1987). *A Taste of Freedom: The ICU in Rural South Africa, 1924–1930*. New Haven: Yale University Press.

Buthelezi, Manas (1973). 'Six Theses: Theological Problems of Evangelism in the South African Context.' *Journal of Theology for Southern Africa* 3: 55–56.

Buthelezi, Manas (1976). 'The Christian Presence in Today's South Africa.' *Journal of Theology for Southern Africa* 16: 5–8.

Chikane, Frank (1987). 'Where the Debate Ends.' In: Charles Villa-Vicencio (ed.) *Theology and Violence: The South African Debate*. Johannesburg: Skotaville: 301–9.

Chikane, Frank (1988). 'Church and State in Apartheid South Africa.' *Sechaba* July: 4.

Cone, James. H. (1970). *A Black Theology of Liberation*. Philadelphia: Lippincourt.

Cuthbertson, Greg (1985). 'Christians and Structural Violence in South Africa in the 1970s.' In W. S. Vorster (ed.) *Views on Violence*. Pretoria: University of South Africa. 43–61.

Davis, R. Hunt (1975). 'John L. Dube: A South African Exponent of Booker T. Washington.' *Journal of African Studies* 2: 497–528.

Durand, Jaap, and Dirkie Smit (1987). 'The Afrikaner Churches on War and Violence.' In: Charles Villa-Vicencio (ed.) *Theology and Violence: The South African Debate*. Johannesburg: Skotaville. 31–49.

Fatton, Robert, Jr. (1986). *Black Consciousness in South Africa: The Dialectics of Ideological Resistance and White Supremacy*. New York: State University of New York Press.

Ferris, W. H. (ed.) (1913). *The African Abroad*. New Haven: Yale University Press.

French, Kevin (1983). 'James Mpanza and the Sofazonke Party in the Development of Local Politics in Soweto.' MA thesis, University of the Witwatersrand.

Gerhart, Gail M. (1978). *Black Power in South Africa: The Evolution of an Ideology*. Berkeley: University of California Press.

Germond, Paul A. (1987). 'Liberation Theology: Theology in the Service of Justice.' In: Charles Villa-Vicencio (ed.) *Theology and Violence: The South African Debate*. Johannesburg: Skotaville. 215–32.

Goba, Bonganjalo (1974). 'Corporate Personality: Ancient Israel and Africa.' In: Basil Moore (ed.) (1974) *The Challenge of Black Theology in South Africa*, 2nd edn. Atlanta: George Knox Press: 65–73. 1st edn London: Hurst 1973 (orig. edn Mokgethi Motlhabi (ed.) *Essays in Black Theology*. Johannesburg: Ravan Press, 1972.)

Jabavu, D.D.T. (1928). *The Segregation Fallacy, and Other Papers*. Lovedale: Lovedale Press.

Karis, Thomas, and Gwendolen M. Carter (eds) (1972–77). *From Protest to Challenge: A Documentary History of African Politics in South Africa 1882–1964*. 4 vols. Stanford: Hoover Institution Press.

King, Kenneth (1970). 'James E. K. Aggrey: Collaborator, Nationalist, Pan-Africanist.' *Canadian Journal of African Studies* 3: 511–30.

Kretzschmar, Louise (1986). *The Voice of Black Theology in South Africa*. Johannesburg: Ravan Press.

Kuper, Leo (1957). *Passive Resistance in South Africa*. New Haven: Yale University Press.

Lamola, John (1987). 'Churches Identify with Peoples in Struggle.' *Sechaba* July: 21–3.

Lamola, John (1988). 'Does the Church Lead the Struggle? A Caution.' *Sechaba* June: 7–11.

Legassick, Martin (1973). *Class and Nationalism in South African Protest: The South African Communist Party and the 'Native Republic,' 1928–1934*. Syracuse: Syracuse University Press.

Lembede, Anton M. (1945). 'The Conception of God as Expounded By or As It Emerges From the Writings of Philosophers From Descartes to the Present Day.' MA thesis, University of South Africa.

Lerumo, A. (pseud. of Michael Harmel). (1971). *Fifty Fighting Years: The Communist Party of South Africa*. London: Inkululeko Publications.

Lodge, Tom (1977). '"Izwe-Lethu" (The Land is Ours): Poqo, the Politics of Despair.' In: Anne V. Akeroyd and Christopher R. Hill (eds) *Southern African Research in Progress: Collected Papers.* Vol. 3. York: University of York, Centre for Southern African Studies. 93–115.

Lodge, Tom (1978). 'The Rural Struggle: Poqo and Transkei Resistance, 1960–65.' In: *Conference on History of Opposition in South Africa.* Johannesburg: Development Studies Group, University of the Witwatersrand. 224–34.

Lodge, Tom (1983). *Black Politics in South Africa Since 1945.* Johannesburg: Ravan Press.

Lodge, Tom (1983–84). 'The African National Congress in South Africa, 1976–1983: Guerrilla War and Armed Propaganda.' *Journal of Contemporary African Studies* 3: 153–80.

Lodge, Tom (1984). 'Insurrectionism in South Africa: The Pan-Africanist Congress and the Poqo Movement.' PhD thesis, University of York.

Lodge, Tom (1988). 'State of Exile: The African National Congress of South Africa.' In: Philip Frankel, Noam Pines, and Mark Swilling (eds) *State, Resistance, and Change in South Africa.* London: Croom Helm. 229–58.

Luckhoff, A. H. (1978). *Cottesloe.* Cape Town: Tafelberg.

Luthuli, Albert (1962). *Let My People Go: An Autobiography.* London: Collins.

Mahabane, Zaccheus R. (1966). *The Good Fight: Selected Speeches of Rev. Zaccheus R. Mahabane.* Evanston: Program of African Studies, Northwestern University.

Marks, Shula (1975). 'The Ambiguities of Dependence: John L. Dube of Natal.' *Journal of South African Studies* 1: 162–80.

Marks, Shula (1984). *The Ambiguities of Dependence in South Africa: State, Class and Nationalism in Early Twentieth-Century Natal.* Johannesburg: Ravan Press.

Marks, Shula, and Richard Rathbone (eds) (1982). *Industrialization and Social Change in South Africa.* London: Longman.

Marks, Shula, and Stanley Trapido (eds) (1987). *The Politics of Race, Class and Nationalism in Twentieth-Century South Africa.* London: Longman.

Mayson, Cedric (1985). *A Certain Sound: The Struggle for Liberation in South Africa.* Maryknoll, NY: Orbis.

Mayson, Cedric (1987a). 'The Comradeship of Marx and Jesus.' *The African Communist* 110: 52–63.

Mayson, Cedric (1987b). 'Converting Christian Subversives.' *Sechaba* September: 29.

Mbiti, John (1979). 'An African Views American Black Theology.' In: Gayraud S. Wilmore and James H. Cone (eds) *Black Theology: A Documentary History, 1966–1979.* Maryknoll, NY: Orbis. 477–81.

Molteno, Frank (1979). 'The Uprising of 16th June: A Review of the Literature on Events in South Africa 1976.' *Social Dynamics* 5(1): 54–76.

Moore, Basil (ed.) (1974). *The Challenge of Black Theology in South Africa.* 2nd edn Atlanta: George Knox Press; 1st edn London: Hurst, 1973 (orig. edn Mokgethi Motlhabi (ed.) *Essays in Black Theology.* Johannesburg: Ravan Press, 1972).

Murray, Martin J. (1987). *South Africa: Time of Agony, Time of Destiny. The Upsurge of Popular Protest.* London: Verso.

Ngcongco, L. D. (1979). 'John Tengo Jabavu, 1858–1921.' In: Christopher Saunders (ed.) *Black Leaders in Southern African History.* London: Heinemann. 142–55.

Novicki, Margaret A. (1983). 'Interview: The Reverend Allan Boesak, President, World Alliance of Reformed Churches.' *Africa Report* 28(4): 7–22.

Ntwasa, Sebelo (1974). 'The Training of Black Ministers Today.' In: Basil Moore (ed.) *The Challenge of Black Theology in South Africa*. 2nd edn Atlanta: George Knox Press: 141–61; 1st edn London: Hurst, 1973 (orig. edn Mokgethi Motlhabi (ed.) *Essays in Black Theology*. Johannesburg: Ravan Press, 1972).

Okafor, S. O. (1982). 'Bantu Philosophy: Placide Tempels Revisited.' *Journal of Religion in Africa* 13(2): 83–100.

Parry, Richard (1983). '"In a Sense Citizens, but not altogether Citizens...": Rhodes, Race and the Ideology of Segregation at the Cape in the Late Nineteenth Century.' *Canadian Journal of African Studies*. 17: 377–91.

Phillips, Norman (1960). *The Tragedy of Apartheid: A Journalist's Experiences in the South African Riots*. New York: McKay.

Pityana, Nyameko (1974). 'What is Black Consciousness?' In: Basil Moore (ed.) *The Challenge of Black Theology in South Africa*. 2nd edn. Atlanta: George Knox Press: 58–63; 1st edn London: Hurst, 1973 (orig. edn Mokgethi Motlhabi (ed.) *Essays in Black Theology*. Johannesburg: Ravan Press, 1972).

Plaatje, Solomon T. (1982). *Native Life in South Africa: Before and Since the European War and the Boer Rebellion*. Johannesburg: Ravan Press (orig. edn 1916).

Ralston, Richard D. (1973). 'American Episodes in the Making of an African Leader: A Case Study of Alfred B. Xuma (1893–1962).' *International Journal of African Historical Studies* 6: 72–93.

Reeves, Ambrose (1960). *Shooting at Sharpeville: The Agony of South Africa*. London: Victor Gollancz.

Schoffeleers, Matthew (1988). 'Black and African Theology in Southern Africa: A Controversy Re-examined.' *Journal of Religion in Africa* 18: 99–124.

Setiloane, Gabriel (1973). *The Image of God Amongst the Sotho–Tswana*. Rotterdam: A. A. Balkema.

Setiloane, Gabriel (1979). 'Where are we in African Theology?' In: Kofi Appiah-Kubi and Sergio Torres (eds) *African Theology en route*. Maryknoll, NY: Orbis Books. 59–66.

Small, Adam (1974). 'Blackness versus Nihilism: Black Racism Rejected.' In: Basil Moore (ed.) *The Challenge of Black Theology in South Africa*. 2nd edn. Atlanta: George Knox Press. 11–17; 1st edn London: Hurst, 1973 (orig. edn Mokgethi Motlhabi (ed.) *Essays in Black Theology*. Johannesburg: Ravan Press, 1972).

Smith, Edwin W. (ed.) (1950). *African Ideas of God*. London: Edinburgh House Press.

Tambo, Oliver (1985). 'President's Message.' *Sechaba* March: 5.

Tambo, Oliver (1990). 'President's Message.' *Sechaba* February: 11.

Tempels, Placide (1959). *Bantu Philosophy*. Paris: Présence Africaine (orig. edn 1945).

Tutu, Desmond (1984). *Hope and Suffering*. Grand Rapids, MI: Eerdmans.

Villa-Vicencio, Charles (ed.) (1986). *Between Christ and Caesar: Classic and Contemporary Texts on Church and State*. Grand Rapids, MI: Eerdmans.

Villa-Vicencio, Charles (ed.) (1987). *Theology and Violence: The South African Debate*. Johannesburg: Skotaville.

Walshe, Peter (1970). *The Rise of African Nationalism in South Africa: The African National Congress, 1912–1952*. Berkeley: University of California Press.

Walshe, Peter (1983). *Church versus State in South Africa: The Case of the Christian Institute*. Maryknoll, NY: Orbis.

Wilmore, Gayraud S. and James H. Cone (eds) (1979). *Black Theology: A Documentary History, 1966–1979*. Maryknoll, NY: Orbis.

Wilson, Monica, and Archie Mafeje (1963). *Langa: A Study of Social Groups in an African Township*. Cape Town: Oxford University Press.

Woodson, Dorothy (1982). 'The Speeches of Albert J. Luthuli.' *Africana Journal* 13: 41–9.

Woodson, Dorothy (1986). 'Albert Luthuli and the African National Congress: A Bio-bibliography.' *History in Africa* 13: 345–62.

Name index

Subject index